# Issues in 21st Century World Politics

**Second Edition**

**Edited by**

**Mark Beeson**
**and**
**Nick Bisley**

palgrave
macmillan

First published 2010
Second edition 2013

Published by
PALGRAVE MACMILLAN

Palgrave Macmillan in the UK is an imprint of Macmillan Publishers Limited, registered in England, company number 785998, of Houndmills, Basingstoke,
Hampshire RG21 6XS.

Palgrave Macmillan in the US is a division of St Martin's Press LLC,
175 Fifth Avenue, New York, NY 10010.

Palgrave Macmillan is the global academic imprint of the above companies
and has companies and representatives throughout the world.

Palgrave® and Macmillan® are registered trademarks in the United States,
the United Kingdom, Europe and other countries

ISBN 978–0–230–36286–4  hardback
ISBN 978–0–230–36287–1  paperback

This book is printed on paper suitable for recycling and made from fully
managed and sustained forest sources. Logging, pulping and manufacturing
processes are expected to conform to the environmental regulations of the
country of origin.

A catalogue record for this book is available from the British Library.

A catalog record for this book is available from the Library of Congress.

10   9   8   7   6   5   4   3   2   1
22  21  20  19  18  17  16  15  14  13

Printed in China

# Contents

*List of Contributors*    vii

1   Issues in 21st Century World Politics: An Introduction    1
*Mark Beeson and Nick Bisley*

2   Emerging Powers and the Changing Landscape of World Politics    13
*Nick Bisley*

3   Globalization and Statehood    30
*Philip G. Cerny*

4   Governing the Global Economy: Multilateral Economic
Institutions    47
*Richard Higgott*

5   Regions and Regionalism in World Politics    60
*Shaun Breslin*

6   Global Financial Crises    80
*Timothy J. Sinclair*

7   Ways of War in the 21st Century    92
*Caroline Kennedy and Thomas Waldman*

8   Peace Operations and Humanitarian Intervention    106
*Alex J. Bellamy*

9   Transnational Terrorism    120
*Andrew Phillips*

10   New Forms of Security and the Challenge for Human Security    135
*Edward Newman*

11   Inequality and Underdevelopment    149
*Ray Kiely*

12   Population Movement and its Impact on World Politics    162
*Anne Hammerstad*

13   Climate Change and the Politics of the Global Environment    177
*Neil Carter*

14   Energy Security and World Politics                                    192
     *Amelia Hadfield*

15   Nationalism and Ethnicity                                             210
     *Richard W. Mansbach*

16   Gendering World Politics in the 21st Century                          225
     *Rahel Kunz and Marianne H. Marchand*

17   Democracy and Democratic Change                                       235
     *William Case*

18   International Law, Justice and World Politics                         251
     *Aidan Hehir*

19   Media and World Politics                                              263
     *Peter van Onselen*

20   After Neoliberalism: Varieties of Capitalism in World Politics        277
     *Mark Beeson*

21   Conclusion: Paradoxes, Problems, Prospects                            290
     *Mark Beeson and Nick Bisley*

*References*                                                               299
*Index*                                                                    341

**Issues in 21st Century World Politics**

# List of Contributors

**Mark Beeson** is Winthrop Professor of Political Science and International Studies at the University of Western Australia.

**Alex J. Bellamy** is Professor of International Security, Griffith University, Australia.

**Nick Bisley** is Professor of International Relations at La Trobe University, Australia.

**Shaun Breslin** is Professor of Politics and International Studies, Warwick University, UK.

**Neil Carter** is Professor of Politics, York University, UK.

**William Case** is Professor in the Department of Asian and International Studies at City University of Hong Kong.

**Philip G. Cerny** is Professor Emeritus of Politics and Global Affairs at the University of Manchester and Rutgers University.

**Amelia Hadfield** is Professor of European Affairs at Vrije Universiteit, Brussel.

**Anne Hammerstad** is Lecturer in International Relations at the University of Kent, UK.

**Aidan Hehir** is Senior Lecturer in International Relations at the University of Westminster, UK.

**Richard Higgott** is Vice-Chancellor of Murdoch University, Australia.

**Caroline Kennedy** is Professor of War Studies at the University of Hull, UK.

**Ray Kiely** is Professor of International Politics at Queen Mary, University of London.

**Rahel Kunz** is Lecturer at the Institute for Political and International Studies at the University of Lausanne.

**Richard W. Mansbach** is Professor of Political Science at Iowa State University, US.

**Marianne H. Marchand** is Professor of International Relations at the University of the Americas, Puebla, Mexico.

**Edward Newman** is Senior Lecturer in International Relations at the University of Birmingham.

**Peter van Onselen** is Winthrop Professor of Journalism at the University of Western Australia.

**Andrew Phillips** is Senior Lecturer in International Relations and Strategic Studies at the University of Queensland, Australia.

**Timothy J. Sinclair** is Associate Professor of International Political Economy, Warwick University, UK.

**Thomas Waldman** is Research Fellow in the Department of Politics at the University of York, UK.

# Chapter 1

# Issues in 21st Century World Politics: An Introduction

MARK BEESON AND NICK BISLEY

On 17 December 2010 a street vendor, Mohammed Bouazizi, set himself on fire to protest years of harassment and petty corruption on the streets of Tunis. His act became the trigger that launched what has come to be known as the Arab Spring. Driven by a diverse set of grievances ranging from high rates of unemployment, sky-rocketing food prices and human rights violations to government corruption, states across North Africa and the Middle East were rocked by mass protests and social revolt. In Tunisia, Egypt, Libya and Yemen long-standing and much despised dictatorships were overthrown. The downfall of the Qaddafi regime was made possible by international intervention in the first high-profile invocation of the 'responsibility to protect' doctrine. In some cases, such as Algeria and Oman, governments made concessions to dissipate popular discontent while in others, most notably Syria, the protests have spiralled into outright civil war. The Syrian conflict continues at the time of writing and threatens not just to draw Turkey and Syria into outright war but also to exacerbate broader international tensions as the West, led by the US, attempts to bring international pressure to bear on the Assad government, while Russia and China deflect this criticism.

The Arab Spring is a crucial issue in world politics not simply because of the way in which mass movements can overturn even the strongest of authoritarian states, but also because of the way in which they illustrate the blend of old and new factors that are so crucial to contemporary events. While popular protests are time-less, those in the Arab Spring had a 21st-century dimension, with protests organized through social media and international sympathy mobilized through broadcast images taken with mobile phones and published through the Internet. They also show how domestic circumstances in one state can have consequences that spread rapidly, are unpredictable and are hard to control. Moreover, the protests have led to a range of political and economic changes in the region whose long-term consequences are very difficult to predict. Just what the fall of the Mubarak regime will mean for Israeli and US policy in the Middle East, for instance, is very difficult to ascertain.

Elsewhere in world politics the sense of the novel and the unexpected is evident. The richest and most powerful country the world has ever seen, one endowed with unparalleled military, technological and cultural advantages has not, in spite of these advantages, managed to achieve its strategic objectives in its military adventures in Iraq and Afghanistan. It is also largely responsible for the financial crisis that prompted what has come to be known as the Great Recession. In 2012 the US economy was roughly where it had been in 2002 – a decade of growth lost – while Greece and Iceland had gone even further backwards and major developed economies such as Britain, Italy and France had lost between eight and six years of growth (*Economist*, 2012). Elsewhere, the growing affluence of Asia's massive societies, India and China, alongside the already developed Japan, is beginning to make humanity acknowledge the environmental consequences of rapid, widespread industrialization. This is not to downplay the environmental impact of earlier periods of industrialization, such as the enormous devastation caused during Britain's Industrial Revolution or the Stalinist modernization programmes in the USSR; rather it is to emphasize that the speed and scale of development in Asia makes the stark realities of environmental constraint unarguably clear-cut. The sustainability of the way human beings currently arrange their lives, especially in the West, appears to be under very real threat (Homer-Dixon 2006). Equally novel are the sources of insecurity which peoples the world over face. For most states and societies the most pressing threats to their well-being and sense of security do not come from neighbouring states invading their land and stealing resources but rather from such issues as infectious diseases and transnational criminality, including drug smuggling, money laundering, people trafficking and transnational political movements, particularly those which use terrorist methods.

All of this seems to imply that world politics in this century will be marked by rather different trends and issues than in the past. Yet not all would agree with this observation. For many, international politics will be no different in this century from those gone by; as in the past it will be driven by contests for power, survival and advancement. Whether the game is played with ships of the line or thermonuclear weapons is immaterial to the underlying rules. From this point of view, 21st-century world politics will be characterized by rivalry, competition and only very limited forms of cooperation between international actors (see, for example, Ross 2006; Waltz 2000). In the rise of China and its challenge to American dominance, one sees only the latest variation in the endless drama of great power politics (Mearsheimer 2001). Others see continuity in the larger themes of world politics, but for different and more optimistic reasons. At the close of the Cold War, Francis Fukuyama (1992) declared that the victory of liberal democratic capitalism over its challengers – first fascism and latterly Soviet-led communism – had brought about the end of history. By this he meant that the historical contest about the best way to arrange human societies, both politically and economically, had come to an end as liberal democratic capitalism had vanquished all comers. Other liberals saw the emergence of globalization – a process binding societies across the globe ever closer into a network of financial, trade, cultural, political and strategic linkages – as reinforcing the trend of democratization, expanding the reach of global capitalism in ways that improved the lot of people the world over and homogenizing cultures. Globalization was touted as driving a convergence of political and economic systems, dramatically reducing the differences among states and societies, making people economically better off and reducing their prospects for conflict (Ohmae 1990). For these liberals, world politics in the new century appeared to be marked for a good deal of continuity with the last, understood as the perpetuation of the twin trends of globalization and democratization that had been dominant in the last century's final decade.

Yet over a decade into the 21st century, even the most optimistic of liberals recognizes that while economic globalization has powered on, much of the world remains locked in seemingly inescapable poverty, exclusion and conflict (Collier 2008), a rather more depressing line of continuity with the past. Equally, democracy seems to have taken a distinct step backwards with democratic reversals, the consolidation of sham democracies and the rise of highly successful authoritarian powers (Diamond 2008). National borders retain their salience, particularly with regard to the movement of peoples, and the economic disaster of the global finan-' cial crisis and the Great Recession has severely dented the appeal of the Western economic template, while China's economic success, in spite of the Great Recession, is seen by many in the developing world as an appealing alternative to the Western orthodoxy.

While the 20th century opened as largely a continuation of the 19th's preoccupations – colonial rivalries, rising nationalism, and complex diplomatic manoeuvring around marginal shifts in the balance of power – the 21st appears to contain a set of threats and risks that are as frightening as they are unprecedented. World politics in the 21st century will be shaped by both new and old challenges, whether in the economic, political or military realm. And yet, notwithstanding the novelty and risk of climate change, pandemics, energy security and violent transnational terrorism, world politics is still driven by many of the same forces as in the past. States seek security and prosperity in an uncertain and anarchic political environment. The uneven distribution of power and resources prompts rivalry, fear and ambition among states and peoples. The manifest material inequalities among and between states continues to be a determinant of the prospects of people the world over. As the events in the Middle East have once again reminded us, the hopes and dreams of people to remake the world in ways which they believe to be more just, more moral or simply their own continue, as ever they did, to disrupt the plans, maps and power structures of the established order.

Many of the key problems facing world politics fly in the face of existing structures of political authority. For example, even if we might agree in principle that climate change is a threat which necessitates some form of collaborative action, it is far from clear what form this action should take, who should pay for it, how it should be done, or what the underlying rationale for such action should be. At the heart of such problems lies the continuing salience of national forms of politics and the robust reality of sovereignty in the minds of so many. The environment and our response to it is not only one of the most pressing problems of our times, it also serves as a reminder of the enduring nature of some underlying realities. Karl Marx (1913) suggested that men – his word, not ours – make their own history, but 'under circumstances existing already, given and transmitted from the past'.

Marx's ideas have become rather unfashionable, an ironic reminder of the importance and indeterminacy of non-material forces, but his basic insight into the 'dialectical' nature of our collective relationship with material reality continues to resonate: if the planet were a little larger, if there were more resources to distribute, if our impact on the environment was not as great as it is, the contemporary world might look rather different. The scarcity of desirable goods does remain a profound influence on human beings' acquisitive behaviour, as economists are right to point out. Whether we take such behaviour to be learned or innate, beneficial or harmful, or ultimately subject to change, are rather different questions, of course.

Equally, the financial crisis that erupted in 2008 served as a powerful reminder of the cyclical nature of economic crises and also vividly illustrated the speed with which economic problems can spread due to globalization. The crisis highlighted a number of issues that are particularly salient for the concerns of this book. First, it is a crisis of capitalism, and a particular form of 'Western' capitalism at that. Not only are there different ways of organizing broadly capitalist economic activities, but there are alternatives to capitalism itself. While we may all inhabit states of one sort or another these days, the domestic political systems within those states, the ideologies that populations may subscribe to and the very capacity of the states themselves vary tremendously and continue to throw up different answers to the basic questions of social organization, economic development and political stability (see Hollingsworth and Boyer 1997). The point to emphasize at the outset, however, is that the world continues to be characterized by major disparities of political and economic power, and major divisions in thinking about the way the international system should be organized. These differences have been thrown into sharp relief by the recent crisis because it is entirely possible that the dominant distribution of power and influence in the international system is about to be transformed. Second, the crisis and its ongoing effects illustrate how, in spite of distinct forms of national politics, rules and regulations, actions in one part of the world can, courtesy of globalization, have profound consequences for states and peoples all over the planet. That questionable regulation in America's banking sector can play a tangential role in the near collapse of the Greek economy is testimony to the complex political and social consequences of contemporary globalization.

The old order, established under the auspices of American power in the aftermath of the Second World War, has been challenged by the apparent economic fragility of the US itself and by the emergence of a range of rising powers, including India, Brazil and Russia. The most important of these emerging powers is of course China. The ascendancy of China is such an important development that it is worth making a few observations about it at the outset. Like the environment, China's rise seems a definitively contemporary issue, but China's past is a reminder that current developments have extremely long histories. China is the world's most enduring civilization, but one that has experienced major historical fluctuations in its power and influence. It is easy to forget that for the vast bulk of the past two thousand years, China has been the world's richest and most important power. Its marginalization by imperialism only dates from the early 19th century. China's rise is thus better understood as a revival of its long-term position of power and prestige (Morris 2010). Indeed redeeming the past is a central part of the domestic legitimacy of the Chinese Communist Party in which the party is presented as the only body capable of ensuring that China takes its historically rightful place at the centre of world affairs.

Such an outcome would not surprise some scholars, of course, and there is a substantial literature that discusses the prospects for 'power transition' and competition between the US and China for global leadership (see, for example, Chan 2008; Beeson 2009). Many influential observers – especially in the US – think that inter-state competition is the inescapable consequence of changes in the relative standing of major powers (see, e.g., Mearsheimer 2006; Friedberg 2011). As China becomes more powerful relative to the US it will inevitably want to challenge the dominance of the US, so the argument goes. However, other scholars argue that China's policy-making elites are being 'socialized' into different forms of behaviour. As they become more familiar with the international system and its rules and procedures, they will begin to adopt the habits of normal members of the system (Johnston 2007). Other liberals argue that greater economic interdependence and participation in the liberal system will change the calculation of national interests and through this cause China's leaders to recognize their own growing stake in the existing order (Ikenberry and Wright, 2008).

When we look at the massive expansion in the size of China's economy and the growing and increasingly complex links it has to the rest of the world, such an interpretation of events seems persuasive. The fact that China is developing increasingly cordial relations with Taiwan suggests that economic considerations may indeed be on the verge of becoming more important than strategic concerns in the minds of policymakers in precisely the way liberals would expect. If the implacable logic of economic interdependence seems to be influencing state behaviour at the local level, there is little doubt that states are being profoundly influenced by changes at both the international and the transnational levels. On the other hand, since 2009 China has taken on a more assertive approach to its foreign dealings, with many within the party elite convinced that the West and the US in particular will do what it can to prevent China reaching its potential (Bisley 2011). Equally, nationalism has been a central device used by the government to legitimate itself, and powerful forces unleashed by the party may spin beyond their control to foster a more belligerent approach to the outside world. How the existing order copes with China's emergence and the extent to which China can be satisfied with that order is likely to be one of the most important determinants of the path 21st-century world politics takes.

A further distinctive change to the contemporary international system is the emergence of a plethora of new transnational actors that have appeared on the international stage. Multinational corporations (MNCs) are recognized as some of the world's most important economic entities. Given their wealth it is not hard to see why many feel that ExxonMobil, Goldman Sachs or Microsoft are more important than many states. Unsurprisingly, perhaps, some of these corporations are able to exercise a good deal more influence over the behaviour of states in particular and the operation of the international political economy more generally than many individual states do. But MNCs are not the only new forces that are shaping economic and political outcomes. The massive expansion of international financial markets has placed constraints on the autonomy of even the most powerful states, as it seems policymakers must tailor their decisions with one eye on the markets. And yet the current crisis is a reminder of how rapidly apparent certainties can change. The balance of power between market and political power remains fluid: if policymakers have the requisite will and motivation it is apparent that they can quite quickly legislate to change the nature of the international political economy and the key relationships of which it is constituted – especially if they act in concert.

Key questions in this context are which countries should initiate such changes and which institutions should implement them. Here we see a further key component of the contemporary international scene. International institutions have become major, functionally necessary parts of what has increasingly come to be known as 'global governance'. While there are some enduring theoretical and practical problems about the way we think about and operationalize global governance (Sinclair 2004), it does draw our attention to the array of new inter-governmental organizations that have become such prominent parts of international life. The Bretton Woods institutions – the International Monetary Fund, the World Bank and the World Trade Organization (WTO) – created after the Second World War are the most important and enduring organizations of this sort. But there are many others, including those that represent the interests of the private sector, such as business lobby groups, and those that represent civil society.

A further recent development has been the idea that civil society – that sphere of collective action that exists outside the family and the state – has become transnational (Keane 2003). The expectation or hope that 'global civil society' could give political expression to issues that are either not taken seriously by national elites or which are inherently transnational and thus outside the realm of national politics, seems intuitively persuasive. Some of the most high-profile actors on the international stage these days are, after all, organizations like Greenpeace or the myriad anti-globalization groups that have become prominent features of most conventional international political gatherings. Civil society groups are, however, not all liberal, progressive and making up the shortcomings of Western states. They include such decidedly illiberal entities as Hezbollah and al-Qaeda. Yet although there are major questions about the legitimacy of unelected actors that may represent single issues, there is a growing sense among many scholars and participants that only unconventional politics can actually achieve the political outcomes they desire, whether that means action on climate change, human rights advancement or a caliphate in Southeast Asia (O'Brien *et al.* 2000). They may have a point: would we take environmental issues as seriously as we do if it had not been for the tireless efforts of non-governmental organizations that have agitated about their importance for so long? Would the much invoked but rather nebulous 'international community' have got around to banning the use of landmines if this cause had not been championed by civil society groups? Indeed, are such groups any less legitimate than the unelected technocratic elites that populate the Western-dominated international financial institutions?

Even if the extent and implications of globalization are overstated, the idea that some issues are beyond the capability of individual states to deal with has become firmly established. The fact that some states have no desire to deal with certain issues is also clear. Consequently, one of the defining issues of the 21st century is deciding how – perhaps even whether – certain problems and challenges are even capable of being addressed with the sorts of political mechanisms and processes that we have developed collectively thus far. Even the organizations or institutions that have been created with a specific mission in mind – like the World Bank or the WTO – often seem incapable of furthering their central goals, be it poverty reduction or trade liberalization (Woods 2000). Adding to the problem is the fact that the goals themselves may be contentious and not representative of the interests of 'the international community'. All of which should caution us against using unspecific phrases like 'the international community' in the first place. While some scholars might like to promote the idea of a 'cosmopolitan' future shaped by collectively derived, universally applicable notions of justice and equality (Pogge 2002), achieving such noble goals remains depressingly elusive; wishful thinking will not make it so.

None of this should be taken to mean that we should abandon hope about our ability to bring about change. One of the most striking recent events in world politics was the Arab Spring of 2011, sometimes also called the 'Arab Awakening'. The popular overthrow of seemingly well entrenched and powerful despotic regimes in the Middle East took observers and indeed participants by surprise. The downfalls of Qaddafi in Libya, Ben Ali in Tunisia and Mubarak in Egypt, illustrates that change is the one certainty in international life. But we need to think about who 'we' are and whether 'our' views and thinking even accurately reflect the reality that we experience as individuals, much less that of the planet's population as a whole. The very fact that there are a number of competing perspectives about the apparently fundamental realities of international life is a reminder of how much remains uncertain, contested and unknowable. This may seem a strange observation for the editors of a book about the key issues of the 21st century to make, but experience dictates that we assume a little intellectual modesty as we try to pick our way through the foothills of this still new century. What we can do is to try to identify the key issues and recognize that the way we feel about them will reflect our geographical position, our gender, our age, our class and ultimately, perhaps, that idiosyncratic amalgam of memories, impressions and experiences that make us who we are as individuals. We cannot tell you what to make of all this, but we can introduce you to the forces and actors that will shape your world and ours.

## Overview of the book

The aim of this book is to identify the issues that are and look likely to remain significant influences on the international system, both those that are novel challenges that break with the pattern of the past and those that provide lines of continuity. The chapters in this book attempt to provide a detailed introduction to nineteen of the major issues that influence the dynamics of world politics and over which there is considerable social and political contestation in the contemporary world. Of course we cannot hope to provide exhaustive coverage of every issue that matters; rather we have selected what we feel are the most important of these issues at present and which are likely to remain of considerable salience in the coming years. Many of these issues are to some degree inter-connected; for example, climate change is contributing to the increasing politicization of security questions, such as energy security and population movement, while globalization is amplifying the rate, incidence and consequences of financial crises. However, each is sufficiently discrete to warrant specific treatment.

Chapter 2 examines the prospects of a shift in the basic pattern of power distribution among states and its implications for the structure of world politics. Nick Bisley provides an overview and assessment of the arguments that the rise of China and India, alongside the hydrocarbon-fuelled wealth of Russia and a number of other powers presages a shift in power and influence from the North Atlantic to the Asian continent. He presents an overview of the origins of the West's dominance and the different ways in which relative power seems to be changing. While he argues that Western decline can be overstated, and has been in the past, he concludes that on balance there are good reasons for thinking that world politics will be shaped by the interplay of a larger number of closely inter-related major powers than in the past sixty years. This is likely to make world politics a more unstable, complex and unpredictable place.

In the third chapter, Philip Cerny examines what has become one of the central questions in contemporary politics: the relationship between globalization and the state. States are the foundation stones of the international system and many have argued that the powerful transnational forces of globalization threaten not only the power of states but the very functioning of the international system itself. Cerny observes that the state faces a crisis in its traditional function and that this is prompting a transformation of governance and authority structures which will produce a much more complex and multilayered system of world politics over the coming years. The chapter examines the origins of this crisis, its contemporary manifestations and the place of globalization in this process. He argues that the state will increasingly be hamstrung as webs of authority networks limit its ability to fulfil its traditional governance function.

Richard Higgott's subsequent chapter examines efforts to provide governance to aspects of the global economy with an examination of the current state of multilateral economic institutions. This fourth chapter charts the rise of multilateralism in world politics and particularly the emergence and transformation of the Bretton Woods system. It then examines the emergence of a range of newer multilateral organizations, such as the G20, as well as the questions increasingly being asked of these institutions about the legitimacy and efficacy of their policy-making. The chapter then considers the prospects of improved economic governance and overviews a number of changes that policy advocates have put forward to make the global economy function more efficiently and more fairly. Higgott observes that the prospects for greater governance are subject to the willingness of the powerful to concede the need to change.

In Chapter 5 Shaun Breslin examines the growing role of regional cooperation in world politics. He argues that geographically constrained forms of inter-governmental cooperation are a central feature of the current order and are likely to remain so for many years to come. They will not, however, supersede the state and often operate in an uneasy and sometimes antagonistic relationship with global multilateral mechanisms. The chapter charts the emergence of regionalism in the 20th century and particularly the centrality of the European experience in shaping both the theory and practice of regional cooperation, its transformation in response to changing circumstances and its likely future trajectory. The sixth chapter examines financial crises. Here Timothy Sinclair first considers the differing ways financial crises are understood and explained and then examines the reasons for the increasing volatility of global finance following the breakdown of the Bretton Woods monetary order. He then looks at the origins of the 2008 global financial crisis and concludes by reflecting on the prospects for regulatory reform of the global financial system. Sinclair argues that while it is not necessarily inevitable, the political reality is that we are unlikely to see the kind of governmental cooperation and coordination as well as shifts in attitude that would be necessary to ensure a significant reduction in the scale and severity of financial crises.

Caroline Kennedy and Thomas Waldman examine the character of war in the 21st century in Chapter 7. It begins with a brief discussion of arguments about the changing forms of war associated with the 'new wars' debate and the West's distaste for involvement in such conflicts. It then examines what the authors call the '9/11 wars', how these represented something of a revival of 'old wars' and the West's ability and interest in undertaking these kinds of conflict. It then shows how the evolution of these conflicts, in particular the changing nature of the engagement and the use of counter-insurgency, opened up a gap between means and the political ends of these conflicts. Attempts to use impersonal means, such as drones, to deal with these conflicts, they argue, will ultimately not resolve the problems that Western powers face in 'new war' contexts. In Chapter 8, Alex Bellamy discusses how the increasing sense that international society should breach the core non-intervention norm for humanitarian reasons presents a serious challenge to world politics. Since the creation of the United Nations (UN) in 1945, international society has increasingly devised military means to try to manage international conflict and its consequences. The chapter charts this practice and particularly focuses on the emergence of peace operations during the Cold War and the turn to more coercive interventionism of the post-Cold War period. The chapter then examines the emerging principle that state sovereignty implies a responsibility to provide a minimum level of protection to citizens, the failure to provide which warrants international action. This principle is not uniformly accepted and has yet to prompt more effective humanitarian action; however, key policymakers at the UN and elsewhere are trying to work out the best way in which this principle can reduce the frequency and impact of humanitarian catastrophe. The chapter includes a consideration of these principles in the 2011 Libya intervention.

In the ninth chapter, Andrew Phillips considers a phenomenon that encapsulates many of the changing facets of contemporary world politics: transnational terrorism. Having distinguished terrorism from other forms of irregular organized violence, and emphasizing its distinctly transnational character, Phillips traces its historical origins and then assesses its contemporary significance. Terrorism is of particular importance, he shows, not because of its strategic threat but because of the destabilizing consequences that reaction to it has brought about and, of course, the intellectual jolt that transnational terrorism has caused to the academic discipline of International Relations. He concludes by arguing that terrorism is likely to remain an important, albeit an indirect, factor in shaping the international order, although the specific threat of al-Qaeda has been significantly reduced in recent years, most obviously symbolized by the death of Osama bin Laden.

In Chapter 10 Edward Newman provides an overview of the vast array of new security challenges emerging in contemporary world politics and some of the policy responses they have prompted. These include the way in which health and other related areas have recently become areas of security concern; the question of human security and the growing role played by private security corporations in contemporary conflicts and post-conflict societies; how this influences the pattern of conflict and cooperation in world politics; and the ethics of the use of force. Ray Kiely examines the staggering material inequality of states and societies, one of the most enduring features of the contemporary world, in Chapter 11. The chapter assesses the competing arguments about the causes of the perpetuation of the, for some, ever-widening gap between rich and poor. It focuses particularly on the debate between those who feel that globalization provides reason to be optimistic about the prospect of the poor being able to improve their lot and those who are more sceptical. After examining a wide range of views, Kiely concludes that, on balance, the evidence seems to support a more pessimistic interpretation. He argues that globalization is, if not exacerbating, then not doing anything to redress the structures of inequality, particularly in power relations, that have produced the current setting and are likely to remain central organizing principles of the world economy.

In the twelfth chapter Anne Hammerstad considers the impact of population movement on the broader dynamics of world politics and why it is that population movement is thought to be such a contentious issue in so many countries. She first investigates perceptions that the present is an unparalleled 'great age' of migration, as some have claimed, looking then at what is old and what is new about migration trends, and arguing that today's population movements do pose some distinctive challenges, particularly as they relate to the way in which globalization is blending questions of identity with often acute problems of security. She concludes that the hard realities of demographic change are likely to ensure that migration continues to occur, but that with it will come continued political and cultural contestation and resistance.

Climate change, and the diplomatic and institutional dealings that try to cope with or mitigate it, has become one of the most important issues in world politics.

In Chapter 13, Neil Carter examines efforts to respond to climate change, assesses their strengths and weaknesses and reflects on the extent to which environmental questions have transcended their traditional location as 'low' politics to become major national interest concerns. He argues that central to the, so far, inadequate response to the profound challenge presented by environmental transformation is the predominance of territorial conceptions of sovereignty. Until such time as this is overcome, prospects for ameliorating the worst consequences of climate change remain slim. This was perhaps nowhere more evident than in the failed international conference held in Copenhagen to devise a post-Kyoto regime in late 2009. Chapter 14 examines the dynamics of energy and resource security and their impact on the patterns of world politics. Here Amelia Hadfield assesses the emergence of concerns around energy and resource security, the policy responses from key states and the way in which these processes are contributing to the growing rivalry among many states, as well as the new political alliances and relationships that are being forged by the politics of energy and resources.

In Chapter 15 Richard Mansbach analyses the role of nationalism and ethnicity in world politics. He considers the extent to which these remarkably powerful forces of particularism are able to find such traction in an era when states and societies are increasingly deeply inter-connected. Mansbach provides an overview of theories of nation, nationalism and ethnicity and the historical development of these ideas in practice in the political as well as the economic realm. He draws attention to the way in which these ideas have always been subversive of existing practices but shows that they can play out in both positive and negative ways: they can unify disparate peoples into a functioning society or equally be the source of strife and conflict. He concludes that in spite of the unifying tendencies of globalizing forces, the politics of identity as manifested in nationalism and ethnicity are likely to continue to drive conflict and contestation well into the 21st century. The sixteenth chapter considers how questions of gender remain a significant issue in contemporary world politics. Here Marianne Marchand and Rahel Kunz begin by examining the gender dimensions of the global financial crisis, setting out why gender is a salient issue in 21st-century world politics. In particular they examine how gender shapes the concept and practice of security and the gender dimensions of labour, focusing particularly on migrant and domestic workers and the gendered social construction of *maquila* workers and 'care givers' in the global political economy, and the concrete gendered implications of this social construction.

Chapter 17 considers the current state of democracy and democratization and the implications for world politics of the stuttering expansion of democratic systems of political rule. William Case examines the preconditions for democracy that have been identified in the literature as well as the substantive aims of those who seek to bring about democratic change. The chapter assesses the extent to which democratic systems of government affect human welfare and can bring about the improvements that many of its supporters seek. Case argues that some of the shortcomings of democracy relate not simply to the problems of particular countries and their elites but to the transfer of power away from statist forms and thus away from participatory systems of authority. The chapter concludes with a consideration of the recent democracy 'recession' whereby authoritarian governments are increasingly able to resist democratizing impulses and democratic standard bearers, such as the US, have plummeted in popularity. In Chapter 18, Aidan Hehir considers the complex role played by international law in world politics. He examines arguments about the efficacy of international law, charts developments in the recent past that have led to more optimistic conclusions about the positive role law may play in world politics, and discusses the tension between law and morality which gained currency in the late 1990s. The chapter concludes that international law is important both because of the growing purchase it has on international politics and because of the strain of hope and optimism that it reflects.

Peter van Onselen considers the role of the media generally and the 'new' media in particular as a force in international affairs. Chapter 19 analyses the impact of developments such as Wikileaks and new social networking sites. In particular it considers how the increase in the rate of information flow through new modes of communication influences foreign policy and domestic stability and especially the way in which authoritarian regimes are able to use new media to reinforce their position.

In the book's final chapter Beeson argues that the experiences of the past ten to fifteen years have put paid to the idea, so dominant in the 1990s, that an Anglo-American liberal vision of capitalist economic development was the only plausible way in which societies could structure their economies. The predominance of neoliberal capitalism in the economic realm had been matched by the apparent victory of liberal democracy in the light of Soviet Communism's demise. However, not only has the global financial crisis of 2008 seriously undermined arguments in favour of deregulation, privatization and lower social spending, but the dramatic resurgence of a number of developing economies, most notably China, has shown that there is a wide variety of forms of capitalism that can be successful, in some cases spectacularly so. The chapter examines the different types of economic systems and their interaction, and concludes with a consideration of the implications of the recent crisis for economic and political systems, showing that circumstances in the 21st century might be decidedly more conducive to less liberal forms than many had thought.

# Chapter 2

# Emerging Powers and the Changing Landscape of World Politics

*NICK BISLEY*

In late autumn 2011, statesmen and women from the G20 grouping converged on the French Riviera city of Cannes to try to manage Europe's ever-worsening financial meltdown. The global financial crisis of 2008–9 had sparked the worst global downturn since the 1930s, now dubbed the 'Great Recession'. The severe downturn in the global economy had revealed the dreadful finances of many European states, most particularly those who had joined the European single currency and essentially lied about their economic circumstances. Greece was the worst hit. Other small economies, such as Portugal and Ireland, were in dire straits and there were even grave concerns about some of Europe's major players, most immediately Italy. Global markets were on a knife-edge and public anger was at boiling point as heads of state and finance leaders met over the first weekend in November. How could confidence be restored? America was not in a position to bail out the profligate Europeans, nor was the International Monetary Fund (IMF). In one of history's great ironies Europe, which had given birth to modern capitalism and colonized vast tracts of the globe, was hoping that the world's largest communist state would ride to the rescue. China's immense surpluses, the product of the greatest economic expansion in history, seemed to be the only way out of Europe's immediate crisis. Yet China did not oblige and Europe's economic woes continued.

That weekend was of note not only for embodying a striking set of developments: the club of wealthy European countries brought low by underwhelming growth and even worse macroeconomic policy; an emasculated America unable to fix the problem; a cashed-up China confident enough in itself and its broader circumstances to deny the supplicants; and of course the G20 now acting as the forum for economic manoeuvring. It was also illustrative of the ongoing transformation of world politics caused by shifts in power and influence across the world.

For most of the past 200 years, world politics was dominated by powers residing on either side of the North Atlantic. They enjoyed substantially greater wealth, power and influence than all others. By the turn of the millennium, the United States had accumulated such a huge advantage over everyone else, that it had devised a grand strategy premised on a never-ending perpetuation of global

13

military predominance (White House 2002). But just as this prompted debate about the vices and virtues of American empire (Johnston 2004; Ferguson 2004), more profound changes were afoot. On the back of historically unprecedented economic growth, China and India were beginning to exert an international influence to match their demographic scale and historical legacies. China was already the world's factory and a 'Top10' economy. India's information technology and outsourcing was having a global impact and a newly renovated Russia commanded the world's largest reserves of fossil fuels. A famous report published in 2001 by the investment bank Goldman Sachs identified four countries – Brazil, Russia, India and China – as the keys to the future of the global economy. The bank's analysts predicted that by 2035 the four, collectively known as the 'BRICs', would overtake the combined GDP of the G7 (Goldman Sachs, 2001).

Over a decade on, the report's authors have been vindicated. In 2010, China surpassed Japan to become the world's second largest economy in aggregate GDP terms (Hosaka 2010), and the IMF has calculated that if growth patterns continue on current trends, then emerging economies will produce more than half of global GDP by 2016 (cited in O'Sullivan 2011). With this economic success has come confidence and a desire to take a place on the world stage that is matched with creative and pragmatic diplomacy. Where in the past emerging powers had been hamstrung by limited resources and an ideological strait-jacket, their much more pragmatic foreign policies are today showing a distinctly entrepreneurial quality. More disconcertingly, in many parts of the world, growing national prosperity is also leading to growing investment in military modernization, prompting in turn uncertainty among their neighbours and the world more generally. But the rise of the emerging powers is only half the story. Long-term Western economic decline, compounded by the catastrophic events of the global financial crisis and the Great Recession, has saddled wealthy states with mountains of debt. On average wealthy economies have debt worth 100 per cent of their GDP, while emerging economies have around 35 per cent. This has accelerated the narrowing of the gap between aspirant and dominant powers.

It is not surprising that many see these developments as ushering in a period of transformation in world politics. Some feel that the new era will be one of an Asian ascendancy (e.g., Mahbubani 2008), while others feel that the world will have multiple centres of power and influence, in which no one power is able to dominate the others, in a manner not dissimilar to the 19th century (e.g., Bell 2007). This chapter provides an overview of these arguments and assesses the extent to which the 21st century will be shaped by a global power shift and the implications that such a restructuring of the system might have for the pattern and dynamics of world politics.

## The North Atlantic era

Beginning in the mid-16th century, European powers and their offshoots began to dominate the globe. In the Americas, Africa, Asia and the Middle East, Europe's great powers expropriated lands from indigenous populations, subjected these people to their often brutal and arbitrary rule and found new stages on which to play out their rivalries and conflicts. This was made possible by a long phase of technological advance, maritime exploration and industrialization. So wide-ranging was the reach of European imperialism that by the beginning of the First World War, Britain, France, Belgium and the Netherlands ruled around a third of the world's territory and just under 30 per cent of its population (Townsend 1941). During this period European states and their colonial offspring, such as Australia, the US, Canada and New Zealand, dramatically improved their place in the world. By the middle of the 20th century, these states had become substantially better off than all others. They were the most powerful, had a decisive advantage in virtually all technologies and generated the vast bulk of global GDP. At the micro level, their populations enjoyed vastly better standards of living, with higher levels of education spread far more widely across their populations, long life expectancy, significantly reduced infant mortality and widespread control of many diseases such as cholera, typhoid and smallpox which had ravaged humanity for centuries.

The Cold War's end appeared to confirm Western dominance. A liberal model of politics and a capitalist vision of economics ended the century ideologically undefeated. Western ideas also dominated the constitutional structure of the international system and the nascent edifice of global governance. The material dominance of Western states was matched by the apparent monopolization of Western ideas as to how states and societies should be run and how relations between those entities ought to be organized. Even in the efforts to create international mechanisms to limit state power that accelerated after the Cold War, such as the international human rights regime and the International Criminal Court, Western powers and ideas predominated.

But it was not just the West that dominated; one state in particular was of overwhelming importance. For most of the period since the end of the Cold War there has been one unambiguously great power and no-one, alone or collectively, has been in a position to challenge this situation (see Brooks and Wohlforth 2002). The US enjoys massive military advantages, has the world's largest economy, as well as being at the leading edge of technology and innovation, and has a virtual monopoly on the world's best universities as well as a culture that is consumed and enjoyed the world over. It stands at the centre of a global network of military alliances, has the world's largest and most influential diplomatic corps and conceives of its interests and strategy in global terms (see Walt 2004). Not only is the US the system's most important player, but also its underlying values and forms of social organization – democracy and free markets – had seemed to be the only real game in town.

Perhaps the most striking feature of the past several centuries in world politics has been the way in which a very small proportion of the human population has been able to acquire so much wealth, military power and influence. So significant has its influence been that the changing configurations of power within the grouping – from multipolar to unipolar – have become the central organizing principles of the system as a whole. During the period of colonialism Western attitudes to local populations and to other Western rivals was of paramount importance to local conditions all over the world. After the unravelling of Western empires, it was still the cleavages among Western powers that shaped the broader contours of world politics. In the years since the end of the Cold War world politics has again been shaped by the distribution of power and influence among the Western powers. The question that is of paramount importance, then, is whether these circumstances are coming to an end in the face of the emergence of a number of large and dynamic powers.

## Emerging economies, global powers

When viewed from a long historical perspective, the West's ascendency is recent and relatively short-run. For the bulk of the past two thousand years, Asia has accounted for nearly two-thirds of global wealth (Maddison 2001). Economists describe the massive gap that began to open up between the West and the rest from the 18th century as the beginning of an era of great divergence in global economic history. In recent years, the resurgence of India and China, following on from the earlier success of the 'Asian tigers', appears to mark the beginning of a new phase of convergence (Spence 2011). Indeed, some go so far as to argue that the economic forces working to level out the very uneven distribution of wealth across the world will be the most important factors shaping the world in the coming century (Sachs 2008). It is this process of flattening out the economic discrepancies between the rich and at least some of the less well-off which lies at the heart of the arguments about the possible changes to the basic patterns of world politics, a process that has been accelerated by the self-inflicted wounds of the global financial crisis and the Great Recession.

The most obvious reason that many perceive world politics to be changing is as a result of a redistribution of power across the system. The argument is not that the West is on the precipice of terminal irrelevance, rather that it is no longer going to be the monopoly supplier of influence and leadership in the international system. It is, as one leading commentator puts it, not so much a case of the absolute decline of the US or the West, but of 'the rise of everyone else' (Zakaria 2008: 1). At the centre of this is economic performance. Emerging powers have outstripped the growth rates of the US and other wealthy states consistently over a reasonably long period of time. As the Great Recession has taken hold this trend has been accentuated. In 2008 emerging powers grew by 6.1 per cent, while wealthy economies could only manage 0.5 per cent. As the financial crisis began to bite the gap widened further with emerging powers growing by 2.6 per cent and advanced economies shrinking by 3.2 per cent (IMF 2010: 2). Indeed one economist argues that if the emerging powers grow faster than the US by 3 per cent each year, then by 2030 they will account for two-thirds of global output (Subramanian 2011).

The modernization programme launched by the People's Republic of China in 1978 has produced one of the greatest success stories in world economic history (Bergsten *et al.* 2008). Between 1975 and 1999, the average annual GDP growth rate was 8.1 per cent (UNDP 2001: 179). Since 1979, the economic output of the PRC has quadrupled and the government intends for it to quadruple again by 2020 (Hu 2004). It is not only China's dynamism that is so captivating, it is its scale. China is now the second largest economy in the world and, depending on a range of variables, is tipped to become the world's biggest economy sometime between 2016 and 2020 (Arends, 2011). Never in human history have so many people had their life chances changed so dramatically and so quickly. The renowned development economist Jeffrey Sachs claims that 'China is the most successful development story in world history' (quoted in Zakaria 2008: 89). China is the world's largest exporter, it leads the world in manufacturing, creating around two-thirds of the world's electronic goods, and is the world's largest producer of steel, cement and coal. From being a poor and isolated country with few prospects in the mid-1970s, China is a huge and dynamic economy that is fundamental to global supply chains and trade networks in almost all industries. In the aftermath of the 2008 global financial crisis, it is not only the key engine of growth for the world economy, as events at Cannes made clear, but it is also a state with remarkable political clout.

China's economic success has tended to put India's economic modernization into the shade. The contemporaneous economic acceleration of the two Asian giants has shown that China is not unique, and that vast complex societies that many thought of as economic basket cases can very rapidly turn themselves around. Since initiating a series of liberalization reforms in the early 1990s, the Indian economy has been transformed. Although economists point out that growth rates began to pick up in the late 1980s, since the adoption of the reform programme the Indian economy has grown at an average annual rate of just over 6 per cent (Panagariya 2008: 6). Over that time, India has become linked into the global economy through a vast IT industry, it is an increasingly attractive venue for foreign direct investment (FDI) and its productivity, especially in manufacturing, is growing dramatically. The analyst who first devised the notion of the BRIC economies, Jim O'Neill, predicts that India will become the world's second largest economy by 2027 (O'Neill 2011). With the resurgence of India and China, alongside the well-recognized success stories of Japan, South Korea, Taiwan, Singapore and to a lesser extent Thailand and Malaysia, the idea that we are about to enter an Asian century appears compelling. In typically ebullient form, economist Larry Summers is reported to have said: 'At current growth rates in Asia, standards of living may rise 100-fold, 10,000 per cent within a human life span. The rise of Asia and all that follows it will be the dominant story in history books written 300 years from now with the Cold War and the rise of Islam as secondary stories' (cited in Mahbubani 2008: 10).

While India and China are the two most important emerging powers, due both to their size and location, the sense of a global power shift is reinforced by the growing number of states enjoying economic success. From the economic doldrums of the late 1990s, Russia has capitalized on its huge hydrocarbon deposits and the sustained high prices for commodities and become a significant economic power. Since 2000 annual GDP growth has averaged 6.8 per cent with a peak in 2007 of 8.1 per cent. Russia suffered very badly in 2009 with a dramatic contraction but has turned growth rates to around 4 per cent in 2011 (World Bank 2011a). Russia sits on the world's largest known oil and gas reserves, and has a wide range of commodities within its territory, including diamonds and gold, which position it well to enjoy prosperity so long as commodity prices remain buoyant. Brazil is leading a Latin American economic revival and while it is not likely to achieve levels of growth akin to those of China or India, it has nonetheless experienced striking economic prosperity. When adjusted for price differences its economy is ranked eighth largest in the world. Its commodity endowments, strong labour market and excellent returns on FDI mean that Brazil's economic success is likely to continue over the medium term.

Beyond the now well-recognized success of the BRIC economies are a host of other emerging powers that have significantly improved their circumstances. The rapid increase in oil and commodity prices, itself driven to a large degree by the growth in demand caused by India and China, has allowed a number of countries well-endowed with these resources to move up the global influence chain. The oil-rich states of the Gulf region, Iran, Bahrain, the UAE, Kuwait, Saudi Arabia and even, to a lesser degree, Iraq, have all had national coffers hugely inflated by the long-running high oil and gas prices. Elsewhere in the developing world, most notably in Venezuela, Northern Sudan and Nigeria, vast primary resource holdings are generating surprising levels of national wealth in countries that have historically been at the margins of the global economy. Beyond those that have done well out of commodities, and particularly hydrocarbons, are a small group of large economies which many feel will be key drivers of growth in their region and of global significance in the longer term. Mexico, Indonesia, South Korea and Turkey are all large economies (each accounts for around 1 per cent of global GDP), have significant populations and diverse economies, and are all members of the G20. Many analysts feel that the 'MIST' states are likely to be the next tier of influential emerging economies.

The reasons for the economic vitality of the emerging powers are wide-ranging. Some point to elite policy choices, others to cultural matters, while natural advantages are also clearly important. A central theme among some of the more prominent writings is the role played by the application of Western ideas to non-Western societies. Some writers point to things like the embrace of market systems of economic exchange, the adoption of the principle of meritocracy and the rule of law (Mahbubani 2008: 51–99), while others point to clothing, food and business principles as examples of Westernization (Zakaria 2008). However, the most important factor behind the economic success of all the emerging powers, from the big players such as China and India to the more moderately-sized South Korea and Turkey, is globalization. As Phil Cerny's chapter in this volume explains, the linkages between states and societies facilitated by the growth in networks of trade, investment and communication have provided many with economic, political and cultural opportunities that had hitherto not been available. Without the ability to tap into global markets, whether for capital, finished goods, raw inputs or commodity sales, the dramatic changes in economic fortunes in Shanghai, Daegu and Mumbai would have been unimaginable. Equally, as many point out, the technological dimensions of globalization – the rapid reduction in the costs imposed by distance, and particularly the ability of ideas to overcome geographic limitations – have been instrumental in the rise of many powers. The time needed to make good the gap between rich and poor is not only narrower than it has ever been, it is also likely to narrow further still, at least for those countries able to take advantage of the evolving global economy (Pape 2009; Zakaria 2008). Yet as Ray Kiely reminds us in Chapter 11, there will still be many who will not be able to make good on these opportunities.

## Big and ambitious

One of the more striking elements of the emerging powers, most particularly the BRICs, is their physicality. In the first instance, they are geographically substantial and are all located in strategically significant parts of the world. They also all have very large populations. India and China together account for around a third of the world's total population. The BRIC grouping together constitutes nearly three billion people and when combined with the MIST states the eight emerging economies constitute just under half of the human population. Moreover, all, with the exception of Russia, are projected to grow substantially over the next fifty years. While size, location and demographics are very much the stuff of old-fashioned geopolitics, they continue to have salience in a world of globalization. While a large population will not guarantee success, as Pape puts it, China, with four times the population of the US, has the opportunity to create four times the number of knowledge workers (2009: 26). Size provides not only the basic foundation of economic success, it allows opportunities for the benefits of economies of scale and also provides for the possibility of national resilience through greater scope for the domestic economy to withstand international crises. None of these are inevitable, but the benefits of scale continue to matter in world politics. Importantly, the advantage of size is almost entirely in the hands of the emerging economies. Notably, the eight key emerging economies (BRIC and MIST countries) all have trillion dollar economies (adjusted for price differences between countries).

The argument that a new global order is being forged rests not only on traditional power resources that derive from their physical and demographic size, location and the ability to link this with economic success, but also because of an often neglected dimension: will. The emerging powers in the 21st century want to be of global significance. They are actively seeking global influence and have the material ability to begin to make good on this ambition. They not only have the capacity to be very powerful, they want to wield this to shape the broader international environment in their favour. Precisely how they will do this is not clear but it is unlikely that they will look to 20th-century Western liberal ideas for a model. Perhaps most importantly, there is a growing confidence that many emerging powers have not just an ambition to guide events, but that they can do so rather better than their erstwhile masters. As Mahbubani puts it, 'any lingering Western assumption that the developed Western countries will naturally do a better job in managing global challenges than any of their Asian counterparts will have to be rethought. An objective assessment would show that Asians are proving to be capable of delivering a more stable world order' (2008: 234).

## Western decline

The ongoing economic achievements of the emerging economies are a compelling story. But the sense of change is underlined by the shortcomings of the wealthy West, and in particular the US. This involves both longer-term problems of under-performance as well as more immediate and in some cases very acute problems caused by the financial crisis and the Great Recession. The West's share of global output is declining and will continue to do so for so long as its growth rates are outstripped by the emerging economies. Between 1990 and 2008 America's share of global output declined by about 12 per cent while China's rose by over 300 per cent (Pape 2009: 23). This rests on the longer-run drop in American growth rates, which have declined by 30 to 40 per cent since the mid-1990s. These trends are evident across the Western world, with a number of minor exceptions. Since 2009 the output gap has grown considerably.

A related problem for Western countries, and particularly for the US, is their growing dependence on credit from emerging economies. Even prior to the massive bailout packages that were adopted after the global financial crisis, America and most of the G7 economies were badly in debt. In 2008, the American government recorded a budget deficit of US$454.8 billion (Treasury 2008), and by 2011 this had blown up to US$1.299 trillion (Treasury 2011). This debt is largely financed by high domestic savings in Asia, particularly in China and Japan. Prior to this huge expansion prompted by the financial crisis, concerns about growing government debt were evident, with many concerned about both dependence on external credit and that Western countries were not using debt especially produc-tively. That is, they were relying on external savings to fuel domestic consumption. In Europe, massive government debt was taken on after 2009, often on the back of already substantial government deficits. The rise of the emerging powers has turned the traditional patterns of debt and surplus on their heads. Where in the past developing economies were mired in debt and the wealthy had surpluses the reverse is now the case.

The West relies not only on the credit of the rest of the world to fund much of its standard of living, it is also increasingly dependent on importing cheap manufac-tured goods and energy. The significant savings produced by shifting productive processes to very low labour cost countries, such as China or Vietnam, has helped Western countries maintain their economic well-being at relatively low cost. They have also been able to export pollution through the movement of many dirty indus-tries to developing economies. Effectively, the labour force of the emerging economies has acted as a global deflationary force lowering consumer good prices and freeing up considerable volumes of wealth in Western economies. To some degree one consequence of this was to allow speculation in property markets that led to the bubbles in the US and UK. Another central component of Western success has been relatively low energy prices. The United States imports nearly two-thirds of its petroleum needs. Interestingly, China and Japan rely to an even greater degree on imported petroleum and natural gas than the US or Western Europe. Not only is this a significant drain on importing countries' national coffers, but as prices have risen – and they are likely to remain high over the longer run – it has undermined an important foundation of Western prosperity. Equally it has also distributed wealth from the importers to those sitting on significant energy reserves. The most notable beneficiary of this process in recent years has been Russia.

The apparent vulnerability of America's place in the world, and more broadly that of the Western world, is also a function of some self-inflicted wounds (Mason 2008). Many believe that the difficulties facing the US and its allies as a result of their two long and expensive conflicts in Iraq and Afghanistan are entirely of their own making. They have spent considerable amounts of money, blood and political capital to no great benefit to their interests. Moreover, they have stretched their defence forces very thinly and have provided many in the Islamic world and elsewhere with much fodder for anti-Western sentiment. Many have therefore been led to argue that the West is to a large extent responsible for its own decline. No less a figure of the American foreign policy establishment than Richard Haass puts it succinctly: 'by both what it has done and what it has failed to do, the United States has accelerated the emergence of alternative power centers in the world and has weakened its own position relative to them' (Haass 2008).

But it is not only the costs of West Asian follies that make many feel that the West may be past its use-by date. There are a number of pressing problems which the institutional structures dominated by the West have simply failed to manage. The two most commonly pointed to are the shortcomings of the nuclear non-proliferation regime and climate change (Mahbubani 2008; Emmott 2008). Other problems include the inability of the UN Security Council to resolve long-running conflicts, particularly the Israeli–Palestinian dispute, and the perpetuation of wasteful agricultural subsidy programmes in Europe and the US. In essence, the argument goes, the West has been shaping the contours of the international system for well over 100 years and the legacy of that custodianship has some very significant black marks.

## Is it real this time?

Before considering the implications of the shift in power and fortune it is worth reflecting upon the underlying claims of Western decline. In the 1970s, many predicted the end of Western dominance after the Vietnam War and the oil shocks. Again in the 1980s as Japan seemed about to overhaul the US, many expressed doubts about America's competitiveness (e.g., Rosecrance 1976; Kennedy 1987).

But debates about American decline rapidly became passé (Cox 2001) as a long boom began in 1992 which lasted nearly 15 years, with only a minor downturn in 2001. Yet in barely five years the US found itself entrenched in two long-running and expensive wars which revealed starkly the policy limitations of massive military power. Most importantly, the US was squarely responsible for the worst economic crisis in seventy years. It has taken on epic levels of debt as a result of this and continues to suffer its consequences, including high unemployment levels, depressed demand and a weak housing market. Indeed so parlous is the government position that even the Department of Defence is experiencing cuts.

Is Western decline real this time around? Previous experiences with this kind of debate make clear that one should not discount America's capacity to rebound from economic malaise. Nor should one ignore America's retention of significant degrees of structural power. Most obviously, the US maintains its position as the most important military power on the planet and the only state capable of projecting significant force over any great distance. Equally, its diplomatic networks, cultural appeal and advantages in innovation and research and development investment seem likely to last. No country even begins to approach America's ability to influence other states, nor does the US appear at all interested in changing its broader place in the world (Lynch and Singh 2008). President Obama's election removed much of the international opprobrium associated with his predecessor's foreign policy. Moreover, as some point out, the challengers are considerably weaker than is often realized, many have key structural problems in their economies and they appear too dependent on servicing the needs of wealthy states and societies. Economists point out that many emerging powers risk being caught in a 'middle income trap' as the steps that need to be taken to move to the next economic level for China, India and the rest are much more difficult and historically unusual than the ones taken to date (O'Sullivan 2011).

Others also point out that while the size and scale of many emerging powers is remarkable, the nature of power is changing so as to negate many of the advantages of scale. Slaughter argues that it is the ability to harness informational networks that will be the key to success in the 21st century and because of this the US is very well positioned to maintain its advantage in world politics (Slaughter 2009). One must also recognize that, to a great degree, economic success in the emerging economies was a function of American prosperity and consumption. Prior to the Great Recession, scholars debated the extent to which the emerging economies were becoming economically less reliant on linkages with the West (becoming 'decoupled' from one another). In the light of recent events, this debate has cooled as it has become clear that the links are still very strong (Rossi 2008). Beckley shows that the US continues to dominate in the three key areas of national power, wealth, innovation and conventional military capability and is not likely to be surpassed in these areas in the foreseeable future (Beckley 2012). As such, while Western power may be reduced and US influence in world politics will decline to some degree, for the foreseeable future the US is likely to continue to be the most important power in the system (Halliday 2009).

There are, however, a number of reasons why one should take seriously the argument that, at the very least, the rest will become significantly more important than in the past. First, the emerging powers are not only gaining in material strength; they are also increasing their influence in the structures of the international system and forging new networks to advance their interests and leverage their strengths. In the international response to the global financial crisis, not only has the G20 grouping of industrial and emerging economies demonstrated that it is best placed to coordinate international responses to economic crises, but the increased leverage that China, India and others have has also been shown. All of the key emerging powers are conducting activist and multilaterally engaged diplomacy that is intended not only to maximize their domestic economic and modernization ambitions, but also to promote their influence (discussed further below). On top of this, these powers are creating new bodies, such as the Shanghai Cooperation Organization, that will further this end. If working through networks and cooperation is key to success in the coming century, then the adept diplomacy of many emerging powers means they can more than hold their own. To point out that China's, India's or Russia's economic growth may not be as significant as one thought, and hence their influence curtailed, is to miss a very substantial set of diplomatic efforts that will noticeably enhance their stature and contribute to a significant restructuring of the international system.

Second, the emerging powers want to have a global influence commensurate with their growing size. Where in the past prognostications of transformation of structural change in world politics have fallen short, in part this has been because the named emerging powers have lacked the requisite ambition. For example, during the 1980s, much was made of Japan's remarkable economic success, and that it was likely to compete with the US for influence at the global level. Not only did Japan's economy slump at a crucial point, there was little appetite among Japanese elites to undertake a diplomatic or strategic leadership position. The contemporary circumstances could hardly be more different. China, India and Russia, as well as a number of the smaller emerging powers such as Brazil, aspire to be major players in world politics in the coming century. Precisely what they imagine this to involve varies, and there are different assumptions about what being a great power might actually mean in the 21st century, but the ambition of the emerging powers and their desire to reshape aspects of the international system to suit their interests and values mean that the current period of transformation will produce greater change than any seen since 1945.

The contemporary context of world politics, most particularly the processes of globalization – that is, the reduction in the cost imposed by geography on the movement of people, goods, capital and, most importantly, ideas – makes the arguments in favour of some kind of shift in the patterns of world politics more compelling. It does so primarily because it works to increase the leverage of smaller-scale actors in the international system (Bisley 2007). This will have several important consequences. First, it will help emerging powers accelerate their development and increase the speed with which they will be able to have global strategic heft. Second, it means not only that transnational groups such as activists and terrorists can have an influence that belies their small scale but also that the emerging powers will be able to have global influence with fewer resources. This is due to the ways in which globalization enmeshes states' interests, reduces the policy efficacy of traditional forms of state power and promotes the need to collaborate and cooperate among states, peoples and groupings. In the terrorist attacks of 2001 and the manifest failings of American policy in Afghanistan, one sees the two faces of this phenomenon. On that autumn morning a small group acting on the fringes of international society caused an astonishing degree of psychological trauma to the world's most powerful country. In Southwest Asia, the application of massive and highly expensive military power is unlikely ever to produce the kind of policy outcomes that the US desires. While the US may maintain its military might, recent events have cast real doubt on the ability of such forms of power to protect national interests at home and advance policy goals abroad. Thus, it is not merely the size and scale of the emerging powers, nor a simple linear projection of their economic success thus far out into the future which means world politics is in for a significant shake-up. Rather it is how these states are handling themselves, their ambitions as well as changes in the context of world politics affecting how power can be used to advance national interests that together mean that it is reasonable to conclude that over the next fifteen to twenty years the stage of world politics and the identity of the major players is unlikely to resemble that which has been in place over the past half a century.

## Consequences of a changing world

World politics is clearly in a period of transformation and while it is far from certain what the longer-run consequences of these changes will be, nonetheless one can already identify a number of ways in which the success of the emerging powers, alongside the relative decline of the West, is having important effects. Perhaps the most obvious immediate consequence of the emerging powers' prosperity is the significant price increases that have occurred in key areas, most particularly commodities and food. As China and India urbanize, the need for the infrastructure of modern societies – roads, bridges, sewerage systems, electricity and so on – has pushed prices of commodities such as iron ore, aluminium, coal, copper and zinc to record highs. As these societies get richer they consume more energy and this has pushed the price of oil, gas and coal upwards as well. While this benefits commodity suppliers like Australia, Kuwait and Brazil, it also has very significant consequences for the rest of the world. The economic success of the rich world was built on the back of cheap energy and part of the ongoing problems in the West derives from sustained high oil prices. Increases in energy prices depress global output and significantly hinder economic activity in developed economies. Moreover, these prices seem likely to remain high for as long as growth continues in the emerging world. Record high prices for food in recent years, particularly staples such as wheat, rice and maize, have been driven in part by bad weather but also by rising demand from emerging powers (Dupont and

Thirlwell 2009). Historically, high food prices have been closely associated with periods of political volatility. Some have argued that they were, at least in part, a trigger for the Arab Spring of 2011 (Johnstone and Mazo 2011). Emerging powers have put new pressures on natural resources. High prices are a reflection of inadequate supply and concerns about supply have prompted a degree of international competition over resources. India and China are scouring the world in search of secure supplies for their resource needs and have thus added a hue of political contestation to questions of commodity production and distribution.

A second way in which the emergence of new powers is having a tangible consequence is in the realm of geopolitics. Growing wealth, prosperity and ambition is producing increased tension among states, most particularly in Asia. The emerging and dominant powers have key interests that intersect, if not overlap, in the region, which is prompting a strong sense of unease. This discomfort is being translated into increased defence spending across Asia and particularly an expansion of offensive weapons capabilities (IISS 2012). For at least thirty years, the US has been Asia's pre-eminent military power. As China becomes more prosperous and more militarily capable, it is less willing to be beholden to American primacy and is increasingly using military means to claim and defend its interests. India is likewise expanding its military capacity with a particular focus on being able to protect its interests in the Indian Ocean and beyond. Whether in maritime clashes in Southeast Asia, or Sino-Indian maritime rivalry in the Indian Ocean, one sees evidence of the growing geopolitical friction that has been created by the emergence of these new powers.

On the diplomatic front there is also considerable new activity as the emerging powers seek to advance their interests in novel ways. Given that the bulk of the institutional efforts to try to manage world politics were created in the wake of the Second World War their membership and mandate reflect a North Atlantic view of power and interest. Efforts to reform existing mechanisms, most obviously the creation of the more expansive G20 and reform of voting procedures at the IMF, reflect a realization of the need to change these bodies to respond to changing circumstances. But there is also a growth of new institutions and networks of influence that derive from the activism of the emerging powers and the belief that existing bodies do not advance their interests especially well. There is a wide array of these but some of the more prominent include the annual BRIC summit, first held in Yekaterinburg, Russia in 2009. The India–Brazil–South Africa (IBSA) summit has met annually since 2006 and has been meeting at ministerial level since 2003 to advance what the group calls 'South–South cooperation'. IBSA was first formed to coordinate efforts at the WTO but has expanded to discuss a wide array of issues, including reform of multilateral economic institutions (on which see Higgott in this volume) and the reconstruction efforts in Afghanistan, and has even discussed an IBSA satellite programme. A further grouping, BASIC (China, Brazil, South Africa and India), was first seen flexing its muscles at Copenhagen as the countries collectively stymied a face-saving President's statement to the climate change conference in 2009. Elsewhere organizations like ASEAN (Association of Southeast Asian Nations) and the Shanghai Cooperation

Organization embody non-Western institutional efforts to manage and advance collective interests. One can see also in bilateral initiatives like the Turkey–Brazil gambit to manage Iran's nuclear ambitions, the China–Africa summits and the G20 lobby at the WTO inklings of move away from a Western-centric world order (Barma *et al.* 2007). The emerging powers are not only becoming more prosperous, they are stepping out onto the stage of international society to try to shape their broader environment. These efforts have become more obvious and indeed more necessary due to the Great Recession as it weakened existing powers and demonstrated the shortcomings of the existing institutional framework.

Finally, as Mark Beeson's chapter in this book shows, the success of China, Russia, India and a host of other emerging powers has significantly eroded the ideological power of the Western, broadly liberal, model of economic development. China and others embody what has come to be known as state capitalism, in which a mix of political authoritarianism, selective use of market mechanisms, and a highly active state role in economic dealings has proven to be remarkably effective (Wooldridge 2012). Where in the past Western success was seen to provide the ultimate example of the power of liberal thinking, its recent failings alongside the striking achievements of China and the like have underlined the appeal of state capitalism.

The emerging powers' influence on world politics is already evident. In their impact on resource consumption and the knock-on effects on price and competition, in geopolitics, institutions and networks of influence and the ideas of how economic and political life should be managed, the new kids on the block are already of global importance.

## Visions of the future

So what are the longer-term structural implications of rise of the rest for world politics? While prediction is a fraught business, the literature has thus far identified three main ways in which things may evolve. First, there is the chance of the creation of a multipolar world order in which the basic structure and patterns of world politics are shaped by the interplay of five or six great powers (e.g., Bell 2007). The changing distribution of power is most likely to create a world in which the US still predominates, but one in which it is joined at the top table by China, India, Russia, Japan and the EU (NIC 2008). The range of great powers is thought to be a clear parallel with the pentarchy of great powers in Europe's 19th-century international order. As then, the world will see a range of roughly equivalent powers; some are ambitious and rising, while some are declining, with much friction caused by overlapping and intersecting sets of interests (Emmott 2008). But unlike that time, there will also be a large number of major powers who will be of sufficient heft to affect the character of relations among the top tier, such as Mexico, Indonesia, Brazil, Nigeria, Turkey and South Africa.

Second, not only is the US in relative decline and new powers are emerging, but also non-state actors and concentrations of power will matter in ways that are entirely new. This leads some to argue that the 21st century will be the first period of nonpolarity in the modern era (Haass 2008). Here globalization will dramatically reduce the effective power of large states and will significantly increase the leverage of non-state actors, whether firm, criminal or activist. Nonpolarity means that states will have to forge networks or coalitions of other states, institutions and non-state actors to coordinate policy so as to advance their interests. Haass goes so far as to argue that this new world order will make alliances lose much of their salience and instead demand that states become much more nimble and pragmatic in their network building.

Both of these visions of the future assume that the rising powers have chosen to accept the basic structures of the existing international order and avoid contesting leadership of the system with the US and the West. A third alternative sees the emerging powers turning their back on the Western-centric world order and moving to establish a new setting for world politics. In the new institutions and networks of influence mentioned above, one sees evidence of this new world in the offing. The non-Western world commands the majority of the world's resources, most particularly its energy deposits, it has the lion's share of foreign exchange reserves (around two-thirds), it dominates manufacturing, has abundant labour pools and has shown a capacity to compete in complex globalized business operations. While the new powers accept some of the basic principles of the international system, most notably a strict understanding of sovereignty and the centrality of the state, a non-Western world will involve more than just a redistribution of power. It would most likely lead to a shift in the institutional structures of world politics, such as the UN and the multilateral economic institutions, and perhaps more importantly, a change in the values and norms that underpin that order.

In the early years of the 21st century the landscape of world politics is in a state of flux. While the basic features of the international system pertain, the distribution of power within the system, the number of states with influence, the way they advance their interests, and indeed the content of the norms and principles underpinning the system are all set to change to some degree. American predominance of the kind which was the hallmark of the recent past will come to an end over the next thirty years (see Walt 2011). America is likely to remain among, if not still, the most important power in the system; however, the gap between it and the other major powers will have narrowed substantially.

Alongside the United States, India, China, Russia and Japan will comprise the five most important power centres in world politics. The geographic concentration of these powers' interests in Asia means that world politics in the coming years is going to become Asian-centric. Just below them will be a wide array of major powers of substantial size and influence who may lack the wherewithal for global influence, but who will nonetheless be of great importance within their regions and will shape the preferences of the five top states. These include the EU, Britain, France, Germany, Brazil, Turkey, South Africa, Nigeria, Australia, Mexico, South Korea, Egypt and Indonesia. The institutional setting of world politics will remain fraught as the emerging powers' preferences for a more traditional understanding of sovereignty sit uneasily with the growing need to cooperate and coordinate policies. Geopolitical instability will be a hallmark of this new order. In the first instance it will be due to the uncertainty that emerges in times of transition, as previously damped down security dilemmas resurface. The increase in defence spending in Asia in the past decade or so is a leading indicator of these trends. As this new setting becomes more consolidated, instability will become the strategic norm. The world's major powers will all have significant nuclear arsenals, major militaries and most importantly, overlapping and physically contiguous security and economic interests. In the sea lanes of the Indian Ocean, fossil fuel links from the Gulf region, Russia or Central Asia or the choke points of maritime Southeast Asia, the number of powers and the scope of their intersecting interests will make the management of disputes and conflicts more complex and thus less stable.

On the economic front a number of trends are evident, although their trajectory is somewhat harder to ascertain. First, increased uncertainty and economic maturation are going to produce lower levels of economic growth over the longer run with considerable variation in growth rates across the world (Spence 2011). As India and China mature, they will not sustain their current effervescent rates of growth and will struggle to overcome the middle income gap. How the world will cope with such a slowdown is by no means certain and recent experience of such events in emerging markets is not at all good. This means that it is likely that world politics will experience the unusual circumstance of 'poor' great powers. That is, states of global importance but who lack the resources to behave as great powers of previous eras. Second, it is more than likely that the openness that has been the hallmark of globalization – an openness to trade, investment and ideas – will be significantly reduced. Regulations on investment, protectionism in trade and labour markets and restrictions on population flows are much more likely over the coming years. This means that economic growth is likely to be slower and prices higher than they have been for the past twenty years. It is also likely that inequality will have increased and that environmental problems will remain largely unaddressed.

The world appears to be on the cusp of a qualitatively new phase. National interests across the world have never experienced the degrees of connectedness of the present. Yet the geopolitical and geoeconomic consequences of this appear to be somewhat counter-intuitive as linkages are coupled with increasing uncertainty, rivalry and animosity. The shift from a world dominated by Western power and ideas appears to be driven by a broader distribution of power and a dilution of Western ideas. Precisely how this will play out is impossible to determine; however, it is clear that world politics is entering a much riskier and more complex context than at any point since 1945.

## Guide to further reading

The Goldman Sachs 'BRICs' report was one of the first to alert people to the magnitude of change that appeared to be in train (2001) and so successful has it been that the firm produces regular follow-up publications (Goldman Sachs 2007) with Jim O'Neill's *Wealth Map* (2011) the most detailed and recent version of this perspective. The literature assessing change in the structures of the international system is rapidly expanding. Some of the interesting examples include: the Singaporean diplomat and academic Kishore Mahbubani's argument that the coming century will belong to Asia (2008), the former editor of *The Economist*, Bill Emmott's nuanced argument that Asian rivalry will be the central concern for the coming quarter of a century (Emmott 2008) and Martin Jacques' gloomy prognostications about China (Jacques 2009). A number of government reports and strategy documents have also contributed to this debate, most notably National Intelligence Council global trends report (NIC 2008). The leading policy journals are a main forum for this debate and are the likely venue for cutting-edge assessments in the coming years. These include *Foreign Affairs*, *Foreign Policy*, *The National Interest*, *The Washington Quarterly* and *Survival*.

# Chapter 3

# Globalization and Statehood

PHILIP G. CERNY

## States and statehood in world politics

States have been the fundamental building blocks of modern world politics. They have formed a dualistic structure reminiscent of the role of the Roman god Janus. Statues of Janus were placed at the gates to the city. The god had two faces, one looking inwards to guard the social, economic and political life of the city, to give it unity and a sense of the common good and public interest. The second face looked outwards, to protect the city from external threats and predators, to pursue the city's interests in a hostile world and to interact with other cities. In today's collective choice literature, the first face or function of the state is said to be an 'arena of collective action' amongst its inhabitants and citizens. The second face or function was to permit the state to make – or break – 'credible commitments' to other states, what Kenneth Waltz, in his magisterial *Theory of International Politics*, called 'like units' (Waltz 1979). The capacity of a set of political institutions to play such 'two-level games' (Putnam 1988) effectively – i.e., to do both things successfully at the same time – is what is called 'statehood' (Brenner 2004).

'Statehood', therefore, is defined as the capacity to fulfill these two different and sometimes conflicting functions simultaneously. It is the central *problématique* or analytical puzzle of the modern world system itself. States frequently cannot do either of these tasks very well, much less do them both successfully at the same time. States have always been consolidating, fragmenting, experiencing both domestic conflict and upheaval and international weakness and subordination throughout what historians label the 'modern' period, that is, from (broadly speaking) the 17th century to the mid-20th century, as well as the 'contemporary' period, that is, from the late 20th century until today. Today, a process of adaptation to what are sometimes loosely called 'global realities' has presented a challenge both to older post-feudal states and quasi-states that have been absorbed into larger units, as in 18th- to 20th-century Europe, and today to 'new' and 'postcolonial' states.

More powerful older nation-states like Britain, France, Germany and, more recently, the United States have normally been seen to have a comparative institutional advantage in terms of embodying 'statehood'. This advantage is said to be rooted in the association of several factors, including their long-term historical development, their relative wealth and power in an industrializing world, their governments' increasing bureaucratization and state intervention and regulation to promote economic growth, prosperity and welfare – or what French social philosopher Michel Foucault has called 'biopolitics' (Foucault 2008; Gallarotti 2000) – and their inhabitants' sense of common sociological or ideological identity or belonging, whether instilled and indoctrinated from above or spontaneously emerging from below. In contrast, states that have *not* had strong centralizing institutions, political processes, economic development and/or cultural identity – 'weak' states generally, especially what are today called 'failed' or 'collapsed' states – are seen as failing to fulfill the fundamental requirements of statehood (Badie and Birnbaum 1983; Migdal 1988).

Thus the way most academic analysts as well as policymakers and mass publics conceive of 'modern' world politics has centred on the roles of states as the core political-organizational units. These have often been called 'nation-states', on the assumption that some sort of social and economic, *grass-roots* 'nation' had either pre-existed, or been constructed from above or below and justified through nationalism, to underpin and empower state institutions and political processes. Yet that very form of organization has been problematic from the start, and is becoming even more problematic in an age of globalization, from the mid-to-late 20th century to today. In the 21st century, what is often called 'globalization' presents a particular challenge to this modern 'multifunctional' conception of the state and statehood through a range of top-down and cross-cutting structural transformations, from the integration of global markets and production chains to rapid technological innovation, the growth of complex 'multi-level governance' surrounding and cutting across the state, the convergence of economic policies around varieties of 'neoliberalism', the increasing influence of transnational interest groups and social movements, the emergence of a 'global village' linking societies and identities across borders, and the like. This process is at an early stage, but 'statehood' is being stretched, relocated, broken up and put back together in new, often experimental ways.

In the 21st century, then, the capacity of traditional nation-states to act in effective 'state-like' fashion is increasingly being challenged by a range of factors. The transnational and global nature of the most pressing problems being faced by policymakers and publics, from globalized financial markets to endemic economic crises to the challenges of the environment, makes it difficult for state actors to make coherent and effective policy at the nation-state level. The transnationalization of technology, from the Internet to transport to flexible production techniques, creates and strengthens all sorts of cross-border economic, political and social linkages and processes. Changing political attitudes towards the human and economic costs of traditional interstate wars, from the rapid exhaustion of domestic public support to the rise of ethnic and religious conflict, including terrorism, mean that the nature of warfare is undermining traditional state-based military hierarchies and methods (Cerny 2012).

Furthermore, growing awareness of the complexity of political and social identities, from ever-increasing migration and multiculturalism to the capacity of groups to maintain and intensify cross-border social and political linkages (for example, through the Internet and the growing ease of international travel), challenges the fundamental sense of national identity and belonging that is essential to the social coherence and effectiveness of the 'nation' that the nation-state relies upon for stability, accountability and legitimacy. Transnational economic stresses, from factory closings and job losses seen to stem from the globalization of multinational firms and production chains to trade and financial flows, particularly in the current environment of financial crisis and recession, highlight the interdependence of economic processes across borders and make it more and more difficult to make effective economic policy in isolation. Lifestyle issues from consumerism and the media 'global village' (McLuhan 1964) to today's 'green' consciousness make ordinary people, as well as elites, increasingly aware of the global and transnational significance and consequences of these challenges. And a fundamental shift is taking place from mindless patriotism and jingoistic nationalism to an awareness of the need for transnational and global responses to a whole range of other issues that were traditionally seen to be the job of nation-states to tackle.

Indeed, the problem of statehood itself is at the centre of political debate, as various kinds of 'multi-level governance' crystallize and proliferate in a globalizing world. More formal international regimes, institutions and quasi-supranational bodies have been set up and are increasingly influential, if still in somewhat fragmentary form, from the United Nations and the International Monetary Fund, the World Bank, the World Trade Organization, the Bank for International Settlements and the like to regional institutions like the European Union, as well as urban and other subnational or cross-national regions sometimes reaching across borders (Brenner 2004).

A range of less formal transnational processes are also emerging, including the crystallization and intertwining of 'transgovernmental networks' among national regulators, legislators and legal specialists whose cross-border links increasingly take priority in terms of policy development over domestic hierarchies (Slaughter 2004); the development of 'global civil society', especially with regard to NGOs (non-governmental organizations); and the growing role of 'summits' and other *ad hoc* or semi-formal intergovernmental negotiating fora like the G7/8 and especially the G20 (Beeson and Bell 2009). 'Issue areas' are increasingly globalized, such as the question of whether an 'international financial architecture' is developing, especially in the context of the continuing global financial crisis, including the transformation of the Financial Stability Forum into the Financial Stability Board, the convergence of public policies across borders through imitation, policy learning and 'policy transfer' (Evans 2005).

Thus there is a crisis of statehood in today's world. Some see the solution in resurrecting the nation-state – whether through religious identity (Israel, Iran), 'nation-building' or 'state-building' (Fukuyama 2004), the reinvention of various forms of 'state capitalism' and the 'return of the state' (Plender 2008), or the renewal of American hegemony through 'soft power' or economic leadership (Nye 2004; Gallarotti 2009; Cerny 2006). Others look to a range of more specific organizational alternatives:

- strengthening existing international institutions such as the United Nations (United Nations Commission of Experts on Reforms of the International Monetary and Financial System 2009);
- working through regional organizations like the European Union (de Larosière 2009);
- encouraging the development of a new multilateralism of 'civilian states' (Sheehan 2008) or a more pluralistic 'society of states' (Hurrell 2007);
- the creation of new forms of transnational 'regulatory capitalism' (Braithwaite 2008);
- the spread of such intermediate sub-state or cross-state organizational levels as urban, subnational and cross-border regional governance (Brenner 2004);
- 'global civil society' (Edwards 2004);
- the spread of democratization and cosmopolitanism (Held 1995; Archibugi 2008); and/or
- the 'bottom-up' development of new forms of social globalism based on translocal initiatives or 'glocalization', i.e. cross-cutting local initiatives (Sassen 2007).

There are also more pessimistic interpretations that argue that we are entering a world of greater volatility, competing institutions, overlapping jurisdictions and greater instability reflecting a general 'disarticulation of political power' and statehood in a more open ended, destabilizing way sometimes referred to as 'neomedievalism' (Cerny 2000a).

Therefore the future of statehood itself – not merely of states or nation-states – is increasingly uncertain and *contested* at a number of levels in a world characterized by increasing transnational and global problems, cross-cutting political alliances and the emergence of more complex forms of awareness and expectations that new kinds of political action and policy-making are necessary. This chapter will examine the background to this development – the growth and decline of the states system and of states themselves – and reinterpret the *problématique* of statehood in the light of the central challenges facing world politics (*not* International Relations) in the 21st century. I will argue that future structural and organizational developments will depend on the kinds of political coalitions that can be built to confront and deal with those challenges, especially those involving cross-border networks. The result is likely to be a more complex form of world politics that is not only *multi-level* but also *multi-nodal* (Cerny 2010). States are enmeshed in increasingly dense webs of power and politicking, as well as economic and social connections, that, in the continued absence of a world government or a world state, diffuse 'statehood' unevenly through differently structured points of access and decision making. This process sometimes leads to conflict and stalemate, but also sometimes to new, innovative forms of governance and a kind of multi-dimensional statehood within an ongoing process of construction and evolution.

## The distorted development of the nation-state and the states system

The state has been the predominant organizational unit for political, social and economic life in the modern world. Paradoxically, the development of the modern state has historically gone hand in hand with the long-term globalization of world politics and the international economy. Globalization itself in its earlier manifestations was primarily organized and structured by and through the division of the world into states. The effective division of Europe into the first post-feudal states in the 16th and 17th centuries stemmed from a territorial stalemate among competing monarchs. Since that time, ambitious national elites have sought not only to consolidate their rule domestically but also to keep up with other states, especially their neighbours, both politically and economically, through imperialism, trade and other forms of outward expansion and linkages. The development of the leading states has been inextricably intertwined with their imperial expansion and global reach.

From the first European colonial empires in the 15th century to the spread of globalization in the late 20th century, the development and institutionalization of states as such and the states system has been inextricably intertwined with a range of profound transformative changes at various levels:

- the spread of international trade and finance;
- the promotion of industrialization, economic growth and technological change;
- underdevelopment and development;
- the construction of social identity;
- the establishment of international institutions; and
- political modernization, including democratization.

Until the late 20th century, therefore, the very organization of world politics itself and the global political economy was rooted in the emergence, consolidation and interaction of nation-states. Those states still remain. Despite the flaws in the system, which will be dealt with in more detail below, it must be stressed that states also have deeply entrenched sources of institutional and organizational strength. The legacy of the states system is embedded in both perception and practice. Nevertheless, contemporary forms of globalization are challenging the predominant role of the state and transforming it in numerous ways.

In long-term historical perspective, of course, the nation-state is only one of a wide range of alternative political-organizational forms, including village societies, tribal societies, city states, multilayered feudal and warlord-dominated societies, federations and confederations of various kinds, and empires. These other forms have characterized most historical epochs. Nevertheless, the nation-state form is inextricably linked with the concept of *modernity* and thus with an evolutionary conception of political change leading to 'higher' forms of organizational, institutional and socio-economic development. However, with the emergence of new forms of complex interdependence in the late 20th and early 21st centuries – including global markets, networks of firms, transnational pressure groups (NGOs), international regimes, the rise of world cities and urban regions, and the like – states have found themselves increasingly enmeshed in cross-cutting or 'transnational' political, social and economic structures and processes. Rather than constituting the natural 'container' for social life, as much modern social and political theory and ideology has suggested, the nation-state today is highly contingent and in flux (Brenner *et al.* 2003).

Social and political bonds, once rooted in fixed concepts of social status and kinship hierarchies, were increasingly seen from the 17th century onward to derive from a 'social contract', and such contracts were embodied in and constituted through the state (Barker 1962). In turn, political actors representing both old and new socio-economic forces sought to construct new institutional forms to replace the failed feudal system. This process has been called 'institutional selection' (Spruyt 1994). Foucault sees it as representing a particular 'governmentality' or 'governmental rationality' rooted in what in France is called *raison d'État* or what others have called a 'shared mental model' (Roy *et al.* 2007) that takes the state for granted as the normal way to organize social life, effectively the only option (Foucault 2007 and 2008; Burchell *et al.* 1991). Powerful new European state elites – monarchs, bureaucrats, and lower-level administrators and politicians, allied to the new wealthy classes called *bourgeoisie* (city-dwellers) – increasingly defeated attempts to set up alternative organizational forms such as city states and city leagues.

These increasingly centralized states had, or appeared to have, a 'differentiated' organizational structure – that is to say, each had its own set of relatively autonomous officeholders outside other socio-economic hierarchies, with its own rules and resources coming more and more from taxes rather than from feudal, personal or religious obligations. State actors were able collectively to claim 'sovereignty' (Hinsley 1966). Sovereignty, originally rule or supreme power and authority from above, was a more legalistic, centralized, formal and normative version of what is here called statehood. The original European states derived key aspects of their power from the 1648 Peace of Westphalia. This treaty, which ended decades of religious warfare in the wake of the collapse of feudalism and the Holy Roman Empire, indirectly enshrined the twin principles of (a) the territorial integrity of the state and (b) non-intervention in the internal affairs of other states. Together these principles have become the fundamental organizing doctrine of an international system rooted in the *de jure* sovereignty and *de facto* autonomy of states. Sovereignty in the ideal-type sense has therefore been more a political objective than a fact on the ground, and the ideology of the sovereign nation-state has been called a form of 'organised hypocrisy' (Krasner 1999). Nevertheless the principle of national (or state) sovereignty has been at the heart of both domestic state building and international relations throughout the modern era (James 1986).

Nation-states had to be consciously *constructed* precisely because they did *not* constitute self-evident 'natural containers'. Rather they were complex, historically contingent playing fields for political, social and economic power struggles. They were products of discourse, manipulation and institutionalization – the cornerstone of a wider project of political modernization. In this process, European states and later the United States and Japan turned themselves into 'Great Powers' that together dominated world politics and the international political economy, whether through imperial expansion, political influence, economic clout or social imitation. Britain and France were the first effective nation-states (Kohn 1955); much of their strength later came from their world-wide empires. Germany and Italy were only unified in the late 19th century but sought to become empires thereafter. Russia remained a loose, quasi-feudal empire until the Soviet era and retained many of its characteristics thereafter. The United States saw itself originally as a quasi-democratic continental empire that needed to avoid 'foreign entanglements' and had a complex federal structure, but it increasingly expanded outwards and centralized from the end of the 19th century. Japan moved rapidly from isolationist empire to expansionist empire in the 20th century.

Therefore imperial expansion was crucial in providing a resource base for 'core' states to spread the states system around the world through both imposition, on the one hand, and a mixture of resistance and emulation, especially by national liberation movements, on the other. In turn, the most dramatic phases of the global extension of the states system came with decolonization – the end of Spain's empire in Latin America in the 1820s and the dismantling of the British and French Empires from the end of the Second World War through the mid-1960s. Leaders of independence movements and postcolonial governments tried to emulate the European nation-state model as the road to progress and modernity, what has been called 'nation-building' (Bendix 1964), although this process often did not include democratization.

In this context, attempts at post-independence democratization merely opened the way for zero-sum social and economic struggles to be introduced into the core of the institutionalized political process without sufficient capacity for conflict resolution or pursuit of the common good, leading to predatory politics, corruption and authoritarian takeovers (Cerny 2009a). Only a few postcolonial states (especially India) stayed democratic for long, although since 1990 most former Communist states have become democratic and attempts to spread democracy in Asia, Latin America, Africa, and the Middle East have also multiplied in that time, sometimes successfully, sometimes unsuccessfully. Nevertheless, by the end of the 1960s virtually the entire world was divided up into supposedly sovereign states, democratic or not. International arrangements reinforced this trend, as the membership and institutional structures of the United Nations and other formal international organizations are essentially composed of sovereign states. Ironically, it was at this time that the system of states started to decay as the first shoots of a new, transnational form of globalization emerged in the mid-to-late 20th century.

## The state as a contested organization

The capacity of the state to embody and exercise effective statehood rests on two analytically distinct but inextricably intertwined foundations. In the first place, the state, as an *organization* or *institution*, is embodied in particular factors including: (a) a set of generally accepted 'rules of the game'; (b) the distribution of resources in a particular society; (c) a dominant ideology; and (d) the capacity of the state to use force, whether 'the monopoly of legitimate violence' (Max Weber) or a range of legal, economic and social sanctions, to impose particular decisions and ways of doing things upon both individuals and the society as a whole. In the second place, the state, like other organizations and institutions, is populated by a range of *actors* within and around the state apparatus. These 'state actors' make decisions and attempt to impose outcomes on non-state actors. In other words, the state is both a structured field of institutionalized power on the one hand and a structured *playing field* for the exercise of social or personal power on the other.

The most important organizational characteristic of states is that they are – ostensibly at least – so-called '*differentiated*' organizations. In other words, ideal-type states are organizationally distinct from families, churches, classes, races and the like; from economic institutions like firms or markets; and indeed, from non-state political organizations such as interest and pressure groups or social movements. They are in legal and philosophical principle (and to some extent in practice) both discrete and autonomous, in that they are not subordinate to, nor incorporated within, nor morphologically determined by (structurally subsumed into) other organizations, institutions or structures. The state, in theory at least, stands on its own. Nevertheless, both conceptually and in practice the 'state' is also a deeply contested category. The modern state as it has evolved in recent centuries is often taken as a 'given' of political, social and economic life. However, the very notion of the state can be thought of as what philosophers call a form of 'reifica-tion', that is, seeing an abstract concept as if it were a material thing. But states, like ideas, have real consequences. The state can be seen as contested on at least three levels.

First, the state is an *economically* contested organization. As noted above, it is organized around relationships of power as well as political ideas such as fairness and justice, whereas economic organizations like firms and markets are organized in principle at least around material criteria and relations of profit, exchange and economic efficiency. Nevertheless, firms and markets also involve inherent *de facto* relationships of power. In particular, states and state actors have been increasingly involved historically in trying to promote economic growth and modernization. This deeply embedded organizational relationship between state and economy has been the subject of intense debates and conflicts, both academic and political, private and public.

Second, the state is a *socially* contested organization. States are not natural, spontaneous emanations from a taken-for-granted, pre-existing 'society', 'people' or 'public'. States are political superstructures that are historically constructed by real people and political forces around and over often deep divisions such as class, clans and extended families, ethnicity, religion, geography, gender and ideology, usually in an attempt precisely to mitigate, counteract or even violently repress those divisions. People are regularly forced or indoctrinated into acquiescing to the rules, ideas, power structures and policy decisions of the state. 'Citizens' are made, not born. This often entrenches deep conflicts of identity and interest actually *within* the state itself, whether right at the apex or on different levels of the state apparatus.

Finally, the state is a *politically* contested organization. States are constructed in the first place and controlled and/or fought over by political, social and economic actors – from absolutist monarchs and national revolutionaries to various bureaucrats, officials, patrons and clients, from corporate elites to popular movements, and from religious movements to corrupt and even criminal gangs. States can be organizationally 'strong' in the sense that they can be rooted in widely accepted social identities and bonds, or that their institutions are effective and efficiently run, or that their 'writ' runs throughout the territory. They can also be powerful internationally. However, states can also be weak on both levels. All states have particular strengths and weaknesses along various dimensions, often cutting across the so-called 'inside/outside distinction' (Walker 1992).

Nevertheless, as noted earlier, what is distinct about states in the modern world is that the state form of political organization has at least until recently prevailed historically over *other* forms, which have been relatively weak and vulnerable in comparison. The combination of hierarchical power inside the state and the spread of the state form of organized governance across the globe – along with the rise of modern political ideologies and the strategic and tactical focus of political, economic and social actors on gaining power and influence within the state – have led to the widespread assertion and belief that states are, and should be, genuinely 'sovereign'. Whether that sovereignty is thought to start from the top down, as in 'the divine right of kings', or from the bottom up, as in 'popular sovereignty', state organizations in the final analysis are said to represent a holistic concentration and centralization of generalized, overarching and legitimate political power that is unique among organizations – what the political philosopher Michael Oakeshott called a 'civil association', as distinct from an 'enterprise association' that has specific purposes and a limited remit (Oakeshott 1976).

State sovereignty is also Janus-faced, as noted at the beginning of this chapter. At the international level of analysis, there is supposedly no international 'state' or authority structure that has the kind of legal, political, social, economic or cultural reality, claim to primacy or legitimacy that the state possesses. The international system of states – that is, the claim that the international system itself is composed of and constructed by (and *for?*) states above and beyond any other institutions or structures – is seen as the norm. The international balance of power, the territorial division of the world and international law are therefore in theory all constituted by and through relations among states. Each state is in principle, in international law, founded upon a unique base – a specific geographical territory, a specific people or recognized group of citizens, a specific organizational structure or set of institutions, a specific legal personality and a specific sociological identity. Such distinctions, however, have historically often been constructed upon shaky foundations. More important for this book, however, is that the inside/outside distinction rests on foundations that are increasingly problematic in the context of globalization.

## Contemporary challenges to the organizational capacity of the state

Both dimensions of the inside/outside distinction are rooted in the *organizational capacity* of states – that is, the ability of states and state actors to act autonomously and simultaneously both in domestic politics and in the external states system. This is problematic in two main ways. On the one hand, various international, transnational and global structures and processes have competed with, cut across, and constrained, as well as empowered, states and state actors throughout modern history. As noted earlier, the most successful European states throughout the early modern and modern periods were ones whose power and prosperity were rooted in international trade and imperial expansion as well as domestic consolidation, including the United States once it had expanded across the American continent. Indeed, globalization itself has often been seen as the externalization of a mix of hegemonic British and later American patterns of open capitalism, trade liberalization and monetary and financial hegemony, not to mention military success in defeating more authoritarian and corporatist states like Germany and Japan and even the Soviet Union in the Cold War. But in working to expand and extend such patterns globally, state organizational power has paradoxically boxed itself in by promoting its own subsumption in the globalization process.

States and the states system thus do not exist in a vacuum, but are increasingly cut across by a range of 'complex interdependencies' (Keohane and Nye 1977). Globalization theorists suggest that these interdependencies constitute a rather different infrastructure of the international or global. This structure is based on cross-cutting linkages that states have both ridden on the back of and struggled to control – whether multinational corporations, international production chains, the increasing international division of labour rooted in trade interdependence, globalizing financial markets, the spread of advanced information and communications technologies (Marshall McLuhan's 'global village'), rapidly growing patterns of migration and diasporas, and the emergence of diverse forms of 'global governance' and international regimes, not to mention the rapidly evolving field of international law.

For example, the core of domestic state power – what is called in legal terms the 'police power' – is becoming more problematic in this world, where borders are often helpless in controlling the movement of people, information, goods and ideas (Mostov 2008). These highly structured linkages and patterns of behaviour have encompassed and shaped the ways states are born, develop and operate in practice – and they are becoming increasingly institutionalized. They have their own organizational characteristics, power structures and agents that shape the world in ways even apparently strong governments must work harder and harder to catch up with. They may not exhibit the same holistic, hierarchical institutions and processes that developed states do, but they are often more structurally mobile and organizationally flexible than states. In the 21st century, states are increasingly seen as a kind of organizational Maginot Line of global politics.

On the other hand, states are rapidly evolving in their role as domestic or endogenous arenas of collective action in ways that also are inextricably intertwined with complex interdependence and globalization rather than holistic autonomy. Paradoxically, as stated earlier, the world as a whole was only finally divided up into nation states in the mid-to-late twentieth century, just as globalization was starting to change the organizational parameters of the world; in the 1950s and 1960s, when the British and French empires shed their final colonies; and in the 1980s and 1990s, when the Soviet Union lost its Eastern European empire and itself dissolved into the Russian Federation and other post-Soviet states. However, many newer states, as well as older states that had in the past been part of quasi-imperial spheres of influence like that of the United States in Latin America or of Britain and France in Africa, have not 'developed' into bureaucratically effective, politically unified, socially homogeneous, or economically more prosperous and/or fairer societies. Some have thrown in their lot with regional organizations like the European Union, while others have stagnated and become more corrupt, for example suffering from the 'resource curse' or the 'aid curse' (Moyo 2009), and some have become 'failed' or 'collapsed' states, descending into quasi-anarchy, like Somalia.

States are also exogenously diverse and highly unequal. Some are relatively effective, efficient and/or powerful, while others are weak, collapsed or failed. But even in relatively developed and powerful states like the United States, a combination of economic problems and the increasing difficulty of controlling external events has led to what the historian Paul Kennedy called 'imperial overstretch' (Kennedy 1987). These developments involve not only the lack of capability to project military and economic power abroad, but also what in the Vietnam War was symbolized by the 'body bag syndrome', that is, the unwillingness of the American public to see American soldiers die for either unwinnable or inappropriate foreign adventures – a syndrome that has been revived by today's wars in Iraq and Afghanistan. Indeed, military historian James Sheehan has argued that precisely because of its extreme experience of war in the 20th century, Europe, that cauldron of international imperialism in the modern era, has simply lost its taste for war and evolved into a grouping of 'civilian states', more concerned with promoting transnational economic prosperity than seeing their survival and success as bound up in warfare and the external projection of power (Sheehan 2008).

In this context, states are also endogenously – domestically – diverse. They consist of a bewildering variety of institutions and practices – democratic, authoritarian, egalitarian, exploitative, etc. – that have very different consequences both for their inhabitants or citizens, on the one hand, and for other states and their inhabitants/citizens, on the other. No state can fail to be ensnared in the global web in one way or another. Each state combines with and internalizes globalizing trends in somewhat different ways (Soederberg *et al.* 2005). Sometimes this enables them to exploit the opportunities presented by the opening up of particular international markets, for example the so-called 'BRICs' (Brazil, Russia, India, and China), but sometimes they find their international linkages exacerbating domestic problems by aggravating social or ethnic conflicts, hindering or even reversing economic development, or undermining political stability and leading to violent conflict, civil wars and terrorism. At the same time, these transnational linkages can lead to emergent groups, especially a new, often young, increasingly globally aware and technologically skilled bourgeoisie, demanding a greater democratic say, as exemplified in recent years by the 'colour revolutions' of Eastern Europe and the Arab Spring.

Of course, to paraphrase Churchill on democracy, states are still the central and predominant political organization of the modern era, compared with all the others. Markets and other economic organizational structures are concerned with material outcomes, not basic social or political organization. Ethnic groups pursue their own cultural goals, whether inside or outside existing political structures and processes. Only in theocracies do religious organizations claim political sovereignty, and even in the leading theocracy of the 21st century, Iran, religious claims to political authority are contested at various levels. International institutions and regimes are fragmented and lack sanctioning power, although a certain neoliberal hegemony increasingly pertains. Nevertheless, as a result of variables discussed here, the role of the state is increasingly contested both inside and outside. States are the conventional product of history and social forces, not a 'given' or 'natural' phenomenon, and statehood is continuing to evolve in a more open and interdependent world.

## Key issues in the relationship between globalization and statehood

It is possible to identify a range of organizational issues crucial to any understanding of how states work both internally and externally (and in between) in this more complex environment. The first of these is what traditional 'Realist' International Relations theorists call 'capabilities'. This term originally covered mainly military resources but has been extended more and more to include social and economic organization. States that could marshal concentrated military power to defend their national territory and, especially, to conquer or exercise effective influence over other states and/or power sources have, over the course of modern history, been likely to exercise disproportionate influence over outcomes at the international as well as the domestic level. Such powerful states could use their organizational capacity to control other states and the evolution of the international system in general, whether through alliances or more direct forms of domination or hegemony. However, these states were also very vulnerable to complex shifts in the 'balance of power' and often found that others could 'balance' against them by forming alliances as well. Technological changes can also upset such existing balances or relations of capabilities. And diplomacy or international bargaining and politicking among states could constrain or effectively alter existing balances too (Little 2007).

Although the possession of such capabilities has been the main underpinning of national strength or power in the modern era, today it is often seen that other forms of capacity or effectiveness are far more important. As noted above, people, especially in liberal democratic states, are more aware, particularly because of the development of the 'global village', not only of the downside of military involvement in other parts of the world but also of the possibilities of increased popular influence through pluralism and democratization. Paradoxically, this globalization of awareness has led to a growing unwillingness to get involved in military operations abroad unless they are relatively costless. Historians usually see the Tet Offensive by the Vietcong against American military forces in Vietnam starting in January 1968 as the cultural watershed here, when for the first time in history images of battles apparently being lost (although historians disagree on who won or lost Tet) were viewed over the breakfast table by ordinary people and fed into a mass movement against the war.

At the same time, the costs of war, like the costs of empire in the 1950s, are increasingly seen by economists to be counterproductive of economic development, growth, and prosperity – in other words a drain on the state (and the country) rather than a benefit. Debates are raging over whether the costs of the war in Iraq, often estimated at US$ 2 to 3 trillion, have in turn prevented the United States from tackling a range of other problems, both domestic (health care, rebuilding infrastructure, social security, employment) and foreign (development aid, fighting disease, etc.) (Bilmes and Stiglitz 2008). In this context, the maintenance or expansion of military and related capabilities are increasingly seen as having negative consequences for state, society and economy. The implications of this shift for the organization of the state are enormous, both in opening the state up to new international economic and institutional opportunities and constraints and in expanding the economic regulatory/domestic state. The continuing financial crisis has accelerated awareness of these issues at all levels across the globe.

For these and other reasons, war as an instrument of statehood has declined dramatically since the Second World War. And despite the increased prominence and visibility of civil wars, ethnic conflicts and terrorism in recent years, especially as the result of the widely televised and dramatic destruction of the World Trade Center in New York by al-Qaeda militants on 11 September 2001, those sorts of wars have significantly decreased too. Some analysts stress the role of global awareness and the role of norms of peace and security in this previously understated development (Pinker 2011), while others stress – paradoxically, at first glance – the very success of the states system itself. As state borders have become more fixed and mutually recognized, as states themselves have become more firmly rooted domestically and concerned with economic issues in a globalizing world, and as intergovernmental regimes have become more developed and accepted, so foreign conquest, empire building and other forms of war have come to be seen as a pathological rather than normal state of affairs. Indeed, United

Nations peacekeeping has played a significant role in this transformation, especially with regard to civil wars and ethnic conflict (Goldstein 2011). Whereas in the post-feudal European context, as Charles Tilly so famously wrote, 'war made the state, and the state made war' (Tilly 1975), today states, especially 'civilian states', are expected to make peace and cooperate in order to grow and prosper (Kaplan 2012). 'The story is more one of war's containment than expansion' (Strachan and Scheipers 2011: 21).

The second major organizational issue facing the state in the 21st century involves the internal coherence and hierarchical effectiveness of states in both domestic and foreign policy-type decision making. States that are internally divided, bureaucratically weak, torn asunder by civil conflict, and/or subject to the influence of special interests of various kinds, may be ineffective in pursuing so-called 'national interests' and may even be themselves the cause of destabilization processes that limit or even destroy state capacity and therefore undermine statehood itself. All states are facing analogous pressures, including the strongest. Competing domestic interests have often been at odds with the 'national interest' in the modern era, and in the age of globalization, that conflict of interests is expanding rapidly.

The competition of interests has previously been analysed primarily at domestic level but is becoming increasingly transnationalized (Cerny 2010). Some critical analysts have identified the formation of a 'transnational capitalist class' – or at least a 'transnational elite' linked with multinational corporations, global financial markets, various transnational 'policy networks' and 'epistemic communities' and the like, and further associated with hegemonic opinion formers – especially in developed states (Sklair 2000; Pijl 1998; Gill 2003). These groups are more than mere competing actors. Indeed, they are said to have a common interest in the spread of a neoliberal model of globalizing capitalism. Not only do they have common goals across borders, but they also have resource power and a set of institutional bases and linkages that go from the local to the global (sometimes called 'glocalization'), not to mention the kinds of personal connections traditionally associated in domestic-level political sociology with class and elite analysis. Even if they do not in fact possess this kind of organizational coherence and instead are seen as a set of competing pluralistic interests, however, their common concern with developing transnational power bases – cross-border sources of income and influence – gives them a kind of collective political muscle that parochial domestic groups cannot match.

The most powerful interest groups are increasingly those that can mobilize resources transnationally and not just internally – multinational corporations, global financial market actors, social networks that cut across borders like ethnic and/or religious diasporas, and even consumers who don't care where particular goods are made provided the price and quality are right for the means at their disposal. Nation-states represent sociological 'nations' less and less, increasingly resembling associations of consumers (Ostrom *et al.* 1961) trying to get the best product at the best price in the international marketplace. They are characterized by domestic fragmentation and cross-border linkages – what Rosenau calls 'fragmegration', or transnational integration alongside domestic fragmentation (Rosenau 2003). In this context, neoliberal globalization has become the 'common sense' of a wide range of otherwise competing interests and factions (Cerny 2010).

The third major organizational issue of the 21st century concerns whether the state itself is increasingly becoming 'splintered' or 'disaggregated'. In studies of bureaucracy in the 20th-century tradition of Max Weber, the key to effective rule was said to require a hierarchically organized state in which officials knew their roles and functions in the larger structure. Although a full command hierarchy in the authoritarian or Soviet planning modes was seen to be counterproductive, the state required a great deal of centrally organized institutional coherence and administrative efficiency in order to develop and prosper. Today, that logic has been turned on its head. The most effective bureaucratic structures and processes are those that link officials in particular issue areas with their counterparts in other countries, in order that they might design and implement converging international standards, whether for global financial market regulation and trade rules or accounting and auditing standards and the like. Expanding 'transgovernmental networks' among regulators, legislators and legal officials are effectively transnationalizing such issue areas, red-lining them from domestic protectionist interests, dominating policy-making processes, and globalizing the most important parts of the state in order to promote economic growth and other key policy goals (Slaughter 2004).

A fourth level of internal organizational change concerns the so-called 'competition state' (Cerny 2000b, 2009b). Modern nation-states, in the pursuit of the public interest or the 'general welfare', have traditionally sought to 'decommodify' key areas of public policy – to take them out of the market through some form of direct state intervention – in order to protect strategic industries or financial institutions, bail out consumers or investors, build infrastructure, counteract business cycles and integrate workers into cooperating with the capitalist process through unionization, corporatism, the welfare state and the like. This process in the 20th century was linked with the growing social and economic functions of the state – the industrial state and the welfare state – and tended to come about through the expansion of what have been called 'one-size-fits-all' bureaucracies for the delivery of public and social services.

Today governments are more concerned not with decommodification of social and economic policy but with the 'commodification of the state' itself (Cerny 1990). This has two goals. The first is to promote the international competitiveness of domestically based (although often transnationally organized) industries. Domestic sources of inputs and domestic markets for products are too small to be economically efficient. Only competitiveness in the international marketplace will do. The second is to reduce the costs of the state – what is called 'reinventing government' – or 'getting more for less' (Osborne and Gaebler 1992). These two processes are aimed both at streamlining and marketizing state intervention in the economy and at reorganizing the state itself according to organizational practices and procedures drawn from private business. The welfare state is increasingly under cost pressure in the developed world, and developing states are often not able to provide meaningful welfare systems at all. The current financial crisis is only exacerbating this trend, despite Keynesian stimulus policies, which are seen as short-term remedies intended to 'save capitalism from the capitalists' (Cerny 2011). Economic growth in general is today more the result of global economic trends and developments than of state policies.

This combination of the transformation of capabilities through complex interdependence, the transnationalization of interests, the disaggregation of the state and the coming of the competition state has fundamentally transformed how the state itself works, eroding, undermining and making 'end runs' around the traditional Weberian state. Of course, different states have distinct institutional (or organizational) logics. Each is subject to a form of path dependency in which historical developments create both specific constraints and specific opportunities that become embedded in the way states work. Nevertheless, there is a rapidly growing trend towards the erosion of national varieties of capitalism and the rise of a new neoliberal hegemony rooted in globalization (Soederberg *et al.* 2005; Cerny 2010).

## Conclusion: statehood as the predominant problématique of 21st-century world politics

Statehood is not a given, the exclusive property and distinguishing feature of modern nation-states, but a *problématique* or analytical puzzle, the parameters of which are continually evolving. Organizationally strong states may to some extent be able both to internalize and to resist the pressures of economic, social and political globalization, although that capacity is increasingly hedged around by complex interdependence. Organizationally weak states are undermined by globalization and crisis becomes endemic. Most states are in between these two extremes, with state actors and various kinds of interest groups – crucial players in the international system of states as well as in the expanding globalization process – seeking to alter, reform or completely restructure states in order to cope with the challenges of a globalizing world. In this context, effective statehood is becoming more and more difficult to achieve at the level of the nation-state, while multi-level and multi-nodal politics are creating new and complex forms of latent, embryonic and indeed emergent forms of statehood that have increasingly come to dominate politics in the first decade of the 21st century. The statue of Janus increasingly resembles a kind of Gulliver, pinned down by the Liliputians of globalization, while people cast about for new ways of organizing their relationships and going about their business.

## Guide to further reading

These issues are covered more comprehensively in Cerny (2010). A classic work developing concepts such as 'transnational networks' and 'complex interdependence' is Keohane and Nye (1977). Foucault (2008) provides a highly insightful discussion of concepts like 'neoliberalism' and 'governmentality', that is, how statehood changed fundamentally in the 20th century. Hurrell (2007) is an excellent contrasting perspective from a leading member of the English School of International Relations, while Gallarotti (2009) shows how attempts by states to develop traditional power capabilities in a context of growing interdependence can backfire – the 'power curse'. Pinker (2011) and Goldstein (2011) have initiated a major debate on the decline of war and violence in the 21st century. A range of key public policy issues are analysed in innovative ways in Evans (2005). Sassen (2007) looks at micro-level developments that underpin the kind of transformation of statehood addressed here, Slaughter (2004) shows how governments themselves are increasingly inextricably intertwined with each other, and Soederberg *et al.* (2005) argue that 'globalization' is increasingly 'internalized' in the domestic politics of states, interest groups and other actors, that is, it is not an 'outside in' or 'top-down' phenomenon, but one that shapes daily life and politics at all levels, leading to a new, variegated statehood that transcends and absorbs the nation-state.

Chapter 4

# Governing the Global Economy: Multilateral Economic Institutions

*RICHARD HIGGOTT*

In July 1944 delegates from all 44 Allied nations in the Second World War met at the Mount Washington Hotel in Bretton Woods, New Hampshire to discuss the reconstruction of the international economic and financial systems after the war. The goal of the participants was to create a system which would avoid the financial instability that followed the First World War – and contributed to the start of the Second World War – as well as to support the reconstruction of economies ravaged by conflict. A final, more contentious aim was to lay the foundations of a liberal multilateral trading system. These three aims resulted in the three institutions which were agreed upon at Bretton Woods: the International Monetary Fund (IMF), the International Bank for Reconstruction and Development (IBRD), more commonly known as the World Bank, and the General Agreement on Tariffs and Trade (GATT) initially a set of bargained agreements which eventually became the World Trade Organisation (WTO). These institutions have become central parts of an international order that aspires to be multilateral in form and global in scope. Indeed, it is difficult to imagine quite what 'globalization' might look like without the existence of international organizations generally or of the international economic (financial and trade) institutions (IFTIs or IEIs) in particular. However, the continuation of the global financial crisis that began in 2008 (see Sinclair, this volume) has caused some observers to question whether the international economic institutions are still 'fit for purpose': if they are repeatedly unable to prevent economic crises or facilitate long-term collective action economic problem solving, then what are they for? Such questions oversimplify the problems of managing the global economy.

The struggle between power and rules-based behaviour is the primary hallmark of the present system of global economic governance. The challenge of marrying the two in a meaningful and legitimate manner remains the perennial concern of those attempting to grapple with politics and economics at the international level. The multilateral financial institutions are undoubtedly imperfect. However, they represent an important step in the development of global economic governance, the ultimate goal of which is a more stable and equitable international economy. In an era characterized by higher levels of economic interdependence the need for multilateral economic institutions will only grow.

In order to develop this argument the chapter proceeds as follows. First, it provides some initial clarification of terms and concepts. Second, it sketches the general historical contours and dynamics that have made multilateral institutions quintessential agents of the post-Second World War international system. Third, it outlines the role of the original Bretton Woods institutions and the GATT and explains how their missions have changed over time and attracted criticism. Fourth, it describes some newer multilateral organizational activity and suggests why issues of authority and accountability have become increasingly contested as – often unelected – policymakers (public and private) and economic actors accrue greater decision-making authority. Finally, the chapter assesses the prospects for global economic governance and the ability of multilateral institutions to participate in the management of the complexity and uncertainty that is an endemic part of the current world order.

## Conceptualizing multilateralism

The key aim of multilateralism, according to the theoretical literature, is overcoming collective action problems in the absence of enforcement (for a review see Martin 2006). Robert Keohane (1990) and John Ruggie (1993: 14), in their influential analyses of multilateralism, describe it as a process that 'coordinates behaviour among three or more states on the basis of generalised principles of conduct'. This description raises a series of further questions: upon which (or whose) principles or norms will the process be based? How should the norms that shape behaviour actually be operationalized? And how should decision-making authority be allocated? Empirically, we can observe that the institutionalization over time of bodies such as the IMF and the World Bank has seen a greater degree of decision-making autonomy pass to the institution than their membership had initially anticipated.

The growth of new state-sponsored and non-governmental organizations has been a defining feature of the international system for decades, and such organizations have played a crucial role in institutionalizing particular ideas and practices (Meyer *et al.* 1997). However, there is an important distinction between organizations and institutions: all organizations are institutions, but not all institutions are organizations (see Higgott 2006). International organizations have a formal identity, staff, budgets and a potential capacity to act in the international system that in some ways mirrors or even stands in for the actions of states. Institutions, by contrast, may also refer to cognitive and regulatory structures that inform more general social behaviour, and which may be carried by cultures and routine patterns of behaviour (Scott 1995). The intersection of formal organizational or state power and more informal cultural or social influences was central to early attempts to theorize emerging practices of 'governance without government' (Rosenau 1992).

A final point to note about multilateral organizations in particular and their potential for exerting influence relates to their composition and role. Some organizations are established to serve a specific purpose, and the IFTIs are especially important illustrations of this possibility. Others may have a circumscribed regional identity; organizations like the North America Free Trade Agreement, the Asia Pacific Economic Cooperation forum and especially the European Union (EU) are important in this regard. Thus, an emerging 'conventional wisdom' now has it that international multilateral institutions and organizations provide global public goods, or the sorts of benefits that potentially accrue from effective trade or monetary regimes that states acting alone could simply not provide (Kaul *et al.* 1999). A brief look at the history of multilateralism suggests why this view prevails.

## Economic multilateralism in historical context

The number of international organizations grew dramatically during the course of the 20th century (for a review see Armstrong *et al.* 2004). There was, and is, a strong link between incipient forms of 'globalization' and the growth of international cooperation and institutionalization. The fact that what is widely regarded as the first international organization was the International Telegraph Union (founded in 1865) is reminder also of the enduring links between technological development, functional necessity and political cooperation (Hirst and Thompson, 1999). Less happily, the often unsuccessful pursuit of peace has also been a major spur for international cooperation: the Concert of Europe in the 19th century and the League of Nations in the first half of the 20th arc sobering reminders of the difficulty of creating lasting and effective institutions. While the links between conflict and cooperation might seem most immediate and obvious, warfare and its aftermath have also been responsible for much more encompassing forms of institutionalized cooperation, including economic policy coordination (Ikenberry, 2001).

The most important and enduring example of this possibility is the international order created under the auspices of US 'hegemony' in the aftermath of the Second World War (see Beeson and Higgott 2005). As already suggested, the organizations established at this time were primarily concerned with the management of the international economy. This should not surprise us: the principal lesson that policymakers in the Anglo-American alliance took from history, specifically the period between the two world wars, was that a failure to maintain an 'open', liberal economic order was a recipe for international economic disorder and possibly outright military conflict. Consequently the IEIs were charged with maintaining a stable monetary order (the IMF), post-war economic rebuilding (the IBRD), liberalizing trade via the reduction of tariffs (the GATT) and encouraging economic development more generally (the IBRD). Their obvious wider aggregate welfare-enhancing utility notwithstanding, such policies have been interpreted by some analysts as reflecting the normative preferences of American policymakers and even actively advantaging US-based economic interests (Kolko 1988; Harvey 2003).

There are a number of general points to note about this historical context. First it is important to re-emphasize just how rapidly organizational development has occurred. International Governmental Organizations (IGOs) increased from 37 to well over 400 by the end of the 20th century (Schiavone 2001). The second point to stress is that there has been a continuing shift of authority from states to non-government or government-sponsored organizations which are assuming greater responsibility for making and enacting policy in areas of presumed competence. Bodies like the Bank for International Settlements (BIS) (formed in 1930), the International Organization of Securities Commissions (IOSCO) (formed in 1983), Institute of International Finance (IIF) (formed in 1983) or the International Swaps and Derivatives Association (ISDA) (formed in1985), are good examples of organizations that are products of their era, and composed of specialist industry representatives or unelected technocrats (see Helleiner *et al.* 2010). Braithwaite and Drahos's review of the growth of business regulation describes the way in which new organizations have emerged to address novel problems and issue areas. Unsurprisingly, these organizational activities, like those from an earlier era, were found to reflect the prevailing configurations of power (Braithwaite and Drahos, 2000: 583).

## The evolving roles of the Bretton Woods institutions (and the WTO)

The Bretton Woods institutions have assumed such a prominent and often contentious place in the history of economic multilateralism and cooperation that it is worth spelling out their roles in more detail. There are two general points to make at the outset. First, the original IFIs established after the Second World War were products of specific economic and geopolitical circumstances. They reflected US (and British) desires to rebuild successful capitalist economies in the face of what was then a credible 'communist' competition from the Soviet Union. Secondly, the roles of the IFIs evolve with the changing geopolitical environment as new generations rise to positions of institutional leadership and as the issues on the international agenda change.

The role of the IMF has changed significantly since its creation. Originally established to manage and oversee a system of more or less fixed exchange rates, the IMF's mandate was fundamentally undermined by the evolving geopolitical context in which it was embedded. The expense of the Vietnam War and intensified international economic competition led to the US 'closing the gold window' in 1971, thus ending the relationship between the US dollar and the value of gold (Gowa 1983) which led to the dismantling of the system of fixed exchange rates. This in turn led to the growth of international money markets in a new era of 'floating' exchange rates. In response to this changing environment, the IMF reinvented itself in several ways. For instance, the 1970s saw its mission transformed from one of the arbiter of global monetary stability to that of arbiter of developing country macro-economic rectitude (Elliott and Hufbauer 2002) as it began making concessional loans to poor countries experiencing balance of payment problems.

In 1986 the IMF created a new concessional loan programme called the Structural Adjustment Facility. Mainly as a result of this programme, the IMF in the 1980s and 1990s became primarily associated with crisis management and the enforcement of a 'neoliberal' agenda of economic liberalization (Chwieroth 2007). In order to receive loans, countries in economic crisis were required to privatize public assets, cut government spending, reduce regulation and liberalize their capital accounts. These 'conditionalities' were highly controversial for the way they involved the IMF in the domestic affairs of some of its members. The IMF response to the Asian Financial Crisis of the late 1990s marked the apogee of IMF interventionism. As a result of its handling of the crisis 'the IMF came under criticism that was more intense and widespread than at any other time in its history' (IMF 2011). This criticism spanned the political spectrum from high priests of the anti-globalization movement (see Bello 1998) through to impeccably credentialed Nobel laureates in economics (see Stiglitz 2002). In particular it was criticized for its close relationship with the US government (Wade and Veneroso 1998): 'from this experience, the IMF drew several lessons that would alter its responses to future events' (IMF, 2011). In effect, the IMF's role as the arbiter of global macro-economic rectitude, especially in the developing world, disappeared in the wake of its sub-optimal performance in the financial crises of the late 20th century. However, the crises of the early 20th century have prompted the role of the IMF in the global economy to evolve once again. The 2009 G20 summit in London tasked the IMF with developing guidelines for the supervision of the financial sector, and the European sovereign debt crisis has led the IMF to reprise its role as arbiter of macro-economic rectitude but with Greece playing the part of the developing country.

The role of the World Bank, like that of the IMF, has evolved significantly over time. Beginning as a facilitator of European reconstruction following the Second World War, its mission today is to reduce poverty and support development (World Bank 2012). This transformation had a natural logic to it in the era of decolonization. While its organizational evolution should not simply be read as a reformulation of the IMF's neoliberal template (Rodrik 2006), it clearly has supported neoliberal reform in the developing world. Indeed, one of the reasons the Bank has attracted so much attention has been because its 'structural adjustment' policies – which tied financial assistance to far-reaching reforms designed to reconfigure the political economies of its client states – complemented IMF policy in the 1980s and 1990s. Since that time the Bank has undergone a process of self-evaluation and change re-shaped by a changing international environment in which strategic factors and ideas about development have changed over time.

The preoccupation with 'modernization' and the pursuit of massive, often inappropriate development projects gave way in the late 1990s to a more technocratic approach that stresses its role as a 'knowledge bank' (Stone 2001), with an emphasis on institutional reform, the provision of 'good governance' and a rhetorical commitment to greater inclusiveness and engagement (Stone and Wright 2006). The Bank's intellectual and practical transition, although more widely accepted and less controversial than that of the IMF, has not been without its internal governance failures and critics (see, for example, Weaver 2008 and Woods 2006). Concerns about their often unaccountable forms of internal organization, especially with regard to voting rights, continue to reflect the entrenched nature of the political influence of major powers, as indeed is the case in many international organizations more generally (see Keohane *et al.* 2009).

Consequently, despite the Bank's efforts to differentiate itself from the IMF and respond more effectively to criticisms from 'global civil society' and client states over the decade 1998–2007, there remains a good deal of dissatisfaction with both the ideational and practical roles of the two principal IFIs. The financial crisis of 2007–9 has exacerbated the dissatisfaction in many quarters. Calls for the reform and/or the development of a new institutional architecture continue unabated, notwithstanding the regular G20 summits held since November 2008.

The third leg of the post-Second World War international multilateral economic architectural triangle, the GATT, had as its original mandate the reduction of those barriers to trade (then principally tariffs) that were seen to have played a destructive role in causing and prolonging the Great Depression of the inter-war years. Not only was increased trade thought likely to spur the reconstruction of the western world's battered economies, but greater economic interdependence was also seen as a way of reducing the prospect of conflict. This position is supported by strong prima facie evidence that economic interdependence does indeed have pacific effects and is associated with, if not responsible for, higher economic growth (Keohane and Nye 1977; Mousseau 2009). The GATT, through a series of post-Second World War multilateral trade negotiation rounds, successfully and substantially reduced the role of the tariff as an instrument of protection and instilled a series of norms and principles into the multilateral trade regime (notably the norms of most favoured nation status and national treatment) (see Hoekman and Kostecki 2001; Narliker 2005; WTO 2007:179–201). It also fulfilled some of the generally unstated Cold War geopolitical goals that underpinned its rationale, along with that of the IMF and the World Bank.

In the decades following the end of the war the GATT developed major capacity constraints. Patterns of global trade evolved (trade in services in particular grew in importance) and the favoured methods of economic protectionism shifted from tariff to non-tariff barriers. The reduction in tariffs opened up the US economy more than that of many of its trading partners at the same time as the rise of non-tariff barriers affecting its developing sectors (service and intellectual property) became less effective. Throughout the 1970s and early 1980s the US trade policy community saw that GATT rules and procedures would do nothing to redress these imbalances. This led to the introduction of a policy of 'aggressive unilateralism' intended to prise open markets, especially in the face of mounting trade deficits with Japan, the principal beneficiary in the economic and strategic environment the US had effectively underwritten (see Bhagwati and Patrick 1990).

While aggressive trade rhetoric exceeded practice it nevertheless secured an adjustment in the incentive structures of US trading partners and a willingness to contemplate a new trade round to address those interests deemed essential by the US. Hence, when the Uruguay Round of trade negotiations commenced in 1986, the agenda covered virtually every outstanding trade issue, aimed to review all the original articles of the GATT and was expected to extend the trading system to cover services and intellectual property for the first time (WTO 2012). Talks took twice as long as originally scheduled and involved 123 countries, but were successfully concluded in 1994, resulting in the creation of the WTO, a new organization including not only GATT but agreements on services (GATS), intellectual property (TRIPS) and a dispute settlement mechanism (see Croome 1995) giving the WTO a significantly greater capacity to enforce compliance with its resolutions. In addition, the ambit of issues that the WTO seeks to manage has expanded significantly in line with the evolving international political economy. However, the Uruguay Round was criticized because the new agreements on services and intellectual property reflected the economic interests of the most economically developed countries, especially the US. Partly in response to this perceived imbalance the subsequent round of trade negotiations, launched in Doha in 2001, explicitly aimed to engage with trade issues of concern to developing countries.

Liberalizing international trade, the fundamental purpose of the GATT/WTO, is a highly contentious and emotive policy area, because it deals with the most basic concerns of everyday life and questions central to cultural identity. Many of these issues are perceived to be of the highest national interest. Criticism of the GATT and WTO has come from analysts across the political spectrum, from what we might call 'right nationalists' in the US and parts of Europe, to the left developmentalist and anti-globalization movements of the South. Both groups, from their different perspectives, see the WTO as an excessively intrusive, sovereignty-challenging back door to global governance and would have it abolished. The WTO's supporters, however, occupy the pivotal positions in the global policy community (both public and private); although they too do not adopt a uniform position and range across a spectrum from market privileging neo-classicists to interventionist Keynesians. But they too recognize that the WTO faces serious problems in maintaining its global economic institutional relevance in the early 21st century.

## A new institutional architecture?

As argued, discontent over the roles of the IEIs, in both the analytical and policy communities, has been a continuing theme in the post-war period. The East Asian crisis of the late 1990s brought dissatisfaction with the so-called 'international financial architecture' to something of a head. In retrospect this should not surprise us. A number of regional economies that were formerly objects of admiration because of their economic achievements were suddenly thrown into chaos and many among their populations were thrown back into the poverty from which they had recently escaped. Observers felt that if the IFIs were not in some way responsible for the crisis by encouraging premature economic liberalization, they were certainly culpable in failing to manage the impact of and recovery from the crisis. Indeed, one of the big lessons that East Asian economic and political elites drew from the crisis was that the region rapidly needed to develop its own economic institutions if it wanted to be able to respond more effectively to future crises (Grimes 2009). As a consequence, there have been accelerated efforts to develop new, regionally based economic mechanisms (Deiter and Higgott 2003.) One of the great paradoxes of globalization, therefore, has been a noteworthy proliferation of institutions to either encourage regional integration or to generate regional responses to specific problems (see Breslin, this volume). Given Ruggie's understanding of multilateralism, as cooperation between two or more states, we should recognize these regional activities for what they also are – exercises in multilateralism.

Indeed, the growth of regional multilateral economic institutions must be seen as the other side of the coin of global multilateralism (on aspects of this, see Warwick Commission 2007: 45-53; Frankel 1997). The growth of regional multi-lateral institutions is not an exclusively East Asian phenomenon. On the contrary, it is a strong characteristic of post-Second World War international economic rela-tions. Such processes are most fully developed in Western Europe (see Telo 2009) notwithstanding a lack of enthusiasm about the European project amongst large sections of its own populations at the end of the first decade of the 21st century. Indeed, doubts have been expressed about the EU's capacity to survive, much less effectively manage the current global economic crisis (Erlanger and Castle 2009), particularly as the European sovereign debt crisis has unfolded.

Similar doubts about our abilities to provide an appropriate multilateral regu-latory framework for the management of the economy at the global level abound in the wake of the great recession of 2007–9 – even by prominent former cham-pions of the free market (Turner 2009; Wolf 2009). Although the arguments of would-be reformers are at least being heard, it is not clear whether the crisis at the end of the first decade of the 21st century will lead to major changes in the existing system of regulation. Precisely the same arguments were heard after the Asian crisis when there were widespread calls for institutional reform and tighter control of the activities of banks and financial markets (Armijo 2002; Kenen 2001). In reality, little has changed. Indeed, many of the restrictions that had formerly been put in place to control the activities of banks at a national level were repealed, as policymakers in the Anglo-American economies became locked in a competition to provide 'light-touch', business-friendly regulation (see Sinclair, this volume).

The dialectical interaction, broadly conceived, between states and markets has been one of the central dynamics driving the evolution of the international econ-omy, and the institutions that seek to manage it, for the last 60 years. One perennial problem, as economic historian Niall Ferguson opines (Ferguson 2009) seems to be the failure to learn the lessons of history: policymakers in the US and the UK in particular have ignored the experiences of the Great Depression, the saving and loans crisis in the US, the Asian crisis and so on. However, it is important to emphasize that the most recent crisis did not come as a complete surprise to everyone. In addition to the long-standing warnings of some academics (Strange 1998), more institutionalized forms of policy advice were also ignored. The Bank for International Settlements (BIS) a key source of independent policy advice for policymakers around the world, despite raising concerns about the dangers associated with the new financial instruments central to the most recent crisis, was continuously ignored (Giles 2009).

That policymakers choose to ignore advice that is unwelcome or at odds with pre-existing ideological prejudices should not surprise us. Nevertheless, it raises important questions about the role that extant or new institutions can actually play in any putative processes of global governance. One key issue, as we have seen, is the unrepresentative nature of existing international institutions. Recently there have been attempts to expand the club of 'developed' economies beyond the confines of the G7 and G8 groupings which have dominated inter-governmental discussions for decades. The prominence achieved by the G20, which includes key actors from the 'global South' like Brazil, China and India, in the wake of the recent crisis should be seen as part of a genuine push to develop more representative multilateral institutions. An idea developed from an earlier Canadian initiative (see Higgott 2005), the G20 failed to gain momentum until the crises of 2007–9. And yet it remains far from clear how effective such a group might be in the long term. There remains a reluctance on the part of the major powers, especially the US, and indeed some declining former major powers (especially in Europe) to concede the need to share power with the new actors from the South (see Beeson and Bell 2009). Indeed, the apparent difficulties of state-based, inter-governmental organizations in securing effective collective action problem solving in times of crisis helps to account for the rise of other novel forms of governance.

One of the most striking aspects of what passes for global economic governance at present is just how much of it is becoming increasingly decentralized and network-based. From the closing decades of the 20th century we have seen a proliferation in the number of non-state, specialist agencies and organizations playing an increasingly prominent role in international standard setting. Inherently elitist, the principal claim for inclusion in these new informal and often uncoordinated networks of governance is technocratic competence or specialist expertise. The development of the BIS prior to the crises of 2007–9 is a classic example of what we might call a transnational executive network (TEN) and reflects a more generalized ideological preference for light touch regulation on the parts of many OECD governments; in this case as they delegated responsibility for monetary policy to (unelected) central bankers (Tsingou 2004, 2010). This process is mirrored by a similar, and simultaneous, process of regulatory diffusion occurring in the private sector as different actors develop a responsibility for setting regulatory standards for codes of conduct, production standards and the like (Braithwaite and Drahos 2000). The interesting normative question posed by these developments is the degree to which these actors are contributing to the delivery of global public goods (as public goods theory would have it) or whether they are in fact engaged in the provision of club goods for their respective clientele. The empirical evidence from the financial crises of 2007–9 would suggest that private interest has prevailed over public good.

For some observers the growth of TENs is both predictable and  appropriate, and marks a functional response to demands for regulation and governance that can no longer be met by states in an era of globalization (Slaughter 2004.) For others this is part of a long-running debate between those who see states as taking part in a process in which they have voluntarily ceded power to other actors, and those who view state authority as being inexorably undermined by technological developments and intensifying transnational economic and political processes (see Cerny, this volume; Cooper *et al.* 2008). What is novel and potentially important now, however, is the possibility that the very nature of the 'knowledge economy' is generating new patterns of governance in which informal ties and expertise are generating new networks that help explain the way in which policy is made at the global level (Stone 2008) and, at a more macro-theoretical level for some, even the way the economy is conceived as an object of governance (Haas 1990; Rose 1993).

Of one thing there is little doubt. One effect of the crises of the early 21st century is that the state has made a major comeback as a key stakeholder in the unfolding process of economic reform. Although it is too soon to know what the long-term impacts of the current crisis will be, it has challenged the credibility of the hands-off, light-touch style of neoliberal-inspired economic regulation that characterized the last two decades of the 20th century and the early years of the 21st and which, especially, justified and actively encouraged the growing role of self-regulation by the private sector in the Anglo-American economies (see Gamble 2009).

## The contingent future of multilateral economic governance

The multilateral economic institutions have long been criticized for lacking polit-ical legitimacy. The argument that some forms of regulation are so specialized that only a handful of experts, practitioners or other insiders can claim to understand their intricacies, does not overcome the fundamental problems that flow from a legitimacy deficit (Hurd 1999). For all their shortcomings, the saving grace of democratically elected bodies is that they can claim a popular mandate for their actions. This has never been the case with the multilateral institutions. Their legit-imacy as agents of global governance is still drawn only indirectly from the legiti-macy of their member states.

Theoretical endeavours to enhance legitimacy at the global level, emanating from essentially cosmopolitan views of global civil society, have invariably assumed an extension of the 'domestic analogy' to the extra-territorial, or global, context. That is, the extension of the model of democratic accountability that we have come to accept in the advanced countries of the developed world to the wider global context. The weakness of the domestic analogy is that only the most mini-mal of democratic constraints present within a domestic polity are present at the global level (Dahl 1999.) There is no serious institutionalized system of checks and balances at the global level. Institutional constraints that do exist have little purchase on the behaviour of major powers, especially a hegemon, should they choose to ignore them, and to speak of a *global* public sphere or *global* polity, in a legal or a sociological sense, has little meaning (see Ougaard and Higgott 2002).

There are, of course, sophisticated cosmopolitan democratic theories which have problematized the domestic analogy in the attempt to elaborate which elements of 'traditional' democratic theory – that presuppose a national *demos* (people) and a nation-state context – are feasible and desirable on the global level of politics (Held 2002, 2005; Archibugi *et al.* 2000; Archibugi 2000). But in these theories, which are principally normative, feasibility tends to give way to desirability. Liberal cosmopolitan theorists start from the individual as a member of humanity as a whole, rather than the state, and the idea that we as members deserve equal political treatment. They emphasize the importance of individual rights claims and wish to replace the state-based system of international relations with a new set of cosmopolitan principles, laying out a moral standard that sets limits to what people and political authorities are allowed to do through international institutions (for examples see Held 2002: 23–4). Sovereignty, the idea of rightful authority, is thus divorced from the idea of fixed territorial boundaries and thought of as an *attribute of basic cosmopolitan law* (Held 2002: 32).

Of course, contemporary multilateral institutions and multilateralism as practice do not operate with these normative assumptions. The legitimacy of multilateralism, to the extent that it exists, is embedded in shared norms (usually of elites, rather than wider national publics) and is underwritten by judicial instruments (such as the International Criminal Court or the Dispute Settlement Mechanism of the WTO). But contrary to many assumptions in both the scholarly and the policy world that excessively privilege an increasingly dynamic role for civil society and non-state actors, effective multilateral governance at the global level remains with states as the principal (although not exclusive) actors.

However, recognizing the central role for states does not mean yielding to a purely statist view of legitimacy. States are not the sole actors in global governance. Global institutions involve and reflect the perspectives of individuals as well as states. To have the right to rule means that institutional agents are morally justified in making rules and that people subject to those rules have moral reasons for complying with them or at least not preventing others from doing so (Buchanan and Keohane 2006: 411). Legitimate global governance must thus understand state actions within a global framework of international law and *common norms of action*. What Keohane (2005) calls the increasingly 'contingent' nature of multilateralism has meant that the multilateral aspirations of the second half of the 20th century are more muted in the 21st. What can be done multilaterally (in an inclusive sense of the word) is being recast in more restrictive terms. This is clearly a factor behind the emergence of other approaches to and exercises in collective action. This chapter has already identified the growing trend towards regional economic cooperation in the rise of preferential trading arrangements.

The growth of regionalism in recent years has clearly been sub-optimal in systemic and political terms in a number of ways. Specifically, regionalism has diverted attention from multilateral negotiations. Governments may believe, or be lulled politically into the conviction, that they can acquire all they need by way of trade policy through regional arrangements. This has led to, and is likely to continue to lead to, neglect of the relative costs and benefits, especially over time, of regional versus multilateral approaches to trade relations. As a consequence, some recent theorizing in the trade domain has also led scholars to identify the need, in the words of Richard Baldwin and his colleagues, to 'multilateralize regionalism' (see Baldwin 2006; Baldwin *et al.* 2007). These calls reflect the reality that while regional preferentialism in trade might be sub-optimal to acting multilaterally through the WTO, it will not be going away; hence the exhortation to multilateralize it.

At another level, but related, we are also seeing a growing interest in what Moisés Naim (2009) calls 'minilateralism'. Minilateralism is a response to a growing recognition that large-scale multilateral agreements – whether they are, for example, in pursuit of trade liberalization, the attainment of Millennium Development Goals or the reduction of greenhouse gas emissions (GHGs) – have all seen deadlines missed and policy execution stalled. The recognized limits of multilateralism are leading to the advocacy and practice of more targeted approaches to collective action problem solving. The correct number in any given problem area is 'the smallest possible number of countries needed to ensure the largest possible impact'. This number will, of course, vary from issue area to issue area. The theory was, for example, developed in the area of trade in the recommendations of the first Warwick Commission for the development of a process of critical mass decision making at the WTO (Warwick Commission 2007: 27–36; see also Gallagher and Stoler 2009). As is well known, a small number of states (about 20) count for 85–90 per cent of total world trade. A deal made by them – with appropriate safeguards and non-discriminatory access to the deal for late-comer signatories and smaller players – could offer a way forward in certain contested areas of trade policy without trammelling the consensus decision-making principle that prevails in the organization. Similarly, the world's top 20 polluters account for 75–80 per cent of the world's GHG emissions. Rather than being thought of as anti-democratic and exclusionary, such minilateral agreements could be thought of as 'deadlock busters' that can be open to other states in an inclusive non-discriminatory fashion after the event. Such approaches are undoubtedly controversial but without such innovations, international collective action decision making will become progressively more difficult.

## Conclusion

The dramatic rise of globalization in general over the last several decades, and the economic crises of the early 21st century in particular, have challenged the efficacy and legitimacy of multilateralism as both institutional practice and principle.

It has also raised more general meta-theoretical questions. One of the most important long-term successes of the 20th century has been to make market principles an accepted and authoritative part of everyday existence (Hall 2007). A consequence of the most recent crisis has been to damage the authority of both the actors and agencies that had assumed responsibility for managing economic processes, and – more fundamentally – the stability of markets themselves. The rapid transformation of the terms of the debate over economic management in the wake of the crises of 2007–9 must remind us that the processes and practices of governance remain temporally and politically contingent. The economic crises of the early 21st century have once again highlighted Harold Lasswell's (1935) perennial questions of modern politics: who gets what and how; governance for whom; and in whose interest? These remain essentially contested questions.

A reformist approach to the current system is not entirely out of the question, as attempts to marshal a G20 approach towards global economic cooperation, the growth of minilateralism, multilateral regionalism and transnational network activities identified in this chapter attest. But we are not yet at a stage where the major players will easily share power with emerging actors or indeed with various and increasingly active strata of an emerging global civil society. The generic challenge is to adapt multilateralism to the dynamics of a world battling to come to terms with changing power balances and emerging policy agendas that do not lend themselves to the kinds of collective action problem solving that prevailed in the second half of the 20th century.

## Guide to further reading

For a good historical and analytical introduction to international organization see Armstrong *et al.* (2004), but see also Schiavone (2004) for an empirical guide. Ruggie (1993) remains the essential theoretical introduction to multilateralism but see also Keohane (1989). On international economic institutions generally, see Martin (2006); on the World Bank, see Weaver (2008); on the IMF, see Woods (2006); and on the WTO, see Hoekman and Kostecki (2001) and Narlikar (2005). On new forms of international governance, see Slaughter (2004) and Stone (2008).

## Chapter 5

# Regions and Regionalism in World Politics

SHAUN BRESLIN

In the mid-2000s, some analysts were seriously debating whether a united Europe might emerge as the next global superpower (Schnabel and Rocca 2005; Leonard 2005; Reid 2005). By the end of the decade, the focus had switched from Europe's potential power to Europe's crisis and the 'struggle against global irrelevance' (Youngs 2010). This is not entirely new – indeed, in many respects the history of regional integration in Europe can be read as an almost continuing response to crises (Kühnhardt 2008). Nevertheless, the speed of this turnaround suggests that we are at the start of a new chapter in the study of the importance of regions in world politics.

Or at least, we are at the start of the latest wave of European regionalism. And it is important to remember that while Europe remains perhaps the dominant focus, there is much more to the study of regions than simply the European experience. There have been a number of waves of regionalization across the globe – particularly in the post-Cold War era. And even as Europe debated its future in the wake of the global financial crisis, the logic of deeper financial cooperation was back on the agenda in Asia and Latin America, while the African Union and the Arab League were significant players in the process of political change in Libya.

The first purpose of this chapter is to identify both what drives regional processes forward, and what are the constraints that obstruct or slow regional integration in different parts of the world. The second objective is to consider the implications of the rise and fall of regions for individual states, the people who live in them, and the functioning of world politics in general; not so much to ask if regionalism is a good thing or not, but rather to ask who (or what) benefits from regional integration projects and processes, and who (or what) loses out.

It does this by identifying different historical waves of regionalism (with a focus on the post-Second World War period) as a way of identifying commonalities in the different regional projects, and the accompanying different waves of theoretical innovations. The extent to which the development of a regional identity matters (and whose identities matter) is one such common thread. What regions mean for the future of the sovereign state is a second. The importance of hegemony and hegemons in driving or blocking regional processes is also rarely wholly absent. And the possibility of building national security through regional cooperation provides a fourth important strand. But the single most important recurring concern brings us back to economics and responses to the internationalization of economic activity beyond the national scale.

Although this chapter utilizes examples from across the world, it acknowledges that the European case has occupied a particularly important position – not least in the development of different theoretical explanations of regional integration. As such, it begins with a brief outline of how the study of Europe has influenced the evolution of approaches to regionalism and regional integration *per se*, and a categorization of different types of scholarship on regionalism.

## European integration and the study of regions in world politics

Since the 1980s, there has been an upsurge in the number of regional projects being negotiated and enacted across the world, and the study of regionalism has reflected these innovations; regionalism has become a truly global issue rather than just a European one. Nevertheless, Europe remains by far the most studied and debated case and in some ways this dominance has obstructed the emergence of a holistic and comparative study of regions and regionalism in general (Breslin *et al.* 2002). There are three main reasons for this.

First, Europe has become something of a benchmark against which other processes of integration are sometimes viewed and evaluated. From the creation of the European Coal and Steel Community (ECSC) in 1951, regionalism in Europe has been characterized by a high degree of institutionalization and the creation of formal regional bodies and entities (the European Community, the Euro, the European Parliament, and so on). For a number of analysts, this created the expectation that regional integration elsewhere would result in the establishment of similar institutions (and conversely that the absence of such institutions reflected a lack of integration). This can result in a tendency to focus on *institutions* rather than *processes*, and overlook the real and significant integration across national borders that occurs in many parts of the world even if there are no regional bodies to organize and regulate it.

Second, where comparisons have been made, there has been a tendency to use Europe as the primary point of reference. It is rather rare to see studies that compare cases across regions – to compare African regional experiences with those of Latin America, for example (Soderbaum 2008). But while these first two concerns point to Europe being a dominant presence in the study of regions in world politics, the third relates to the isolation of Europe from broader and more comparative analyses. The study of Europe has also all but generated its own academic sub-discipline – specialist journals, conferences, book series and associations that locate the study of European regionalism as separate from the study of regional integration *per se* (Rosamond, 2007). Here there is a focus on major concerns within Europe that are a consequence of long-term and deep integration – such as the potential for a federal Europe superseding the state, the relationship between different agencies, and the viability of maintaining a single currency in light of the impact of the global financial crisis.

Of course, Europe is not the only case of a relatively long-standing regional organization. The Association of Southeast Asian Nations (ASEAN), established in 1967, is a good example. But even though ASEAN has shared some of the experiences of the EU – most notably expansion to include former communist party states – ASEAN has always been characterized by looser linkages than the more legally formalized European project. Its operating principle, the 'ASEAN way', is defined in terms of consensus building rather than formal rules and a strict acceptance of the ultimate sovereignty of member states (Henry 2007). Moreover, much of the current discussion over the future of Asian regionalism is concerned with the formation of a larger East Asian region of which ASEAN is only one constituent part.

So with the possible exception of ASEAN, for the majority of students of regionalism beyond Europe, the focus is not on *consequences* of regionalism, but on *causes* and *processes* – what makes a region come into existence, cohere and have longevity. Or even more fundamentally, it is often on the prior question of what the region actually is (or should be) – which states are part of it, and which are extra-regional?

Bearing in mind both the importance of Europe as a generator of ideas, theories and experiences, but also that there is much more to regional integration than just the European case, the study of regionalism in world politics today can be divided into seven sub-groups:

- Theory building. This work considers how we define a region, how and why regional integration takes place, and what forces a region to cohere, consolidate/institutionalize and survive (and the counterfactual question of why regional integration does not/has not occurred in some places).
- The study of Europe. An isolated and discrete sub-discipline, this includes theories of European integration, analyses of the consequences of regionalism, studies of the machinery and processes of EU policy-making, the relationship between the regional and national levels of governance, and prospects for future integration. These studies might have significance for the wider study of regionalism *per se*, but are conceived of as being part of the EU studies sub-discipline.
- Case-specific studies of individual regions. Conducted by specialists in those regions, these case studies are informed by wider theoretical understandings of regional integration and often explicitly seek to contribute to theory and comparative understandings, rather than simply being concerned with events in the region under discussion. Whilst economic issues tend to loom large in these studies, the importance of dealing with non-traditional challenges to security has an increasingly strong focus (the environment, infectious diseases, movement of people, drug trafficking, and so on).
- Comparative studies of different regional processes. These typically focus on different types or levels of institutionalization of regional cooperation, and there is a tendency in these for the EU to be the constant against which other

regional forms are compared. Non-European regions are much more rarely compared to each other. These comparisons often imply that Europe is the norm that others diverge from, rather than perhaps Europe being the exception and informality and shallow integration the norm in most of the world.

- The relationship between regionalism and world order. Here the main focus is the relationship between regionalism and global multilateralism. The question is whether regional forms of cooperation are a 'building block or stumbling block' to global solutions, particularly in terms of regional free trade arrangements and global free trade agendas. There is also a strong focus on the extent to which regions can provide forms of economic supervision and regulation that either protect the region from unregulated global capitalism or provide regional alternatives to global regulatory forms and developmental strategies.

- Regions as actors in international relations. Perhaps really a sub-set of considerations of global order, this work focuses on how, if at all, regions can develop and promote a common/single interest in international relations – the 'actorness' of regions. The majority of this work, unsurprisingly, focuses on the actions and self-identity of the EU which has done more than most to promote itself as an actor; for example, through adopting a single EU position in trade negotiations and by promoting international 'strategic partnerships'. There is also increasing interest in how regions interact with each other – inter-regionalism.

- Regions and security. Ensuring security in Europe was a key impulse in Jean Monnet's thinking (one of the original architects of European integration), especially about the extent to which economic interactions decrease the possibility of conflict remains important in explaining regional initiatives in other parts of the world. To this extent, security issues have always been at the heart of theories and processes of regional integration. But there is also a strand of research that focuses specifically on regional security alliances, communities and cultures that has become a separate strand of the study of regionalism – a sub-sub-discipline that is not covered in any detail in this chapter.

These categories are not always mutually exclusive. Work on security regions, for example, may well also fit into one or more of the first four categories. But while the boundaries might sometimes be a little blurred, this typology nevertheless provides a rough overview of the different ways in which regionalism impacts on international politics today.

Rather than run through each of these different categories in turn, this chapter now moves on to show how the balance of interest in these seven areas has changed over time by tracing the evolution of approaches to studying regions since the end of the Second World War. Despite the above caveats about the dangers of focusing too strongly on the European case, it is simply not possible to ignore the importance of Europe in helping shape the main theories developed to explain regional integration processes, and this Eurocentricism is reflected in what follows here.

## Contextualizing the study of regionalism

### Region as empire/empire as region

In many respects, the focus on states rather than 'higher' levels of authority in world politics is a relatively new phenomenon. But rather than talk in terms of 'region', these older studies focused instead on 'empire' – empires that typically rose and fell through the success and failure of military adventures. Such military expansionism often resulted in the creation of new economic spaces that served at least some of the functions of contemporary regions. For example, the Napoleonic Continental System (1806–14) established a common customs policy of sorts in French-controlled Europe and Russia (in the form of a blockade against goods from Britain or British colonies). There is also a strong case for arguing that the idea of a discrete region called Southeast Asia (as opposed to the larger understanding of Asia as a whole) originated in the integrative strategies of the French colonial powers, later reinforced by the establishment of the Allied South-East Asia Command to fight Japan in 1943 (Charrier 2001). More recently, the creation of both security and economic regions in Eastern Europe – the Warsaw Pact and COMECON – owed more than a little to the military activities of the Soviet Red Army.

Region as empire retains some importance – but more in terms of the consequences of colonial rule and decolonization than as a force for regional integration in itself. For example, the two Franc Zones that created shared currencies (and fixed exchange rates with first the Franc and now the Euro) in Western and Central Africa have their origins in French colonial rule in Africa. After the dissolution of the Soviet Union, a number of regional organizations were established to try to coordinate political and economic relations between the newly independent states: the Commonwealth of Independent States, the Organization of Central Asian Cooperation, the Eurasion Economic Community and the proposed Common Economic Space (Kubicek 2009). The idea of something called 'Latin' America also has its origins in the commonalities of colonial experiences on the continent that continue to exercise some influence over region-building projects today (Mignolo 2005).

### Identifying regions

These historical examples draw our attention to the importance of how we identify and conceptualize the constituent members and boundaries of different regions – and perhaps more importantly, how those who are engaged in processes of regional integration identify to which region they think they (should) belong. This might sound a little strange. Surely we can identify regions simply by looking at a map. But while continents are formed by nature, regions are formed by people; they are politically and socially constructed. And these political constructs are as likely to sub-divide continents as they are to work on continent-wide levels.

For example, despite attempts to build a continent-wide Free Trade Area of the Americas, the majority of region-building projects in the Americas have been at the sub-continent level. And notwithstanding shared histories of colonization (of sorts) in Latin America, the question of what countries constitute the 'region' is yet to be fully resolved. For example, Mexico might be part of 'Latin America' in terms of culture and a history of Spanish colonization, or Central America/ Mesoamerica in terms of the population settlements that spanned this part of the continent before the arrival of the colonial powers. But largely because of its position as a major producer of goods for the US market, Mexico became part of a different region in the shape of the North America Free Trade Agreement (NAFTA) in 1994. Further south, the continent is further divided by different conceptions of region – perhaps most importantly the Andean Community of Nations and Mercosur.

Similar observations can be made about Africa, where continent-wide regionalism in the form of the African Union coexists with numerous sub-continental projects; for example, the South African Development Community (SADC), the Economic Community of West African States (ECOWAS), the East African Community, and so on. If anything, identifying the Asian region (or regions) is even more problematic. For example, does the region called East Asia include India and Australasia as it does in the form of the East Asia Summit (EAS), or exclude them as it does in ASEAN plus Three meetings (AEAN plus China, Japan and South Korea)? Or should the region actually be something else – the idea of Asia-Pacific as embodied by Asia Pacific Economic Cooperation (APEC) which excludes India, but brings in countries like the US and Canada that have a Pacific coastline?

To add an extra level of complexity, regions change over time. The six founder members of the ECSC expanded to be 12 members of the European Economic Community by the late 1980s, through to the expansion of the EU to 27 member states in 2007. Similarly, ASEAN expanded to add Vietnam, Burma/Myanmar, Laos and Cambodia to the original six member states in the 1990s. Regions also change as members leave – for example, Venezuela's withdrawal from the Andean Community in 2006 – and occasionally as regional organizations fail or dissolve. For example, the Central American Common Market dissolved in 1969 (but reformed in 1991) and regional cooperation between the Soviet Union and Eastern Europe did not survive the end of communist party rule.

Perhaps what comes across most clearly from this short discussion is the potentially bewildering array of organizations – and an even more bewildering array of acronyms of organizations! Moreover, it is not always easy to identify what is a truly regional organization. For example, APEC explicitly refers to 'the region' as the focus of its activities, but in many respects looks like an arena for different regions to come together to discuss cooperation. Occasionally linguistic (Portuguese, French and the Union of Latin Speaking States) or religious-based communities (such as the Organization of the Islamic Conference) are included in lists of regional organizations even though they have members from across the world and do not occupy distinct and observable cartographic spaces. There are also a number of regional development banks that play a role in promoting regional integration, but which have members from across the world and therefore occupy something of a blurred space between being a regional or global organization. If we ignore these groups (but include those regional organizations subsequently subsumed into the EU), a total of 76 regional organizations can be identified as being in operation since the Second World War (each with its own acronym).

## Regional identities

So both regional identities and regional formations are fluid. What is Europe and who is European does not have to be defined by membership of the EU, but the idea of 'Europe' as a political entity in the guise of the EU has gained currency – and as we have seen, the membership of this idea of 'Europe' has changed considerably over time. Moreover, multiple identities are common and do not always map with the boundaries of formal regional organizations. So if we go back to the example of Mexico and ask if Mexicans are part of North America, Mesoamerica or Latin America, the answer is probably all three at different times depending on the issue at hand that requires people to think of their identity (and against which 'other' this identity is constructed).

There is a relatively strong consensus that a shared regional identity helps a region cohere – a feeling of being part of the region knits people and thus economies and societies together, and makes the regional sphere of governance legitimate (see Adler 1997). However, there is less unanimity over what is cause and what effect. Does the existence of a shared identity lead to people coming together in a shared regional effort? Or does the creation of a region for other reasons establish common laws and borders and facilitate the flow of goods and people that subsequently leads to the emergence of a regional identity? For the first generation of students of European regionalism, the creation of new regional identities was an essential part of the transition from national to regional levels of political activity. Crucially, however, this was a shift that was conceived to first take place in the minds and actions of key political and economic elites rather than in the general population. So are popular identities important? Or, put another way, whose identity matters? These questions are not only important for understanding how regions emerge or consolidate, but also for highlighting arguably the single most important example of regionalism (when calculated by newspaper column inches at least).

The feeling that the regional project is being driven by business and political elites in opposition to the more national(ist) identities and aspirations of the general public has long become part and parcel of political debates in many European states. As political leaders resigned in Greece and Italy in the wake of the financial crises in 2011, their replacements were widely considered to be technocrats rather that politicians put in place under pressure from the EU to bring in economic reforms designed to 'dislodge the entrenched cultures of political patronage that experts largely blame for the slow growth and financial crises that plague both countries' (Donadio 2011).

## Theorizing the study of regionalism

This concern that the response to financial crisis in Europe is leading to techno-cratic rule that undermines the power of sovereign nation-states brings us full circle back to the origins of theorizing about regional integration in the 1940s. But rather than fearing the reduced power of nation-states, in the early post-war years the erosion of state sovereignty was considered a good thing. The state, after all, had been the key source of instability and war in Europe in the 1930s and 1940s – or more correctly, competition between states and nationalism had been the cause of the problem. Moreover, once the early experiment in collaboration in the form of the ECSC seemed to be a success, ceding some state authority to a higher authority seemed sensible from an economic as well as security viewpoint.

The idea that the state was being transcended was an important component in the emergence of 'functional' interpretations of international relations that have become firmly embedded as means of understanding regional integration in Europe and elsewhere. Most often associated with the work of David Mitrany, functionalists assumed that the common transnational issues that states faced, combined with an increase in scientific knowledge about the nature of these problems and how to deal with them, would result in cooperation. Territorial organization (states) would be transcended and replaced by functional organization (transnational bodies) with competence in specific areas – for example, one dealing with finance, another for education, and another specializing in trade.

With competence in regulation transferring from the national scale to suprana-tional specialist agencies, nationally based identities and nationalism would decline, resulting in what Mitrany (1943) called 'a working peace system'. Indeed, at a time when debates over the future of European regionalism are dominated by economic concerns, it is salient to remember that the architects of the initial impulse towards regional cooperation started from primarily security concerns. This cooperation would ensure that 'war between France and Germany becomes not merely unthinkable, but materially impossible' (Schuman 1950) – and the prospect of a peaceful (North)West Europe stood in stark contrast to the almost permanent state of Franco-German conflict which had been all but the 'normal' situation in the previous century and a half.

Whilst sharing the basic assumption about the need to cooperate beyond national borders, the functional division of authority was questioned by neofunc-tionalists. Most closely associated with the early work of Ernst Haas (perhaps most famously Haas 1958), neofunctionalists concentrated on the idea that functional cooperation on technical issues would ' spill over' into other forms of integration. For example, it is simply impossible to deal with issues relating to coal and steel production without also considering wider trade and investment rules, and the domestic social and economic policies of the states involved in this functional collaboration. Thus, cooperation on narrow functional areas would inevitably lead to the new organizations extending their reach into other areas of authority and governance. So for neofunctionalists, it was essential to have an institution above the state level supported by a regional elite that could take the lead in pushing the regional project forwards. In the early years of the European project, for example, the ECSC was assumed to fulfil this role and the Europeanization agenda of people like Robert Schuman and Jean Monnet personified the idea of regionalizing elites.

As with earlier functional understandings, the shift of identification from the national to the regional scale is seen as a crucial dynamic. Integration occurs as the political sphere of action moves from the national to the regional level – individuals and groups increasingly realize that national governments are unable to meet their demands and so instead move the focus of their action and allegiances to new regional bodies. For Walter Mattli (1999), integration is most likely to occur and cohere when the supply of supranational institutions by regionalizing political elites meets the demand for regional level coordination and action by primarily economic elites. Most often, economics is seen as the driver, with individual states simply unable to manage the ever-increasing complexity of international financial and trade flows on their own. The logical end point of this process is that the state is ultimately replaced by a new locus of power at the regional level – a single holistic regional organization that becomes a single political union.

## States, intergovernmentalism and national interests

States, however, have not simply withered away. Individual states have retained most of the traditional functions of international relations, even in Europe. Indeed, by the mid-1970s, even the firmest proponents of a new world of regions were admitting that they had been too enthusiastic (Haas 1975). Not only were states still the key actors *within* the European project, but the rest of the world had stubbornly resisted following the European model of even this level of integration.

Nevertheless, some of the core concerns that informed the original neofunctional approaches not only remain, but were reinvigorated by the shift in the pace of European integration from the mid-1980s. The emergence of an activist European Commission under Jacques Delors appeared to provide the regionalizing institutions and elites that were necessary for the promotion of further integration (Ross 1995). The prospects of spillover into a new federalist Europe were enhanced when the Maastricht Treaty of 1992 established the transition from a European Economic Community to a European Union, laying the foundations for monetary union, and theoretically at least creating the basis for a common foreign and security policy. With more and more regulation and legislation occurring at the regional level, an additional regional level of political activity, such as lobbying, was added to existing national foci.

But there are two important differences between these two phases. First, whilst some still think of Europe as the blueprint that other regional projects will follow, there is a growing acceptance that Europe is not *the* model of regional integration, but simply *a* model (albeit an extremely important case study). In the late 1980s and early 1990s, a slew of new regional organizations either came into being or reformed themselves with new agendas that increased the pool of case studies for students of regionalism. The creation of Mercusor (1991) and the North American Free Trade Area (signed 1992, enforced 1994) in the Americas; the resurgence and expansion of the Association of South East Asian Nations and the creation of the Pacific Islands Forum (1995) in Asia and the Pacific; and the transition of the Southern African Development Community in 1992 from an organization designed to resist South Africa into a development community are all important examples of new 'non-European' forms of regional integration projects.

Second, the appeal of Europe as a model has been tarnished and the logic of pursuing ever-deeper regional integration has been seriously questioned. Part of this stems from the failure of Europe to act with a common, clear and coherent foreign policy in times of military crisis. The invasion of Iraq might have done most damage to the reputation of the US, but it also reflected back on those European states that participated in support of the US, and raised questions about some of the liberal assumptions that supposedly underpin the European project. More important, the economic troubles that hit many European economies (and the Euro as a whole) in and after 2008 have undermined the idea of a European model to be emulated by others.

Third, the residual role of states as the key locus of authority and action in international relations has been re-imposed in debates over regionalism. This has included attempts to reconcile neofunctional assumptions of the inevitability of 'spillover' with an understanding of how states mediate, manage and in some ways govern these processes of spillover (Cameron 1991). For others, the significance of regional institutions and elites in promoting integration has been replaced by a more singular focus on the region as a political space occupied by states. For those scholars who come to regionalism from a broadly liberal perspective, thinking about how states act at the regional level is relatively straightforward. What happens at the European level, for example, is intergovernmental bargaining by different national governments, with each government's position on any given issue primarily a consequence of bargaining within the national political sphere. Regionalism creates rules of the games and other mechanisms that make coming together to negotiate less costly and more predictable, and over time, the success of the regional level in solving problems grants further legitimacy to the regional level as an arena for problem solving (Moravcsik 1993).

But for those from other traditions, cooperation in Europe and in particular the move towards monetary union 'pose a serious challenge to neorealist arguments about international institutions' (Grieco 1995: 24). The solution was to find ways of explaining why assumptions that states act to maximize their national interests were not contradicted by the reality of cooperation and even the pooling of sovereignty at the regional level. One of the earliest attempts to do so entailed a synthesis of sorts between realist and liberal positions through the idea of 'complex interdependence' (Keohane and Nye 1977), where cooperation at the regional level was seen as just one means deployed by states to rationally manage their interests through varieties of intergovernmental cooperation. Thus, regionalism is seen as a statist response to an increasingly complex world where the activities of non-state actors (primarily companies) operating beyond the national sphere resist the control of national-level legislation and action alone (Keohane 1988).

## Regionalism beyond Europe: common enemies, common responses?

Whilst the relative importance of states and national interests remains hotly debated in the European case, the focus on the role of states promoting their interests through regional cooperation becomes stronger when analysis moves away from Europe. For example, China's promotion of regional integration in East Asia has been depicted as a process of 'cooperating to compete' (Moore 2008) – establishing good relations with neighbours in an attempt to align them to Chinese interests and to undermine support for Japan and the US in the region. In short, regionalism is promoted by those states that have most to gain from it. Indeed, different powers will promote different understandings of what the region is (or should be) based on how this understanding of the region maximizes the national interest.

Returning to the case outlined earlier in the chapter, the competing understandings of what the Asian region is or should be (see p. xx), we see different national understandings of the region mirrored in preferences for regional organizations. The US preferred understanding of the region as the Asia-Pacific is embodied in APEC; China's narrower East Asian understanding of the region is evident in their preference for ASEAN Plus Three and Japan's view is reflected in the East Asia Summit which balances out China's influence. In this last case, China then responded by supporting the further expansion of the EAS to bring in more 'big powers' like the US and Russia – not to make it more powerful but rather to reduce the chances of it acting with authority by making it too big to work effectively. So rather than thinking of this new bigger EAS as a region, perhaps we should instead think of it as an 'anti-region' – an organization designed to prevent another form of region cohering and prospering.

Alternatively, states might choose regionalism as a means of serving the national interest by combining to fight a common enemy. This common foe is often conceived in terms of a common military threat (or potential threat). Examples include ASEAN's role as a mutual defence against communism, the Gulf Cooperation Council as a means of resisting Iran, and the Southern African Development Coordination Conference's role as a bulwark against apartheid-era South Africa. But this does not always have to be a common defence against military power. For example, after the Asian financial crisis of 1997, there was a relatively strong feeling in East Asia that the West was imposing unfair and inappropriate reforms on the region designed to serve Western interests. The solution was to build a regional-level mechanism – the Chiang Mai Initiative – through which Asian states agree to support each others' currencies in any future financial crisis. So a regional identity and regional cooperation can be built on a shared understanding of what 'we' are not, an identification that requires an 'other' from which to be different.

### Regionalism, realism and hegemony

Such a focus on alliances against common enemies draws attention to the importance of conceptions of hegemony in explaining the motivation for regional interaction. In his analysis of different theories of regionalism, Hurrell (1995) distilled four dominant approaches. First, the above-mentioned common defence against a common enemy – the basic idea that the power of the many is greater than the power of one. The second involves incorporating and socializing potentially dangerous hegemons into a favoured regional order – for example, enmeshing West Germany into the European project or shaping the nature of China's rise through engagement in regional projects and processes. Here, there is sometimes a blurring of realist and liberal positions as the enmeshment idea has commonalities with liberal institutional understandings of how states can be 'socialized' into preferred ways of doing things through participation in liberal regional integration projects.

Third, weaker states 'band-wagon' in regional projects with dominant powers – either to gain special preferential treatment by being seen to support their prefer- ences, or by trying to ensure access to their lucrative economies (or both). In short, it is seen as in the national interest to link the state in an asymmetric relationship with the hegemon. This approach has been used to explain the regional strategies of a number of Latin American states towards the US – although not always with successful outcomes (Mera 2005).

The fourth sees regionalism as a function of hegemonic preferences. Thus, American support for European regionalism and ASEAN can be explained because of the way in which these efforts helped achieve Washington's security and, to a lesser extent, economic objectives. But those regional projects in Latin America that might obstruct the aims of the US were not exactly encouraged. Similarly, we might suggest that the changing stance towards regionalism in China from scepticism to active engagement provided a new stimulus towards integra- tion in Asia – and fears about a China-dominated Asian region has at least some- thing to do with the differing visions of region promoted by the US and Japan (Breslin 2009).

## Actors and processes: towards 'new regionalism'

When it comes to considering the relationship between hegemony and region- alism, the focus on regional actors is very clearly on the state. In the other understandings of regionalism that we have briefly surveyed, the role of the state is less absolute. For example, some see a role for supranational agencies and actors in higher authorities 'above' the state. Furthermore, to varying degrees neofunctional, intergovernmental and institutional approaches all see a role for non-state actors in moving the regional project forwards, be this in economic elites seeking new regional sites of governance, or regionalism as a result of states coming together to deal with common governance issues caused by the transnational activities of economic actors. Nevertheless, while the state is not the only actor, it is the state that ultimately signs treaties and international agreements that bring into force formal regional organizations. And in this respect the study of regionalism has been dominated by what we might call broadly 'statist' approaches.

But from the mid-1990s, this twin focus on states as actors and formal institution building as the end point of regional integration appeared out of step with what was happening in many parts of the world. As such, there was a turn towards what came to be known then as a 'new regionalism'. 'New' because it emerged from dissatisfaction with the 'older' waves of theorizing about regionalism and also because it drew from a range of contemporary regional experiences beyond just the European case (Gamble and Payne 1996).

In order to have a more holistic study of regions that allowed for a more comprehensive understanding of what a full range of regional integration processes mean for international politics, the analysis was divided into form and process. On one side, what might be called the 'idea' or 'ideology' of region or the conscious and deliberate attempts to create formal regional institutions – regionalism. On the other side, those real interactions that bind not just states, but people, economic activity, ecosystems and so on – processes of 'regionalization that fills the region with substance such as economic interdependence, institutional ties, political trust, and cultural belonging' (Vayrynen 2003: 39).

In many respects, the study of how regionalization resulted in regionalism is exactly what earlier studies had been all about – and this remains a focus of new approaches. But for new regional theorists, there is no reason to expect that regionalization will necessarily lead to institutional forms of regionalism – and certainly no reason why these processes will result in anything that resembles European-style regionalism. Rather, the study of the processes themselves are important and interesting in their own right, irrespective of where these processes lead. Furthermore, as Bull's (1999) analysis of various regionalism initiatives in Central America found, even where there are formal regional bodies, this is no guarantee that actual regionalization will take place if market actors prefer to seek economic interactions with extra-regional economies.

So it is the regional 'space' that is important in new studies rather than the institutions of regionalism – the creation of regional spaces of activity that do not replace the nation-state as a site of governance and action, but typically coexist alongside territorial/statist spaces. Indeed, rather than just being seen as something that occurs 'above' the nation-state, regional integration can also occur 'below' the national scale. For example, the way in which the economies of San Diego and Tijuana have become economically interlinked across the US–Mexico border is a form of micro-regional integration that exists at a different level of integration to US–Mexican integration through NAFTA. Both of these occur alongside the very real continued importance of both nation-states (Grimes 2002).

Because there is no expectation of an inevitable end form of integration, and through the use of a wider variety of cases, new regionalism has in many ways become a search for the causes of diversity. Nevertheless, within this diversity, we can identify a number of common strands. For example, the role of non-state actors takes on a greater significance than in earlier studies of regionalism. Moreover, it is not just a case of non-state actors as sources of integration – for example, through transnational economic activity – but also as providing regional responses to regionalization. Non-governmental organizations (NGOs) and grass-roots movements have particularly important roles to play when it comes to coordinating regional responses to shared environmental and developmental challenges – a relatively common focus in the study of regionalization in Latin America, for example (Grugel 2006). Regionalization is also driven by the relationship between migrant workers and diasporas – a form of financial regionalization that emerges from the remittance of salaries and/or investments in the 'homeland' (Read 2004).

## Why regionalism matters: still all about the economy?

Whilst the environment and broadly defined development issues are clearly important, economic concerns have not lost their place as the primary point of interest for students of regionalism. And in terms of identifying non-state actors, this means concentrating on those who move money and goods across national boundaries, creating new regional spaces. For Kenichi Ohmae (1995), the power of these economic actors means that states have become irrelevant. Economic activity will occur where it is most conducive and profitable, crossing national borders and jurisdictions at will and creating new loci of economic activity based on what the market wants. This extreme position is perhaps a deliberate exaggeration to try and prove a point. Governments continue to be key actors not just in bringing formal regions into existence, but in facilitating regionalization as well. It is governments that change fiscal, financial and currency regimes that allow others to move goods and money across borders. It is also governments that typically create the hard infrastructure of regional integration – building roads, railways and ports that allow for the transfer of goods and commodities. Thus, states are seen as paving the way for real economic integration that is driven by the actions and interests of non-state economic actors.

So the key question is: why would governments act in this way? The answer partly lies in conceptions of the state – not the state as rational actor pursuing the 'national' interest in international relations, but the state as representative of the interests of those who favour free markets and globalization. Moreover, by the mid-1990s, engagement with the global economy was increasingly seen as the best – perhaps even the only – way of promoting economic growth and development. Key elites in developing countries that had previously sought to establish defences against the global economy and to avoid dependence on core economies now thought that linking to those core economies through participation in regional forums and domestic liberalization was essential (Bowles 1997). This context is a crucial component in understanding this new turn in regional integration (and the study of this integration) – liberalization that was occurring through the end of communist party rule in Europe, through the decline in communist ideology as China engaged the capitalist global economy, and through the retreat from dependency perspectives in Latin America.

## The regional and the global

### Regional Free Trade Agreements (FTAs): building blocks or stumbling blocks?

Although the phrase 'fortress Europe' might have gone out of fashion somewhat, it was once a powerful metaphor for the concept of the European project as a means of protecting Europe from outside intruders – whether would-be migrants, or producers from other parts of the world. This Europe was one where domestic producers (particularly farmers) received massive subsidies to keep them afloat. And this Europe had removed internal barriers to international contacts that made it much easier and more profitable for those within the fortress to trade with each other than it was to pierce the fortress from without.

The idea of region as fortress has also been deployed to explain the creation of NAFTA. This was a region that could thus compete internationally in terms of the production of goods for itself and for other markets, and protect key groups from potentially damaging competition from a truly global (and truly) free market. The NAFTA treaty was signed in 1992, the same year as the Maastricht Treaty moved Europe from a Community to a Union, and the then six members of ASEAN agreed to set up a Free Trade Area. The emergence of a world of competing regional blocs might not have been imminent, but nor was it wholly impossible (Frankel 1997).

The establishment of FTAs remains an important part of contemporary region building and they have become central pillars of common regional governance in most of the world. But the extent to which this shows that regionalism is in opposition to globalization is open to question for three main reasons. First, while FTAs are indeed often built around wider understandings of regional integration, there is more to preferential trade agreements than geographic regions. The Israel–Mexico Free Trade Agreement (2000), for example, would pretty much defy any definition of what constitutes a region. So perhaps the real issue is not so much the benefits of regionalism, but instead the failings of multilateralism at the global level that have created the need to seek alternatives at both bilateral and regional levels.

Second, in making the reforms required to meet the criteria required to join regional organizations like the EU or to reach agreement over FTAs, states engage in processes of economic liberalization. To be sure, they might become more open and liberal to each other than to non-partners in the first instance, but the end result is both greater economic liberalization across the world and, perhaps more important, the increasing predominance of the 'idea' of liberalization. Global liberalization can thus proceed through overlapping and intertwined regional processes (Mansfield and Milner 1999).

Finally, we should consider the extent to which regional processes are driven by and perhaps even dependent on wider global processes. Take, for example, economic integration in East Asia. Here we see investment from the rest of the region into China resulting in increased trade flows as the rest of Asia provides Chinese factories with resources and components. The creation of an ASEAN–China Free Trade Area not only facilitates these flows, but also makes it easier for Chinese interests to access the region – a relatively new and fast-growing element of regional integration in Asia. But this very real regional integration has in no small part been driven by the production of goods that are sold in other parts of the world, often with money that has its origins outside the region as well. Thus regional integration in Asia and indeed also in other parts of the world is essentially the local manifestation of wider global processes, often driven by the production decisions of major global corporations, and based on demand in key markets in the West.

But the need for regional arrangements to maintain a level of openness to the global economy does not mean that they will be totally open. In Europe, regional organizations had been playing an important role as a 'filter' for globalization for many years by protecting European social welfare systems from pressure to liberalize and privatize (Wallace 2002: 149). In other parts of the world, the financial crises of 1997 in East Asia, Russia and Argentina revealed for many the dangers of unregulated global capitalism and the problem of trying to impose solutions at the global level. With global multilateralism found wanting and reflecting the neoliberal preferences of the West, and most individual states seen as lacking the power and resources to do things on their own, regional solutions became increasingly attractive. National-level legislation alone was not able to deal with transnational problems, and global-level solutions were simply inappropriate. As such, for Katzenstein (2002), regionalism was attractive because it was neither too local nor too global but 'just right'. This lesson was reinforced by the global financial crisis that started in the US and Europe in 2008. The extent to which this really was a 'global' crisis rather than simply a crisis for the West has been questioned (Mahbubani 2011). Nevertheless, it is a crisis that has undermined the legitimacy of neoliberal capitalism which could have important consequences for the organization of regional economies in the long run.

## Conclusions: the future of regionalism(s)

What this suggests, then, is that the regional level is in some cases seen as the most effective site of authority for collective action above the national level. It is also sometimes seen as more legitimate than other levels of power and authority – particularly if global institutions are thought to be dominated by the US and the West. Such legitimacy has two dimensions. Internally, states and influential non-state actors must be prepared to empower the region to act – and also to give it the capacity to do so through the provision of finances, personnel, information and so on. Externally, the regional body needs to be accepted as a legitimate and representative actor (though as we have already noted, whose interests are being represented is not always wholly clear). Thus, for example, when China did not veto UN action in Libya in 2011, despite its stated opposition to infringing state sovereignty, officials explained China's (in)action by referring to the Arab League's support for the resolution and the importance of listening to regional voices (China UN Mission 2011).

Here we see the importance of the region as a security actor. And despite the dominance of transnational economic issues as drivers of regional cooperation and integration, dealing with shared transnational security issues is likely to be an important component of regionalism in the future. In particular, non-traditional security challenges and growing societal concern with human security issues suggests that 'people-centred' issues and actors could become ever more significant for regions in the future. A key question here is what Young (2002) referred to as the right 'fit' for regional organizations – whether the region as defined by shared environmental concerns occupies the same geographical space as the region defined by economic considerations. And this brings us back to Mitrany and the early debates over the nature of regionalism – do we need single 'catch-all' regional organizations or different bodies with different memberships and forms to deal with functionally discrete policy areas and issues?

The sad reality is that the impulse towards regional security cooperation is often driven by disasters and crises – the perceived significance of regional anti-terrorist activity after 9/11 and the response to the SARS outbreak in Asia in 2003 are just two examples. Crises are also key determinants of regional activity when it comes to economics. It will still take some time for the implications of the financial crisis to play out, but given the history of regionalism and regionalization in the post-war period that this chapter has briefly covered, then we can make some predictions with a degree of certainty.

First, despite the observations of early theorists, and the aspirations of some practitioners, the state seems destined to survive and coexist alongside regional (and other) sites of governance and authority. Second, the search for the right balance between different levels or authority in global politics will continue. As Nordbeck (2011: 37) puts it:

> The rationale for 'going regional' is ... linked to the belief that the right combination of country-based and transnational measures in turn leads to outcomes that are superior to those that are achievable based on national measures alone.

Thus, we can expect tensions between global and regional levels of regulation and governance to continue, and the balance between national, regional and global levels to be formed and reformed in response to key changes in global politics; not just economic crisis, but more 'normal' changes such as the increasing global significance of countries like China and India and those Gulf states that have financial power that far outweighs their formal power in organizations like the IMF.

Third, regions themselves will also continue to be formed and reformed. Even in Europe, the most established of all regional bodies, the question of what the region is or should be is still fluid and contested. And while for many years the question in Europe has been who should be allowed to join, the financial crisis has raised other questions over whether some countries should leave the Euro and the extent to which different countries have different 'depths' of integration.

Elsewhere the understanding and parameters of what regions should (and could) look like is even more unclear and fluid. Great power politics and strategic considerations are clearly important here as states seek to engage, enmesh, resist, block or sideline other regional powers. So too are new patterns of transnational interactions which create and re-create new regional spaces and actual processes of integration through regionalization.

Finally, the extent to which regions can be considered to be key actors in international relations is likely to evolve. Not surprisingly, the EU has been the major regional actor in this way, acting with a single voice in establishing common external tariffs and in trade negotiations – both bilaterally and in international forums such as the WTO. It has developed what Hill (1994) called a level of 'actorness' – though the retention of foreign policy authority in key areas by member states means that the emergence of a truly European single common foreign and security policy still looks like an aspiration rather than a reality.

More importantly, there has been the emergence of 'inter-regionalism' where regions come together in various forms to primarily discuss issues of common interest and to explore ways of working together (as opposed to signing treaties). Again, the EU is the key actor here, establishing formal arrangements with regional groups in Africa, South Asia and East Asia, Latin America, South Asia and Oceania (Söderbaum and Van Langenhove 2005). But there are also cases of inter-regional meetings between non-European regions – for example, between ASEAN and the Gulf Cooperation Council and between Mercusor and the Australia–New Zealand CER. The expansion and consolidation of such inter-regional dialogues (indeed, to become more than just dialogue) – particularly between non-European regions – would mark a significant new turn in the importance of regions for the modern world order in the future.

## Organizations and memberships

Table 5.1 summarizes the membership of the regional organizations and agreements mentioned in this chapter as at 2012.

## Guide to further reading

Early post-war theorizing about European integration continues to play a role in thinking about regional integration today. In addition to reading the texts cited in the body of this chapter, see Ruggie *et al.* (2005), and for an appreciation of Mitrany's contribution including a full list of publications, see Anderson (1998). Rosamond (2000) provides a succinct introduction to various theories of European integration. For a classic discussion of the relationship between realism and neoliberal institutionalism, see Jervis (1999). On realism and regionalism, Grieco (1999) is a good introduction to realism, while a combination of Keohane and Nye (1977) and Moravcsik (1993),

*Table 5.1* Membership of regional organizations and agreements, 2012

| Acronym | Full name | Members |
|---|---|---|
| APEC | Asia Pacific Economic Cooperation | Australia, Brunei, Canada, Chile, PR China, Hong Kong, Indonesia, Japan, South Korea, Malaysia, Mexico, New Zealand, Papua New Guinea, Peru, Philippines, Russia, Singapore, Chinese Taipei, Thailand, US, Vietnam |
| ASEAN | Association of Southeast Asian Nations | Brunei, Cambodia, Indonesia, Laos, Malaysia, Myanmar, Philippines, Singapore, Thailand, Vietnam |
| CACM | Central American Common Market | Costa Rica, Guatemala, Honduras, El Salvador, Nicaragua |
| CIS | Commonwealth of Independent States | Armenia, Azerbaijan, Belarus, Kazakhstan, Kyrgyzstan, Moldova, Russia, Tajikistan, Uzbekistan |
| COMECON | Council for Mutual Economic Assistance (now defunct) | Albania, Bulgaria, Cuba, Czechoslovakia, East Germany, Hungary, Mongolia, Poland, Romania, Soviet Union, Vietnam |
| EAEC | Eurasian Economic Community | Belarus, Kazakhstan, Kyrgyzstan, Russia, Tajikistan, Uzbekistan |
| EAS | East Asia Summit | Australia, Brunei, Cambodia, China, India, Indonesia, Japan, Laos, Malaysia, Myanmar, New Zealand, Philippines, Russia, Singapore, South Korea, Thailand, United States, Vietnam |
| ECOWAS | Economic Community of West African States | Benin, Burkina Faso, Cape Verde, Cote d'Ivoire, Gambia, Ghana, Guinea, Guinea-Bissau, Liberia, Mali, Niger, Nigeria, Senegal, Sierra Leone, Togo |
| EU | European Union | Austria, Belgium, Bulgaria, Cyprus, Czech Republic, Denmark, Estonia, Finland, France, Germany, Greece, Hungary, Ireland, Italy, Latvia, Lithuania, Luxembourg, Malta, Netherlands, Poland, Portugal. Romania, Slovakia, Slovenia, Spain, Sweden, United Kingdom |
| GCC | Gulf Cooperation Council | Bahrain, Kuwait, Oman, Qatar, Saudi Arabia, United Arab Emirates |
| MERCOSUR | Mercado Comun del Sur, Southern Common Market | Argentina, Brazil, Paraguay, Uruguay, Venezuela |
| NAFTA | North American Free Trade Agreement | Canada, Mexico, United States of America |
| OIC | Organization of the Islamic Conference | Algeria, Albania, Afghanistan, Azerbaijan, Bahrain, Bangladesh, Benin, Brunei, Burkina Faso, Cameroon, Chad, Comoros, Cote d'Ivoire, Djibouti, Egypt, Gabon, Gambia, Guyana, Guinea, Guinea-Bissau, Indonesia, Iran, Iraq, Jordan, Kazakhstan, Kuwait, Kyrgyzstan, Lebanon, Libya, Malaysia, Maldives, Mali, Mauritania, Morocco, Mozambique, Niger, Nigeria, Oman, Palestine, Pakistan, Qatar, Saudi Arabia, Senegal, Sierra Leone, Somalia, Sudan, Suriname, Syria, Tajikistan, Togo, Turkey, Turkmenistan, Tunisia, Uganda United Arab Emirates, Uzbekistan, Yemen |
| PIF | Pacific Islands Forum | Australia, Cook Islands, Fiji, Kiribati, Micronesia, Nauru, New Zealand, Niue, Palau, Papua New Guinea, Marshall Islands, Samoa, Solomon Islands, Tonga, Tuvalu, Vanuatu |
| SADC | Southern African Development Community | Angola, Botswana, DR Congo, Lesotho, Madagascar, Malawi, Mauritius, Mozambique, Namibia, Seychelles, South Africa, Swaziland, Tanzania, Zambia, Zimbabwe |

though now somewhat dated, remain essential starting points for understanding varieties of institutionalist positions.

There have been a number of attempts to provide overviews of interpretations of understandings of regionalism. Hurrell (1995), Mansfield and Milner (1999) and Pangiriya (1999) remain influential attempts to interpret what was at the time considered a radical 'new' wave of regional projects. Edited collections not only provide more space to explore different approaches, but also allow detailed analysis of particular dimensions of regional cooperation. For good examples of this see Jayasuriya (2004), Cooper *et al.* (2008) and Breslin *et al.* (2002). This includes work that moves beyond economics to consider environmental regionalism (Elliott and Breslin 2011) and regional security governance (Breslin and Croft 2012).

# Chapter 6

# Global Financial Crises

*TIMOTHY J. SINCLAIR*

One of the realities of global politics is that the most important things are often overshadowed by what, on a dispassionate analysis, are really much less significant issues. Financial crises, for example, are increasingly frequent and can pose challenges to the established order of global politics. But even though financial volatility seriously affects governments and the lives of billions, it is typically relegated to the business pages by the drama of terrorism or the high politics of trade negotiations, until it bursts forth as a global financial crisis, such as the one that began in 2007. This is unfortunate because it means that what is happening in the 'engine room' of globalization is often poorly understood by those in power and by those who wish to change the policies of those in power.

Some of this can be attributed to the cheap thrills of sensationalism. But much of this neglect is a result of the mythic technical character of finance, especially as it is talked about by business people, and written about by most journalists, government officials and even some scholars. Finance and money are discussed as if they are purely technical matters that those without the requisite training cannot hope to understand. The widespread propagation and acceptance of this falsehood makes it easy for those with policy control to pursue their objectives without the constraint of informed democratic debate.

An accessible introduction to global financial crises is offered here. I start by examining the competing ways financial crises are understood and comment on the merits of these perspectives, beginning with the market advocates' account of crisis, then moving on to critical views. In the second part I review the renewed financial volatility that followed the end of the Bretton Woods system and the liberalization of financial regimes in the developed countries starting in the 1980s. This includes the Asian financial crisis of 1997–8 and the Enron bankruptcy of 2001–2. The chapter then considers the global financial crisis that began in 2007, suggesting that the immediate causes of the crisis are quite different from those commonly assumed. After this discussion, I consider the prospects for regulatory reform based on the example of the credit rating agencies, and then offer a series of conclusions on global financial crises and world politics at the start of the 21st century.

## Perspectives

It is possible to distinguish between two main ways of understanding financial crises that compete for scholarly and political pre-eminence. The first of these has dominated economic thought about finance for thirty years and has had a major influence on policymakers. This stream of thought I call the 'exogenous approach', that is, an account in which the explanation is dominated by the role played by external influences. Although invoking the legacy of Adam Smith, this tradition's modern founders include Friedrich von Hayek and Milton Friedman. Their views are associated with attacks on the 'mixed economy' model, which emerged after the Great Depression of the 1930s and which was distinguished by high levels of state intervention in the economy. The likes of Hayek and Friedman took it as axiomatic that markets, when left to their own devices, are efficient allocators of resources. For them, financial crisis is a deviation from the normal state of the market, that is, when external forces get in the way of the proper functioning of the marketplace.

Eugene Fama's 'efficient markets hypothesis' (EMH) has come to represent this tradition of thought (Fama 1970). The basic idea of the EMH is that because prices for stocks, bonds, derivatives and so on are always based on all the available information they therefore reflect the fundamental value of these securities. Real-world markets are efficient because securities trade at equilibrium between supply and demand. No price gouging or market manipulation is possible if the EMH holds true. It is a remarkable claim about the importance and availability of information and how it is incorporated into market prices.

The case for EMH is built on three assumptions. First, investors are said to be rational and to value their potential purchases accordingly. So investors are not likely to buy before finding out about what they are buying and thinking about how to maximize their return. Second, if there are irrational investors their random trades will cancel each other out, leaving prices unaffected. Irrationality is the exception and it is of no consequence. Last, even if there is a completely irrational approach to investing, based on non-factual or irrelevant information, amongst a group of investors (known as rational arbitrageurs), players will meet them in the market and eliminate their influence on prices, which will return to fundamental or 'real' values.

The EMH consequently has two main implications for financial markets (Sinclair 2009). First, because asset prices for stocks and bonds supposedly incorporate all information they provide very accurate signals to buyers and sellers. If this is correct, asset price bubbles are simply not possible. The very notion of a bubble or inflated price cannot survive. The second implication is that traders cannot beat the market. If everyone in the market has the information any cheap or expensive assets will be rapidly identified by traders, and arbitraged away. Just as it is difficult to beat the house at roulette, it is hard to beat the market under these assumptions.

What are the problems with EMH? Firstly, what is known as an ergodic axiom underpins EMH. This awkward-sounding phrase actually underpins a range of features of the international financial system, such as collateralized debt obligations. The ergodic axiom simply assumes that given time, things will return to 'normal'; the future is essentially a repeat of the past. As a result, financial economists calculate probable future risks based on historical data. Unfortunately, human societies are not quite so stable and repetitive. Our communities are more like living things than automobile engines. They grow, change, adjust and over time are transformed. They are, in fact, non-ergodic. Adopting a fundamental axiom drawn from analyses of the physical world is a potential problem when trying to analyze complex *social* processes.

Eliminating uncertainty from the lexicon of the financial markets has arguably been a mistake. EMH encourages altogether too much confidence in financial engineering. If more of our financial activities assumed uncertainty, meaning that we would have to be more risk-averse, we would live in a world of more conservatively managed companies, governments and individuals. Of course, the trade-off would be a society more like that of our grandparents, in which getting a mortgage is a struggle and the standard of living is lower. But the global financial crisis has forcibly recreated that world for a good portion of us now in any case.

Assuming that markets are always efficient leads to neglect of the regulation of key institutions like banks and credit rating agencies that actually make our markets work. EMH encourages neglect of the role of institutions because it says that information works to automatically impose the disciplines of the market, a bit like an operating system in a computer. But in a world populated by people rather than abstractions and ideal-types, institutions are fundamental to instilling confidence in market participants about the future. In an uncertain world we need institutions we feel we can trust in order to engage in financial transactions.

Thinkers in what I have described as the exogenous tradition assume markets work efficiently, and thus focus on 'external', non-market-based factors, especially government failure, as the cause of crisis. Friedman, for example, blamed the Great Depression of the 1930s on what he considered to be incorrect Federal Reserve policy in 1929 and 1930, rather than the effects of the stock market crash in October 1929 (Kindleberger and Aliber 2011: 72). Such accounts of financial crisis assume, following EMH, that market participants are constantly adjusting their behaviour – for example, whether they buy or sell financial instruments like bonds and stocks – based on new information from outside the market. In this context, market prices are assumed to always reflect what other market participants are prepared to pay. If this is the case, reason exogenous thinkers, prices are never inflated or false. They must always be correct. So the idea of a 'bubble economy', in which assets like houses, stocks and oil futures deviate from true value to a higher, false value, is rejected. There can be no 'true value' other than what the market is prepared to pay.

The other main approach, by contrast, says that financial crises begin primarily inside finance; this is known as the endogenous perspective. Writers such as Marx and Polanyi, for example, see crises as caused by the internal 'laws of motion' of the capitalist mode of production. These produce constant change and upheaval, not equilibrium between demand and supply. For Keynes, the 'animal spirits' or passions of speculation give rise to risky gambits. Typical of this perspective is the idea that market traders do not merely integrate information coming from outside the markets in the wider, real economy, but are focused on what other traders are doing, in an effort to anticipate their buying and selling, and thus make money from them (or at least avoid losing more money than the market average). Given this, rumours, norms and other features of social life are part of their understanding of how finance works. On this account, finance is subject to the pathologies of social life, like any other activity in which humans engage. This is an image of finance in which markets are not the self-regulating mechanisms that figure in the exogenous view.

Keynes provided what remains perhaps the best intuitive illustration of the importance of this internal, social understanding of finance and financial crises in his tabloid beauty contest metaphor, first published in 1936 (Akerlof and Shiller 2009: 133). Keynes suggested that the essence of finance is not, as most supposed, a matter of picking the best stocks, based on an economic analysis of which should rise in value in future. Anticipating what other traders in the market were likely to do was actually more relevant. Keynes compared finance to beauty contests that ran in the popular newspapers of the time. These contests were not, as might be assumed, about picking the most attractive face. Success was achieved by estimating how *others* would vote and voting with them, although as Keynes pointed out, others would be trying to do the same, hence the complexity and volatility of financial markets.

More specifically, in a useful synthesis of some of the writings that fall within what I have termed the endogenous approach to global finance, Cooper has argued that the traditional assumptions made about markets and their tendency to equilibrium between demand and supply do not work for assets like houses or financial instruments like stocks, bonds and derivatives (Cooper 2008: 9–13). In the market for goods, greater demand can be met with greater supply or higher prices. But this logic does not work for assets. Instead, demand for assets often grows in response to price increases. The 'animal spirits' identified by Keynes and elaborated on by Akerlof and Shiller do not produce stability in the market for assets as they do in the market for goods. In the absence of equilibrium, there is no limit to the expansion of market enthusiasm for financial assets or houses, producing what we have come to call a 'bubble' economy. Unfortunately, as we know, bubbles tend to deflate in an unpredictable manner, with very negative consequences for economic activity.

## A brief history of financial crises

The history of financial crises shows that they are always shocking events, as they typically occur after long periods of affluence. The reversal which crises represent seems incomprehensible to those at the centre of things, never mind the general public. The standard against which all financial crises are measured is, of course, the Great Depression of the 1930s. At the height of the Depression a quarter of

American workers were unemployed (Galbraith 1997 [1955]: 168). As a quick perusal of the Dow Jones Industrial Average shows, the New York Stock Exchange did not return to its summer 1929 value until the early 1950s, almost a quarter of a century after the crash of October 1929 (www.djindexes.com). However, financial crises did not start in the 20th century. The Dutch 'tulip mania' of the 1630s, in which tulip bulbs greatly appreciated in value, is usually cited as the first such boom and bust. At the time tulips were exotic imports from the eastern Mediterranean. 'Mass mania' for the bulbs led to massive price inflation, so that some tulip bulbs were worth the equivalent of $50,000 or more each. When the crash came and the bubble deflated 'not with a whimper but with a bang', many who had invested their life savings in tulips lost everything (Galbraith 1993: 4). Mass default ensured a depression in the Netherlands in the years after 1637 (Galbraith 1993: 26–33). More recently, the 1907 financial panic came about after the failure of a trust company at the centre of Wall Street speculation (Bruner and Carr 2007). Calamity was avoided by cooperation between major banks, led by J.P. Morgan, perhaps the world's best-known and most powerful financier at the time.

After the Great Depression and the Second World War, the Bretton Woods system was created to bring greater order to the global financial system. As much a political as a financial system, Bretton Woods was intended to avoid rapid and unsettling economic adjustment within countries. The hope was that this would avoid the sort of economic problems which contributed to the Second World War and which would, no doubt, increase support for the communist system in Russia. Although the intention behind Bretton Woods was to avoid crises and the political conflict that followed, despite US assistance, it had few resources at its disposal. Given considerable protectionism in trade after the Second World War, countries were frequently either in significant surplus or deficit in the national accounts that measured their trade and payments with the rest of the world. This led to crisis-driven efforts to restore balance, often aggravating relations with other states.

The Bretton Woods system, with fixed exchange rates and controls over the movement of capital, was gradually abandoned in the developed world during the fifteen years after 1970. What emerged was a new system in which floating exchange rates were increasingly the norm, at least in developed countries, and in which capital could flow freely around the world to find the highest returns (see also Higgott, this volume). A floating exchange rate regime should rapidly and effectively adjust to reflect the changing economic conditions in a country, that is, reflecting real interest rates, inflation, profit margins, regulations and political stability. However, this system proved less than perfect. The 1980s was marked by a series of currency crises, as the values of major currencies like the Japanese yen appreciated, causing trouble for their trade partners. Perhaps the most dramatic of these crises was the ERM crisis of 1992, in which currency traders, especially George Soros, placed bets on the ability of the British government to keep the pound sterling within the European Exchange Rate Mechanism. At the end of the crisis the British government abandoned the defence of sterling, which depreciated substantially and had to be removed from the ERM.

The Asian Financial Crisis of 1997–8 was the culmination of a boom in East Asia that led to what in hindsight turned out to be excessive short-term lending and risky pegging of national currencies to the US dollar, a problem also for Argentina in 2001. As in Holland in the 1630s, the result of the crisis was economic depression in some countries, notably Indonesia, where the price of basic foodstuffs and other costs increased dramatically. The Asian crisis, like the financial crisis that began in 2007, led to criticism of lax regulation, fraud and corruption. In Malaysia, despite a barrage of criticism, controls on the movement of capital were reintroduced until the panic pressures eased.

## Global financial crisis

The subprime crisis that began in the summer of 2007 may rank as one of the most traumatic global developments since the Second World War. Unlike wars and famine, this crisis and its causes seem to have caught the governing elites in rich countries completely unawares. The crisis and the deep recession it generated have caused dismay and at times panic as the depth of the problem revealed itself, especially in September 2008 with the bankruptcy of investment bank Lehman Brothers. These events led to the realization amongst policymakers that there was a profound problem with what banks do and how they operate (Rethel and Sinclair 2012).

As with most financial crises, the origins of the crisis can be found in the ending of the previous boom, with the bursting of the stock market mania for dot-com stocks in 2000. The US Federal Reserve responded to this market reversal with a low interest rate policy intended to make the cost of borrowing cheaper. The policy worked and interest rates fell. But the fall in rates had unanticipated effects. Looking for higher returns in a low yield environment, bankers sought out financial instruments that would deliver better profits. 'Structured finance' had been around for several years but now it became the financial instrument of choice. Structured finance works by packaging the debt most of us incur – such as credit card borrowings, car loans, mortgages – into securities that can be traded in financial markets. These securities gave their owners a claim on the revenues that those with the car loans, credit card debt and mortgages repay. This process was called 'securitization'. At a stroke, a whole world of illiquid consumer debt was turned into financial market assets. Traders were then able to trade these new securities in the markets, just as they traded the more traditional bonds issued by corporations, municipalities and national governments.

The usual claim made about securitization is that it led to a breakdown in the relationship between the originators of mortgages and those in the financial markets creating and trading in the bonds and derivatives that pooled the stream of income from these mortgages. Because people in the financial markets were so distant from the actual credit risk of the individual mortgage payers and may have been poorly advised by credit rating agencies, they underestimated the riskiness of the assets they were buying. This eventually created a financial system that was full of 'toxic assets', that is, assets not generating promised revenues. Once this was fully appreciated by markets in the summer of 2007 as a result of increasing mortgage defaults by subprime borrowers, panic developed, followed by the collapse of a number of major financial institutions, worldwide government intervention to prop up the markets, and the subsequent recession. Many popular accounts such as Baker assert that too much debt was accumulated, and that therefore it was inevitable that the boom would collapse into bust (Baker 2009). These depictions do not typically identify the mechanism through which this took place.

This view suggests that the crisis occurred because some people were not doing their jobs properly, and that if we can just make sure people do what they are supposed to do, another financial crisis like this can be avoided. Given that the subprime securities market was worth only US$0.7 trillion in mid-2007, out of total global capital markets of US$175 trillion, the supposed impact of subprime assets is out of all proportion to their actual weight in the financial system (Bank of England 2008: 20). This strongly suggests that another explanation for the global financial crisis is needed. The crisis developed not because subprime lending was so important. The paralysis or 'valuation crisis' that came over global finance in 2007–9, in which banks were unwilling to trade with each other or lend money, had no specific relationship to subprime lending. Other bad news might have had the same effect on the markets (Galbraith 1993: 4).

An interpretation that fits the facts better is that the confidence in financial markets had, prior to 2007, reached such a frenzy that it became an episode of 'irrational exuberance', like so many financial manias before. But like other forms of over-indulgence, the hangover the next day is unpleasant. The 'bad news' about subprime lending was actually quite modest in summer 2007, predicting a higher rate of mortgage foreclosures than anticipated, but not a crisis. But in the context of the preceding mania this was enough to cause panic. The panic, which so typically follows financial expansions, created widespread uncertainty about the quality of financial institutions and their balance sheets. It is this uncertainty or panic that effectively brought the financial markets to a halt, forcing government intervention.

## Attributing blame

Since the 1930s, financial crises have almost always been accompanied by public controversy over who was at fault. Before the 1930s, governments were not generally held responsible for economic conditions, but since the 1930s the public have increasingly expected governments to manage problems in the financial system. Inevitably, efforts to defuse or redirect blame develop. During the Asian crisis, corrupt Asian governments and business leaders were held responsible, even though just a few years before, 'Asian values' were supposedly responsible for the unprecedented growth in the region. During the Enron scandal of 2001–2 auditors were blamed for not revealing the financial chicanery of the corporation. The subprime crisis has been no different, with rating agencies, mortgage lenders, 'greedy' bankers and 'weak' regulators all subject to very strong attacks for not doing their jobs.

The rating agencies have been subject to unprecedented criticism and investigation in the midst of the subprime meltdown. Congressional committees, the Securities and Exchange Commission, the European Parliament and Commission, and the Committee of European Securities Regulators all conducted investigations. A very senior rating official indicated that the crisis over subprime ratings is the most threatening yet experienced by the agencies in their century of activity. This effort to blame the agencies is a curious reaction, given that the rating agency business is now open to greater competition since the passage of the Credit Rating Agency Reform Act of 2006. It suggests that the movement from regulation to self-regulation – from 'police patrol' to 'fire alarm' approaches – has not eliminated the role of the state. Governments are still expected by their citizens to deal with market failure, and when necessary act as lenders of last resort, and they know it.

Three groups seem to have got away with little criticism: politicians themselves, although responsible as law makers for the design of regulation; the academic discipline of economics, which generally opposed the notion of asset price bubbles and neglected the role of social dynamics such as market confidence in the working of financial markets; and consumers and home-owners, who created the debt in the first place and thought it normal, for no good reason, that house values should increase forever at rates well in excess of inflation.

## Regulatory reform

Financial crises stimulate demand for new government intervention in markets to prevent a similar problem from occurring again. They also stimulate internal mobilization as a political strategy on the part of governments to show they are taking responsibility. The slow development of the central bank role of the Bank of England is an example of these processes over time. The New Deal reforms of 1930s America are an example of rapid reaction to very threatening conditions. The global financial crisis has seen much regulatory action, such as the massive Dodd-Frank Act of 2010 in the US. Whether this is really substantive or not can be gauged by examining the prospects for regulation of the major credit rating agencies, who have, as we have seen, been blamed in part for the development of the crisis.

The activities of rating agencies have been largely free of regulation (Sinclair 2005). Starting in the 1930s, the ratings produced by the agencies in the United States have been incorporated into the prudential regulation of pension funds so as to provide a benchmark for their investment. This required pension funds to invest their resources in those bonds rated 'investment grade' and avoid lower-rated, 'speculative grade' bonds. Regulation of the agencies themselves only started in the 1970s, with the Securities and Exchange Commission's (SEC) Net Capital Rule in 1975. This gave a discount or 'haircut' to issuers whose bonds are rated by Nationally Recognized Statistical Rating Organizations (NRSROs). No criteria were established for NRSROs in the 1970s, and this status was determined by the SEC in a largely informal way. NRSRO designation acted as a barrier to entry until the Rating Agency Reform Act of 2006, passed in the wake of the Enron scandal, created criteria and a recognized path to NRSRO recognition.

Two major sets of concerns have dominated discussions about the rating agencies in the wake of the global financial crisis. The first are to do with the competence of the agencies and the effectiveness of their work. The second relate to broader, structural issues. Critics have frequently attacked the timeliness of rating downgrades, suggesting that the agencies do not use appropriate methods and fail to ask the sort of forensic questions needed to properly investigate a company. Concerns about staffing, training and resourcing are associated with these problems. Since the Enron scandal, critics such as Partnoy have attacked what are perceived to be broader, structural problems in how the agencies do business (Partnoy 2006). These problems, suggest the critics, create poor incentives and undermine the quality of the work the agencies undertake.

The first of these broader structural issues is the legacy of weak competition between rating agencies as a result of the introduction of the NRSRO designation. Although several new agencies were designated NRSRO after the passage of the Rating Agency Reform Act, many critics would like NRSRO status abolished, removing any reference to ratings from law. The view implicit here is that weak competition has led to poor analysis, as the rating agencies have had few incentives to reinvest in their product. In this view, the revenues flowing to rating agencies are rents from a government-generated monopoly.

Concerns about how the agencies are funded became widespread with the onset of the subprime crisis. The idea was that the 'issuer-pays' model, although established for 40 years, was a scandalous conflict of interest because it means that the agencies have incentives to make their ratings less critical than they would if they were paid by investors, the ultimate users of ratings. Many critics called for an end not only to NRSRO status but also to the issuer-pays model of rating agency funding.

A vigorous if often poorly informed debate about the merits of regulating rating agencies took place from the onset of the crisis in spring 2007. Behind the rhetoric, it is apparent that both the American SEC and European Commission officials are reluctant to regulate either the analytics of the rating process itself or the business models of the major rating agencies. In amendments to NRSRO rules announced in February 2009, the SEC required enhanced data disclosures about performance statistics and methodology, and prohibited credit analysts from fee setting and negotiation, or from receiving gifts from those they rate (SEC 2009). How ratings are made and who pays for them are materially unaffected by these changes.

Much the same can be said for European efforts. Hampered by the reality that Moody's and Standard & Poor's (S&P) are both headquartered in the United States, for many years rating agencies were little more than 'recognized' in European states by local regulators free-riding on American regulatory efforts. With the Enron crisis concern about rating agencies grew and the industry codes of conduct were increasingly used as a useful form of self-regulation. With the onset of the global financial crisis European Commission officials have sought to regulate the agencies in Europe with proposed new laws passed by the European Parliament for referral to the Council of Ministers (EU Commission 2008; European Parliament 2009). This legislation, which is premised on local enforcement, creates a registration process like the NRSRO system and addresses issues of disclosure and transparency in the rating process. But it does not change rating analytics nor effectively challenge the issuer-pays model of rating funding.

It is intriguing that despite the worst financial crisis since the 1930s, and the identification of a suitable culprit in the rating agencies, proposed regulation should be so insubstantial, doing little to alter the rating system that has been in place in the US since 1909 and Europe since the mid-1980s. Part of this can be put down to a lack of confidence on the part of regulators and politicians in the efficacy of traditional state-centric solutions to market failure. It may also reflect the apparent weakness of already heavily regulated institutions such as commercial banks, and an understanding that the financial system is, despite the rating crisis, likely to continue to move in a more market- and more rating-dependent direction in future.

## Conclusions

There are two very different, competing understandings of financial crises. The first, the exogenous view, sees finance itself as a natural phenomenon, a smoothly oiled machine that only breaks down when governments interfere, or as a result of events that nobody can anticipate, such as war or famine. The other perspective, the endogenous view, argues that the machine-like view of finance is a myth. Like all other human institutions, finance is a world made by people, in which collective understandings, norms and assumptions give rise periodically to manias, panics and crashes. On this account, financial crises are normal. What is not normal, concede those who support the endogenous perspective, is the expansion of financial crises into global events that threaten to destabilize world politics, as did the Great Depression of the 1930s.

Whether you adopt an exogenous or endogenous view of financial crises, the necessity for international cooperation to combat them is essential. In the first instance, this probably amounts to no more than ensuring that governments and central banks communicate about their efforts to support vulnerable financial institutions, especially when those institutions operate, as so many do, in multiple jurisdictions. While there is evidence of this in recent times, there was also much unilateral, uncoordinated action intended for national advantage, such as the Irish Government's guarantee of all funds deposited in domestic banks. Building up the institutional capacity for cooperation between finance ministries and central banks should be a priority.

Political management will remain at the centre of financial crises. Governments, whether they like it or not, know they have responsibility for financial stability and they have become adept at identifying and disciplining institutions that do not seem to serve their purpose within the financial system. As a result, 'witch hunts' will continue to be a key feature of the fallout of financial crises, as governments attempt to offload as much of the liability for crises as possible.

Substantive regulatory change is likely to be muted by the lack of confidence amongst law makers in the US and Europe in the efficacy of regulation in the face of rapid financial change. The weakness of the regulatory response is already evident in the character of the initiatives developed to 'regulate' the credit rating agencies.

Intellectually, recent financial crises do not seem to have had much impact on the assumptions of academic disciplines like economics that provided the justification for the financial innovations at the heart of the subprime crisis. This means that even now the idea of asset price bubbles remains at odds with established thinking in the field, as promoted by financial economists. Inevitably, this means another generation of self-confident financial 'rocket scientists' is being trained ready to pursue financial innovation once memories of the current crisis fade.

While truly global financial crises are thankfully rare, we understand so little about the mechanisms that cause crises that much greater modesty about how finance works seems sensible. I argue we should abandon our assumption that finance is natural, like the movements of the planets, and instead embrace the lesson of Keynes' beauty contest and recognize that  financial markets are social phenomena in which collective understandings, especially confidence, may be more important than ostensibly technical considerations.

Although many academic assumptions remain resilient to change, it is apparent that, at least for now, the global financial crisis that started in 2007 created a much greater sense of uncertainty in the world, and challenged the idea that globalization will deliver us all from want in a risk-free way. This sense of unease has been deepened by the European sovereign debt crisis. It turns out that globalization is something that is unpredictable, that lurches in ways we cannot guess, and that even at the very heart of the global system can imperil great fortunes.

The relationship between global finance and politics has changed over the past hundred years. Before the 20th century governments had an interest in the smooth working of finance to fund the activities of the state, especially in relation to war. After 1929, governments, especially in the developed world, had a new role in preserving financial stability. After the Second World War, because of the absence of leadership between the wars, the United States assumed the central role in the design and implementation of a new global financial architecture of rules and institutions in support of an increasingly liberal order, but also one that at least in principle valued stability. After the Bretton Woods system of fixed exchange rates came to an end in the 1970s, the US played a strong coordinating role in response to the increased financial volatility that went with renewed international capital mobility, especially in relation to exchange rate fluctuations. Given the unprecedented circumstances of the global financial crisis that started in 2007, it is likely that a more activist stance on the part of the United States will be evident in the future. Whether US leadership and interstate cooperation will be as effective today as they were in the 1940s and the 1980s remains to be seen.

Unfortunately, the pressure to return to asset price booms (and thus inevitably, busts) remains very strong. People seem attached to the empirically false proposition that property values only increase in real terms. But given the degree to which western governments promoted home ownership as a route to prosperity after the Second World War, it is no wonder that people think this way. When we take the likelihood of future asset price bubbles into account, add in perennial developing country crises, and note the uncertain nature of the market response when bubbles burst, it seems almost inevitable that we will be dealing with financial crises on a regular basis in the future. Only through cooperation between major governments can we hope to ameliorate their worst effects and minimize their duration.

## Guide to further reading

A quick, readable introduction to financial crises is John Kenneth Galbraith's *A Short History of Financial Euphoria* (1993). His equally readable history of the Great Depression is *The Great Crash 1929* (1997 [1955]). The standard history is Charles P. Kindleberger and Robert Z. Aliber's *Manias, Panics and Crashes: A History of Financial Crises* (2011). Influential arguments about crisis in capitalism can be found in Polanyi's *The Great Transformation* (1957 [1944]), Schumpeter's *Capitalism, Socialism and Democracy* (2010 [1943]), Friedman and Schwartz's *A Monetary History of the United States, 1857–1960* (1963), and Minsky's *John Maynard Keynes* (2008). An excellent review of the economic literature on the Great Depression is Bernanke, *Essays on the Great Depression* (2000). On the global financial crisis that started in 2007 the reader should examine Krugman, *The Return of Depression Economics* (2nd edition, 2008); Cooper, *The Origin of Financial Crises* (2008); and Akerlof and Shiller, *Animal Spirits* (2009). The most readable accounts for the non-economist are Gamble's excellent *The Spectre at the Feast* (2009) and Germain's thoughtful and well-informed *Global Politics and Financial Governance* (2010). On banks and their troubles, see Rethel and Sinclair, *The Problem with Banks* (2012). Upton Sinclair's entertaining novel, *The Moneychangers*, based on events leading up to the 1907 panic, is well worth reading for a comparison with the past (2001 [1908]).

# Chapter 7

# Ways of War in the 21st Century

CAROLINE KENNEDY AND THOMAS WALDMAN

After the end of the Cold War, contradictory trends in warfare became apparent. During the 1990s many scholars thought that the demise of the Soviet Union had brought about a new world order in which international politics had taken on a new and more optimistic shape. Some even expressed the sentiment that war itself had passed into history alongside other practices such as duelling and slavery (Mueller 1985). Indeed, it became commonplace to argue that hard military power had been replaced by 'soft' power (Keohane and Nye 1998). Thus it appeared the scholarly community was hopeful that more peaceful modes of transformation would dominate international relations. This lack of interest in war-making, however, ran headlong into the reality of the 1990s as civil and ethnic wars proliferated across the globe, from the Balkans through Africa.

These 'new wars', characterized by ethnic cleansing, identity politics and endemic violence, demanded action, in some cases even military action on humanitarian grounds (see Bellamy, this volume). It was immediately apparent, though, that the Western powers preferred not to engage with these wars and sought to avoid military action, especially after the ill-fated US intervention in Somalia in 1993. However, when conflict erupted in both Rwanda and the Balkans, intervention appeared necessary, not because of specific state interests but for humanitarian reasons. This was the case in the Balkan Wars and the subsequent war against Serbia. While Western powers prided themselves on the defeat of Serbia and the liberation of Kosovo (Blair 2011), the manner in which the conflicts were waged was especially striking. The Kosovo War did not lead to a single combat fatality on the Western side. This and the mode of war from the air led to the label 'virtual war' (Ignatieff 2001). Liberal states preferred to wage war at a distance with as few sacrifices for their troops and as little disruption for domestic politics as possible. There were, of course, many casualties on the other side, some caused by NATO's bombing campaign against Serbia.

Civilian casualties have always formed part of the tapestry of war. But by the end of the 20th century civilians, as opposed to regular troops, were unquestionably bearing the brunt of conflict (Black 2004). It appeared that we had moved from an era of total wars such as 1914 and 1939 through the nuclear age to an era of selective war for the West, but still wars which were total for those on the receiving end. Wars in which the West was involved, it was predicted, would be wars of humanitarian intervention or wars of conscience (Wheeler 2000) fought from the air and waged with technological superiority. They would be short, sharp and distant.

Yet 9/11 transformed the international context. Rather than forgetting war, states such as the US and the UK proved enthusiastic for military action against not just those who had perpetrated terrorist attacks but those they deemed to be a threat. Hence, with the wars in Iraq and Afghanistan, what was a fairly traditional type of warfare returned. Yet, the opening episodes in these new trends in war resurfaced; the Afghan campaign reflected in many ways the Kosovo war, fought by the West largely from the air with the added involvement of special operations teams working with local Afghan forces. Iraq involved a larger deployment but air power was crucial; planners expected a short, decisive campaign with relatively little serious resistance. In the first phase at least this proved largely correct.

It was only when both these wars began to falter that large numbers of boots were put on the ground for a sustained period and with significant losses for Western states. The '9/11 wars', as they have been dubbed, have not proved easy (Burke 2011) because, as we go on to argue, these wars were, despite expectations, in essence types of new wars. The insurgents in Iraq and more recently in Afghanistan have turned these theatres of war for democratic states into the type of quagmire where the West meets not just insurgency but the brutality of endemic violence waged by a variety of sub-state actors. So how did we get here?

The interaction of the West with the new wars can be broken down into five rough phases. First, the early 1990s witnessed an uneasy confrontation with the new wars. There were many mixed lessons but overall an increasing awareness of the costs, both human and material, of direct involvement. Second, around the turn of the millennium, the combination of growing humanitarian sentiment encouraging action and the seemingly endless possibilities implied in the Revolution in Military Affairs (RMA) suggested a possible solution to the problem of these costs: humanitarian wars fought at a distance. Third, the early 9/11 wars saw the return of more traditional forms of war and an awareness of the utility of force as demonstrated in Afghanistan in 2001 and Iraq in 2003. Humanitarian intervention seemed to be replaced by short, sharp and largely effective wars of national interest for traditional reasons of state security. Yet the hope was that these wars, exploiting the opportunities provided by defence transformation, could be executed with little risk to Western forces. But fourth, Western forces found themselves caught up in the wars they had spent the 1990s trying to keep at a distance – the result was a rediscovery of counter-insurgency war as embodied in the twin surges of Iraq and then Afghanistan. A fifth phase has been one typified by retreat from war and a reversion to the trend of the late 1990s, but in a new context. The IED (improvised explosive device) and its use by the insurgents put pressure on Western forces to shift their mode of operations both in Iraq and in Afghanistan. After a decade of bloody wars and increasing casualties on all sides this has led to an emergent paradigm that we dub 'war at a distance'.

The desire not to commit manpower into theatre was reinforced during the so-called 'Arab Spring'. The uprisings across the Arab world in 2011 against brutal and corrupt leaderships, such as the Qaddafi regime in Libya, were characterized in the West by a willingness to encourage the overthrow of the regimes but without committing significant manpower other than small special operations teams and intelligence units. In the Libyan action therefore, like Kosovo, there were few casualties for the United States or the European powers. The conflict in Syria which began in 2012 too has been characterized by an American reluctance to commit troops coupled with an overt encouragement of the rebels, although there has been a desire within some circles for the United States to 'do more' militarily to prevent the abuse of the civilian population (Slaughter 2012).

The way of war is now, as it was in Kosovo, increasingly military action at a distance. The increasing use of drones in both Afghanistan and Pakistan, as well as the reliance on local forces and private security contractors, demonstrates a preference for technology and a dependence on surrogate forces over national sacrifice. This chapter goes on to argue that we will continue to see at least two contradictory trends in war this century: liberal powers loth to sacrifice and opponents increasingly finding novel ways to exploit the weak spots of the West and the vulnerabilities of this technology-dependent approach.

Looking to the future, we argue that liberal democracies will find it increasingly difficult to use traditional military methods to achieve foreign policy objectives. We argue that the wars in Iraq and Afghanistan which have characterized the early years of this century will be viewed as aberrations and that we will see an attempt to rely on technological fixes, local proxies, private military contractors and special forces. National sacrifice is an increasingly unpopular sentiment and liberal states seem to lack the durability, finance and commitment to wage lengthy wars. The way of war will be preferably wars at a distance for those in the West but not for the rest of the world.

## Feeling out the new wars

While the end of the Cold War did not bring about the kind of new world order which George Bush envisaged, it certainly marked the closing chapter of the old order. What have usefully, if controversially, been described as 'new wars' (Kaldor 2012) flared up or morphed out of earlier frozen conflicts. Just how 'new' these wars were in historical terms, given their eerie similarity to the religious wars Europe experienced in the first half of the 17th century (Münkler 2005), need not distract us here, but for Western militaries, the problems they posed were certainly not like those for which they had spent the last half-century preparing. Gray describes the conflicts of the 1990s as 'in-the-face personally primitive and postmodern. Chechnya, Bosnia, Rwanda, and Somalia comprised a ghastly combination of Homer and Tom Clancy' (Gray 1999). Other commentators spoke of 'destructured conflict' (Shawcross 2000).

These new conflicts displayed a disturbing mix of characteristics; they were seemingly inconclusive and intractable; often identity-based; and a mixture of old and new forms (primitive and modern). These were conflicts that more resembled guerrilla raids and massacres than set-piece confrontations between clearly identifiable armed groups as in the past. Battle lines were often blurred with high levels of collusion between supposed antagonists. Violence was often directed at civilians in the form of massacre, mutilations, rape and pillage. Child soldiers, mercenaries, arms dealers and criminal gangs all made their way into the landscape of these conflicts. Conflicts such as those in Sierra Leone, Liberia, Somalia, Chechnya, Sri Lanka and Nepal were characteristic of this period.

With the United Nations ostensibly no longer constrained by the great power politics of the Cold War and a growing global 24-hour media relaying images of suffering from these conflict zones, the pressure among populations in the West to 'do something' increased. Humanitarian actors flooded into these zones of conflict; aid workers, non-governmental organizations (NGOs) and peacekeepers became a distinctive feature of the 1990s wars. But just what the appropriate military and political responses should be remained uncertain in these 'wars amongst the people' (Smith 2006). A series of questions were posed over both whether and how to intervene. Peacekeeping and intervention proved problematic, as was witnessed both during the US intervention in Somalia and the obvious failure of will to defend the people of Srebrenica during the Balkan Wars. The perils of doing nothing were laid bare in Rwanda when around one million people were slaughtered. So the West ignored new wars for the most part, largely dismissing them as the atavistic eruptions of innate tribalism in the Third World or seeing them as unconnected to their own strategic concerns, apart perhaps from those conflicts closer to home or where colonial legacies prompted involvement, such as for the UK in Sierra Leone and the US in Liberia. The huge and destructive wars in sub-Saharan Africa were considered largely out of bounds or beyond the capabilities of Western military forces.

However, a number of trends evident through the 1990s prompted policymakers to shape a response to the chaos apparently continuing unabated around the globe. Western military institutions began seriously to reflect on the experiences of the early 1990s, specifically those of Bosnia and the use of air power above Iraq in no-fly zones. New technologies encapsulated in the Revolution in Military Affairs (RMA) seemed to hold out the possibility of risk-free but effective warfare. It was thought that the West could, where certain conditions were met, intervene to rescue societies from themselves by employing advanced weaponry and sophisticated communications technology. These became the West's answer to some but not all of the atrocities of the 1990s – humanitarian war fought at some cost but with little or no risk to Western soldiers, utilizing the latest technology and satisfying mounting public pressure to respond to the slaughter (Ignatieff 2000). Yet, this response remained highly selective – the West was by no means suggesting it could respond wherever crimes against humanity were being perpetrated. And, while it might have had an answer to Serbia's nationalistic campaign in Kosovo, the intractable and brutal civil wars in the heart of Africa represented a different order of problem and one with which the West showed little enthusiasm to engage. Given the trends of the 1990s, some commentators went so far as to suggest that war had become a 'spectator sport' (McInnes 2002). But then came 9/11.

## The 9/11 wars

The phrase 'war on terror' is not one that was dreamt up by George W. Bush. It was used as far back as the 19th century to refer to attempts by anarchists to attack and assassinate political leaders. After the attacks of 9/11, President Bush resurrected the term and argued that the war on terror would begin with the group which had perpetrated them, al-Qaeda, but that it would certainly not end with al-Qaeda. It was used not only to justify the use of war in Afghanistan and Iraq but also to underpin a series of controversial activities including 'extraordinary rendition' and the widespread use of torture at detention facilities in both Iraq and Guantanamo in Cuba. These initial wars of the 21st century have so far rendered permissible a range of activities which were prohibited after 1945, raising serious concerns about the breaching of human rights.

Initially, both the Afghan and Iraqi invasions suggested that Western militaries had not lost their touch for war. Those two very different campaigns were fought, at least initially, with remarkable flair and efficiency. Despite the warnings and doubts of some commentators, the campaigns proved relatively unproblematic to conduct. In many ways, the 2001 Afghan incursion laid the ground for Iraq – such political and legal concerns as surrounded the removal of Saddam Hussein were offset by the confirmation of a notable level of military effectiveness displayed in the decisive victory over the Taliban (Aylwin-Foster 2005).

Immediately after the events of 9/11, the US worked with the Northern Alliance in a bid to depose the Taliban's Islamic Emirate of Afghanistan which was credited with sheltering and supporting al-Qaeda (Burke 2011). The radical mullahs in Afghanistan had offered sanctuary to Osama bin Laden, the leader of al-Qaeda (Giustozzi 2009). In the last few months of 2001, the US delivered 767 tonnes of supplies and US$70 million to equip and fund some 50,000 militiamen to fight Taliban forces. The US air force also proved decisive in this first phase. B52s launched assaults on the caves of Tora Bora, dropping 'daisy cutter' bombs onto the insurgents below. Bin Laden later recounted how the *mujahedeen* had attempted to dig themselves into trenches to avoid losses (Wright 2006).

While requiring much greater concentrations of force and thousands of troops on the ground, the 2003 Iraq War underlined Western military dominance when employed in conventional wars for national interests (however contested those supposed 'interests' might be). Where Iraq was more problematic initially was in the political realm. The decision to make war over Iraq's putative weapons of mass destruction (WMD) programme split the Western alliance, with relationships between Washington and its allies more fractious than they had been for many years (Kagan 2003). But for neoconservative ideologues, this objection would amount to a footnote in the long sweep of history once the military had deposed a hated regime and democracy precipitated the flourishing of peace and stability in the Middle East, not to mention a steady supply of oil to the American economy (Muttitt 2011).

Afghanistan and Iraq were purportedly wars of necessity. At the outset Western military forces proudly displayed the agility, flexibility and superiority they would employ to defeat a regular enemy. Yet, in both theatres the nature of the battle soon changed. By 2005, in both countries, worrying signs were emerging. In Iraq, the 'descent into chaos' was relatively rapid. As John Nagl puts it, 'what was supposed to be a cakewalk became a rebellion exacerbated by mistakes' (Slaughter 2011); before long, the US found itself in the midst of emergent civil wars. Iraq between 2004 and 2006 was a hellish place. Meanwhile, in Afghanistan – as the West's gaze was firmly fixed on the chaos unfolding in Mesopotamia – the Taliban was infiltrating provinces in the south and east of the country. What had started as wars waged with air power, special forces and general 'shock and awe' rapidly turned into insurgency and counter-insurgency.

## The new wars: Iraq and Afghanistan

Events in both Iraq and Afghanistan did not play out according to the script. What were meant to be post-conflict state-building scenarios typified by gradual stabilization and democratic consolidation moved in the opposite direction. Iraq was beset by the ugly spectre of sectarian strife, death squads, beheadings, suicide attacks and human rights abuses (Ricks 2009). New wars had arrived in these two countries and the West found itself up to its neck in the quicksand of post-modern conflict – the very scenario it had tried its best to avoid in the 1990s. Of course, the 9/11 wars were also fuelled by resistance to perceived occupation, but this only served to heighten passions. Western forces, finding themselves embroiled in conflicts they did not fully understand, searched for solutions in works that had barely been dusted off since the 1970s: the classics of counter-insurgency. Drawing inspiration from these books, but revising them for a very different age, the US Army's new Counter-insurgency Field Manual, FM 3-40, essentially took on an exalted status and General David Petraeus – one of its lead authors – assumed the role of 'counter-insurgency prophet' (Ricks 2009). The subsequent Iraq surge between 2006 and 2008 became the exemplar of how to fight modern war. With the situation deteriorating in the Pashtun belt of Afghanistan, it was only a matter of time before the book and its prophet moved east to proselytize. Moreover, the US military was riding the wave of a new sense of purpose and self-belief that had so nearly been buried in the rubble of the Iraqi Sunni Triangle.

Counter-insurgency is certainly not for the faint-hearted and the twin surges of Iraq in 2006 and Afghanistan in 2009–10 suggested that the war-at-a-distance, risk-free paradigm of the 1990s had been discarded and 'real' war had returned. The contrast with the engagements of the 1990s was palpable. The fighting in, for instance, the Iraqi city of Fallujah or Afghanistan's remote Korengal Valley were but the most stark manifestations of this return to visceral warfare (McCarthy and Beaumont 2004). These deployments underlined the renewed willingness of Western states to commit troops and put them in harm's way. This undoubtedly reflected the sense to which strategic interest, however considered, had found its way back into war post-9/11, as well as the extent to which, as Clausewitz might have had it, the passions of the American people had been aroused by the 9/11 attacks (Waldman 2012).

Yet the Iraq model set the scene for the failures of counter-insurgency in Afghanistan. Not only were the counter-insurgency lessons from Iraq highly tentative, the Afghanistan context presented deep challenges that were shrugged off by the new legions of counter-insurgency experts, self-described as COIN experts, stalking the corridors of the Pentagon. Two chief obstacles stood out. First, elements in Pakistan continued to provide extensive support as well as sanctuary to Afghan insurgents (Waldman, M 2010). Second, the regime in Kabul that the West was supporting, and to which it was essentially attempting to win the Afghan people over, was ineffective, and patently corrupt and predatory. Considering that FM 3-40 had stated that the 'primary objective of any COIN operation is to foster development of effective governance by a legitimate government', the situation was not promising. What we witnessed instead was the death of counter-insurgency.

## The death of COIN

In Afghanistan, the situation deteriorated in slow motion. By 2005, the war was proving problematic on a number of counts and by the time President Obama was elected in late 2008 there was a widespread view that the US was, if not losing the war in Afghanistan, than certainly not winning it. The Taliban and associated insurgent groups had proved resilient, resourceful and operationally flexible. O'Hanlon argued that the Taliban had become a 'smarter insurgent' force (O'Hanlon 2010). Rather than engaging in large-scale assaults on NATO forces, they targeted instead smaller, more vulnerable NATO enclaves. This proved lethal with the widespread use of roadside bombs and suicide attacks, often combined with follow-up attacks using small arms. The Taliban generally eschewed attacks on civilians and concentrated attention on 'foreign' troops and Afghan security personnel.

The Obama response to the Taliban resurgence was a surge of 30,000 additional troops combined with an operational approach put together by General Stanley McChrystal. The strategy was to implement a limited degree of state building which placed the onus on Afghan forces to eventually control territory in the south and the east of the country. Building institutions at the national and sub-national levels was designed primarily to win the population over to the government by providing them with security and services. McChrystal also emphasized the limiting of casualties in a bid to win over more of the civilian population.

Counter-insurgency in the Afghan theatre, despite the much talked about previous experience of the Americans and British, certainly proved unable to bring about easy victories. Indeed, after over ten years, the decision to 'draw down' troops in Afghanistan demonstrates that the Western powers would prefer not to prolong the presence of boots on the ground. The Obama surge had become highly contested and the political calculus began to change, due to electoral considerations, economic woes and, of course, mounting casualties sacrificed for increasingly uncertain objectives. This became even more the case after bin

Laden, the architect of 9/11, was assassinated by US Special Forces in May 2011. Furthermore, in response to the surge, in 2010 the Taliban launched its 'victory' campaign and adapted its operations. The movement managed to spread further into the north and, throughout 2011, launched daring and sophisticated attacks in Kabul and elsewhere.

Under Obama a degree of fatigue at the ongoing and seemingly inconclusive war set in. With 100,000 troops deployed, fewer than half of Americans supported the war when he took office, a trend that has continued (CNN Politics 2011). Allies proved far from durable as casualties and costs mounted. While it is true that the International Security Assistance Force (ISAF) in Afghanistan initially involved some 40 countries, by 2012 many had left or signalled their intention to do so, leaving some twelve countries continuing to contribute troops.

The weight of professional opinion, from seasoned Afghan watchers to even those within military circles, suggests there is no purely military solution to the conflict. It is also clear that a genuine appetite for counter-insurgency has diminished. This has been evidenced by the increasing reliance on force protection, a retreat into fortified outposts, the use of drones, special forces and private military corporations. It has also become apparent that the very real gains the troop surge allowed in the south were offset by insurgent intensification in the east. 2010 was an exceptionally bloody year for the United States in Afghanistan, with 499 American dead, 5,182 wounded and a notable increase in Afghan casualties (Congressional Research Service 2011). A decade after the terrorist attacks on the United States the cost of the 9/11 wars was estimated to be around US$300 trillion (*New York Times*, 2011).

The perfect storm of contextual determinants weighing against the chances of successful execution of COIN was powerfully on display in Afghanistan. A distinct lack of political and strategic direction has meant that an overwhelmingly kinetic and militarized approach, guided by considerations of casualty avoidance, has served to intensify the conflict and undermine exploratory moves in relation to negotiations with the Taliban. The military dominated decision making and inevitably sought military solutions to problems that are overwhelmingly political in nature: as Paul Cornish argues, counter-insurgency 'must be political first, political last, political always' (Cornish 2009). Deriving from the almost universal military proclivity to seek solutions through technological elixirs and 'magic bullets', the military domination of policy and strategy led to an approach focused on attrition and material factors over more nuanced, sophisticated political and diplomatic solutions. The increasing reliance of the United States on drone technology is a clear manifestation of a desire to resolve what are essentially political issues with a short, sharp fix that ignores not only some parts of international law but also the broader strategic picture.

## Drones and increasing lethality

As P.W. Singer points out, 'the introduction of unmanned systems to the battlefield doesn't change simply how we fight, but for the first time changes who fights at the most fundamental level. It transforms the very agent of war, rather than just its capabilities' (Singer 2009). The use of drones is increasing. Initially used for reconnaissance purposes, they began to be used in combat missions after President Bush's Secret Memorandum of Notification authorizing the CIA to kill members of al-Qaeda in what was termed 'anticipatory self-defence'. Drone technology is now possessed by the US, the UK, China, France, Italy, Iran, Israel, Russia, South Korea and Turkey, with others about to join the club (Radio Free Europe 2012). Non-state groups such as Hamas have also experimented with drones.

The growing sophistication and increasing use of the technology promote the assumption among many that drones are adding to the 'de-humanization of war', as Christopher Coker might put it (Coker 2001). Evidence of this view is omnipresent in military and political circles, where the effects of drones on reducing 'our' combat deaths are emphasized and the capacity of the technology to be ever more precise is often lauded, as in Kenneth Anderson's claim that drones are a major step forward towards a much more discriminating use of violence in war and self-defence – a step forward in humanitarian technology (Anderson, 2010). A counterview, however, is also present and certainly seems as plausible. This is simply the fact that, in practice, drones are a very blunt weapon. As the growth in so-called 'collateral damage' (Caputi 2012) as a result of US drone strikes in Afghanistan and Pakistan shows, the technology is not always good at sorting out the combatant wheat from the non-combatant chaff and when it fails to do so the political – as well as the human – consequences can be very severe. As David Kilcullen, one of the most astute contemporary commentators on counter-terrorism, pointed out in his testimony to Congress in April 2009, drone strikes often 'give rise to a feeling of anger that coalesces the population around the extremists' (Kilcullen 2009). In other words, the political costs of using the technology may well outweigh any military benefits.

The likely result of this phenomenon, as drones become more common in the practice of modern war, can be readily imagined – a perfect storm of resentment and grievance that is likely to sour relations between allies (as it has done between the US and Pakistan, though to be sure there are many other reasons for that), worsen and prolong conflicts and impede the prospects of diplomacy and conciliation. Thus, even at the practical political level it would seem that drones are, to put it charitably, a double-edged sword. This issue is raised very obviously by drones now, but will become more pressing still when the next generation of drones appears – which, if reports are to be believed, will be completely autonomous and not even controlled by remote operators (Singer 2009). In his book on 'post human war' in the 21st century, Coker (2002) points out that we are witnessing the slow elimination of the characteristics that have marked out the idea of the Warrior over the centuries and across cultures. The idea of the Warrior, he suggests (echoing a phrase of Michael Ignatieff) is inseparable from the idea of the Warrior's honour. But the point is how to fight with honour against insurgents and terrorists playing by a different set of rules in a range of complex environments.

## Slaughterhouse

The Western confrontation with new wars over the last decade has been a sobering one. There is a palpable sense of exhaustion among policymakers and soldiers in the West, a situation not dissimilar to the compassion fatigue of the mid-1990s described by Ignatieff (1998). Combined with warnings of strategic overstretch and, in America, the existence of a bloated defence establishment sticking out like a sore thumb in an age of austerity, politicians and soldiers could do with a 'holiday from history' to rest and recuperate from a period of tireless activity. Yet, as the 1990s taught us, withdrawal and inaction are hardly options in an era when Western populations – confronted daily with media reports of conflict around the world – demand that their representatives intervene to put a halt to injustice, suffering and violence. Perhaps this is true; however, a happy coincidence has been observed by some commentators keen to note the decline in the number of civil and ethnic conflicts over the last two decades. These trends are certainly to be welcomed and the optimism generated by renewed emphasis on conflict prevention among Western states and international institutions is perhaps warranted. If conflict really is fading into obsolescence, the American global policeman and supporting retinue will not only be able to take pause to rest, but could soon be out of a job – a rosy outlook for cash-strapped governments, perhaps less so for those, such as defence contractors and mercenaries, whose livelihoods depend on conflict.

However, it is well to be sceptical about the prospect of such a scenario actually unfolding. A number of developments suggest the West cannot wave goodbye to the new wars of this century just yet. The observed decline in the number of conflicts cannot hide the burning reality of the many new wars that rage unabated in Africa, the Middle East and Asia and that show little sign of imminent resolution. Instances of conflict in Kenya, Georgia, Kyrgyzstan and elsewhere, despite being short, are redolent of a world pervaded by political, ethnic and tribal tension that can quickly turn ugly. The wars the West has waged for stability and democracy in Iraq and Afghanistan risk reverting back to the terrible spectacle of sectarian bloodshed and warlordism once international troops leave. Many commentators fear a return to the multi-sided civil war that racked Afghanistan in the early 1990s. Authoritarian regimes resisting reform constitute pressure cookers of popular discontent and future civil strife (as witnessed in Libya and now Syria). Drug-related gang violence is endemic in parts of South and Central America. Essentially, it would be presumptuous to predict the near-demise of the new wars just yet, despite whatever comfort positive trends and global activism might provide.

Furthermore, in a global age, the militant groups, criminal gangs and pirates operating on the fringes of the civilized world repeatedly confront Westerners in multiple contexts: crews on ships navigating the Indian Ocean, consultants in north-east Nigeria, aid workers in Somalia. The activities of pirates operating across thousands of miles of water not only pose a considerable threat to commercial activities globally but point to the ingenuity of these actors who target the material and human resources of wealthy states (Gettleman 2008). In this way, the West will constantly find itself having to respond to the effects of regional instability, civil conflict and state failure. Also, as articulated in various Western government policy papers with increasing amplitude over the last two decades, there has been a realization that these wars represent not only threats to the human security of local populations, but also compromise their own security and interests, be it in the form of creating breeding grounds for terrorists, the supply of narcotics onto Western streets, human trafficking, disruption of energy supplies, nuclear proliferation or more generally as threats to regional and international security. The West is not immune to these forms of war and this fact will continue to prompt governments to react, sometimes militarily.

There is thus much to suggest that an assortment of terrorists, gangs, militias, hostage takers, hackers and pirates will be confronted by an equally diverse array of special forces, drone operators, private security contractors, military advisers, foreign-trained local proxies and cyber-warriors. Large concentrations of troops may be deployed from time to time but in the long sweep of this century, it is the mixed bag of actors described above that are likely to be the prominent protagonists of the 21st-century battlefield. The battlefield will be multidimensional with one side tending to confine themselves to urban sprawl, dense jungles and mountain caves, and the other preferring to fight from air-conditioned converted trailers and fortified regional bases, as well as from sea, air and space. Rarely will the belligerents come face to face.

## Counter-insurgency and the liberal predicament

Counter-insurgency has been shown to be a hazardous military road to take, full of the chance and uncertainty which the West so desperately seeks to control, but that Clausewitz taught us two centuries ago is an inescapable element of war. It is unwise to hold up the case of Iraq as proof that counter-insurgency can work and that the United States has been able to 'relearn' (if ever it knew) the fundamentals of this type of war. Indeed, it was perhaps this mistaken optimism that led American generals to believe it could successfully conduct counter-insurgency in Afghanistan. Abandoning counter-insurgency again, Western states will most likely find themselves embroiled in an era of clandestine war, special operations, counter-terrorism, secretive intelligence operations and proxy conflicts involving the training and equipping of foreign armed forces or rebel groups tentatively aligned with the West. The use of force for security reasons will likely be supplemented by humanitarian interventions characterized by precision bombing, no-fly zones, naval blockades and covert action, often followed by multilateral peace operations and security sector reform programmes. These deployments will be accompanied by a wider array of counter-piracy, hostage rescue, defence diplomacy and other smaller-scale missions. Putting such operations into practice will require investment in hugely expensive technologies, the management of a network of outposts and secure bases from which to house teams of trainers, advisers and specialists, as well as complex contractual arrangements with an array of private organizations.

Prominent events in recent years certainly point to the future: anti-piracy operations off the Horn of Africa; the special forces raid which led to the killing of Osama bin Laden; the US military advisers sent to assist in the hunt for Ugandan war criminal Joseph Kony; the failed British Special Boat Service hostage-rescue raid in northern Nigeria of March 2012; the expansion of America's Africa command and security sector programmes throughout the continent; the continuing drone strikes in Pakistan's tribal regions; and much more. The difficulties encountered in some of these examples suggest this type of war by no means offers neat and easy answers to strategic problems. The political fall-out from both the bin Laden raid and the failed Nigerian hostage rescue underlines the inescapable truth of Clausewitz's contention regarding the political nature of war, even with respect to such limited uses of force (Waldman, T. 2010).

## Patterns of war: virtual, vicious and vicarious

These conclusions, we think, reflect not simply the legacy of two difficult, costly wars fought over the first decade of the 21st century. They are that, but more importantly, they derive from deeper, more fundamental patterns that pre-date the experiences of Iraq and Afghanistan (wars which only served to consolidate underlying realities). These trends are rooted in a certain attitude to war that is unique to liberal societies, and which has been compounded as a result of profound changes in modern popular attitudes to the use of force.

A dominant feature of modern Western culture is the profound 'debellicization' of society. The perception of war as a virtuous activity was gradually delegitimized during the 20th century, and although war continued to fascinate, it was no longer deemed desirable. These attitudes were consolidated through post-war social trends of mass consumerism, shrinking family sizes, the decline of civic militarism, democratization, redefinitions of masculinity and the growth of an individualistic youth culture (Waldman 2007). Other cultural patterns include the growing concern for human rights and the emergence of prosperity as a dominant socio-political value. Such popular norms have increased restrictions on when and how war is waged.

Also, as militaries have become increasingly professionalized, societies have diminishing contact with them, thus further separating publics from the experience of conflict, contributing to what has been termed a 'revolution' in attitudes towards the military (Black 2004). Advances in science and medicine have led to a rejection of fatalism and a greater reluctance to accept the hazards of conflict – a fact embodied in the growing casualty sensitivity of Western publics, particularly when the justice and probability of success are in question (Gelpi *et al.* 2005/6), or when the war is one of choice rather than necessity. Further, even though war directly affects only small proportions of Western society in a post-conscription age, the media saturation of modern wars has meant the suffering of grieving families, wounded soldiers and those who experience ongoing psychological problems on their return are relayed to millions in intimate, agonizing detail. So, any greater acceptance of military sacrifice due to professionalization has been offset by the media impact.

No doubt Western states will take to the battlefield again – especially where state interest appears to demand action on security grounds – hoping the use of large-scale force will solve whatever pressing problem they are confronted with. In some cases an Iraq-style campaign may serve objectives, but as Rupert Smith and others have pointed out, such campaigns are less and less likely in this age (Smith 2006). Furthermore, given the trends outlined above, not only will the large-scale deployment of forces prove harder to effect but the pressures to find alternative solutions is only increasing. For most Western states, counter-insurgency wars like those fought in Iraq and Afghanistan will be rare and increasingly hard to countenance, justify and sustain. With low-level, irregular and 'small' wars (rather than national wars of interest) likely dominating the strategic landscape, the kind of large-scale wars of the 2000s are not likely to be a regular feature of the 21st century. As Anne-Marie Slaughter (2011) has put it, 'historians will see 9/11 as the catalyst for the end of twentieth-century warfare: large-scale, multi-year deployments requiring conquest, control and long-term stabilization and reconstruction of foreign territory … The second Iraq war and the war in Afghanistan are ending boots-on-the-ground wars of counter-insurgency and regime change.'

It is perhaps misleading to term the types of war that are likely to dominate this century as 'virtual', because not only will the West's opponents and citizens caught in the cross-fire suffer the very real effects of war, but so too will the West's surrogate agents of war; the local proxies and private specialists in violence to whom it increasingly subcontracts its war-fighting. This way of war will be fought in a manner that limits risk and is at arm's length, at a distance. It will be an age of vicarious war.

## Guide to further reading

One of the best accounts of the consequences of 9/11 both militarily and politically is to be found in *The 9/11 Wars* (Burke 2011), while an impressive account of how al-Qaeda came to attack the United States is *The Looming Tower* (Wright 2006). For a detailed assessment of the conduct and command of the Western powers in Iraq see *The Gamble* (Ricks 2009). Perhaps the most authoritative account of the impact of technology on future battlefields and the prospects for a revolution in military affairs is *Wired For War* (Singer 2009). To understand the complex nature of soldiering amongst the new wars of the 1990s, see *The Warrior's Honor* (Ignatieff 1998) and also *Blood and Belonging: Journeys into the New Nationalism* (Ignatieff 1993). To really understand the complex nature of politics within Afghanistan see *Empires of Mud: Wars and Warlords in Afghanistan* (Giustozzi 2009), while for predictions about the nature of future challenges and theatres of conflict in the coming century see Black (2004). Clausewitz's writings provide a steady objective lens through which to view all the complex contortions of contemporary war; for a clear exposition of his central theoretical device, see *War, Clausewitz and the Trinity* (Waldman 2012).

# Chapter 8

# Peace Operations and Humanitarian Intervention

ALEX J. BELLAMY

Since the 19th-century 'atrocitarians' lobbied for the great powers to intervene in the Balkans to put an end to Ottoman massacres (Bass 2008), the commission of genocide and mass atrocities has tended to provoke calls for international society to act. In the 1990s, genocide in Rwanda (1994) killed at least 800,000, war in the former Yugoslavia (1992–95) left at least 250,000 dead and forced thousands more to flee. Protracted conflicts in Sierra Leone, Sudan, Haiti, Somalia, Liberia, East Timor, the Democratic Republic of Congo (DRC) and elsewhere killed millions more. More recently, thousands more civilians have recently been killed by their own governments in Libya, Syria, Yemen and elsewhere in the Middle East during the 'Arab Spring'. Historically, however, genocides have ended in one of two ways: either the *genocidaires* succeed in destroying their target group or they are defeated in battle. This cold fact is borne out by recent cases. The Rwandan genocide ended with the defeat of the Rwandan government and *interehamwe* militia at the hands of the Rwandan Patriotic Front (RPF); the carnage in Bosnia came to an end when the military balance turned in favour of a Croat-Muslim coalition backed by NATO airpower; and the bloodshed in Darfur declined after 2005 primarily because the *janjaweed* militia and their government backers succeeded in forcing their opponents into exile.

Facts like this pose a major challenge to world politics. Contemporary international order is based on a society of states that enjoy exclusive jurisdiction over a particular piece of territory and rights to non-interference and non-intervention that are enshrined in the Charter of the United Nations. Article 2(4) of the UN Charter forbids the use of force as an instrument of state policy with only two exceptions – each state's inherent right to self-defence (Article 51) and enforcement measures authorized by the UN Security Council. This system is in turn prefaced on the assumption that states exist primarily to protect the security of their citizens. In other words, the security of the state is considered important, and worth protecting, because states provide security to individuals. Moreover, the principles of non-intervention and non-interference have helped international society dramatically reduce the number of inter-state conflicts. Although inter-state war is not yet obsolete, it is very rare thanks in part to this normative order. However, it should be clear from the preceding paragraph that although the norms of non-intervention and non-interference have helped reduce inter-state war, the assumption that states are always the best providers of security to individuals is often found wanting. In the past century, threats to individual security have tended to come more from an individual's own state than from other states. Whilst states are often the main perpetrators of genocide and mass atrocities, there are also cases where states are simply incapable of protecting their populations – either because the state has collapsed entirely, as in Somalia in the early 1990s, or because it lacks the capacity to defeat or make peace with rebel groups.

All this raises questions about the role of international society in mitigating the worst effects of armed conflict and protecting populations from genocide and mass atrocities. In the 1950s, the UN began to develop peacekeeping operations aimed at providing impartial monitoring of ceasefires, political transitions and assistance to states to maintain order. In the decades since, the fate of peace operations has ebbed and flowed and different types have emerged, ranging from small monitoring missions (e.g., UNTSO in the Middle East) through to large and complex multidimensional operations with a range of different military, policing, civilian and humanitarian tasks (e.g., MONUC in the DRC) and transitional administrations where the UN assumes temporary sovereign control over a territory (e.g., Kosovo). In the main, these peace operations are conducted with the consent – albeit sometimes coerced consent – of the host state. This leaves the thorny question of what should happen when the host state is the main perpetrator of genocide and mass atrocities and refuses to consent to the deployment of multinational forces, as in the case of Syria in early 2012. In those circumstances, should the security of individuals be privileged over the security of states? Should a state's right to be secure and free from armed attack be dependent on its fulfillment of certain responsibilities to its citizens, not least a responsibility to protect them from mass killing? Or should the imperative of maintaining international order override concerns about human security? It is these questions that animate the contemporary debate about humanitarian intervention.

This chapter provides an overview of the military tools that international society uses to manage and mitigate armed conflict. It begins by briefly surveying the development of peace operations conducted largely with the consent of the host authorities. The second part of the chapter turns to the question of what should happen when the state refuses to grant its consent or is the main perpetrator of mass atrocities. The third and final part of the chapter focuses on the emergence of a new international principle which seeks to reframe the way that international society protects populations from genocide and mass atrocities. This new principle, called the 'responsibility to protect' (R2P) holds that states have a responsibility to protect populations from genocide and mass atrocities, that international society has a duty to assist them, and that when the host state manifestly fails to do so, the international community has a responsibility to take timely and decisive action. The challenge now, I argue, is to clarify the R2P principle and develop practical measures for translating it from words to deeds.

## Peace operations

### Historical evolution

Although the term 'peacekeeping' was invented in the 1950s, the international management of armed conflict has a far longer history. In the 19th century, the Concert of Europe managed political violence by intervening against revolutionaries and to protect Christians in the Ottoman Empire. Between 1919 and 1939, the League of Nations oversaw plebiscites in contested territories and deployed peacekeepers to the Ruhr and Danzig (see Schmidl 2000). The development of peace operations conducted by the UN after the Second World War needs to be seen against the backdrop of the Cold War. It was initially conceived that the UN would be a collective security institution. However, Cold War politics stymied the UN's efforts to adopt this role, forcing it to develop alternative ways of contributing to international peace and security. Peacekeeping – a term not envisaged by the UN Charter – was one of the principal means of doing this. In 1947, the General Assembly dispatched an observation mission (UNSCOB) to report on cross-border movements during the Greek Civil War. The following year, the Security Council also began to be engaged in two of the world's most pressing crises, the Palestinian conflict and the struggle over Kashmir (Luck 2006: 32), leading to the deployment of two further observation missions. These ad hoc missions began to be conceptualized into a coherent role for the UN. The terms of reference for what was widely regarded as the UN's first self-styled peace operation, UNEF I – deployed to the Sinai to help defuse the Suez Crisis of 1956 – contributed to the establishment of core principles of consent, impartiality and minimum use of force.

In total, the UN conducted fourteen missions during the Cold War. All were intimately connected with decolonization. UN peace operations during the Cold War were therefore a tool for managing one of the most significant structural shifts in world politics – the globalization of the sovereign state. Closer attention also reveals that almost half of all the UN operations deployed in this period were in the Middle East. This supports the view that peace operations were an important part of the UN's 'preventive diplomacy' role, seeking to prevent local conflicts escalating into a global imbroglio. In the Middle East case, both superpowers recognized the potential for escalation but neither was prepared to wage war in order to defend their claims and allies in the region. This created an opening for consensus in the Security Council and helps explain the strong regional bias in the deployment of peace operations towards the Middle East. It is worth noting that, by contrast, the same period saw only one UN operation (ONUC) deployed to sub-Saharan Africa and this too came in relation to a crisis that divided the superpowers (Bellamy and Williams 2009).

As the Cold War came to an end between 1988 and 1993, peace operations underwent a triple transformation (Bellamy and Williams 2009). First, there was a *quantitative transformation*. During this period, the UN conducted more peace operations than it had undertaken in its previous forty years. Moreover, traditional peacekeeping contributors were augmented by a flood of new countries, including great powers such as the US, France and the UK, prepared to deploy their troops as UN peacekeepers. Second, there was a *normative transformation* catalysed by a growing belief among some member states that the remit for peace operations should be broadened to include the promotion of humanitarian values and human rights. Finally – and as a result of the normative transformation – there was a *qualitative transformation*. The UN was asked to carry out complex missions reminiscent of ONUC in the 1960s but on a far more regular basis. In places such as Cambodia, Bosnia and Somalia, the UN launched operations that were qualitatively different from earlier missions, marrying peacekeeping with the delivery of humanitarian aid, state-building programmes, local peacemaking and elements of peace enforcement. These missions were also much larger and more expensive than anything the UN had attempted before, with the exception of ONUC.

Still operating on the basis of Cold War ideas about peacekeeping, these new missions lacked the resources, doctrine and institutional capacity they needed to succeed, and led to a series of high-profile failures. In Angola, peacekeepers were forced to stand aside as a peace deal collapsed and bloody war recommenced. In Somalia, American peacekeepers became the targets of militia violence and the mission there collapsed after the US sustained casualties in the infamous 'Black Hawk Down' incident. In Bosnia, four years of dithering was capped off with the collapse of a UN 'safe area' in Srebrenica and the massacre of 7,600 men and boys. Worst of all, however, in Rwanda an ill-equipped UN force was instructed to stand aside during the genocide. By 1995, the catastrophes in Angola, Somalia, Bosnia and Rwanda had prompted many states to re-evaluate the value of peace operations and the nature of their contribution to it. The number of UN peacekeepers deployed around the world fell dramatically as member states expressed a preference for working through regional organizations and alliances, such as Economic Community of West African States (ECOWAS) and NATO, and the Security Council became reluctant to create new missions. This ushered in a period of hesitant introspection at the UN, during which the organization produced reports detailing its failings in Rwanda and Bosnia. These reports identified serious problems with the way that the UN mandated, organized and conducted its peace operations and exposed gaps between the tasks peacekeepers were expected to fulfill in the post-Cold War era and the conceptual and material resources made available to them (Bellamy and Williams 2009).

Attitudes began to change in 1999 with high-profile and largely successful interventions in Kosovo and East Timor. In the months that followed, the Security Council authorized new missions to Sierra Leone and the DRC. This renewed demand for peace operations helped prompt the UN Secretary-General to commission a major report into the conduct and management of peace operations. Commonly referred to as the Brahimi Report after its chairman Lakhdar Brahimi, this panel of experts made a series of recommendations which laid the groundwork for a new approach to UN peace operations (UN 2000). The panel called for improved decision making at UN headquarters, a better fit between mandate and means to ensure that operations have the resources they need to succeed, measures to improve the rapidity and effectiveness of deployment as well as the profession-alism of the mission itself. The panel also argued that the UN should reconfigure its understanding of consent and impartiality so that it be presumed that UN forces have a mandate to protect civilians from harm. UN operations, the panel argued, should be capable of protecting themselves, their mandate and civilians under their care, using force if necessary.

Although not all of the recommendations have been put into practice, the Brahimi Report helped transform UN operations. Not only was there a 'surge' in the number of UN peacekeeping operations, up to a peak of seventeen such opera-tions which together deployed over 120,000 troops at the end of the century's first decade, but typically these newer operations are larger and more robust than their predecessors. For example, in the DRC and Haiti the UN used force against rebel militia groups that refused to disarm and engaged in hostage taking. Moreover, contemporary operations are more complex and multidimensional, incorporating a wider range of civilian personnel – including larger numbers of police – in order to close the 'public security gap' in the aftermath of war. It is now widely under-stood that the principal purpose of peace operations is to create self-sustaining peace and that this requires the building of legitimate and capable local institu-tions. Military peacekeepers can help facilitate the conditions conducive to such capacity building, but civilians working with the local authorities and population to construct these institutions are also needed. As we will see below, all of this has improved the effectiveness of UN forces. It has also stimulated fresh demands for new and larger missions that the UN will struggle to satisfy unless member states are more forthcoming with troops and material resources. This brings us to the question of whether peace operations are an effective tool of conflict management.

## Does peacekeeping work?

According to data gathered by the Uppsala Conflict Data Program (UCDP), since the early 1990s, the number and intensity of state-based armed conflicts involving the world's governments has reduced by as much as 40 percent. Some analysts have argued that a significant part of the credit for this should be given to peace operations (Mack 2007). Peace operations significantly reduce the likelihood of wars reigniting after such agreements have been concluded (Fortna 2003, 2004, 2008). Where peacekeepers are deployed, the likelihood of war reigniting falls by at least 75%–85% compared to those cases where no peacekeepers are deployed (Fortna 2008: 171).

In the post-Cold War era, traditional peacekeeping operations deployed with the consent of the belligerents reduced the likelihood of war reigniting by as much as 86 per cent. For large and complex multidimensional operations – often deployed in regions with unstable consent and lingering violence – the figure remained above 50 per cent (Fortna 2004: 283). In addition, since 1990, peace operations have become more efficient in reducing the likelihood of war reigniting (Fortna 2004: 283). This is all the more important if we consider that the single most important factor in determining a country's risk of descending into war is whether it has endured war in the past five years (Collier *et al*. 2003). By dramatically reducing the risk of war reigniting, peace operations make a vital contribution to reducing the frequency and lethality of war in our world.

But the contribution of peace operations does not end there. Statistical analyses also support Samantha Power's claim that 'for all the talk of the futility of foreign involvement' in cases of genocide and mass killing, the evidence categorically points to the fact that even small steps by concerned outsiders save lives (Power 2002: 73). Big steps, properly coordinated and executed, save lots of lives. In only a third of cases has outside intervention either had no effect in terms of saving lives or made matters worse (Seybolt 2007: 270). In these cases, there is a correlation between the size, composition and legitimacy of an operation and its ability to save lives. Well-equipped operations dispatched with the broad-ranging support of international society are much more likely to save lives than contentious, ill-equipped and ill-conceived operations.

None of this is meant to obscure the myriad problems that are clearly part of the history of peace operations but it is clear that, overall, peace operations are an effective tool of crisis management. The problem, however, is that in many cases it is the host state itself that is perpetrating grave crimes. In such cases, the state is unlikely to give its consent to the deployment of UN peacekeepers and, guided by the principle of non-interference, the UN Security Council has been reluctant to authorize operations without the consent of the host state. This brings us to the difficult question of when, if ever, states should intervene to put an end to genocide and mass atrocities without the consent of the host state and sometimes without the authorization of the UN Security Council.

## Humanitarian intervention

When states kill large numbers of their own population or prove incapable of protecting them from other groups intent on doing them harm, the question of humanitarian intervention arises. Because states very rarely consent in such cases to the deployment of peacekeepers, and because the UN Security Council remains reluctant to authorize armed intervention in fully functioning states without the consent of the government, the protection of populations from mass killing may sometimes require intervention without either host state consent or Security Council authority. This section surveys the debate about whether, and in what circumstances, such humanitarian intervention might be legitimate.

### The case for intervention

The case for intervention is typically premised on the idea that external actors have a *duty* as well as a *right* to intervene to halt genocide and mass atrocities. For advocates of this position, sovereignty should be understood as an instrumental value because it derives from a state's responsibility to protect the welfare of its citizens. As such, when states fail in their duty, they lose their sovereign right to non-interference and non-intervention (Tesón 2003: 93). There are a variety of ways of arriving at this conclusion. Some liberal cosmopolitans draw on Kant to insist that all individuals have certain pre-political rights that deserve protection (Caney 1997: 34). Many advocates of the Just War tradition writers arrive at a broadly similar position but ground their arguments in theology. Paul Ramsey (2002: 20), for instance, used Augustine's insistence that force be used to defend or uphold justice to argue that intervention to end injustice was 'among the rights and duties of states until and unless supplanted by superior government'.

Political leaders who adopt this position tend to maintain that today's globalized world is so integrated that massive human rights violations in one part of the world have an effect on every other part and that social interconnectedness itself creates moral obligations. The most prominent proponent of this view was former British Prime Minister, Tony Blair. Shortly after NATO began its 1999 intervention in Kosovo, Blair gave a landmark speech setting out his 'doctrine of the international community' and endorsing the concept of sovereignty as responsibility (Blair 1999). Blair maintained that sovereignty should be reconceptualized because globalization was changing the world in ways that rendered traditional views of sovereignty anachronistic. Enlightened self-interest created international responsibilities for dealing with egregious human suffering, and sovereigns had responsibilities to the society of states because problems caused by massive human rights abuse in one place tended to spread across borders.

A further line of argument is to point to the fact that states have already agreed to certain minimum standards of behaviour and that humanitarian intervention is not about imposing the will of a few upon the many, but about protecting and enforcing the collective will of international society. Advocates of this position argue that there is a customary right (but not duty) of intervention in supreme humanitarian emergencies (Wheeler 2000: 14). They argue that there is agreement in international society that cases of genocide, mass killing and ethnic cleansing constitute grave humanitarian crises warranting intervention (see Arend and Beck 1993). They point to state practice since the 19th century to suggest that there is a customary right of humanitarian intervention (Finnemore 2003). In particular, they point to the justifications offered to defend the American- and British-led intervention in Northern Iraq in 1991 to support their case (see Roberts 1993: 436–7).

This movement towards acceptance of a customary right of humanitarian intervention was reinforced by state practice after Northern Iraq. Throughout the Security Council's deliberations about how to respond to the Rwandan genocide in 1994, no state argued that either the ban on force (Article 2(4)) or the non-intervention rule (Article 2(7)) prohibited armed action to halt the bloodshed, suggesting tacit recognition that armed intervention would have been legitimate in that case. Throughout the 1990s, the Security Council expanded its interpretation of 'international peace and security' and authorized interventions to protect civilians in safe areas (Bosnia), maintain law and order and protect aid supplies (Somalia), and restore an elected government toppled by a coup (Haiti). These instances prompted Richard Falk (2003) to describe the 1990s as 'undoubtedly the golden age of humanitarian diplomacy', whilst Thomas Weiss (2004) argued that 'the notion that human beings matter more than sovereignty radiated brightly, albeit briefly, across the international political horizon of the 1990s'. Progress did not stop, however, at the turn of the century. Since 2000 the Security Council has on several occasions mandated peacekeepers to protect civilians under threat in the Democratic Republic of Congo, Burundi, Cote d'Ivoire, Liberia and Darfur. Furthermore, since 2002 the UN's standard rules of engagement have permitted peacekeepers to use force for this purpose.

Although appealing, several aspects of this defence of humanitarian intervention are problematic. First, it is not self-evident that individuals *do* have pre-political rights. Parekh (1997: 54–5), for example, argues that liberal rights cannot provide the basis for a theory of humanitarian intervention because liberalism itself is rejected in many parts of the world. Second, critics argue that any norm endorsing the use of force to protect individual rights would be abused by powerful states, making armed conflict more frequent by relaxing the rules prohibiting it but without making humanitarian intervention any more likely (Chesterman 2001; Thakur 2004).

Above all, however, is the charge that advocates of humanitarian intervention exaggerate the extent of consensus about the use of force to protect human rights. There is a gap between what advocates would like to be the norm and what the norm actually is. We should remember that the putative 'golden era' of humanitarianism included the world's failure to halt the Rwandan genocide, the UN's failure to protect civilians sheltering in its 'safe areas' in Bosnia and the failure to prevent the widely predicted mass murder that followed East Timor's referendum on independence in 1999. The world stood aside as Congo destroyed itself, taking four million lives, and – more recently – failed to halt the mass killing in Darfur. Moreover, closer inspection of the relevant cases from the 1990s suggests that the advances were more hesitant than implied by advocates of intervention. Most notably, the Security Council still has yet to authorize intervention against the wishes of a fully functioning sovereign state. Finally, with a few partial exceptions, interveners themselves have typically chosen not to justify their actions by reference to a new norm of humanitarian intervention, lest they encourage others to do likewise (see Wheeler 2000).

## The case against intervention

Nowadays, only a handful of marginal states (e.g., Cuba, Iran, Venezuela, Zimbabwe) are prepared to argue that humanitarian intervention is *never* warranted. Even China (2005), the state most closely associated with the principle of non-interference, publicly acknowledges that massive humanitarian crises are a 'legitimate concern' for international society and that the Security Council is entitled to take action in such cases. By and large, therefore, contemporary opposition to humanitarian intervention focuses not on this, but on the questions of *who* can legitimately authorize intervention and *in what circumstances*.

Whilst advocates of intervention are prepared to acknowledge its legitimacy in certain cases even when it is not authorized by the Security Council, opponents maintain that international order requires something approximating to an absolute ban on the use of force outside the two exceptions set out by the UN Charter. The starting point for this position is the assumption that international society comprises a plurality of diverse communities, each with different ideas about the best way to live. According to this view, international society is based on rules – the UN Charter's rules on the use of force first among them – that permit coexistence (see Jackson 2002). In a world characterized by radical disagreements about how societies should govern themselves, proponents of this view hold that unfettered humanitarian intervention would create disorder as states waged wars to protect and violently export their own cultural preferences.

What is more, a right of unauthorized humanitarian intervention would open the door to potential abuse. Historically, states have shown a distinct predilection towards 'abusing' humanitarian justifications to legitimize wars that were anything but humanitarian. Most notoriously, Hitler insisted that the 1939 invasion of Czechoslovakia was inspired by a desire to protect Czechoslovak citizens whose 'life and liberty' were threatened by their own government (in Brownlie 1974: 217–21). More recently, some commentators have argued that the US and UK abused humanitarian justifications in an ill-fated attempt to legitimize the 2003 invasion of Iraq, emphasizing the humanitarian case for war as it became clear that the legal reasons given (the existence of Iraqi weapons of mass destruction) were ill-founded (see Bellamy 2004). It was precisely because of the fear that states would exploit any loophole in the ban on the use of force that the delegates who wrote the UN Charter issued a comprehensive ban with only two limited exceptions – force used in self-defence and under the authority of the Security Council. According to Chesterman, without this general ban there would be more war in international society but not necessarily more genuine humanitarian interventions. Chesterman argues that states do not refrain from intervening in humanitarian emergencies because they are constrained by law, but 'because states do not want them to take place' (2003: 231). Creating a humanitarian exception to the ban on force would not enable more humanitarian interventions, but it would make it easier for states to justify self-interested invasions through spurious humanitarian arguments.

Finally, it is important to note that a majority of states continue to oppose humanitarian intervention, seeing it as a dangerous affront to another core principle, self-determination, which underpinned post-war decolonization. This position was clearly in the ascendancy during the Cold War. In 1977, when Vietnam invaded Cambodia and ousted the murderous Pol Pot regime, responsible for the death of some two million Cambodians, it was condemned for violating Cambodian sovereignty (Wheeler 2000: 90–1). These sentiments persist today. Nearly thirty years after the Vietnamese experiences, Pakistan argued against collective action to halt the Sudanese government-sponsored mass killing and expulsion of civilians in Darfur on the grounds that 'the Sudan has all the rights and privileges incumbent under the United Nations Charter, including sovereignty, political independence, unity and territorial integrity' (UNSC 2004).

Unsurprisingly, there are also a number of problems with these positions. First, its overriding assumption that states protect their citizens does not hold in every case, as the examples offered at the beginning of this chapter attest. Second, critics argue that this perspective overlooks the wealth of customary practice suggesting that sovereignty carries responsibilities as well as rights (see Tesón 1997). Third, although there are a number of notorious historical cases, the fear of abuse is exaggerated (Weiss 2004: 135). It is fanciful to argue that denying a state recourse to humanitarian justifications for war would make them less war-prone – it is unlikely that either Hitler in 1939 or Bush and Blair in 2003 would have been deterred from waging war by the absence of a plausible humanitarian justification. Fourth, this position overlooks the wide body of international law relating to basic human rights and the consensus on grave crimes such as genocide.

## Summary: the irresolvable debate?

Almost all governments recognize that crimes such as genocide and mass killing are a legitimate concern for international society. Some governments, international officials, activists and analysts argue that sovereigns have a responsibility to protect their citizens from mass killing and other abuses and when they fail to do so, others acquire a right to intervene. A majority of the world's governments, however, argue that this responsibility does not translate into a right of humanitarian intervention without the authority of the UN Security Council, because that would contradict other cherished principles of international order, including the rule of non-aggression and the right to self-determination. Since the end of the Cold War, the UN Security Council has authorized collective intervention to protect populations from mass killing. In this sense, there is a norm of UN-sanctioned humanitarian intervention (Wheeler 2000) but it is heavily circumscribed in practice to cases where the host state has collapsed or where the recognized government is not the target of intervention and lends its support. This presents a dilemma about what to do in cases where some governments believe that intervention is warranted to save people from genocide and mass atrocities but where there is no consensus in the Security Council. This dilemma was exposed by NATO's decision to intervene in Kosovo in 1999. The debate sparked by this provided a catalyst for a fundamental rethink of the way that international society conceptualizes the problem of sovereignty and the protection of citizens.

## Towards responsibility to protect

The humanitarian crises of the 1990s prompted new thinking about the nature of sovereignty which developed some old ideas about the sovereign's responsibility to protect its citizens. The first person to begin thinking along these lines was Francis Deng, a former Sudanese diplomat who was appointed the UN Secretary-

General's special representative on internally displaced people in 1992. In a book published in 1996, Deng and his co-authors argued that 'sovereignty carries with it certain responsibilities for which governments must be held accountable. And they are accountable not only to their own national constituencies but ultimately to the international community' (Deng *et al*. 1996: 1). According to Deng, legitimate sovereignty required a demonstration of responsibility. Conceptualizing sovereignty as responsibility removed the validity of objections to international assistance and mediation based on the principle of non-interference.

NATO's intervention in Kosovo prompted UN Secretary-General Kofi Annan to enter the debate and make a vital contribution. In 1999 he insisted that 'state sovereignty, in its most basic sense, is being redefined by the forces of globalization and international cooperation'. He continued, 'the state is now widely understood to be the servant of its people, and not vice versa. At the same time, individual sovereignty — and by this I mean the human rights and fundamental freedoms of each and every individual as enshrined in our Charter — has been enhanced by a renewed consciousness of the right of every individual to control his or her own destiny' (Annan 1999).

Together, Deng and Annan pointed towards a new way of thinking about sovereignty as responsibility. The Canadian government then created the International Commission on Intervention and State Sovereignty (ICISS) to develop a way of reconciling sovereignty and human rights (see Evans 2008). The Commission's report was premised on the notion that when states are unwilling or unable to protect their citizens from grave harm, the principle of non-interference 'yields to the responsibility to protect' (ICISS 2001: xi). The concept of R2P that it put forward was intended as a way of escaping the logic of 'intervention versus sovereignty' by focusing not on what interveners were entitled to do ('a right of intervention') but on what was necessary to protect civilians threatened by genocide and mass atrocities. Influenced by Annan and Deng, the ICISS argued that the R2P was about much more than just military intervention. Appropriate responses to humanitarian emergencies included non-violent measures such as diplomacy, sanctions and embargoes, and legal measures such as referring crimes to the International Criminal Court. Furthermore, in addition to the 'responsibility to react' to massive human suffering, the ICISS insisted that international society also had responsibilities to rebuild polities and societies afterwards. Of the three responsibilities, the Commission identified that the 'responsibility to prevent' was the single most important (ICISS 2001: xi). The Commission also proposed the adoption of criteria to guide decision making about when to intervene.

At the 2005 World Summit, over 150 world leaders adopted a declaration affirming the R2P which was itself subsequently reaffirmed by the UN Security Council in 2006. According to the UN Secretary-General, Ban Ki-moon, who succeeded Kofi Annan in 2007, the R2P principle adopted by states in 2005 rests on three pillars. First, the responsibility of the state to protect its own populations from genocide, war crimes, ethnic cleansing and crimes against humanity. Second, the international community's duty to assist states to fulfill their responsibilities. Third, the international community's responsibility to respond in a timely and decisive manner when a state is manifestly failing to protect its population, using Chapters VI (peaceful means), VII (coercive means authorized by the UN Security Council) and VIII (regional arrangements) of the UN Charter (Luck 2006).

The approach adopted by the UN Secretary-General has been described as 'narrow but deep' (Luck 2006: 1) in that it applies only to a narrow category of cases but requires a deep commitment from states. International society is expected to shoulder the responsibility of preventing genocide and mass atrocities by helping states to build the necessary capacities, developing early warning systems and being prepared to act 'up-stream' of an outbreak of violence with a range of diplomatic, humanitarian, legal and other peaceful measures. Heeding the concerns of states such as Russia and China, the R2P insists that military intervention be authorized by the UN Security Council and rules out unilateral force.

The World Summit's declaration on the R2P received a mixed reception. Todd Lindberg (2005) described it as nothing less than a 'revolution in consciousness in international affairs'. Prominent international lawyer Simon Chesterman agreed, arguing that 'what we're seeing is a progressive redefinition of sovereignty in a way that would have been outrageous sixty years ago' (in Turner 2005). Others were more equivocal. John Bolton, the American Ambassador to the UN and a well-known realist and UN-sceptic, described the R2P as 'a moveable feast of an idea that was the High Minded *cause du jour*' and said of the World Summit Outcome Document: 'I plan never to read it again. I doubt many others will either' (Bolton 2007: 213–4).

To what extent has the R2P advanced and replaced debates about humanitarian intervention? One group of critics complain that the principle is an assault on state sovereignty. They argue that it is little different from the interventionist doctrines put forward by liberals in the 1990s and has all the negative connotations associated with humanitarian intervention (e.g., Chandler 2005). A second group of critics make the opposite point. Michael Byers (2005a), for example, argued that the 2005 World Summit Outcome Document watered down the original R2P concept to such an extent that the new principle would not advance the humanitarian intervention debate or protect threatened populations.

Whilst the first group of critics ignores the fact that the R2P has been adopted by world leaders of all stripes and carefully limits the scope for armed intervention, the second group focuses too heavily on the question of armed intervention and underestimates the potential impact of R2P. Thus, whilst we need to be mindful of the principle's limitations, as the UN Secretary-General's special adviser, Edward Luck, has pointed out, there are several good reasons for thinking that the R2P is likely to make a lasting impact on international peace and security. First, R2P is a politically potent concept based on a consensus produced by one of the largest gatherings of heads of state ever seen. Second, the Outcome Document specifically pointed to the prevention of genocide, war crimes, ethnic cleansing and crimes against humanity, creating a mandate for renewed attention to prevention. Third, the Outcome Document points to the kinds of tools, actors and procedures that could form the basis for operationalizing the R2P. As such, it provides a blueprint for future policy initiatives. Finally, the process of negotiating the Document and forging consensus required compromise by both sides of the intervention debate and produced a shared conception of sovereignty as responsibility that bridges the divide (Luck 2006: 3).

Ultimately, however, the R2P will be judged not according to its ability to help finesse difficult judgments about humanitarian intervention but by the extent to which it improves the way in which the world responds to cases of unconscionable inhumanity. Here there are important signs of progress. In 2007–8, the international community responded in a timely and effective manner to prevent the further escalation of violence in Kenya after disputed elections there. A few years later, in 2011, UN peacekeepers in Cote d'Ivoire cooperated with French troops to remove Laurent Gbagbo from power after he lost an election and refused to step down, triggering widespread violence and threatening a return to civil war. At around the same time, the UN Security Council passed the landmark Resolution 1973 on Libya – the first time the Council has authorized the use of force against a functioning state for human protection purposes. Major challenges remain, however. The crisis in Somalia which has exerted a terrible human toll continues to elude resolution; the world's newest state – South Sudan – teeters on the brink of collapse and conflict; and the Security Council has found it difficult to reach a consensus on responding to the Syrian government's attacks on its own population. Clearly, agreeing on a principle is one thing but agreeing on how to implement it in practice is another thing entirely. Much progress has been made, but the challenges remain formidable.

## Conclusion

The challenge now, as the current UN Secretary-General Ban Ki-moon has argued, is to translate R2P from words into deeds and to change the practice of how the world responds to genocide and mass atrocities. This will necessarily involve measures to enhance the effectiveness of peace operations conducted with the consent of the host state but must also involve fresh thinking and new practice in relation to non-consensual intervention. If the principle continues to develop and gain momentum, chapters about humanitarian intervention might become obsolete as global institutions, regional organizations and individual states develop the capacities to better prevent and respond to such crimes. It is not yet clear, however, whether changing the terms of debate has altered its fundamental logic. The test will come partly in how the world responds to new and emerging crises – in Libya, Cote d'Ivoire and Kenya there were clear signs of improvement, but in Somalia, Syria and South Sudan familiar problems remain – and partly in how successful UN reform is in building the necessary capacities and decision-making capabilities.

# Guide to further reading

Several works offer a comprehensive introduction to peacekeeping, including its history, theory, key challenges and specific cases (Bellamy and Williams 2009). This could be augmented with specific studies on contemporary peace operations (Durch 2006) and detailed study of what makes peace operations more – and less – effective (Fortna 2008). There are a number of very good books tracing the norm of humanitarian intervention since the Cold War (Wheeler 2000), the place of intervention in international law (Chesterman 2001) and the more recent politics of humanitarian intervention (Welsh 2004; Weiss 2007). Although the R2P principle is relatively new, there are very good insiders' accounts of the principle's development and application (e.g. Evans 2008) and a study of the principle itself and efforts to operationalize it (Bellamy 2009c).

## Chapter 9

# Transnational Terrorism

*ANDREW PHILLIPS*

On 11 September 2001, history resumed. A mere twelve years earlier, the rubble of the Berlin wall had seemed to symbolize a grand historical terminus. With communism following fascism into oblivion, political theorist Francis Fukuyama speculated about the possible 'end of history' (Fukuyama 1989), with the defeat of America's last remaining totalitarian adversary supposedly heralding the global triumph of open societies constituted around the twin pillars of democracy and capitalism. By the second year of the new millennium, the ruins of the World Trade Centre conversely invited a more sober assessment of history's course. On 9/11, nineteen hijackers from Saudi Arabia and Egypt exploited the very openness and technological sophistication of liberal societies to inflict more destruction on the US mainland than had any of America's totalitarian enemies in the 20th century. The 'Manhattan raid' and the contemporaneous Pentagon attack dramatized the vulnerability of the world's only superpower, and immediately catalysed a profound transformation in the foreign policies of the US and its closest allies. Dismissed by many as a second-order strategic concern in the 1990s, since 9/11 transnational terrorism has been widely regarded as one of the most potent threats to international security. The nature of this threat, its historical evolution, contemporary import and prospective significance form the subjects of this chapter.

## Transnational terrorism defined

Terrorism is understood here to refer to acts of violence (or the threat of violence) that are deliberately directed at non-combatants for the purpose of securing political objectives. Terrorism is a form of compellence, whereby terrorists seek to leverage the distress evoked by acts of indiscriminate violence against non-combatants to extort tangible changes in their adversaries' behaviour. Terrorism can refer to the activities of state as well as non-state actors, as demonstrated in the 'terror bombing' of civilian population centres undertaken by both sides in the Second World War to compel opposing governments to sue for peace. In its contemporary usage, however, terrorism typically refers to actions undertaken by non-state actors, for example the Provisional Irish Republican Army's (PIRA's) use of terrorism in the British Isles as part of its campaign to compel the British government to acquiesce to the six counties' integration into the Republic of Ireland.

Terrorist violence is intentionally provocative in its transgression of moral and legal norms preserving non-combatant immunity, but it is nevertheless almost always driven by actors pursuing coherent political objectives. As such, terrorism comprises a form of violent political contention that is distinguishable from other forms of private international violence, such as piracy, mercenarism, and transnational organized crime, which are driven by predominantly economic motives. Terrorism is additionally distinguishable from both state-based conventional warfare and guerrilla warfare. Terrorism's frequent characterization as a 'weapon of the weak' captures the truth that terrorism is most often embraced by those who have no possibility of prevailing against their opponents in a conventional war (Crenshaw 1981: 387). From the Napoleonic revolution in warfare onwards, state actors have sought victory either through a decisive battle of annihilation (Bond 1996: 43) or by a relentless process of attrition (Gray 2007: 81). Both strategies favour protagonists endowed with great material strength. Conversely, terrorism relies on strategies of provocation, polarization and exhaustion. The selective use of atrocity is thus deployed to goad governments into disproportionate responses to terrorist violence, to polarize populations into pro- and anti-government factions, and eventually to exhaust governments into capitulating to the terrorists' demands (Crenshaw 1981: 387; Harmon 2001: 44).

In its emphasis on corroding the enemy's will to resist through recourse to a protracted armed struggle, terrorism shares affinities with guerrilla warfare. Nevertheless, terrorism remains distinguishable from guerrilla warfare by the disproportionate weight it accords to highly publicized atrocities as a means of shaping target audiences' consciousness and behaviour. Guerrilla warfare routinely involves the cultivation of a mass base of popular support in 'liberated' rural base areas and the incremental expansion of guerrillas' geographic reach and popular appeal over time, with victory expected to materialize once the guerrillas secure sufficient mass support and military wherewithal to defeat government forces in conventional combat (Hoffman 2002: 22). Conversely, terrorists typically seek to exploit the anonymity of urban environments and the opportunities for publicity afforded by mass media outlets to perpetrate shocking acts of 'propaganda by the deed'. In undertaking high-visibility acts of violence such as hijacking airliners, bombing public places or assassinating public officials and community leaders, terrorists hope to dramatize governmental impotence, intimidate rival ethnic or religious communities, and energize popular support behind their cause (Hoffman 2002: 20). The urban terrorist and the rural-based guerrilla thus embody different styles of asymmetric warfare, employing different strategies to mobilize popular support and laying different emphases on the significance of highly publicized atrocities as a means of communicating grievances and catalysing transformations in the consciousness of allies and adversaries. In practice, however, these forms of violence have historically overlapped to a strong degree, as most recently evident in the wars in Afghanistan and Iraq.

Finally, any definitional overview of terrorism must acknowledge its increasingly transnational character under conditions of globalization (Cronin 2002/3). As improvements in transportation and communication technologies have facilitated growing transnational flows of money, *materiel*, people and ideas, a greater proportion of terrorist activities have acquired a transnational dimension. Separatists with geographically limited agendas such as the Liberation Tigers of Tamil Eelam (LTTE) thus made extensive use of diaspora financing in the 1990s to advance their political goals, all while prosecuting military campaigns that remained predominantly confined to their homeland (Gunaratna 2003: 208). The increasing ease with which locally oriented terrorists have been able to access transnational support networks has considerably increased their resilience in the face of government repression (Adamson 2005: 33). Nevertheless, it has been terrorist groups such as al-Qaeda, which are transnational not only in their mobilization of resources, but also in their choice of targets and in the scope of their political ambitions, that have aroused the greatest public consternation. It is this form of terrorism, equally transnational in its means, goals and targets, with which we will be preoccupied for the rest of this chapter.

## The historical evolution of transnational terrorism

Far from emerging *ex nihilo* following the end of the Cold War, transnational terrorism has existed in some form from at least the last quarter of the 19th century. A consideration of the four successive waves of 'rebel terror' (Rapoport 2001) over the last hundred and thirty years illustrates this point. Transnational terrorism's origins can be traced to the anarchist terrorism that convulsed Western Europe, North America and Tsarist Russia from 1880 to 1914 (Rapoport 2001: 419). Facilitated by factors as diverse as the invention of dynamite, the rise of mass circulation newspapers and the wrenching social changes accompanying rapid urbanization and industrialization, the anarchists' campaign of violence constituted the Western public's first sustained exposure to modern terrorism. While insignificant by contemporary standards, the casualties anarchists inflicted in venues as diverse as cafes, parliaments, theatres, and stock exchanges nevertheless terrified the middle classes (Jensen 2004: 135). The resulting scapegoating of immigrant communities by the popular press and government authorities on the basis of largely imagined international anarchist conspiracies provided a foretaste of the polarizing effects of terrorism that would frequently recur in subsequent decades (Jensen 2004: 143). Equally, anarchists' uncritical faith in the catalysing effects of the 'propaganda of the deed' has also found its echoes in succeeding waves of terrorism, as we will shortly see.

The anarchist wave of terrorism sputtered into history after the First World War, but was succeeded by a wave of anti-colonial terrorism that spanned the 20th century's middle decades. Unlike anarchist terrorists, who were uncompromising in their desire to overturn all formal systems of government, anti-colonial terrorists sought the more modest objective of securing national self-determination in territories then subject to foreign rule. While terrorism featured in various wars of decolonization in Africa and Asia, it was in the Middle East that terrorism featured most prominently, playing a critical role in the National Liberation Front's (NLF) successful campaign for Algerian independence, and in the Palestinians' continuing quest for an independent state. Of all the exponents of anti-colonial terrorism, the Palestinians were the most active transnationally, exploiting the enhanced mobility provided by international air travel and the increased propaganda opportunities provided by television to prosecute their struggle against Israel on a global stage (Hoffman 1998: 67). The murder of eleven Israeli athletes by Black September at the Munich Olympics in 1972 provided the most notorious testament to the effectiveness of this new form of warfare. Global revulsion at the terrorists' atrocities notwithstanding, the Munich massacre catapulted the Palestinian cause to worldwide prominence and shortly thereafter yielded Yasser Arafat's Palestinian Liberation Organization (PLO) the prize of widespread diplomatic recognition as the legitimate voice of the Palestinian people (Hoffman 1998: 75).

Reflecting the strength of anti-colonial sentiment generally and the contentious nature of the Israeli–Palestinian conflict specifically, anti-colonial terrorism failed to generate a coordinated response from the international community. Contrarily, the third wave of terror, which struck Western Europe in the 1960s and 1970s, stimulated the development of wide-ranging counter-terrorism measures that bear comparison with analogous initiatives that have developed globally since 9/11. Drawing tactical inspiration from the Palestinians and ideological inspiration from Mao and Lenin, extreme Leftist terrorist groups such as the Baader-Meinhof Group, the Italian Red Brigades and Direct Action perpetrated a series of hijackings, kidnappings, bombings and assassinations from the late 1960s onwards (Rapoport 2001: 421). Hoping to expel the American military presence in Western Europe and to overturn the capitalist system, the chief legacy of these terrorists was rather to inadvertently catalyse international policing and counter-terrorism cooperation between their would-be targets. Like their anarchist predecessors, the radicals of the 1960s and 1970s underestimated the resilience of the established order while also overestimating the transformative potential of 'propaganda by the deed', with the enhanced state repression they elicited accelerating their own demise (Hoffman 1998: 83).

The fourth wave of terror dates from the late 1970s and differs from its predecessors primarily in respect of its religious-ideological colouration. The origins of transnational jihadist terrorism lie in an ongoing crisis of governmental legitimacy that began to engulf large swathes of the Islamic world in the 1970s and 1980s (Doran 2002: 27). During this period, popular frustration mounted towards dictatorships such as that of Anwar Sadat in Egypt and Zia al Huq in Pakistan. These and other repressive regimes had failed to meet their citizens' economic and political aspirations, and had also become reliant on the US for their internal and external security (Bronson 2006: 125–8; Clarke 2004: 36–9). This crisis of legitimacy coincided with increasing US involvement in the Greater Middle East to fill the power vacuum created by Britain's post-1968 withdrawal from all bases east of the Suez Canal. It also coincided with the growth of politically engaged forms of religious fundamentalism in the Islamic world, a trend that accelerated in 1979 with the Islamic revolution in Iran and the onset of the anti-Soviet jihad following the Red Army's invasion of Afghanistan (Kepel 2003: 93–5).

Transnational jihadist terrorism thus emerged out of the intersection of local-ized crises of legitimacy, increasing superpower involvement in the Muslim world, and the coterminous rise of politicized forms of Islamic identity. Their world-views forged in the anti-Soviet Afghan jihad, jihadists such as Osama bin Laden and Ayman al-Zawahiri beheld a global Islamic community (or *ummah*) being victimized by a combination of apostate local tyrants (the 'near' enemy) ruling at the behest of their infidel Western sponsors (the 'far' enemy). For bin Laden and others, the emancipation of the *ummah* could come only once the tyrants had been overthrown and their Western sponsors ejected from Muslim lands (Doran 2002: 31–3). This would in turn permit the destruction of the 'Zionist entity' of Israel and the eventual unification of the *ummah* under the banner of a global Caliphate ruled according to *sharia* law (al-Zawahiri 2005). To this end, al-Qaeda operatives from the 1990s launched a series of terrorist attacks aimed at goading the West into an unwinnable war in the Muslim world that would end with its humiliation, thereby precipitating the collapse of its 'apostate' client regimes throughout the Middle East and beyond. These provocations even-tually succeeded in catalysing the US invasions of Afghanistan and Iraq that followed 9/11, but al-Qaeda's subsequent efforts to commandeer local insurgen-cies have met with limited success, and the jihadists' prospects of long-term victory remain doubtful. This observation notwithstanding, the impact of jihadist terrorism on Western states' foreign policies since 9/11 has been both dramatic and destabilizing, its impact on global politics defying any comparison with earlier manifestations of transnational terrorism.

## The contemporary significance of transnational terrorism

While transnational terrorism had long been recognized as a significant problem internationally, the 9/11 attacks imbued the threat with a historically unprece-dented level of importance. In the years since the attacks, the struggle against jihadist terrorism has been a dominant feature of world politics, characterized by a contradictory mixture of international cooperation and confrontation. On the one hand, the immediate post-9/11 period saw a flurry of initiatives aimed at suppress-ing the threats posed by the entwined challenges of transnational terrorism and the proliferation of weapons of mass destruction (WMD) (Heupel 2008: 8). In contrast to its earlier lackadaisical efforts to curb transnational terrorism, the United Nations Security Council swiftly passed resolutions imposing binding obligations on member states to refrain from providing material sponsorship to terrorists (Rosand 2003: 334). In parallel with this prohibition, the Security Council also imposed positive duties to prevent terrorists from either acquiring WMD or using member states' territory for purposes of either sanctuary or transit (Heupel 2008: 14). With the codification of these norms and the establishment of standing organ-izations within the UN (e.g., the Counter-Terrorism Executive Directorate, the 1540 Committee) to monitor compliance and assist member states in meeting their obligations, the international community's capacity to resist transnational terrorism was significantly strengthened.

The system-strengthening initiatives sketched above were spearheaded by the US, but were overshadowed by the more confrontational and revolutionary strand of American foreign policy that also emerged after 9/11. Seized by the urgency of the terrorist challenge and exasperated by the perceived inadequacy of existing collective security institutions, the Bush administration embraced a strongly unilateralist foreign policy agenda after 9/11, proclaiming the need for pre-emptive strikes and 'regime change' as necessary expedients to prevent the uncontrolled spread of WMD to both 'rogue' states and terrorists (White House 2002: 15). The endorsement of preventive war in particular aroused alarm internationally, given that it dovetailed with pre-existing neo-conservative aspirations to indefinitely preserve America's status as the world's only superpower. More controversial still were attempts to 'drain the swamp' of sentiment for jihadist terrorism through the promotion of a 'forward strategy of freedom' in the Middle East. This strategy of armed democracy promotion reached its apogee with the March 2003 invasion of Iraq, a gambit that perversely reinvigorated the global jihadist movement (National Intelligence Estimate 2006: 2), while simultaneously absorbing American attention for the remainder of the Bush administration.

In the short term, the Iraq invasion significantly increased strains between the US and many of its traditional Western European and Middle Eastern allies. Europeans fretted about the dangerous precedent that they saw being established with the Iraq invasion, which had proceeded without the express consent of the UN Security Council (Gordon and Shapiro 2004: 170). Middle Eastern allies such as Saudi Arabia meanwhile opposed the invasion, both because of an understandable wariness regarding the administration's democracy promotion agenda, and because of prescient fears of the war's potential to destabilize the Middle East and further radicalize domestic Islamist dissidents (Record 2004: 94). By contrast, China made no concerted effort to thwart American plans in Iraq, rather capitalizing on the post-9/11 rapprochement between the two countries to continue its 'peaceful rise' (Gries 2005: 402). Its opposition to the Iraq War notwithstanding, Russia's relations with the US also improved momentarily after 9/11 (Herd and Akerman 2002: 358), with mass casualty attacks by Chechen separatists in Moscow (2002) and Beslan (2004) reinforcing perceptions of a shared interest in suppressing Islamist terrorism in all its forms.

Transnational terrorism's impact on world politics after 9/11 was thus decisively influenced by US reactions to al-Qaeda's provocation, and by the responses that these reactions in turn elicited from other countries. In the short term, the revolutionary turn in US foreign policy strained its traditional alliances, while counter-terrorist concerns provided a focal point for cooperation with countries such as Russia and China that the Bush administration had formerly seen as strategic competitors. But while counter-terrorism concerns lost none of their urgency during the administration's second term, by then older patterns of cooperation and rivalry had begun to reassert themselves. While most of America's NATO allies remained aloof from the Iraq War, mass casualty attacks in Madrid (2004) and

London (2005) as well as numerous foiled terror plots in Germany (2001 and 2007), Britain (2006 and 2007) and elsewhere highlighted the continuing danger posed to Western societies by transnational jihadist terrorism. NATO's assumption of a lead role in prosecuting the struggle against the Taliban and al-Qaeda remnants in Afghanistan further bolstered Western unity in the face of the jihadist threat, while also demonstrating the alliance's capacity to adapt to the challenges of the radically changed security environment of the post-Cold War period. At the same time, the expansion of Western influence in Central and South Asia from 2001 onwards as part of the 'war on terror' aroused both Russian and Chinese suspicions, with the Shanghai Cooperation Organization (SCO) strenuously backing Uzbekistan's demands for the closure of recently established American bases in that country in 2005 (Olcott 2005: 331).

## Debating the 'war on terror': the contemporary intellectual impact of transnational terrorism

Aside from its profound real-world impact on the course of global politics, the 'war on terror' also provided an intellectual jolt to the discipline of International Relations (IR). Given the state-centrism of most IR thinking, the 9/11 attacks exposed IR scholarship as offering an interpretive framework that was at best incomplete and at worst anachronistic in its reading of world affairs. Subsequently, many of the most stimulating debates surrounding transnational terrorism have focused less on its implications for IR theory and more on practical questions relating to the nature of the struggle against jihadist terrorism and the most appropriate means for managing the terrorist threat.

Clausewitz's injunction that victory in any war presupposes that one first understands the nature of the conflict in which one is involved (Clausewitz 1976: 88) provides a useful entrée into debates over both the nature of the anti-jihadist struggle and the means by which it might be best prosecuted. Drawing inspiration from the works of Samuel Huntington, some commentators have characterized the anti-jihadist struggle as constituting merely the most conspicuous manifestation of a larger 'clash of civilizations' between Islam and the West deriving from a combination of innate cultural differences and enduring historical rivalries (Blankley 2005; Hanson 2002; Sullivan 2001). Seen through this lens, the confrontation with jihadist terrorism expresses broader tensions between the Western and Islamic worlds that are insoluble. A civilizational interpretation of the 'war on terror' thus implicitly recommends a policy of both defence and disengagement. Given the jihadists' implacable opposition to Western values, intensified international cooperation in the areas of policing and intelligence sharing is essential to secure citizens' safety from jihadist assaults. Equally, however, given that the jihadists are assumed to embody a broader dissonance in values between Islam and the West, a civilizational approach *à la* Huntington would counsel that this values gap be openly acknowledged and interaction between the two blocs minimized if inter-civilizational friction is to be contained (Huntington 1996: 211).

Civilizational accounts of the 'war on terror' can be criticized on multiple grounds, ranging from their reliance on essentialist characterizations of Western and Islamic 'civilizations', to the manifest impracticality of a policy of civilizational disengagement given the increasingly cosmopolitan nature of open societies under conditions of globalization. Civilizational accounts have also been condemned for their tendency to downplay the more proximate political imperatives underpinning the conflict (Abrahamian 2003: 537–8; Barkawi 2004: 25–6; Tuastad 2003). Critical accounts of the 'war on terror' have thus, conversely, foregrounded the catalysing role of Western foreign policy both in contributing to al-Qaeda's genesis and in sustaining its subsequent expansion (see, for example, Johnson 2002: xiv). Particular emphasis is given to the role played by Western governments in sponsoring corrupt dictatorships in the Middle East to ensure continued access to the region's vital energy supplies (Ali 2002: 265; Scheuer 2007: 258; Chomsky 2003; 214–16). While critical accounts acknowledge the brutal and indiscriminate nature of jihadist terrorism, they identify its root causes in the 'blowback' deriving from self-interested Western foreign policies. The West has sustained repressive autocracies and in so doing inflamed the popular anti-Western sentiments upon which jihadist terrorists have relied in casting themselves as the legitimate defenders of a global Islamic community (the *ummah*). Despite their hostility towards civilizational portrayals of the 'war on terror', critical accounts thus nevertheless frequently implicitly enjoin changes in Western foreign policy (e.g., decreased reliance on Middle Eastern oil and thus on regional autocrats) that bear some resemblance to the former's calls for disengagement, and can be similarly critiqued on pragmatic grounds.

Opposing both civilizational and critical accounts, a third set of approaches has emphasized the ideational roots of the 'war on terror'. Having identified intellectual affinities between jihadist ideology and earlier 20th-century expressions of totalitarianism, some commentators have cast jihadism as a pathological counter-reaction to the global spread of market civilization and the accompanying crisis of traditional values and institutions this has engendered in rapidly modernizing Muslim-majority countries (Berman 2003; Mousseau 2002/3; Podhoretz 2007). Seen through a neo-conservative lens, this characterization has been invoked to justify policies aimed at eradicating jihadism through the coercive transformation of these countries into market democracies, replicating in Iraq and Afghanistan the grand strategy that purged Germany and Japan of their totalitarian tendencies in the Second World War (Podhoretz 2007: 213).

The disappointing results of the neo-conservative strategy in both countries have nevertheless produced more nuanced accounts that have retained an awareness of jihadism's totalitarian complexion, but that have also acknowledged the role played by local grievances in enabling transnational jihadists to extend their geographical reach into strife-torn states and thereby mobilize a global constituency in support of their cause. Casting the jihadists' campaign as a global insurgency, some analysts have advocated a global counter-insurgency campaign based around the concept of 'disaggregation', in which military power would be employed in conjunction with selective political concessions and improvements in local governance to prise transnational jihadists from host communities in countries such as Iraq and Afghanistan (see, for example, Kilcullen 2005: 608). While constituting a less ambitious strategy than the neo-conservatives' advocacy of armed democracy promotion, this strategy nevertheless also acknowledges the need for a counter-terrorism strategy that moves beyond a posture of passive defence, and instead addresses the role played by failures of governance in contributing to the conditions under which jihadist terrorism has thrived.

## The future significance of transnational terrorism for international order

Disagreements concerning the nature of the struggle against jihadist terrorism and the best means of prosecuting it will persist for some time, if only because the 'war on terror' will endure into the near future. This is so for several reasons. Firstly, increasing great power demand for the Middle East's energy reserves is likely to see growing rather than diminishing foreign interference in the region in the next few decades, further inflaming the grievances that sustain the jihadist movement. Revived regional interest in civil nuclear energy programmes will furthermore increase proliferation concerns throughout the region, as well as increasing the likelihood of nuclear knowledge and technologies diffusing to jihadist terrorists and their sympathizers. A combination of surging demographic growth, limited economic opportunities and unresponsive government in many Muslim-majority societies will meanwhile nurture the conditions of political instability and popular despair within which extremism thrives, providing further recruitment opportunities for the jihadists.

These caveats notwithstanding, a decade on from 9/11 it is equally clear that the transnational jihadist movement has failed to accomplish its political objectives, and that continued failure to achieve its goals will condemn jihadism to marginalization and eventual oblivion. The rise and fall of the three prior waves of 'rebel terror' demonstrates that no political movement is capable of indefinitely sustaining itself without the tonic of victory. The jihadist wave of terror is likely to prove no exception to this rule. In the post-9/11 decade, bin Laden and his acolytes succeeded brilliantly in provoking the US and its allies into two protracted and enervating wars that have considerably weakened them. But al-Qaeda's positive objective of unifying the Muslim world under a global Caliphate remains a totalitarian fantasy. Jihadist efforts to carve out stem-lands for a revived Caliphate in Iraq and Afghanistan have enjoyed minimal success, in no small part because of the jihadists' self-defeating efforts to browbeat local populations into conformity with al-Qaeda's brutal and idiosyncratic misreading of Islam (Phillips 2009: 64). Jemaah Islamiyah's parallel campaign to derail Indonesia's democratic transition has meanwhile proved equally unsuccessful. Indeed, the consolidation of democracy in the world's most populous Muslim-majority state constitutes arguably the greatest triumph in the 'war on terror' for the forces of moderation over extremism, albeit one whose significance remains generally under-appreciated in most

Western capitals. Continuing instability and state failure in South Asia and the Horn of Africa, conversely, counsel against premature triumphalism, but even in these zones of instability the jihadists' sectarian bigotry, extremism and penchant for indiscriminate violence will continue to constrain their ability to translate governmental weakness and popular despair into enduring political advantage.

A comprehensive discussion of the causes of the jihadists' strategic failures in the 'war on terror' is beyond the scope of this chapter. Nevertheless, three factors warrant brief acknowledgement. First, al-Qaeda's war against the 'Zionist–Crusader alliance' was marked from the outset by the jihadists' underestimation of the capabilities and resolve of the US as their principal adversary. Anticipating a re-run of the 1980s anti-Soviet jihad, al-Qaeda's strategists were wrong-footed by America's swift toppling of the Taliban in late 2001 and al-Qaeda's ensuing eviction from its Afghan sanctuary. The Bush administration's lateral escalation of the 'war on terror' to Iraq from 2003 onwards admittedly opened a new 'field of jihad' for al-Qaeda and its affiliates, providing the movement with a temporary reprieve. But America's willingness to sustain ruinously costly occupations in two countries for years on end unsettled the jihadist narrative of the West as a 'paper tiger' that would rapidly retreat from confrontation once Western casualties began to mount. Fixated by a belief in the West's innate cowardice and erroneously extrapolating from previous US retreats from Lebanon (1983) and Somalia (1993) in the face of heavy casualties, al-Qaeda strategists proved incapable of appreciating the sacrifices America could absorb once the Bush administration identified the destruction of jihadism as its primary national security priority. The strategic wisdom of according the jihadist threat such an exalted status may be justly disputed in hindsight. But its immediate consequence was to subject the jihadists to a decade of unremitting pressure that has seen their leadership decimated, their primary sanctuary eliminated and their capacity to mount another attack on the scale of 9/11 significantly – and possibly permanently – degraded (Thiessen 2009: 74–5).

In addition to underestimating their adversary, al-Qaeda's leadership also overestimated their ability both to maintain unity of effort among the global jihadist movement and to ensure that Muslim populations apprehended the 'war on terror' on terms favourable to the jihadists. Following their unexpected eviction from Afghanistan, al-Qaeda's always partial ability to provide day-to-day operational guidance to jihadist operatives significantly diminished. Relegated to the role of 'instigator-in-chief', bin Laden became dependent on violent and unpredictable protégés such as Abu-Musab al-Zarqawi to prosecute the jihadist struggle (Fishman 2008: 48). Al-Qaeda's ensuing association with the atrocities of its most brutal franchisees consequently indelibly tarred the al-Qaeda 'brand', severely damaging its outreach efforts towards the broader *ummah*. Outrages such as the November 2005 bombing of a Muslim wedding in Amman, Jordan solidified popular Muslim perceptions of the jihadists as dangerous extremists, crippling al-Qaeda's ability to leverage genuine popular anger at US interventions in Afghanistan and Iraq into broad-based support for the jihadist movement (Fishman 2008: 48–9).

Finally, the jihadists underestimated the capacity and willingness of national governments to rally against private international violence in support of a state-based international order. Notwithstanding the differences in values and interests that continue to bedevil the international system, states after 9/11 found unity in their subscription to a common denominator consensus favouring the suppression of transnational predators and the defence of the state's claim to maintain a monopoly on legitimate violence. In essence, 9/11 struck at the Hobbesian protection bargain underwriting the legitimacy of all modern states. From the mid-17th century onwards, both democracies and dictatorships have grounded their claims on popular loyalty in their ability to provide their citizens with a basic guarantee of freedom from violent death. The 9/11 attacks and their successors in Moscow, Beslan, Madrid and London dramatized the fragility of the state's monopoly on legitimate violence, and the compelling need to urgently reassert states' ability to honour the Hobbesian protection bargain in the face of the jihadist challenge (Phillips 2010: 271). Regardless of whether jihadist terrorism was conceived as the antithesis of liberalism (as it was in the West) or alternatively as one of the 'three evil forces' threatening social order alongside separatism and extremism (as it was among the member states of the Shanghai Cooperation Organization), governments of all ideological complexions recognized the imperative of reasserting states' exclusive control over organized violence during the post-9/11 decade (Lowenheim and Steele 2010: 32–3). The result was the unprecedented surge in global counter-terrorism cooperation described above, constricting the operational environment in which both jihadists and all other violent non-state actors must now operate.

As the 'war on terror' enters its second decade, the global jihadist movement confronts a bleak future. Osama bin Laden's assassination in May 2011 robs the movement of an iconic and in many respects irreplaceable figurehead. Bin Laden's death denies al-Qaeda a leader whose charisma Ayman al-Zawahiri (bin Laden's deputy and now successor) cannot hope to match. More seriously, a significant number of jihadists were bound to al-Qaeda by a personal oath (*bayat*) they had sworn to bin Laden; with bin Laden now dead, the already fragile bonds of fealty linking the jihadist *Internationale* are likely to fray further (Davison 2011). The 'Arab Spring' of 2011 – a tectonic upheaval for the Middle East from which al-Qaeda was conspicuously absent – meanwhile holds out the promise of ushering in an era of more responsive government across large swathes of the Arab world. Democratic transitions in Tunisia, Egypt and Libya are of course tentative, ambiguous and reversible (Zarate and Gordon 2011: 103). But the jihadists' inability to capitalize thus far on the instability that has accompanied these transitions underscores their weakness, as well as highlighting their failure to cultivate a popular support base after supposedly being at the vanguard of resistance to 'infidel' oppression for over a decade. Jihadists became increasingly evident in the Syrian civil war during 2011–12; however, it is too early to draw firm conclusions about their relative importance. US drawdowns from Iraq and Afghanistan finally threaten to further weaken the jihadist cause, as the Obama administration's strategic retrenchment removes the most prominent rallying point for the popular hostility to the West that sustains jihadist extremism.

While it would be premature to write al-Qaeda's epitaph, US Defence Secretary Leon Panetta's prediction that the US is 'within reach of strategically defeating al-Qaeda' seems increasingly plausible (Bumiller 2011). Nevertheless, defeat is by no means synonymous with disappearance. Indeed, the history of prior 'rebel waves' of terror provides ample evidence of bitter-enders fighting for doomed causes long after the futility of further struggle has become obvious. Terrorist violence is irreducibly instrumental in its character, guided as it is in large part by actors' strategic use of force in pursuit of intelligible (if often abhorrent) political objectives. But instrumental motives do not exhaust the range of reasons terrorists take up arms, with expressive motivations also figuring heavily in terrorists' resort to violence. For this reason – because violence has become as much an existential affirmation of jihadists' understandings of their religious identity as it has an instrumental means of advancing their political goals – jihadist violence will persist even following the reversals of the post-9/11 decade. Significantly, however, the defeats of the past decade will dramatically condition jihadism's evolving character in coming decades, rendering it a different if diminished threat to world order in the post-bin Laden era.

Osama bin Laden's greatest achievement was to weld formerly disparate regional groupings of jihadist extremists together in the 1990s into a transnational coalition dedicated to waging global war against the 'far enemy'. Through the force of his personality, the power of his example and the patronage at his disposal, bin Laden briefly mobilized a coalition of jihadist networks against a US-dominated world order. The post-Gulf War expansion of US military power and political influence in the Middle East provided bin Laden with a critical motivation for taking the jihad global, while the growth of global economic integration under US auspices provided him with the resources necessary to wage a worldwide terror campaign against his American nemesis (Doran 2002; Adamson 2005: 41). After 9/11, the US declaration of a 'war on terror' and its ensuing invasions of Afghanistan and Iraq provided the jihadists with continuing impetus, sustaining jihadism's transformation into a global social movement even as al-Qaeda's direct capacity to prosecute the struggle wilted under US pressure. The jihadists' strategic defeats in the post-9/11 decade, however, combined with US drawdowns in Iraq and Afghanistan, will likely see a reversion from the globalism of the post-Cold War and post-9/11 decades and a return to the regionally distinctive threat constellations that previously predominated.

In Iraq and elsewhere throughout the Middle East, jihadist militants will thus continue to play an important though limited spoiler role in seeking to frustrate the region's halting transition to democracy. South Asia, for several years now the global epicentre of jihadist violence, will meanwhile see a further acceleration of Islamist militancy across the broad swathe of territory encompassing Afghanistan, Khyber Pakhtunkwa (formerly Pakistan's North West Frontier Province) and Indian-occupied Kashmir. With the Indo-Pakistani competition for influence in post-ISAF Afghanistan set to intensify, the prospect that jihadists will seek to provoke a renewed armed confrontation between the nuclear-armed neighbours cannot be discounted, and arguably represents the most significant short-term threat to international security posed by jihadist terrorism (Phillips 2012). Finally, in the Western democracies themselves, the threat of 'lone wolf' acts of terror – perpetrated not only by 'home-grown' jihadists but also by anti-Muslim right-wing extremists such as Anders Breivik – will continue to preoccupy governments, who will struggle to balance counter-terrorism imperatives with the need to uphold civil rights and preserve inclusive and harmonious multicultural societies.

As the jihadist terrorist threat assumes a more regionally distinctive character, the global unity that marked international society's immediate post-9/11 response to al-Qaeda will diminish as old inter-state rivalries reassert themselves, and the jihadist threat recedes in importance relative to more traditional security challenges. This observation aside, much of the intensified counter-terrorism cooperation that 9/11 stimulated is likely to remain in place, the attacks having sensitized states to the disproportionate destruction violent non-state actors remain capable of inflicting on even the strongest states. More fundamentally, while jihadism looks set to eventually join preceding waves of 'rebel terror' in the dustbin of history, the 'war on terror' has nevertheless profoundly shaped 21st-century international politics in ways that will endure for decades after jihadism's defeat. On this point, a brief contrast between the 'end of history' Francis Fukuyama confidently forecast following the Cold War and the world we now inhabit is instructive.

Against the expectations of Fukuyama and his liberal fellow travellers, the post-9/11 era has, first, seen a vigorous reassertion of state power in both the developed and the developing world. Far from atrophying in an age of globalization, the state's powers of policing and surveillance have dramatically grown in response to post-9/11 counter-terrorism concerns. Democratic societies have witnessed significant curtailments of civil liberties to suppress the terror threat; meanwhile autocrats have seized on the 'war on terror' as an all-purpose pretext for clamping down on all forms of dissent. State powers to regulate and supervise religious beliefs and practices have likewise expanded, alongside more concerted efforts to codify the nature of the relationship between faith and state identity. In secular societies, where religion has long been regarded as a matter of private conviction and where there has also existed an institutionalized separation between church and state, this encroachment of state power into the 'private' domain has proved particularly controversial. The French 'headscarves affair' provides just one instance of this development, but it is illustrative of a divisive cultural politics that will continue to attend the efforts of traditionally 'post-religious' societies to reconcile respect for cultural diversity with their commitment to maintaining a predominantly secular public sphere (Roy 2007: 26–8).

Following the post-9/11 decade, the continued strengthening of a rules-based international order along liberal lines also now appears far from guaranteed. In particular, the 'war on terror' leaves as one of its legacies an increasingly permissive attitude towards the use of force on the part of Western democracies and a correspondingly weakened commitment to the maintenance of an international order founded on respect for principles of sovereignty and non-intervention. Historically, material constraints on Western military power prevented the sustained projection of force into the African and Asian interior until the mid-19th century (Black 2005: 131). From the mid-20th century onwards, the UN system of collective security institutionalized norms of sovereign equality and non-intervention at a global level, providing weak states with a robust if admittedly imperfect guard against armed encroachments on their territory by the great powers (Cohen, 2006: 492). In the 21st century, military innovations such as pilot-less drones and precision-guided munitions (PGMs) have again conferred upon strong powers the ability to project force swiftly and easily into weaker states. Simultaneously, counter-terrorism and counter-proliferation anxieties have also provided strong states with compelling grounds for unilaterally abridging norms of non-intervention in the name of assuring their citizens' safety from terrorist attack (Nichols 2005: 8–12). In a world where many states lack the capacity and sometimes the political will necessary to suppress terrorist activity within their borders, strong states have proved more likely to resort to armed self-help to compensate for such local shortfalls in capacity and resolve. As the recent deterioration in the US–Pakistan relationship illustrates, this trend is likely only to intensify as ongoing troop drawdowns increase the West's dependence on drones as the arm of decision in counter-terrorism operations, potentially further weakening international constraints on the use of violence while simultaneously exacerbating political instability in fragile states (Hudson *et al.* 2011: 129–30).

Finally, and most importantly, the decade-long diversion of Western resources and attention to prosecute the 'war on terror' has significantly hastened American hegemonic decline, and with it also the ongoing power shift from West to East. This transition was inevitable in the long run. But the 'war on terror' has dramatically brought forward the time at which the Western democracies will be compelled to accept an autocratic China as an equal partner in managing the global order. While proponents of the 'end of history' thesis once confidently predicted that democracy and market capitalism would triumph everywhere following the Cold War's end, it is now clear that this prediction was implicitly predicated on the premise that liberalism's Western state sponsors would indefinitely remain globally pre-eminent.

Instead, it now appears far more likely that an indebted and depleted West will by necessity share global leadership with an economically dynamic and unapologetically autocratic China for the foreseeable future. Future chroniclers of the early 21st century will no doubt note the supreme irony that a nominally Marxist atheist dictatorship proved to be the ultimate beneficiary of the global clash between liberal internationalism and radical Islamic revivalism. As we enter the second decade of the 'war on terror', an interim assessment of its legacy for international order confirms a truth first evident on that terrible Tuesday in September – history has most assuredly resumed.

## Guide to further reading

Excellent general introductions to the study of terrorism as a phenomenon in world politics include Hoffman (2002) and Crenshaw (1981). Rapoport (2001) provides a succinct overview of the history of modern terrorism, while Jensen (2004) is helpful for understanding the often neglected 'first wave' of anarchist terrorism. Hoffman (1998) provides an indispensible overview of the renewed international-ization of terrorism from the late 1960s onwards, while Adamson (2005) and Cronin (2002/3) provide cogent analyses of the complex and evolving relationship between transnational terrorism and globalization.

The 'war on terror' continues to provoke partisan passions, which are reflected in the polemical tone of works by commentators writing from both critical perspectives, such as Ali (2002) and Chomsky (2003), as well as those writing from a neo-conservative position, such as Podhoretz (2007). A more balanced overview of the struggle against jihadist terrorism can be found in Scheuer (2007), while Berman (2003) is useful in illuminating the ideological contours of the struggle between liberalism and jihadist extremism.

The wars in Afghanistan and Iraq have seen transnational jihadist terrorism feature ever more conspicuously in insurgent conflicts in these countries, a theme that is explored in both Kilcullen (2005) and Phillips (2009). Finally, Nichols (2005) provides an interesting perspective on the systemic implications of transna-tional terrorism, according particular emphasis to its impact on the rules governing the use of force in world politics.

## Chapter 10

# New Forms of Security and the Challenge for Human Security

*EDWARD NEWMAN*

Security and insecurity are perennial – and perhaps the most important – challenges in the study and practice of international politics. Concerns over security arguably defined the birth of International Relations as a distinct subject of academic research and teaching, and security issues have been a defining feature of changes within this subject over the last hundred years. Security is also a privileged policy arena, commanding resources and pre-eminent political influence. Yet the study of security in the 21st-century is also defined by fundamental questions and sometimes doubts relating to its disciplinary coherence and identity, its epistemology, its scope and subject matter, and its relationship with evolving real-world challenges. What should the referent object of international security be: states, other human collectivities and societies, identities, individuals, genders, the environment, the planet? What threats to security should define the study and the policies of security: adversarial foreign states employing military might, terrorism, failed states, migration, environmental degradation, cyber-warfare, poverty, underdevelopment, disease? Which actors should be entrusted to respond to security threats: national defence agencies, national intelligence agencies, overseas development agencies, communities, international organizations? What form should this response be: military deterrence, pre-emptive military action, overseas development assistance, multilateral cooperation, the construction of institutions in weak states, international environmental protection? At what cost – in terms of personal liberty and limits to consumption – should security be achieved? How should security be studied and what forms the basis of reliable knowledge in this area: 'scientific' approaches which seek to establish objective 'truth', or critical approaches which see security and securitization as a politicized, subjective process in which the analyst can never be a neutral observer? It can be no surprise that security has been described as an 'essentially contested' subject, defying consensus on its basic parameters and perhaps even its meaning (Buzan and Hansen 2009: 10).

Until the 1980s ideas of security rested upon more solid ontological foundations – in terms of what the world looked like from a security perspective – at least in mainstream academic and policy circles. During the Cold War security studies were largely preoccupied with external, state-centric military threats. However, in recent decades the manner in which security and insecurity have been conceived – both in academic and policy circles – has experienced a radical shake-up. This chapter will consider the evolution of security at a time of huge change in international politics as a range of new – or newly defined – and emerging security challenges have gained greater attention. It will consider whether there has been a fundamental change in how we think about and respond to security and insecurity, and what the future of security studies may look like. The chapter will give special attention to the irreducible referent object of security – the individual – in order to consider whether the concept of 'human security' adequately captures the challenges of security and insecurity in the 21st century.

## The conventional model of security and its critics

The conventional model of security which dominated international studies following the Second World War was premised upon states both as the primary referent object (that is, what should be made secure) and potential threat, and military force as the source of both security and insecurity. Security was therefore defined by deterring and, if necessary, responding to military aggression against national territory by adversarial states. The means to achieve security were through the management of armed force in an anarchical international environment: deterrence, arms control, alliances and the maintenance of a stable balance of power (or hegemonic military supremacy). In academic circles security studies was largely preoccupied with understanding 'the threat, use and control of military force' by and against state actors (Walt 1991: 212). This model of security was embedded in a realist, Westphalian worldview of international politics comprised of rational, viable autonomous states competing for power in an anarchic environment devoid of meaningful norms except those imposed by the constraints of power politics. Clearly this reflected the historical context of the Cold War, bipolarity and the threat of nuclear annihilation, which very much conditioned the academic study of security.

The fact that this model of security did not reflect the experience of 'security' for much of the world's population did not concern those working in security studies in mainstream academic institutions and amongst policy establishments. Security was firmly in the privileged realm of 'high politics', a fact embraced by those in defence establishments and research centres which received funding to analyse these challenges – and which thus had an interest in the perpetuation of this worldview. According to this model, then, the unit of analysis and referent object of security are states, and threats are conceived in state-centric military terms. There were dissenting voices even during the Cold War: some peace researchers promoted human needs and positive peace ideas as an alternative vision for security, and programmes such as the World Order Models Project challenged the realist orthodoxy (Falk 1982; Galtung 1980). 'Dependency' scholars similarly sought to divert attention away from narrow Western military preoccupations and towards a more global perspective of insecurity, including the structural deprivation suffered in the developing world (Bornschier and Chase-Dunn 1985). Moreover, conventional approaches were not entirely unreflective: Wolfers (1952), for example, described security as an 'ambiguous symbol' in the early Cold War period. Nevertheless, the state-centric, military approach to understanding and responding to security was largely prevalent. This worldview arguably never represented a true reflection of the interests of what Booth (2005) has described as 'real people in real places', and yet it had a firm hold on policy establishments and mainstream security studies for decades.

The conventional model of security also tended to privilege a certain epistemic and methodological approach to understanding security and insecurity. Conventional understandings are generally based upon positivist empirical – and sometimes quantitative – approaches to research. That is, they rest mostly upon the identification, measurement and correlation of tangible, material factors and processes, and the investigation of causal relationships. Research agendas were dominated by parsimonious research questions which emphasized the importance of analytical coherence, without reference to broader questions of justice and social context. They were also characterized by their 'problem-solving' nature, taking – and not questioning – prevailing parameters of knowledge and social institutions as the given and inevitable framework for understanding and action (Cox, 1981). Conventional security studies during the Cold War, in line with their broadly positivist approach, were also dominated by the belief that research should and could be about the impartial search for value-free and objective 'truth', unaffected by the biases and interpretations of the individual researcher and his/her institutional context.

A number of processes began to challenge the traditional security model in the years leading up to the end of the Cold War. In academic and policy circles there were a number of movements towards a more inclusive definition and understanding of security that would reflect a broader range of challenges and referents beyond the use of force between states, and towards more plural approaches to understanding security.

A number of processes stimulated this broadening security discourse. The end of the Cold War and the eventual disintegration of the Soviet Union eroded the bipolar construction of international relations and the heightened sense of 'security dilemma' that had provided a context for the narrow national security paradigm in policy and academic circles. This allowed other – although not necessarily 'new' – challenges onto the security agenda, such as intrastate conflict, environmental degradation, communicable disease and weak states. The apparent increase in intrastate conflict and civil war in the early 1990s, in contrast to the relative scarcity of interstate war and the decreasing threat of nuclear war, also suggested that the conventional security paradigm was no longer an accurate reflection of what was occurring in the real world. This new political environment therefore challenged the state-centric, military model of international security. The challenge was both empirical and normative: the conventional model of security simply no longer reflected the entire reality of security and insecurity – if it ever did – and the privileging of a narrow security discourse was a terrible disservice to the millions of people around the world who suffered injustice and personal inse-curity below the radar of 'high politics'. This evolving intellectual environment – which began before the end of the Cold War (see Buzan 1983; Ullman 1983; Independent Commission on Disarmament and Security Issues 1982; Brundtland Commission 1987) – brought an increased opportunity to address this more complex non-traditional security agenda at the international level, within a wider conception of peace and security. What was most conspicuous was that the narrow, conventional security model had little to say on these broader security challenges and the way they affected states and communities.

Globalization has arguably also been important to this evolution of security. The deregulation and marketization of national economies, in the context of networks of interdependence, has encouraged a broadening of the level of analysis in international relations. These processes point to the interconnections of security challenges and the problematic distinction between 'domestic' and 'international' – indeed, environmental degradation, human rights abuses which cause mass forced migration in the developing world, and communicable disease, amongst many other things, threaten the fundamental interests of states far away from their source and defy political boundaries. The technologies of globalization have also arguably had an impact on the evolving security agenda, empowering transna-tional militant groups and facilitating protest and upheaval within and across borders through the use of social media. These technologies also highlight new vulnerabilities to national security broadly defined: the reliance of modern soci-eties upon computer networks and electronic data has exposed them to cyber threats which have the potential to inflict widespread damage and cost. Finally, globalization has also brought social and economic insecurities to the fore and exposed the destabilizing impact of market disruptions, especially in the develop-ing world. In what is widely described as a merging of security and development, extreme poverty, weak state institutions and conflict in the developing world are – given the interconnections of the modern world – widely seen as a challenge to international security.

Normative changes have also had an impact upon the security agenda. The growing prominence of transnational norms relating to human rights and gover-nance is extending political discourse beyond the territorial scope of the state. Egregious abuses of human rights – and sometimes even the denial of democracy – are seen as a challenge for international security, resulting in calls for military humanitarian intervention (see Bellamy, this volume). The clearest expression of this has been the emerging – although still contested – norm of the 'Responsibility to Protect' which suggests that if states are not willing or able to prevent terrible abuses of human rights, that responsibility falls to the international community. The intervention into Libya in 2011 was arguably an illustration of this norm (Bellamy and Williams 2011).

These developments should be seen within a broader context of change in inter-national politics which might be described as a move towards a post-Westphalian world: a world where notions of inviolable and equal state sovereignty – never actually a reality but often respected as a norm – are breaking down; where states are no longer the sole or even the most important actors in certain areas of international politics; where states cannot be assumed to be viable or autonomous agents; where insecurity and conflict is primarily characterized by civil war, state failure and – in a post-9/11 world – terrorism, rather than inter-state war; where the distinction between 'domestic' and 'international' politics is irreversibly blurred in terms of the causes and impacts of conflict and insecurity; where the nature of, and responses to, security challenges hold implications for norms of state sovereignty and territorial integrity; and where solidarist norms related to governance and human rights are slowly – and imperfectly – transcending absolute norms of sovereignty and non-interference.

## 'New' – or newly securitized – challenges

It is worth noting that whilst the end of the Cold War is often presented as a watershed for security studies and the emergence of new approaches, the antecedents were clearly in evidence before the end of the Cold War, and throughout the Cold War the orthodox approach was challenged. According to Buzan and Hansen (2009: 4), the Cold War/post-Cold War juncture in security studies is a 'myth'. Indeed, a number of diplomatic initiatives and international policy landmarks – particularly the Palme Commission and the Brundtland Commission – paved the road for the emergence of widening security ideas. Earlier academic discourses which problematized the conventional view of security and encouraged new thinking also included feminist and gender analysis which argued that conditions of security and insecurity are indivisible from masculine power structures and gendered institutions (Enloe 1990).

Non-traditional security challenges are often described as 'new', but this is a matter for debate: it may often be more accurate to suggest that issues such as environmental degradation, intrastate conflict, weak and failing states, communicable disease and poverty became *newly perceived* to have become international security challenges. Nevertheless, it became increasingly obvious that the narrow, military state-centric model of international security neglected these important challenges, and from the 1980s progressive political leaders and academics increasingly pushed these issues onto policy and academic agendas. Environmental degradation across borders threatens the well-being of societies and economic performance; in the worst cases – low-lying coastal states threatened by climate change – climate change can clearly represent an existential threat. Environmental change and in particular climate change has also been linked to intrastate instability and conflict, since it exacerbates underlying social and economic conflicts. Intrastate conflict and failing states destabilize regions and have wide-reaching spillover effects, including forced migration, the spread of insurgency and weapons, and the disruption of markets which makes the prices of essential commodities soar. According to some scholars, failed states also provide an environment in which terrorist organizations can exploit the vacuum of authority in order to recruit, train and plan attacks (Rotberg 2004). Fukuyama (2004: 92) has argued that 'weak and failing states have arguably become the single most important problem for international order'. Cyber warfare threatens the integrity of a wide range of systems upon which societies rely for their economic prosperity, societal cohesion and security. Communicable diseases spread over borders, threatening to undermine social cohesion as well as destroying individual lives. A range of issues which might at an earlier time have appeared on the development or humanitarian agendas have gradually but permanently moved over to the security agenda.

## Deepening and widening security

These developments have been conceptualized in a number of ways and there have been a number of strands to non-traditional security studies in recent decades. Some analysts have argued that our understanding of security threats should be widened beyond the military sector, to include a range of economic, social and environmental challenges – but with the state essentially remaining the referent object of security (Buzan *et al*. 1998; Krause and Williams 1996; Krause and Williams 1997). Other analysts have argued that the state should no longer be privileged as the object of security, and so the analysis of security should be deepened to embrace other referents and values and a more inclusive ontology. Deepening approaches therefore challenge the state as the referent object, and also seek to understand the values within which ideas of security are embedded. In addition, many scholars have called for more critical methodological approaches to understanding security and insecurity. These seek to deconstruct and problematize prevailing understandings of security and the interests these serve and point the way to a better understanding of what security means. Some non-traditional approaches to security propose a more coherent – and consciously alternative – agenda. Many new approaches reject the dichotomy between 'domestic' and 'international' security challenges. A widely-held belief, within the broad challenge to conventional security studies, is that security is an 'essentially contested concept', in the sense suggested by Gallie (1956), and that there is no basis for an objective understanding of 'security' and no possibility of consensus on what 'security' means.  According to this view, '"Security" is a socially constructed concept. It has a specific meaning only within a particular social context' (Sheehan, 2005: 43).

Some traditionalists mounted a spirited defence of the conventional emphasis upon military security and the state as the referent object. Most notably, perhaps, Stephen Walt (1991) challenged the widening approaches and argued that the coherence – and thus analytical value – of security studies depended upon a clear, delineated focus on armed force. This of course remains an important and popular topic, but it has been increasingly defined as 'strategic studies'. Nevertheless, in the years following the end of the Cold War security studies has reflected a number of developments, many of which have therefore raised questions about the referent object of security, the nature of 'security threats', the processes through which issues are defined as 'security threats' and the impact of this, and the manner in which reliable knowledge about security can be established.

Non-traditional security studies challenge many of the key features of conventional security studies: its emphasis upon parsimony and coherence; its privileging of a rational, state-centric worldview based upon the primacy of military power in an anarchic environment; its emphasis upon order and predictability as positive values; and its structural view of international politics as historical, recurrent, and non-contextual. Many of these new approaches to security studies also tend to challenge the basic assumptions of what the key features of the world are, what we should be studying, and how to generate reliable, legitimate knowledge. Many non-traditional approaches therefore reject positivist, universalizing knowledge claims and the idea of value-free 'truth'. Indeed, some critical approaches go further, arguing that knowledge is always socially contingent. Smith (2005: 28) therefore suggests that there is 'no neutral place to stand to pronounce on the meaning of the concept of security, all definitions are theory-dependent, and all definitions reflect normative commitments'. According to this, the orthodox idea of security belonging to the state and the military is simply a construction, which can and should be challenged. Critical approaches also challenge the material preoccupation of realism, which confines its analysis to the measurement of physical variables and ignores ideational factors. Following from this, some branches of critical security studies do not necessarily see analytical coherence as the primary objective.

However, beyond a common opposition to mainstream assumptions, the non-traditional and critical approaches to security often fundamentally diverge. In particular, they differ on what the referent object of security should be, whether the objective should be to securitize or desecuritize (and the implications of this), and whether the emphasis should be on normative or explanatory theory. Some non-traditional approaches retain the state as the referent object of study, and broaden their analysis of the threats to the state, to include – for example – economic, societal, environmental, and political security challenges. Barry Buzan's landmark book, *People, States and Fear* (1983), suggested that the individual is the 'irreducible base unit' for explorations of security but the referent of security must remain the state as it is the central actor in international politics and the principal agent for addressing insecurity. What some have called 'societal security' focuses upon 'the ability of a society to persist in its essential character under changing conditions and possible or actual threats' (Wæver *et al.* 1993: 23). Other critical approaches fundamentally challenge the state-centricity of security analysis, and argue that individuals or humans collectively should be the referent object of security (Booth 2005: 268; McSweeney 1999: 208; Booth 1997: 111).

A further important debate concerns the consequences of treating an issue as a security threat, which raises the question of negative and positive securitization. Some scholars – inspired by what is known as the Copenhagen School – raise concerns about the securitization process because this process moves issues from 'normal' (accountable, democratic) politics to 'emergency' politics. Securitization thus mobilizes exceptional resources and political powers which are not necessarily positive or proportionate to the security challenges, and are sometimes manipulated for political purposes in order to create fear or curtail freedoms. In this way securitization studies seeks to understand how and which issues are securitized, who acts as securitizing agents, and what the consequences of securitization are (Buzan *et al*. 1998: 32). According to such an approach, securitizing an issue – for example refugees – does not necessarily result in positive outcomes for the human rights of such people (Suhrke 2003; Wœver *et al*. 1993; Ibrahim 2005). This approach has been successfully applied to a number of political challenges – such as conflict resolution – in order to demonstrate how securitization has exacerbated fears and anxieties and entrenched conflict, and how desecuritization can provide incentives for accommodation and cooperation. Other critical approaches to security studies suggest the opposite: that broadening securitization will broaden 'real' security and bring resources and attention to a wider range of problems and actors, beyond the state. In this way, the Welsh School has a more positive view of security, in common with human security approaches (Jones 1999; Booth 2005).

Non-traditional approaches to security also differ in their normative approach. Some critical security perspectives claim that normative claims are baseless because there are no legitimate means of prescribing alternative policy frameworks. In contrast, the Welsh School is strongly normative, seeing security as a means to emancipation: 'freeing people, as individuals and collectivities, from contingent and structural oppressions' (Booth 2005; Booth 1991). Almost all non-traditional approaches see security as socially – and intersubjectively – constructed and discursive. What is described as 'security' is therefore political practice and a discursive process, and thus contingent on the (unequal) power which underpins the relationships between different social actors.

## Human security

Human security suggests that security policy and security analysis, if they are to be effective and legitimate, must focus on the individual as the referent and primary beneficiary. In broad terms human security is 'freedom from want' and 'freedom from fear': positive and negative freedoms and rights as they relate to fundamental individual needs. Human security is normative; it argues that there is an ethical responsibility to re-orient security around the individual in line with internationally recognized standards of human rights and governance. Much human security scholarship is therefore explicitly or implicitly underpinned by a solidarist commitment, and some is cosmopolitan in ethical orientation. Some human security scholarship also seeks to present explanatory arguments concerning the nature of security, deprivation and conflict. In addition, most scholars and practitioners working on human security emphasize the policy orientation of this approach; they believe that the concept of human security can and should result in policy changes which improve the welfare of people.

There is no uncontested definition of, or approach to, human security; few supporters of the concept would describe it as a 'paradigm'. Like all non-traditional security approaches, human security – as a starting point – challenges orthodox neorealist conceptions of international security. Scholars of human security argue that for many people in the world – perhaps even most – the greatest threats to 'security' come from internal conflicts, disease, hunger, environmental contamination or criminal violence. And for others, a greater threat may come from their own state itself, rather than from an 'external' adversary. Human security thus seeks to challenge attitudes and institutions that privilege so-called 'high politics' above individual experiences of deprivation and insecurity. This is not to presume that human security is necessarily in conflict with state security; the state remains the central provider of security in ideal circumstances. Human security does, however, suggest that international security traditionally defined – territorial integrity – does not necessarily correlate with human security, and that an over-emphasis upon state security can be to the detriment of human welfare needs. So, traditional conceptions of state security are a necessary but not sufficient condition of human welfare. The citizens of some states that are 'secure' according to the traditional concept of security can be personally perilously insecure in their everyday lives, to a degree that demands a reappraisal of the concept of security.

Human security also raises important implications for the evolution of state sovereignty. Traditionally, state sovereignty and sovereign legitimacy rest upon a government's control of territory, state independence and recognition by other states. The role of citizens is to support this system. The human security approach reverses this equation: the state – and state sovereignty – must serve and support the people from which it (in theory) draws its legitimacy. The concept of 'conditional sovereignty' has therefore taken on a renewed importance through human security: the international legitimacy of state sovereignty rests not only on control of territory, but also upon fulfilling certain standards of human rights and welfare for citizens. As a corollary, the legitimacy of states that are unwilling or unable to fulfil certain basic standards may be questionable, an idea that is reflected in the emerging norm of a Responsibility to Protect.

All approaches to human security agree that the referent of security policy and analysis should be the individual, but they disagree about which threats the individual should be protected from, and what means should be employed to achieve this protection. There are essentially four different strands – or usages – of human security, the first three of which are inspired by policy concerns. The first approach to human security is broad; it considers all threats to human integrity including – and sometimes especially – underdevelopment, poverty and deprivation (Thakur and Newman 2004; Tadjbakhsh and Chenoy 2006; Commission on Human Security 2003). This approach is a testament to the importance of development in the emergence of human security thinking. The 1994 UNDP Human Development Report popularized, and is representative of, this approach: human security means 'safety from such chronic threats as hunger, disease and repression' and 'protection from sudden and hurtful disruptions in the patterns of daily life – whether in homes, in jobs or in communities' (UNDP 1994: 23). This broad development-oriented approach to human security has found support in policy circles, in particular the Japanese-sponsored Commission on Human Security, which defined human security as the protection of 'the vital core of all human lives in ways that enhance human freedoms and human fulfilment' (Commission on Human Security 2003: 4).

The broad approach to human security sacrifices analytical precision in favour of general normative persuasion: it focuses on the issues which undermine the life chances of the largest numbers of people. The reality is that, by far, the biggest killers in the world are extreme poverty, preventable disease and the consequences of pollution. According to this approach, any conception of security which neglects this reality is conceptually, empirically and ethically inadequate.

The second approach to human security is narrower and focuses on the human consequences of armed conflict and the dangers posed to civilians by repressive governments and situations of state failure (Mack 2004; MacFarlane and Khong 2006). Modern conflict reflects a high level of civil war and state collapse which has resulted in a high rate of victimization and displacement of civilians, especially women and children. According to this approach to human security, conventional security analysis is woefully inadequate for describing and explaining the realities of armed conflict and its impact upon humanity. It is this strand of human security that is most closely associated with the Responsibility to Protect concept.

The third approach – particularly in policy circles and amongst scholars interested in policy – uses human security as an umbrella concept for approaching a range of 'non-traditional' security issues – such as HIV/AIDS, drugs, terrorism, small arms, inhumane weapons such as anti-personnel landmines, and trafficking in human beings – with the simple objective of attracting greater attention and resources for tackling them (Dodds and Pippard 2005; Leen 2004; Najam 2003). In this usage there is little effort made to contribute to theory. Indeed, relabelling such challenges rarely helps to deepen understanding of the nature of these diverse phenomena. The overriding objective is to raise the visibility of neglected problems and to influence policy.

Finally, some scholars seek to understand human security from a theoretical perspective and integrate human security into security studies (Roe 2008; Newman 2001; Newman 2010; Shani *et al.* 2007; Thomas 2002; Grayson, 2008). From this perspective human security is used to explore theoretical debates concerning the nature of security threats, referents and responses to insecurity. This literature raises questions about the sources of insecurity, the nature of the institutions which provide security, and the interests served by them. Within this approach, a small but important focus is upon the gendered aspects of security and insecurity (Gibson and Reardon 2007; Roberts 2008; Truong *et al.* 2007). This suggests that conditions of deprivation can only be understood with reference to gender relations and masculine institutions of power. As Thomas (2000: 4) suggests, insecurity results 'directly from existing power structures that determine who enjoys the entitlement to security and who does not'.

A defining characteristic of human security scholarship is its engagement with policy and its desire to change security policy in 'progressive' ways. The popularity of the concept since the 1990s – at least in the policy world – is partly attributable to the work of the UN Development Programme and other UN agencies, as well as civil society networks. A number of human security initiatives have been led by government-sponsored organizations such as the Commission on Human Security, the Human Security Trust Fund, and the International Commission on Intervention and State Sovereignty (ICISS). The concept has also been adopted as an embryonic foreign policy framework. The Human Security Network is a loose grouping of thirteen governments committed – at least in a declaratory sense – to a number of foreign policy principles including people-centred development and addressing the sources of insecurity. The activist aspect is also embraced by some in the academic world who proclaim that human security is ultimately about justice and dignity: 'We are scholars who want to change the world' (Tadjbakhsh and Chenoy 2006: 5).

A further characteristic of the human security approach is that it seeks to securitize issues as it broadens its approach to security. In addition to observing individuals as the referent object of security, human security seeks to view any critical and widespread challenge to the physical integrity of the individual as a security threat. According to the broad approach to human security, an extremely wide range of issues – including poverty and malnutrition, disease, environmental degradation and climate change – are securitized. The objective of this is explicitly to encourage security providers – and specifically the state – to invest the attention and resources necessary to address these non-traditional security challenges. Some scholars engaged in other non-traditional security approaches are wary of securitizing challenges as the solution and argue that this carries with it its own hazards.

## Defining human security: the problem of analytical value

Human security is normatively attractive, but analytically problematic. Through a broad human security lens anything that presents a critical threat to life and livelihood is a security threat, whatever the source. This presents an unmanageable array of potential security challenges. Arbitrarily drawing lines to include and exclude certain types of threats is equally problematic. The academic treatment of human security has become stuck and divided on this fundamental conceptual point. If there is disagreement on what should be included as a human security threat – or if this is an arbitrary judgement – then how can human security or variations in human security be reliably measured? How, in turn, can human security be analytically useful? The broad approach to human security – which includes social and economic afflictions – has attracted the greatest degree of criticism in this regard. Critics have argued that the broad approach is so inclusive – in considering potentially *any* threat to human safety – that as a concept it becomes meaningless. It does not allow scholars or policymakers to prioritize different types of threats, it confuses sources and consequences of insecurity, and it is too amorphous to allow analysis with any degree of precision (Krause 2004; Mack 2004; MacFarlane and Khong 2006; Buzan 2004). MacFarlane and Khong (2006: 17) also challenge the idea that 'rebranding' development, the environment or health as security challenges has produced a greater flow of resources to addressing them; such a relabelling may therefore, in addition to the conceptual confusion, also produce false hopes.

There have been attempts to overcome the definitional 'problem' and followers of human security have engaged in unresolved debates about the broad versus narrow definitions and the consequences of securitization (*Security Dialogue*, Special Section 2004; Owen 2004; Thomas and Tow 2002; Bellamy and McDonald 2002). King and Murray (2001–2), for example, proposed a quantitative model of human security based upon the 'number of years of future life spent outside a state of generalized poverty'. Roberts (2008) has suggested a measure of human insecurity in terms of 'avoidable civilian deaths'. Tadjbakhsh and Chenoy (2006) have argued that human security must necessarily embrace a broad range of threats because threats are intrinsically linked. Others have suggested that the definition of human security should not be preoccupied with broad and narrow models; instead, the definition should be based upon a threshold. According to this, threats are regarded as *security* challenges when they reach a certain threshold of human impact, whatever the source (Thakur and Newman, 2004).

More established non-traditional security studies circles – such as the Copenhagen School and Critical Security Studies – have been rather ambivalent towards the concept of human security for a number of reasons. In particular, the policy orientation of human security – and its adoption as a policy framework by some governments – has made critical security scholars suspicious of human security as a hegemonic, statist discourse. From this perspective human security does not seek to genuinely interrogate the structural realities of insecurity and deprivation, and perhaps even serves to legitimize these structures.

In addition, human security scholarship has tended to be 'problem solving'. This is an application of Robert Cox's famous analysis (1981). Problem-solving approaches take prevailing social relationships, and the institutions into which they are organized, as the given and inevitable framework for action. In contrast, critical approaches question how institutions emerge and the interests they represent and serve, and do not accept existing policy parameters as a given or necessarily legitimate. Most human security scholarship has been 'problem solving', largely because of its origins in foreign policy initiatives and amongst scholars interested in international organizations and development. Human security is in itself fundamentally 'critical', but this unfortunately is not how most human security arguments have been approached. Human security generally adopts a policy-oriented approach which attempts to improve human welfare within the political, legal and practical parameters of the real world, which is a problem for many in critical security circles. Human security scholarship, whilst promoting the individual as the referent object of security even when this is in tension with the state, is more likely to see a strong state as a necessary requirement for individual security. Human security does not problematize this ontology, but – perhaps paradoxically – still claims to be emancipatory. It would appear that human security can never overcome its central paradox: it apparently calls for a critique of the structures and norms that produce human insecurity, yet the ontological starting point of most human security scholarship and its policy orientation reinforce these structures and norms.

For a large number of people interested in promoting human security as a normative movement the definition debate and the role of human security within broader security studies are incidental. They have a simple objective: to improve the lives of those who are perilously insecure. Conceptual or analytical coherence is not essential for this task. But in the world of scholarship the differences between a broad and narrow approach have undermined the unity and perhaps even the utility of human security. Attempts to overcome this – for example through a threshold approach – have not as yet resolved this debate. But the debate itself is an interesting space for considering competing visions of security and international politics, and the study of these.

## Conclusion and future directions

New – or newly defined – security challenges have ensured that security studies remains vibrant and alluring. However, the future of security studies will be defined by a number of challenges. The disciplinary identity and boundaries of the subject remain contested, including its relationship with International Relations and with the 'real world'. Indeed, disagreements on what should be the appropriate referent object of, and threats to, security – and how, methodologically, to generate reliable and legitimate knowledge on these issues – suggests that security studies is fundamentally divided. This is manifesting itself in a number of core questions or poles. Firstly, what is the role of the state in security in the 21st century? Conventional readings of international security see the state as the primary referent object and the potential threat. Non-traditional security challenges – such as environmental degradation, refugee flows, underdevelopment and weak state capacity, intrastate instability, transnational extremism and terrorism – have risen to prominence as challenges, and in some ways weak rather than strong states are the defining security challenge of the 21st century. Interstate wars have declined sharply in number; large-scale organized violence is almost entirely civil war. And yet this reading of security appears to downplay conventional security challenges in regions such as South Asia and North East Asia, and the security implications of rising powers such as Brazil, India and China. However much public and academic debate appears to prioritize 'new' security challenges, defence establishments in the major countries of the world continue to give very significant attention to conventional challenges. It would be premature to announce the coming of 'post-international' security, even if the boundary between 'domestic' and 'international' security has become fundamentally blurred.

Secondly, in terms of security referents – whether states, individuals or communities – it will become increasingly difficult to prioritize and to define a singular object of security analysis and policy, at least in a generic sense. If priorities are to be defined, they will be done so as a condition of context and interests. For the

Maldives and Bangladesh – and many other low-lying coastal states or those reliant upon agricultural economies – climate change is truly the existential threat. For the inhabitants of South Korea and Japan, the traditional security paradigm – in the form of the North Korean security threat – remains very much relevant. For individuals in Nigeria, Somalia, the Central African Republic and Guatemala, and in all too many other countries, insecurity comes in the form of local violence enabled by weak state institutions and the absence of a rule of law. In many Western societies security establishments are preoccupied with the threat of 'home-grown' radicalization and the threat of terrorism.

Finally, and following from the point above, a key question will therefore remain: is security an objective, material condition or a subjective thing that depends upon perception? The answer to this depends upon one's context and predicament. Many people in the world, including those in defence establishments, can – or so they believe – objectively define threats to their security. However, these will not be uniform, and so in general, academic terms, security will most certainly remain a contested, subjective challenge.

## Guide to further reading

General textbooks and edited collections on international security give significant attention to new or emerging security challenges including environmental degradation, health issues and failed states. See Michael E. Smith, *International Security: Politics, Policy, Prospects* (2010); Alan Collins, *Contemporary Security Studies* (2009); and Paul D. Williams (ed.), *Security Studies: An Introduction* (2008). There are now also many volumes which adopt critical and non-traditional academic approaches, often explicitly challenging or rejecting conventional 'realist' models: for example, Karin M. Fierke, *Critical Approaches to International Security* (2007); Ken Booth (ed.), *Critical Security Studies and World Politics* (2004); and Keith Krause and Michael C. Williams (eds), *Critical Security Studies: Concepts and Cases* (1997). An example of a volume which seeks to explore the broad range of new and emerging security challenges is Michael E. Brown (ed.), *Grave New World: Security Challenges in the Twenty-First Century* (2003). However, there is no consensus on whether these challenges are truly changing the nature of international security. Constructivist scholars would argue that many so-called security challenges reflect a political process of labelling; a recent example of this is Thierry Balzacq (ed.), *Securitization Theory: How Security Problems Emerge and Dissolve* ( 2010). Human security is also a popular challenge to orthodox security ideas and the journal *Security Dialogue* is a key forum for debates on this topic. See also Shahrbanou Tadjbakhsh and Anuradha Chenoy, *Human Security: Concepts and Implications* (2007).

# Chapter 11

# Inequality and Underdevelopment

*RAY KIELY*

Global inequality and underdevelopment are particularly contentious issues in contemporary world politics. In essence, they are issues which ask the following questions: What is the (global) North–South divide? How has it emerged, how is it reproduced, and what can be done about it? Has the recent era of 'globalization' eroded a North–South divide and promoted some forms of convergence, or at least poverty reduction, in the global order? This chapter examines each, but especially the last of these, questions.

Debate over the relationship between globalization, inequality and underdevelopment has been particularly contentious. On the one hand, there are relatively upbeat assessments of a shift towards convergence between rich and poor countries in the global economy. A variant on this argument suggests that while inequality in some forms may not have been reduced in recent years, what matters is the fact that global poverty *has* been reduced, and this has occurred because of the opportunities that globalization presents to developing countries. Not all states have necessarily taken advantage of these opportunities, but it is precisely in these states that rapid economic growth and poverty reduction have not occurred. Related to these upbeat assessments are various arguments concerning the dispersal of capital flows throughout the world, the rise of manufacturing in the developing world, the rise of China and India, and the increase in primary commodity prices in recent years, which in turn have facilitated high growth rates in Latin America and much of Africa.

On the other hand, more sceptical assessments question the extent to which poverty has been reduced, point to the increase in inequality within countries and (at the extremes) between them, the continued concentration of capital and high-value production in the developed countries, the limits of the kind of manufacturing that has taken place in much of the developing world, including in India and China, the continued limits of development based on excessive reliance on primary commodity exports, and thus of growth rates in the so-called periphery. These problems have all been exacerbated, so the sceptics argue, by the economic downturn since 2007–8. The upbeat assessments have thus exaggerated the positives that occurred in the boom years, and anyway now look woefully inadequate as the world moves into a very serious recession.

149

This chapter assesses the claims made by both the 'optimists' and 'sceptics' concerning inequality and underdevelopment. It does so by first briefly outlining the ways in which inequality and underdevelopment were theorized in the post-war era, as part of the 'great development debate'. This section will suggest that notwithstanding the over-generalizations employed by both sides, this debate retains considerable relevance in the era of globalization. The next section examines the position of the optimists, pointing to some of the evidence used to back up this case. It then moves on to consider the more sceptical side, again examining some of the evidence used to back up this case. The chapter then provides a more in-depth analysis of various trends in the global economy, and suggests that these, on the whole, tend to support the more sceptical arguments. The chapter concludes by reflecting on why inequality and underdevelopment are such serious issues of concern.

## The great development debate: inequality and underdevelopment 1945–1982

The post-1945 era was one in which development became a particular area of concern. While the idea certainly pre-dated 1945, it became more prominent in the context of the Cold War and the beginning of the end of formal empires. Both superpowers supported political independence for the colonies, though both of course were concerned that they exercise considerable influence over the political trajectory of the newly independent sovereign states.

It was in this context that the debate over the causes of global inequality and underdevelopment emerged. Though there were considerable variations and nuances in the debate, we can identify two basic positions: modernization and dependency theories. The former was the mainstream theory of development, which essentially argued that developing societies – the 'Third World' – were backward and undeveloped, and therefore in need of development. This position was developed most famously by Walt Rostow (1960), who suggested that all nation-states pass through similar stages of development. So, poorer societies in the 1960s were at a similar stage of development to, say, Britain in the 1780s. The task of development was to hasten the transition to development in the poorer societies. Rostow argued that this was good for developing societies, as they would become richer, but also for the security of the West, as richer societies were less likely to be attracted by the communist alternative. Modernization theory suggested that the task of development could be facilitated by poorer countries embracing Western investment, technology and values such as entrepreneurship and meritocracy. Whether or not this was an accurate portrayal of Western societies (and the diversity among such countries), both in terms of the transition to development and the reality of modernity in the 1950s, is a moot point. Certainly civil rights movements in the 1950s would not have recognized this characterization of the United States.

The crucial argument of modernization theory, then, was that contact with the West was on the whole favourable to the development of the Third World. On the other hand, some structuralist economists had argued that the situation of poorer countries could not be explained in isolation from the richer world, and that contact with the latter was in some respects part of the problem. Thus, one of the legacies of colonialism was that Third World countries specialized in producing primary products, and this led to an excessive dependence on the world price movements of the one or two goods that accounted for most of their foreign exchange earnings. This was in contrast to the developed countries, which were far more industrialized and diversified, and so were not excessively reliant on the price movements of a handful of products. Moreover, Raul Prebisch (1959) and Hans Singer (1950) argued that primary producers faced certain disadvantages which meant that there was a tendency for the terms of trade to decline for primary goods as against industrial goods. What this meant in barter terms is that in, say, a 10-year period, primary producers would have to exchange more tonnes of cocoa in order to buy a similar number of tractors. Prebisch and Singer suggested that this tendency occurred because there was a low income elasticity of demand for primary products; in other words, as average incomes rise, so consumers spend a disproportionate amount of their income on primary products. Furthermore, while the prices of manufactured goods may fall, they are likely to fall more slowly than those of primary goods as there are many primary goods producers but comparatively few producers of industrial goods. Clearly, then, this account of inequality focused on hierarchies in the world economy, and how colonial powers had enforced specialization in lower-value primary production in the colonies. Even in independent Latin America, this practice had occurred as powerful landowners accrued huge wealth from land ownership and used this to import manufactured goods rather than promote domestic manufacturing production. This account thus suggested that the Western-dominated world economy was not the solution to underdevelopment, as modernization theory contended, but, in some respects at least, was part of the problem.

At the same time, this account suggested that development in the Third World could be achieved through pro-industrialization policies designed to overcome the colonial legacy. In this way, poorer countries could reduce their dependence on the import of expensive manufactures and the export of cheap primary goods. This policy of import substitution industrialization (ISI) was the main development strategy employed in the Third World from the 1950s (or earlier) until the late 1970s and early 1980s. Ironically, though the rationale for such a strategy was very different from that associated with modernization theory, in practice on policy the two theories effectively converged around the idea that development and modernization could occur through industrialization.

Dependency theory challenged this view, suggesting that industrialization remained dependent on the West. The mechanisms that sustained dependence included reliance on foreign capital, foreign technology and foreign markets. Furthermore, the industrialization that was said to be occurring in the developing world was highly exploitative and reliant on cheap labour. None of this was leading to convergence with the developed world; instead it was simply promoting new forms of subordination, hierarchy and dependence in the world economy. Some theories of dependency related this to a crude zero-sum game which suggested that the rich world was rich only because it had underdeveloped the poor world, implying that protectionist ISI policies did not go far enough, and that de-linking from the Western-dominated world economy was the only effective way forward for the Third World (Frank 1969). In this account, poorer societies were not so much undeveloped as *under*developed.

This was essentially what was at stake in the debate over inequality and underdevelopment in the period from the 1940s into the 1970s. On the one side, modernization theory: poorer countries should embrace the opportunities provided by the Western-dominated world economy, and in the process hasten the transition to development. On the other side, dependency theory: poorer countries are poor in part because they are in a structurally subordinate and dependent position in the world economy, and thus need to find ways to protect themselves from the constraints that these hierarchies generate. By the 1970s and into the 1980s, it was clear that for all their differences, both sides in the debate suffered from some similar weaknesses. In particular they tended to over-generalize and homogenize a diverse set of countries. In the process they tended to make sweeping predictions concerning the inevitability of development (modernization theory) or stagnation (dependency theory). For instance, the rise of newly industrializing East Asian countries such as South Korea and Taiwan undermined crude versions of dependency theory, as these countries grew rapidly and exported to Western economies. On the other hand, these countries, rather than simply embracing 'the West', protected certain sectors from foreign competition in order to develop their own national industries. Moreover, the success of these countries may have been contingent on certain specific factors that could not easily be replicated elsewhere. It was precisely this focus on contingency and specificity that was missing in the modernization versus dependency theory debate. It was also in this context that some argued that the study of development had reached an impasse, and that from now on we could only focus on specific cases of development without employing the generalizations associated with the modernization and dependency theories (Booth 1985).

Moreover, changes in the global economy led to important changes in development strategy in the Third World. In particular, the debt crisis of 1982 saw a shift from the developmentalist strategies associated with ISI towards neoliberal policies that encouraged trade and investment liberalization, privatization and the rollback of state intervention in the economy (or at least a shift to intervention that extended the market rather than restricted its role). This was justified on the grounds that ISI encouraged the promotion and protection of inefficient industries, rather than facilitating specialization in those sectors where countries were (relatively) most competitive; in other words, it meant the promotion of the principle of comparative advantage. While in the short term, the results of neoliberal policies were disastrous, and living standards for many fell in the lost decade of development (the 1980s), the 1990s saw a new period of optimism about the relationship between development and globalization.

These shifts – from grand theory to local and national development trajectories, from ISI to neoliberalism – appeared to undermine the foundations of the 'great development debate' of the 1940s to the early 1980s. However, while it is certainly true that these theories were guilty of over-generalization, I will suggest below that the optimistic and sceptical accounts of growth, poverty and inequality replicate these older debates, albeit in the new context of (neoliberal) globalization.

## Global inequality and underdevelopment: the optimistic position

This section outlines the optimistic position, which argues that underdevelopment has been reduced in recent years, and this either has reduced global inequality, or has at least reduced absolute poverty. The main evidence used by the optimists is that the number or proportion of people living in absolute poverty has declined since the 1980s.

Claims have been made that the number of people living in absolute poverty has declined over recent years, with figures ranging from 1.8 billion (1990) down to 1.37 billion (2005), to 1.4 billion (1980) down to 1.2 billion or 1 billion (1980), or even lower (Chen and Ravallion 2010; World Bank 2002: 30; Bhalla 2010). This alleged decline is said to be the result of high rates of economic growth, which in turn are said to be caused by policies of trade and investment liberalization. The clear implication is that poverty is a result of insufficient globalization, and that this is a policy choice made by states in developing countries.

On the whole, then, the news is good – the number of people living in absolute poverty is falling (Bhagwati 2004; Wolf 2004). The Millennium Development Goals (MDGs) are thus likely to be fulfilled, or at least they will be in those states that have carried out appropriate policies. These MDGs were adopted by the United Nations General Assembly in September 2000, and they specified eight goals to be achieved by 2015. These included the eradication of extreme hunger and poverty (though in practice this was linked to the target of halving the number of people living on less than a dollar a day); achieving universal primary education; promoting gender equality; and various health and environmental indicators (UN 2000). While these are desirable goals, the main issue is whether and how these can be achieved, how the goals can be measured, and whether or not power relations hinder the success of achieving such goals.

The key point for the optimists, though, is the adoption of the correct policies, which involves the promotion of a 'globalization-friendly' strategy (World Bank 2002). As other chapters in this book have shown (see Cerny, and Higgott, this volume), globalization is a difficult term to define and is used in a variety of ways by both academics and politicians. In this case, being globalization-friendly means adopting policies that allow countries to embrace the opportunities generated by the world economy, and this in practice means liberalization. At the very least, it means policies of trade and investment liberalization, which in practice means policies that encourage competition and specialization, rather than protection, so that tariffs and subsidies are reduced, import controls are removed, and restrictions on foreign investment are loosened. It may also mean financial liberalization in the form of freer movement of money into (and out of) countries, but there is some disagreement over the extent to which this should occur. The basic argument is that trade liberalization will encourage specialization in those sectors in which countries have a comparative advantage, and thus discourage the production of high-cost, inefficient goods. Investment (and possibly financial) liberalization will encourage investment by transnational companies, and thus lead to a shift of investment from capital-rich to capital-poor areas.

This argument would appear to be reinforced by the surge in foreign capital investment, including that into the so-called periphery, since the early 1990s. The total global amount of foreign direct investment (FDI) increased from US$59 billion in 1982 to US$202 billion in 1990 and US$1.2 trillion in 2000, decreased to US$946 billion in 2005, and increased again to US$1.3 trillion in 2006 (UNCTAD 2002b: 3–5; UNCTAD 2007: 9). Developing countries generally accounted for around one-third of this total. The increase in FDI has also led to the growth of manufacturing in the developing world. In 1970, 18.5 per cent of the total exports from the developing world were manufactured goods; by the end of the 1990s it was over 80 per cent (UNCTAD 2002a: 5). Optimists thus contend that industrialization can occur through open investment policies which allow foreign (or national) companies to take advantage of low labour costs, and this promotes properly competitive industrialization rather than the high-cost, white elephant approach associated with ISI. Critics who point to the cheap labour associated with industrialization do not offer a viable alternative, and this should in any case be seen as a necessary stage that developing societies must pass through. In the long run, competitive industrialization will lead to full employment, which in turn will lead to upgrading to more a more developed kind of manufacturing, as occurred in the case of the earlier developers. Though this argument does not follow the rigid stages associated with modernization theory, the broad contentions certainly replicate that approach.

Moreover, the growth of countries such as China has a favourable impact on the rest of the developing world, even if they have not industrialized at comparable levels. China has increasingly relied on the rising import of inputs; the global export value of iron and steel, ores and minerals and non-ferrous metals increased by between 30 and 45 per cent in 2004, which (in part) reflected rising demand from China, now the leading importer of many commodities (WTO 2005: 1–2). In 2004 Latin American exports expanded by 37 per cent, much of which was accounted for by rising demand in East Asia, especially China (WTO 2005: 11). Some African countries, particularly Sudan and Congo, have similarly boosted their sales in the Chinese market, as have some East Asian countries.

# Global inequality and underdevelopment: the sceptical position

The sceptical position challenges this upbeat assessment on both empirical and theoretical grounds. This section concentrates on the former. The first issue is that of poverty reduction, where there are some grounds for questioning the view that absolute poverty has fallen. Absolute poverty is defined as living on less than a dollar a day, adjusted to take account of local purchasing power. Crucial here is the way in which purchasing power parity is measured, and this is done through a system of international price comparisons, which were made in 1985 and 1993, and have since been adjusted to take account of annual changes to particular economies. The alleged decline in poverty cited above partly reflects a shift away from poverty counts made on the basis of international price comparisons in two different periods – 1985 in the case of the first figure, and 1993 in the case of the second, lower figure (Reddy and Pogge 2003; Wade 2003a). The shift from the 1985 count to the 1993 count had the effect of lowering the poverty line in 77 out of 92 countries for which data were available, and these countries contained 82 per cent of the total population of the 92 countries (Reddy and Pogge 2003: 42). The World Bank's *World Development Report* on 1999/2000 was actually far more pessimistic than the optimistic assertions cited above, as it used the 1985 base year calculations to argue that absolute poverty had increased from 1.2 billion in 1987 to 1.5 billion in 1999 (World Bank 1999: 25).

The measure of absolute poverty is also questionable because the calculation is based on purchasing power parity (PPP) and attempts to factor in local variations in the purchasing power of particular goods, a laudable aim, but one that is particularly difficult when measuring poverty (Reddy and Pogge 2003). This is because the basket of goods that is used to make the comparison includes goods which are unlikely to be consumed by the poor, and which measure average income. This underestimates the numbers of people living in poverty, as consumers with rising income (above poverty level) spend a decreasing proportion of their income on food, and an average rise in income over time will therefore translate into smaller comparisons of those goods which the poor actually consume, and whose price differentials may be far more significant (Reddy and Pogge 2003).

Moreover, the data on growth rates and poverty reduction for China are questionable, and yet these alone account for any poverty reduction that has occurred in the world (Milanovic 2007). Indeed, in 2007, the Asian Development Bank presented the first official results based on PPP measures for China, and suggested that China's economy is 40 per cent smaller than was previously suggested, and that the number of people living below the poverty line is 300 million, which is 200 million more than previous estimates. For India revised estimates suggest that the official poverty line is closer to 800 million rather than the previously suggested 400 million (Keidel 2007). World Bank data suggest that the revised figures are not as high as this, but still accept that for China, for instance, there has been an underestimate of around 130 million (Chen and Ravallion 2010). Furthermore, if the poverty headcount is switched from $1 to $2 a day, which is a more realistic measure of poverty for the US than the PPP adjusted poverty figure, then even the Bank's own problematic figures look less promising, for the number in this category *increased* between 1981 and 2001 from 2.45 to 2.74 billion, a rise of 12 per cent. This has enormous implications for assessing the MDGs, because it may be that it is not the case that poverty has actually been reduced, merely *the way in which poverty is calculated.*

What then of the relationship between poverty reduction and globalization? The World Bank 2002 report *Globalization, Growth and Poverty* argues that poverty reduction has taken place because of globalization-friendly policies. However, the central contentions of this work are seriously flawed (Wade 2003a; Kiely 2007a) for at least five reasons: (i) it uses trade/GDP ratios as a proxy for openness, but this measures trade outcomes and not trade policy; (ii) in any case the trade/GDP ratios of many of the poorest countries are not low – the average in 1997–98 for the poorest 39 countries was 43 per cent, about the same as the world average (UNCTAD 2002a: part 2, chapter 3); (iii) the Bank attempts to overcome this problem by measuring changes in trade/GDP ratios (from 1977 to 1997), rather than actual amounts, but this has the effect of excluding those with high but unchanging ratios from the list of high globalizers, and this would include many poor countries with little or no growth in this period; (iv) following on from this point, China and India have seen shifts in these ratios, as well as trade policy such as tariff rates, but they are not more open than some of the poorest developing countries that have experienced little growth. Average tariff rates in India did decline from 80 per cent at the start of the 1990s to 40 per cent at the end of the decade, while China's declined from 42.4 per cent to 31.2 per cent in the same period, but the latter figures remain higher than the average for developing countries (Rodrik 2001); (v) if we measure trade policy indicators such as average tariff rates, then the Bank's own data suggest that if we measure openness not by trade/GDP ratios or changes in these ratios since 1975, but instead focus on trade and investment policies in 1997, allegedly high globalizers had higher average tariffs (35 per cent) than low globalizers (20 per cent) (Sumner 2004: 1174).

The International Monetary Fund's index of trade restrictiveness measures trade policy through quantifying average tariff rates and non-tariff barriers, and there is no evidence of greater trade restrictiveness on the part of the poorest countries. Thus even if there has been poverty reduction, it is unclear that this is because of globalization-friendly policies. Moreover, the assumption that the poor can simply be lifted out of poverty by economic growth, common in popular books like Paul Collier's *The Bottom Billion* (2008), can be challenged. Based on World Bank data, Sumner (2010) estimates that in 1990, 93 per cent of the world's poor lived in low-income countries (that is, the very poorest countries), but by 2007–8, 75 per cent of the world's poor lived in middle-income countries (that is, the next category of poor countries.) To some extent, this reflects the fact that some low-income countries have moved up to middle-income countries between 1990 and 2007–8, but equally, it shows that the benefits of economic growth do not automatically trickle down to the poor.

The boom in foreign investment should also be treated with considerable scepticism. Although foreign investment levels have increased, this often reflected a shift in ownership from the state to private sector, rather than genuinely new, 'greenfield' investment. Indeed, investment/GDP ratios were lower across the board since the reform process started in the early 1980s. Thus, investment/GDP ratios for sub-Saharan Africa fell from a peak of around 23 per cent in the early 1980s to around 15 per cent in 1985, but by 2000 they were only up to around 17 per cent. For the big Latin America five (Argentina, Brazil, Chile, Colombia and Mexico), the investment/GDP ratio peaked at close to 25 per cent in 1981, falling to 16 per cent by 1984. By 1989, just before the FDI boom, it stood at 19 per cent, and by 2000, it had only increased to 20 per cent (Kozul Wright and Rayment 2004: 30). Similarly, while it is true that there has been an increase in manufacturing in the developing world, sceptics suggest that this alone does not constitute 'development'. The issue of Chinese development is also relevant to this point, and both will be discussed in the next section.

Finally, the onset of global recession in 2008 has led to a significant reduction of the capital flows to developing economies, much of which had been used to finance debt-led consumer booms rather than genuine industrial development. Primary commodity prices have remained high due to demand from China and financial speculation in certain commodity markets, but serious questions remain over whether this is sustainable and whether specialization in primary goods can provide sufficient linkages throughout an economy and reduce poverty in any substantial way.

These points reinforce earlier, dependency-oriented views, that while certain policies do affect particular development trajectories, so too do the structured inequalities of the world economy. Some places are in a structurally subordinate and dependent position in the world economy. Just how they are dependent and subordinate is discussed in the next section.

## Explaining inequality and underdevelopment in the world economy

While there is strong evidence to back up the claims of both the optimists and the sceptics, the last section suggested that the latter are on the whole more convincing. The implication that follows, and which in some respects replicates the claims of (some versions of) dependency theory, is that there are structured inequalities that constrain late developers, making it difficult to overcome inequality and underdevelopment. Unlike the claims of cruder versions of dependency theory, however, these are not insurmountable, but (unlike the claims of neoliberalism or modernization theory) they are real obstacles.

The first point to note is that while foreign investment has increased, it remains concentrated in the developed world. As was stated above, about two-thirds of foreign capital goes to the developed, and one-third to the developing world, and this itself is highly concentrated. Between 1993 and 1998, 'developed countries' received 61.2 per cent of world FDI, developing countries 35.3 per cent, and the former communist European countries 3.5 per cent (UNCTAD 2002b: 3–5). For 1999–2000, foreign investment inflows to the developed world constituted 80 per cent of total FDI, and the proportion going to developing countries constituted only 17.9 per cent of the total (UNCTAD 2002b: 5). By 2006, out of a total of US$1.3 trillion, developed countries received US$857 billion and developing countries US$379 billion, with transition economies receiving US$69 billion (UNCTAD 2007: 2–3). By 2009 developing and transition (former socialist) cconomies accounted for almost 50 per cent of the total global share of foreign investment inflows, but this reflects less a convergence between developed and developing countries, and more the significant decline in the amount of foreign investment in recent years. The 16 per cent global decline in 2008 was followed by a 37 per cent fall in 2009: what has happened, then, is that the amount going to developing countries has declined recently, but it has just done so less steeply than the amount received by developed countries (UNCTAD 2010: 2–3), and the opposite trend has occurred in previous periods of economic upturns. On the whole, over a 20-year period, we can say that the direction of foreign investment is highly unequal, with developing countries receiving around one-third of the global total, and of this third, the lion's share goes to only a small number of developing countries.

While foreign investment figures do not tell the whole story, as there may be subcontracting agreements by foreign firms to local firms, it is also the case that on a per capita basis, FDI is even more concentrated, as developing countries make up a large proportion of the population. But perhaps most important, *the type* of manufacturing that is generally occurring in the developing world is not necessarily overcoming underdevelopment. Since the reform period started in the 1980s, while the developed countries' share of manufacturing exports fell (from 82.3 per cent in 1980 to 70.9 per cent by 1997), their share of manufacturing value added actually *increased* over the same period, from 64.5 per cent to 73.3 per cent. Over the same period, Latin America's share of world manufacturing exports increased from 1.5 per cent to 3.5 per cent, but its share of manufacturing value added fell from 7.1 per cent to 6.7 per cent (Kozul Wright and Rayment 2004: 14). For developing countries as a whole, manufacturing output's contribution to GDP has barely changed since 1960: it stood at 21.5 per cent in 1960, and had increased to just 22.7 per cent in 2000. There is significant regional variation, with East Asia particularly expanding, but these figures hardly tell a story of increasing convergence or even the end of inequality. By the end of the 1990s, developing countries as a whole accounted for only 10 per cent of total world exports of goods with a high research and development technological complexity and/or scale component (UNCTAD 2002a: 56).

What these figures suggest is that developed countries still tend to dominate in high-value sectors, based on high barriers to entry, high start-up and running costs, and significant skill levels. In the developing world, where there are large amounts of surplus labour, barriers to entry, skills and wages are low. While this gives such countries considerable competitive advantage in terms of low start-up and labour costs, at the same time the fact that those barriers to entry are low means that competition is particularly intense and largely determined by cost price, which also means low wages. Thus, the clothing industry, where developing countries have achieved considerable increases in world export shares in recent years, has a very low degree of market concentration. In contrast, more capital-intensive or high-tech sectors have very high degrees of market concentration, and are mainly located in the developed world (UNCTAD 2002a: 120–3).

The optimistic, neoliberal, response is that these labour-intensive sectors are only a starting point, allowing countries to upgrade as more developed countries shift to higher-value production. But actually in practice upgrading has occurred by states deliberately protecting themselves from import competition from established producers, via a process of import substitution industrialization. In the context of a tendency towards free trade, upgrading is far from inevitable and indeed, faced with competition from established overseas producers, is unlikely to occur.

We thus return to the claims of the Prebsich-Singer thesis. However, rather than focusing on trade between primary goods and industrial goods, we now need to examine *different kinds of industrial goods*. A number of studies have suggested that the prices of manufacturing exports from developing countries have tended to fall against more complex manufacturing and services from developed countries, including Chinese exports (Maizels *et al.* 1998; Zheng 2002). Intense competition within sectors where barriers to entry are low leads to competition between developing countries all trying to increase their exports in low-value manufacturing. Seen in this way, China's growth is less an opportunity for other developing countries, and more one that resembles a zero-sum game. On the other hand, as we have seen, China's growth has facilitated a primary commodities boom, which optimists claim could lay the basis for development. But over-dependence on one or two primary commodities is always precarious, as countries are adversely affected when demand falls. For development to occur, there needs to be far more diversity in production, and a shift towards scale economies, technological sophistication, skills and infrastructure – neither low-value manufacturing nor primary commodity production can provide this, and neither are they likely to in the future. There are thus indeed structured inequalities in the global economy, and these are particularly acute for would-be late developers.

## Conclusion

This chapter has outlined debates on inequality and underdevelopment, and has shown how earlier debates over modernization and underdevelopment continue to influence current debates over the relationship between globalization and development. In reviewing both optimistic and sceptical accounts concerning a positive relationship between the two, the chapter has suggested that the latter position is more convincing. But there are two further questions that need to be addressed, at least briefly. First, why does inequality matter? And second, what are the alternatives?

In terms of the importance of inequality, the argument is often made that it is an inevitable feature of all societies, and it is better to have a richer but unequal society, than a more egalitarian but poorer society. Related to this point, an additional argument made is that inequality does not matter so long as people are lifted out of poverty. There are three responses to this. First, while it may be the case that inequality is an unintended outcome of the social interaction of millions of individuals, the fact that it is unintended does not mean that efforts should not be made to alleviate it. If we are to take the claims made for democracy and equal opportunity seriously, then there is a need for collective action both nationally, and within the international order, to alleviate inequality. Just because no single individual intended certain unequal outcomes, it does not follow that no-one is responsible for them. Second, inequality may be socially and even economically dysfunctional. This is because it can be linked to crime and anti-social behaviour, and it can undermine sound economic principles. It is clear that the financial crisis of 2007 onwards must in part be linked to attempts to sustain financial expansion through the granting of credit to people (and countries) that could ill afford to pay it back. When this became clear – in the sub-prime mortgage crash in the US and the sovereign debt crisis in Europe – the economic results were devastating. Third, the generation of inequality is cumulative, as capital tends to concentrate in certain areas and bypass or marginalize other parts of the globe. It is therefore wrong to suggest that poverty and inequality can be entirely separated – it is true that the wealth of a specific rich individual is not caused by the poverty of a specific individual in the developing world. But both are part of a social order which encourages the concentration of capital in some areas and marginalization in others.

These points lead to the final issue, which is that of alternatives to neoliberalism. The current economic crisis may lead to a new international order, where a more 'managed' capitalism, perhaps along the lines of the Bretton Woods order, re-emerges (see Bisley, and Beeson, this volume). However, increased state intervention per se does not mean the end of neoliberalism – contrary to neoliberal ideology, neoliberal policy has always included a great deal of state intervention, not least to extend market regulation. Moreover, much of the response to the crisis has been to cut public spending and expand the rule of the market. What then of national alternatives, based on the revival of ISI policies? The World Trade Organization (WTO) rules are far less conducive to such policies than was the case in the era of ISI. Moreover, the domestic social alliances that encouraged ISI policies after 1945 have broken down. It is therefore likely that national capitals, happy with access to global circuits of capital and uninterested in developmentalist policies that would encourage productive investment, would oppose a return to ISI. Recent events in Latin America bear this out: the policies of President Hugo Chávez in Venezuela, for example, have experienced considerable opposition from wealthy elites.

But perhaps most fundamentally, like neoliberalism, ISI is premised on the belief that upgrading to a 'developed capitalism' can occur so long as the correct policies are carried out. The disagreement is over what policies are deemed to be 'correct'. In a context where 'value added', upgrading and thus development is increasingly derived from monopolized information (embedded in WTO rules), it is unclear that technical policies of upgrading will lead to sustained 'modernization' and the eradication of 'underdevelopment'. While policies matter, so do power relations, both at the national and international levels. Only a radical transformation of these relations is likely to seriously challenge inequality and underdevelopment.

## Guide to further reading

Frank (1969) is the major statement of underdevelopment theory. Held and Kaya (eds) (2007) is a useful reader on the debates over the relationship between globalization and inequality. Kiely (2007b) challenges the optimistic account and relates the debates back to older theories of development. Rostow (1960) is the major book associated with modernization theory. UNCTAD (2002a) usefully outlines a sceptical account of the relationship between globalization and inequality, with much useful, if now dated, empirical data. World Bank (2002) is the main official argument that proposes an optimistic account of the relationship between globalization and poverty reduction.

# Chapter 12

# Population Movement and its Impact on World Politics

*ANNE HAMMERSTAD*

The movement of people has helped shape the trajectory of history for as long as human communities have existed. Since the first groups of modern humans left Africa to populate the world some 60,000 years ago, population movements have brought with them prosperity and devastation, cultural enrichment and annihilation, co-operation and conflict. Mass migration has contributed to the collapse of some empires (the migration of Visigoths, Vandals and other peoples leading to the sacking of Rome in the year 410) and the construction of others (the mass emigration to the US from Europe in the 19th and early 20th centuries). More recently, technological innovations have made long-distance relocation cheaper and easier, while the combination of globalization and inequality has primed the world's working-age population to consider migration as a natural path to achieve economic opportunities and betterment. Add to this the political repression and wars that still riddle many parts of the world, ensuring continuing high numbers of refugees, asylum seekers and other forced migrants, and it is safe to say that the movement of people will continue to be a salient feature of global politics throughout the 21st century.

As the dynamics of forced migration makes clear, people do not only move out of desire for a better life. For many the decision to migrate is taken more out of necessity than choice. In the academic literature, there tends to be a distinction between migration studies and forced migration studies – a distinction strengthened by the fact that research on the two areas is often conducted in separate institutes and centres. As has been increasingly recognized over the past decade, the distinctions between different categories of migrants (forced/voluntary, legal/illegal, regular/irregular, economic/political, internal/external) have become increasingly blurred. At one end of the voluntary/forced spectrum we find highly educated professionals moving between countries in pursuit of career opportunities and welcomed by their host country due to the skills and resources they bring with them. At the other end we find poor villagers gathering up their children and fleeing across a border to escape war and ethnic cleansing, who find shelter of a sort in a refugee camp supported by international aid agencies. Between these extremes (each is a minority among international migrants) are a large group of people who migrate for a varied mix of personal, political, economic and security reasons. The reception these migrants get in their host countries is also mixed, but over the past two decades the trend has been one of increasing unease and even fear over immigration levels. This trend has been particularly noticeable in the rich North, but is also found in the developing South.

This chapter will discuss the challenges and opportunities posed by population movement in the 21st century. It asks why population movement is such a contentious issue. It addresses this question by investigating whether the present 'age of migration' (Castles and Miller 2009) is indeed characterized by unprecedented migration levels, or whether our understanding of current migration challenges lacks historical depth. It looks at what is old and what is new about migration trends, and although it argues that today's population movements do pose some unprecedented challenges, this is as much a result of the response to immigration as of the number and characteristics of migrants themselves.

## An age of migration?

International migration – the movement of people across sovereign borders – has caused widespread concern among the public and politicians both in the global North and the global South. The topic receives frequent news coverage, both of the more alarmist and the more supportive kind. According to an *Economist* special report, migrants are a 'new force that is reshaping our world' (Roberts 2008). The report, in line with the magazine's liberal outlook, sees this as a challenging but mostly positive force, but documents the widespread backlash against migration, both in terms of public opinion and policy decisions. This hardening of attitudes has been described by migration analysts as well. Luedtke (2009) shows an increasingly restrictive trend in EU (European Union) policies since 9/11, where EU harmonization in the immigration sphere has mostly meant adopting the practices of the members with the harshest pre-existing rules and practices. In the US, the events of 9/11 induced a narrower focus on border control, and bolstered, however spuriously, a populist backlash aimed more against Mexican illegal immigrants than Islamist terrorists. Attempts at reforming and liberalizing the country's immigration regime in 2006–7 were derailed, and the only policy on which the House of Representatives and the Senate managed to agree was the Secure Fence Act, creating 700 miles of fencing and surveillance along the US–Mexican border (Rosenblum 2009: 13). Similar barriers have gone up in the global South. Regional powers South Africa and India have both erected border fences in an (ineffective) attempt to keep out undocumented immigrants from their poorer and more troubled neighbours, Zimbabwe and Bangladesh, respectively. The rise of violence and hostility against immigrants has been visible across the world. It could be seen in, for example, the xenophobic riots and murders in South Africa in 2008; in the clashes between Bodo 'indigenes' and Bengali 'settlers' in the north-east Indian state of Assam in 2012; in the decision of Bangladesh to push back Rohingyas fleeing ethnic cleansing in Myanmar that same year; in the many attacks on sub-Saharan African migrants during the civil war in Libya in 2011; and in the practice by southern European coastguards in the Mediterranean of forcing back leaking vessels filled to the brim with migrants trying to reach European shores from North Africa, contributing to the loss of hundreds of lives at sea every year.

How has migration, whether of the voluntary, forced or mixed kind, become such a controversial topic in world politics? In order to assess the challenges and opportunities created by international migration, it is useful to ask first in what ways they differ from earlier eras of migration. Are we indeed living in 'an age of migration' (Castles and Miller 2009), characterized by unprecedented levels of population movement? The answer is both yes and no. Immigration levels are high today compared with recent history, and have accelerated in the past couple of decades. Not even the global economic downturn of recent years has made much of a dent in international migration figures, although it has to some extent affected the direction of flows, leaving some countries less sought-after as migration destinations (IOM 2011: 49). In Europe in modern times, immigration is mostly a post-1945 phenomenon (*emigration*, on the other hand, is an age-old European pursuit). In the 1960s, when Enoch Powell made his infamous reference to 'rivers of blood', less than five per cent of Britain's population was foreign born. By 2001, this proportion had increased to 8.3 per cent (ONS 2005: 133), and by 2010, bolstered by the opening of the UK labour market to eastern European EU members, to 11.8 per cent (ONS 2011: 6).

However, if one takes the long view, there is nothing remarkable about today's levels of migration. As de Haas (2005) points out, in proportion to the world's population, migration levels are no higher today than they were at the height of the last great wave of migrants a century ago. Then as now, international migrants constituted 2.5–3 per cent of the world's population (IOM 2008: 4). Even after two decades of fast and sustained immigration growth in the US, the foreign-born proportion of the population was still lower in 2007 (12.6 per cent) than at the previous immigration peak in 1910 (14.7 per cent) (MPI 2007). Looking even further back, the era around 300 to 700 is known as the Migration Period. It ushered in the Middle Ages in Europe and had a far stronger impact on social, economic and political relations than anything seen in the modern age.

Turning to *forced* migration, there is nothing spectacular about today's levels either. Consider, for instance, the human upheavals during and immediately after the Second World War. In May 1945, around 40 million people were displaced in Europe alone. Among them some 13 million ethnic Germans were expelled from the Soviet Union, Poland and other eastern European countries, many of whom perished on their march westwards (UNHCR 2000: 13). Added to this came the millions of Chinese displaced by Japan during the war; the exodus of some 750,000 to 900,000 refugees from Palestine after the creation of Israel in 1947 and the first Arab–Israeli war in 1947–9; and the estimated 14 million uprooted in the violent 'population exchange' after the partition of India in 1947. In other words, rapid and large refugee movements are not a phenomenon unique to the post-Cold War period.

Having provided some historical perspective, there are nevertheless good reasons for arguing that there are distinctive aspects of contemporary migration.

Migration numbers (not proportions) are unprecedented; the direction of migration flows has changed; and migration control and management practices are taking on new dimensions, linked to the criminalization of migration and the rise of a migration security agenda. All are linked to the phenomenon of globalization, which may be argued to have led to unprecedented migration challenges – at least in modern history.

## Migration numbers

Due to massive population growth over the past 100 years, the actual *number* of migrants is vastly higher now than it was in the early 20th century. For instance, the 14.7 per cent of the US population that was foreign born in 1910 amounted to 13.5 million people. In 2007, a proportion of 12.6 per cent equalled a foreign-born population of over 38 million people. The cumulative effect of migration in the post-war period has also led to significant demographic changes in some countries, especially in major cities. In London, one in three residents in 2007 was non-UK born (ONS 2009: 23). In that sense today's mass migration is at an unprecedented level. Most migration, whether internal or international, is towards urban centres, and the world's fast-growing mega-cities are increasingly diverse and multi-ethnic, teeming with new arrivals from nearby rural areas as well as abroad.

Regarding forced migration figures, the trend has been more uneven, with a peak in the early 1990s. As a proportion of overall international migration figures, forced migration remains small. While there are something like 200 million migrants worldwide, the United Nations High Commissioner for Refugees (UNHCR) estimated that, in 2010, there were approximately 11.5 million refugees and asylum seekers (UNHCR 2011b: 21–4). Despite this, the *impact* of displacement across borders on world politics has taken on a new significance. First, although mass and sudden refugee flows are not a new phenomenon, the frequency with which we have seen large-scale refugee flows leading to humanitarian emergencies in the post-Cold War period is unprecedented. Conflicts in Iraq (1991 and 2003), Rwanda (1994), Bosnia (1992–5), Kosovo (1999), East Timor (1999), Darfur/Chad (2003), Libya (2011), Syria (2012), Somalia (over the past two decades) and Afghanistan (over the past three decades) are just some of the post-Cold War world's sources of mass refugee movements.

In addition a new and contested category of forced or partly forced migrants, 'environmentally induced migration', has in recent years been introduced as part of the climate change debate. Influential reports such as the Stern Review (Stern 2007: 6) have cited alarmist estimates of hundreds of millions of people forced on the move by 2050 due to environmental strain. The figure is taken from a widely quoted but methodologically flawed estimation by Norman Myers (see Myers and Kent 1995 and Myers 2002) and has been used to posit climate change-related migration as the next big global security challenge. More methodologically sound and empirically grounded research rejects such claims, but suggests that climate change is likely to add momentum and volume to existing migration patterns (for an overview of this research, see Foresight 2011). It is clear that migration will be an important option for individuals and societies in their responses to worsening environmental conditions such as rising sea levels, melting glaciers and desertification. There are also signs that environmental shocks (tsunamis, typhoons, earthquakes and other natural disasters) are more frequently leading to sudden mass movements of people (IOM 2011: 52–3), although not usually across international borders.

Second, due to the rise of the norm of humanitarian intervention, most recently in the manifestation of a Responsibility to Protect (see Bellamy, this volume), forced migration leads more frequently to international interventions (Roberts 1998). Since the end of the Cold War, refugee movements have been frequently listed in the United Nations Security Council as cause for international action. In the cases of Haiti (1993) and Northern Iraq (1991), refugee situations were determined as a 'threat to international peace and security' and used to justify coercive action under Chapter VII of the UN Charter. Thus, even though the main impact of forced migration continues to be limited to certain regions in the global South, the question of how to respond to this problem has become a dilemma of global politics.

Third, the international refugee regime (consisting of the 1951 UN Convention on the Status of Refugees and its 1967 Protocol, the UNHCR and several regional refugee conventions) asserts the right of individuals to seek asylum and not to be returned to their home country if in danger of persecution (*non-refoulement*). This means that, in the developed world, each asylum application must be treated on an individual basis. Thus asylum seekers cannot be controlled in terms of the numbers and background of those arriving. As legal labour migration channels from the global South to the global North have narrowed, the potential loophole provided by cumbersome asylum determination procedures has been seized on as a way into Northern labour markets. This said, the vast majority of the world's asylum seekers come from war-torn or repressive countries. Although economic betterment constitutes an important reason behind many asylum seekers' decision to make the journey to Europe, North America or Australia, often travelling illegally, it does not follow that they do not also have political or humanitarian claims to remain in their country of destination.

While the dilemma of how to deal with so-called mixed flows of refugees and labour migrants is not an entirely new phenomenon, its scale and political significance have grown dramatically since the end of the Cold War. As refugees and asylum seekers can now be found across the world, they affect a larger number of states in both the North and the South, causing Loescher (1993) to declare a *global* refugee crisis. The early 1990s saw a steep rise in asylum applications in developed countries, especially Europe. From around 20,000 asylum applications in Europe in 1976 (Loescher 1993: 111), numbers peaked in the European Union during the wars in the Balkans, with 667,770 applications in 1992, down to a still high 291,220 in 1998 (UNHCR 1999: Table V1) and, after some fluctuations, 220,360 in 2010 (UNHCR 2011b: Table 1. This figure covers only the 'old' EU countries; including the 12 new EU members, the figure becomes 235,900). In recent years, the European Union's status as the main asylum hot spot has reduced, with South Africa becoming the world's number one asylum destination in 2008, and Turkey transforming from a migrant transition country to a major asylum destination country in its own right in 2011–12 (UNHCR 2012).

To sum up, the world has never before seen so many people on the move, and global migration has accelerated in pace. The trend is linked to the long period of economic growth we have seen in many parts of the developing world, especially Asia, since it is generally not the poorest people of the world who become international migrants. In order to make the journey from one country to another, some resources are necessary. Thus, part of the migration boom since the end of the Cold War should be seen in conjunction with the success of countries such as China and India in lifting millions of people out of abject poverty during the same period. Since high economic growth continues (so far) in these countries, despite the global economic downturn, global migration levels are likely to remain high. Although fewer legal immigrants have arrived in crisis-ridden countries such as Greece and Spain, there are no signs yet of *undocumented* migration from the South to the North Mediterranean abating. Furthermore, a slight slowdown in new arrivals to the global North has not affected the accumulative global stock of international migrants (IOM 2011: 49).

## Direction of flows – still a regional phenomenon

The rise in asylum requests in the North in the 1990s is an example of how the *direction* of migration flows is changing. In the previous age of migration, those on the move were mostly Europeans resettling in the New World or European colonies. Another substantial migrant group were colonial subjects moved from one colony to another, such as the indentured labourers moved by the British from India to African colonies. Today a substantial minority of the world's migrants make their journey from the global South to the global North. The change is particularly visible in Europe, which has gone from a continent of emigration, to one of immigration. As a result, many previously homogeneous states in Europe have, at least in their major cities, attained a multicultural hue.

Despite the picture given by the European media of a relentless flow of rickety boats laden with migrants setting out across the Mediterranean from North Africa to Europe, it should be kept in mind that most international migration remains intra-regional. Only a relatively small proportion of migration flows are South–North. For instance, according to an IOM (2008) presentation, of 8.5 million West African migrants in 2008, 7.5 million had moved within the region and the remaining 1 million to Europe and the US. We can see the same trend for refugees and asylum seekers. Looking at the world's largest refugee population, 96 per cent of the three million Afghan refugees are in neighbouring Pakistan and Iran (UNHCR, 2011a: 26–7).

The inter-regional trend even holds for asylum seekers. South Africa was by far the most popular asylum destination in 2010. 81 per cent (146,600 out of 180,600) of applicants that year came from neighbouring Zimbabwe (UNHCR 2011b: 42). Of the six main countries of origin of asylum seekers in 2005 (Burma, Somalia, Serbia and Montenegro, the Russian Federation, the Democratic Republic of Congo and China), only among the Chinese asylum seekers did the majority travel beyond their own region to apply for asylum. Of the rest, most went no further than a neighbouring state (UNHCR 2006a: Tables 1, 2, 6; UNHCR 2006b: 7–8). The only mass flows of refugees and asylum seekers to European countries in the post-Cold War period have come from within the region – from the countries of the former Yugoslavia and, to a lesser extent, Russia.

The only part of the world in which the direction of international migration is mainly South to North is the Americas. Notably, 87 per cent of total migration in the Americas region is from Latin America and the Caribbean to North America (IOM 2008: 423).

## Responses to migration movements: migration management and control

The responses to challenges posed by international migration have also taken some new forms. Here I will first look at domestic politics, before moving on to the increased international interaction and co-operation to attempt to regulate, manage and control migration flows.

Despite the fact that most migrants stay within their region of origin, the sheer number of people on the move, together with growth in South–North migration, have nevertheless made immigration and asylum a highly salient issue in domestic politics across the globe, from South Africa in the South to Scandinavia in the North. In Western Europe, the steep rise in asylum applications in the early 1990s contributed to strong electoral results for far-right parties in countries such as Austria, Denmark, France, the Netherlands and Norway. Consequently, 'talking tough on immigration' has also become a mainstream pursuit, leading some analysts to argue that the mainstream political parties have allowed the far right too much influence on immigration and asylum agendas (Bralo and Morrison 2005). Since the end of the Cold War there has been a gradual tightening of legal migration routes across the global North, entailing harsher visa regimes and stricter border controls. This has been particularly visible in the case of asylum systems, where preventative (and punitive) measures against asylum seekers have taken the form of detention centres, withdrawal of the right to work pending application outcomes and distributing benefit payments in vouchers instead of money. In South Africa, the authorities' inability to stem the influx of Zimbabweans fleeing economic and political crisis at home (as well as undocumented immigrants from all over southern Africa) contributed to the township riots and xenophobic attacks that left more than 50 people dead in May 2008.

National measures to clamp down on unauthorized migration can be seen as a series of 'beggar-thy-neighbour' strategies with global effects (Hans and Suhrke 1997: 84), where each country tries to make itself less attractive than its neighbour, thus shifting the burden of hosting refugees, asylum seekers and unwanted migrants onto other states. In terms of protection of the human right to seek asylum, this unilateralism has resulted in a race to the bottom, leading the UNHCR to warn about a crisis in the international refugee protection regime (see, e.g., UNHCR 2004: §5) as asylum practices have become more about migration control, spurred by domestic political and security considerations, than about asylum obligations incurred by international law.

One way of avoiding this race to the bottom is through multilateral co-operation and co-ordination, and particularly through strengthening international migration (and forced migration) management regimes and organizations. There has been a flurry of regional and global initiatives in recent years, all with the aim of harnessing the positive aspects of international migration – for migrants themselves and for their host and home communities – and counteracting the negative aspects, especially trafficking and people smuggling. Migration issues are now routinely placed high on the agendas of various regional and global institutions, such as the UN, the EU, the World Bank, the Organization for Security and Cooperation in Europe (OSCE) and the African Union. In addition, migration-specific institutions such as the International Organization for Migration (IOM) have been strengthened and a variety of migration-specific processes have been created to foster international co-operation (Solomon 2005: 1–2).

An overarching international migration regime is difficult to achieve, since states value control over their migration policies in order to be flexible to adapt these to the changing demands of economic and political circumstances (Solomon 2005). An added problem is the schism between the perceptions and needs of developed and developing states in migration management. For instance, while the South voices concern about the effect of a 'brain drain' on their economies, countries in the North usually welcome skilled migrants but put pressure on Southern states to stop undocumented migration of unskilled workers from the South to the North.

The same North–South tension can be seen in the international refugee regime. There have been several attempts at serious reform of the refugee regime in the 21st century in order to achieve better burden sharing and deal more efficiently and humanely with so-called 'mixed flows' of forced and economically motivated migration. None of these efforts have had much success. This has to a large extent been due to the mistrust between the North and the South. Attempts by Northern states, especially in the EU, to contain refugees in regions of origin and to negotiate return agreements with so-called 'safe first countries of asylum', are broadly seen by refugee-hosting countries of the South as attempts at burden shifting rather than burden sharing (Hammerstad 2011; Loescher *et al.* 2008: 62–6). The outcry over asylum seekers in the North is particularly resented in the South, considering that three-quarters of refugees seek shelter no further than across the border to a neighbouring country (UNHCR 2011b: 24) and the vast majority remain in the South, to be cared for by some of the world's poorest countries.

Considering these obstacles, combined with the fact that most migration remains intra-regional, it is not surprising that most migration management initiatives have been regional, rather than global. Regional Consultative Processes

(RCPs) supported by the IOM have sprung up in all parts of the world. These RCPs are not institutions or organizations, but informal, non-binding and open forums for dialogue with low levels of bureaucracy and rules. Such processes aim to foster common understandings, consider policy options and arrive at consensus views which may lay the foundation for subsequent formal regional agreements (Koppenfels 2001: 9; IOM 2011).

Despite difficulties in evaluating achievements of regional and international migration management processes (Koppenfels 2001: 6; Solomon 2005: 4–5), a picture is emerging of an ever denser and more far-reaching web of informal discussion forums, initiatives and Plans of Action. As such, international processes play an increasingly significant role in the migration management strategies of individual states, although there is a long (and probably unrealistic) way to go before it is possible to talk about a global migration regime.

Moving on to *formal* and binding international co-operation on migration policies, the tense climate created by the terror attacks of 9/11, compounded by recession and rising unemployment in many Northern states, have undermined efforts to achieve comprehensive migration management frameworks involving migrant-sending as well as immigrant-receiving states. Instead, agreements have focused largely on *immigration control* – with the aim of deterring and preventing asylum seekers, limiting unskilled immigrants and controlling skilled migration. The fate of the EU's Tampere Conclusions is an illustrative example. In 1999, the EU agreed on an ambitious migration policy integration programme. The Tampere Conclusions affirmed the right to seek asylum, the commitment of EU countries to the UN Refugee Convention, the fair treatment of immigrants, their integration into host societies and the provision of equal rights for immigrants. However, Luedtke (2009: 144) argues that this process was derailed by 9/11, and that the EU's substantial integration of immigration policies since 1999 has become an opportunity for member states to withdraw rather than enhance the rights of non-EU immigrants by setting the lowest common denominator as EU-wide standards, and by doing so in the name of national security and the war against terrorism. However, it should be kept in mind that this tightening of non-EU immigration went hand in hand with an explosion of intra-EU migration after the admission of nine eastern European countries and Malta into the organization in 2004.

## The pros and cons of international migration – why a backlash?

The EU harmonization process has, in common with other recent national and regional efforts at controlling migration, such as the US, Indian and South African border fences against their poorer neighbours, a particular concern with policing and security aspects of migration management. The focus has been on 'irregular' and 'illegal' migration, 'bogus asylum seekers', 'mixed flows' (of refugees and economic migrants), people smuggling, trafficking and in general what has been termed 'the criminalisation of migration' (Haas 2005: 13).

With international terrorism added to this already heady mixture of concern and fear over migration, it can also be argued that there has been a partial *securitization* of population movements. The impact of 9/11 was immediately felt by advocates of the rights of refugees and asylum seekers. Only a few weeks after the terror attacks on New York and Washington, the UNHCR placed states' anti-terror and security-based efforts to restrict asylum within a broader context of the increasing criminalization of asylum seekers and refugees, and called for resolute leadership 'to de-dramatize and de-politicize the essentially humanitarian challenge of protecting refugees and to promote better understanding of refugees and their right to seek asylum' (UNHCR 2001). The next section will address the concerns and fears raised by immigration by investigating its impact on economies, culture/identity and political security. Although I will mainly discuss host communities, as the phenomenon has global reach and consequences, it is also necessary to look at effects on sending states, as well as on global politics.

## Migration's benefits: an uneven picture

It is not straightforward to determine the economic impact of migration, or to assess whether this impact is mainly of a beneficial or harmful nature. This is partly because migration figures are not accurate, a particular problem in the case of irregular migration (defined by IOM (2008: 203) as 'migrants whose status does not conform, for one reason or another, to the norms of the country in which they reside') – which the International Labour Organization (ILO) estimates constitutes around 10–15 per cent of all international migration (IOM 2008: 209). The difficulty is also due to the political controversies surrounding immigration, which have made cost–benefit analyses often highly politicized.

What is safe to say is that migration's benefits are uneven, whether viewed from the perspective of sending country or host country. Focusing on sending countries first, emigration can be a pressure valve for countries such as the Philippines and Morocco with fast-growing and youthful populations and high unemployment – as indeed it was for European countries such as Ireland and Norway in the 19th and early 20th centuries. It can also be a political pressure valve. For instance, a disproportionate number of the estimated 1.5–3 million Zimbabweans living in South Africa come from the south-western parts of Zimbabwe, the stronghold of the opposition Movement for Democratic Change. This constitutes a 'voter drain' that is likely to skew future election results in favour of the ruling ZANU-PF party (Hammerstad 2012).

But emigration can also hamper development. Since it is often the resourceful and educated who take the leap, emigration can rob developing countries of their most valuable workers and entrepreneurs. Some argue that the 'brain drain' hinders development while others point out that it is underdevelopment and poor economic opportunity, corruption and inefficient bureaucracies that lead the bright and the educated to seek greener pastures elsewhere (Roberts 2008).

The question of the value of remittances is another issue that is high on the migration research agenda. First, the levels of remittances cannot be measured straightforwardly, since many are not transferred through official channels. This is especially the case for irregular migrants, but regular migrants may also choose cheaper alternatives to official transfer channels. The World Bank estimated the size of remittances worldwide in 2010 at around US$440 billion, of which US$325 billion went to developing countries. But since this estimate is based on formal transfers the World Bank agrees it is certainly too low (World Bank 2011b: 19). Nevertheless, even if a conservative estimate, this is a significant transfer from North to South, dwarfing that of official Overseas Development Aid (ODI), which stands at around US$100 billion a year, and outpacing the growth of foreign direct investment (FDI) flows globally (World Bank 2011b: 19). Furthermore, remittances have shown themselves to be more resilient to the global downturn than FDI and ODI. From 2008 to 2009, FDI in developing countries fell dramatically from US$593 billion to US$359, while remittances in the same period dipped from US$325 to US$307 billion – only to recover in 2010 and increase again in 2011. In many countries remittances are higher than earnings from major export commodities. In Tajikistan, 35 per cent of GDP came from remittances in 2009, and for 21 further countries remittances constituted ten per cent or more of their GDP (World Bank 2011b: 14).

Early research on remittances tended to dismiss their significance, suggesting that they merely increase immediate consumption among the migrant's friends and family. Today it is clear that remittances can have a strong developmental role. It is a capital flow unhampered by bureaucracy and corruption, which tends to improve nutrition, health and education among recipients. It can also take the form of highly efficient micro-level direct investment when migrants put money into small businesses back home. Due to the size of remittance flows, the question of how to maximize their impact on development is high on the research agenda of the World Bank, IOM and migration research centres across the world.

The economic impact on migrants' host countries is also uneven. In the UK, the anti-immigration think tank Migration Watch released a controversial study in 2007 suggesting that the overall economic contribution of immigrants to GDP per capita was almost negligible. It suggested that the very small 'fiscal benefit to the host population' (Migration Watch 2007a) was far outweighed by the social costs of migration on 'already overburdened infrastructure, housing, health and schools' and 'an increasing impact on employment and added strains on community cohesion' (Migration Watch 2007b). Others argue that the UK economy would not have boomed in the 1990s and the first half of the 2000s, were it not for young and dynamic immigrants working in a range of sectors from construction to banking and hospitals. The strain on infrastructure is mostly a short-term planning problem for local authorities needing to adapt schooling and housing policies to include the new arrivals (Roberts 2008). The fact that even an anti-immigration think tank could not find data to show an outright *negative* economic cost–benefit analysis of migration is a sign that immigration into developed countries has an overall beneficial impact on host economies. Indeed most governments of migrant-receiving states understand well that immigrants contribute substantially to wealth production and welfare provision, even though their public discourse of migration control and reduction could make one conclude otherwise. For instance, a survey of economic growth from 2000 to 2007 in the US found that 17.3 percent of this growth was accounted for by Latin American immigrants (IOM 2011: 29). Research has also shown that migrants are seldom 'job stealers', but complement the domestic workforce by filling skills gaps, taking jobs locals do not want, and adding vitality to the demographics of the otherwise rapidly ageing populations of Northern states (IOM 2011: 28).

This said, the benefits of immigration are unevenly spread, and some groups of society, especially low-skilled workers, may lose out to newcomers. Furthermore, public *perceptions* of the cost of immigration tend to be much more negative than data and research supports (IOM 2011: 5–19). This distinction between overall benefits to the economy and (perceived and real) costs to particular segments of the population has been stark in the case of South Africa, a country of extreme wealth differences, a poor education system and high unemployment among the country's many poor and unskilled workers. The relatively dynamic South African economy has benefited from an influx of skilled and/or cheap African labour immigrants, as the government has acknowledged. However, little has been done by the authorities to dispel the strong feeling among South Africa's unemployed urban poor that migrants are direct competitors, 'job stealers' and criminals, leading to widespread xenophobic violence and vigilantism against African immigrants (Hammerstad 2012).

## From identity concerns to national security

Concerns over immigration levels often relate to identity and culture as much as to the economy. The perceived unmanageability of immigration adds to this unease, as it is difficult for states' border authorities to distinguish between 'deserving' and desired immigrants and 'bogus' and unwanted ones. Both in political and academic debates (see Wæver *et al.* 1993) there have been concerted and partly successful attempts at elevating both economic migration and forced migration onto states' broader security agenda. Huysmans (2006), for instance, has shown how a language of threat and unease permeates EU discourse on immigration. Migration has usually been categorized as a 'societal security' threat, defined by Buzan (1991: 19) as 'the sustainability, within acceptable conditions for evolution, of traditional patterns of language, culture and religious and national identity and custom'.

Anxieties over immigration heightened after 9/11 due to fears over letting in international terrorists through a country's immigration or asylum system (Givens *et al.* 2009). As recession has hit many migrant-receiving countries in recent years, security-related anxieties have been compounded by economic concerns and protectionist instincts as stagnating growth sharpens the sense of competition between locals and new arrivals. In the crisis-ridden countries of southern Europe, politicians have taken a harsh approach to stemming the flow of irregular migrants across the Mediterranean. In Greece, where stranded immigrants live in abject poverty on the streets of Athens, the government plans vast prison-like detention and deportation centres (Smith 2012). Before the Libyan civil war, Italy pursued a policy of intercepting and forcibly returning migrant boats to Libya (Human Rights Watch 2012). While numbers are uncertain, at least 1,500 migrants died attempting to cross the Mediterranean in 2011 (Council of Europe 2012). This human tragedy is also a growing human rights scandal affecting the whole of the EU. As evidence has emerged of merchant ships and even NATO vessels failing to pick up boat migrants in distress, the Council of Europe has issued damning reports and demanded a policy overhaul to safeguard the basic rights of refugees (Council of Europe 2012; Shenker 2012).

## Mixed motives are not a prerogative of immigrants

It is difficult to separate out concerns raised by the economic, cultural/identity and national security impacts of migration. While it is analytically useful to attempt to separate these concerns, in reality the political discourse on immigration tends to include a mix of all types of concerns, where cultural/identity fears provide a vaguely formulated but pervasive background atmosphere to more clearly articulated and specified concerns relating to the national security of the state and the economic welfare of its citizens.

Neither in the case of immigration nor in the case of asylum was 9/11 the starting point for such securitization of population movements. An emerging trend could already be seen in the 1980s, where immigrants, asylum seekers and refugees became increasingly subsumed within a discourse of unease and fear (Huysmans 2006: 63; and on the particular securitization of forced migration, see Hammerstad 2011). This is important for understanding the way in which international migration and international terrorism were quickly grouped together in the aftermath of 9/11. This happened almost automatically and without substantial political debate as the ground had already been laid for perceiving immigrants and asylum seekers within a security perspective. Most recently, this proclivity for framing migration as a security threat can be seen in the discussion of climate change-related migration. This is an important future research agenda, but both migration and conflict experts have cautioned about positing a clear and direct link between climate change, mass migration and conflict (Foresight 2011).

## Conclusion: immigration challenges and opportunities for 21st-century world politics

Migration challenges are not likely to abate in the coming years. Immigration controls have gone some way to reduce some inflows into some countries, but as Harris (2002, mentioned in Haas 2005) points out, immigration correlates more strongly with economic growth than with migration control policies. Near-complete immigration control in a world with an increasingly globalized labour market (IOM 2008: 24) is not possible without creating a politically authoritarian and economically autarkic state disregarding both the rights of the individual and the logic of the market.

Harris also suggested that the global financial crisis might lead to reduced migration flows as labour markets contract and provide fewer opportunities for those seeking economic betterment abroad. But although there has been a small reduction in new migration in recent years, and some examples of migrants returning home – for instance from the UK to Poland (Pollard *et al.* 2008) – most migrants have stayed. Undocumented migration into southern Europe has also continued unabated. There are signs of this leading to a further backlash against immigrants in a harsh economic climate. The administrative war against (certain types of) immigration fought by states in terms of stricter border controls and bureaucratic measures continues unabated, often in the name of national security.

The welcome immigrants receive has always ebbed and flowed. Migration trends are to some extent cyclical, where immigration booms are followed by increasing concern and fear among host populations and ensuing political backlashes. The reaction following the mass influx of economic migrants to the US in the late 19th and early 20th centuries was severe, and more xenophobic and racist than anything we have seen in recent years. The backlash then started with the recession in the 1890s, and by 1930 'the doors to the new world were effectively closed' (Hatton and Williamson 2005: 160). The globalized nature of 21st-century politics and economics makes such draconian reactions unlikely today. A combination of demographic trends and economic realities will ensure that international migration remains a central feature of world politics. Considering the inequalities of the world economy, not even the global financial crisis will stop motivated individuals from wanting to relocate to improve their prospects. And most states acknowledge the importance of immigrants to their economies. In terms of demographics, the combination of youthful and fast-growing populations in many parts of the global South, and an ageing population in many parts of the North, will ensure that a relatively high level of migration remains desirable for both sending and host countries for the foreseeable future.

## Guide to further reading

Migration and forced migration studies are fast-growing academic fields. Because of the policy salience of the topic, a lot of recent research has come out in the form of reports and policy papers from migration organizations such as IOM (www.iom.int) and UNHCR (www.unhcr.org), and think tanks and research centres such as the Migration Policy Institute (www.migrationpolicy.org); the Center for Immigration Studies (www.cis.org); and Oxford University's Centre on Migration Policy and Society (www.compas.ox.ac.uk) and Refugee Studies Centre (www.rsc.ox.ac.uk). Hatton and Williamson (2005) provide an impressive overview of the economics and history of international migration over the past two centuries, giving the reader a much-needed sense of perspective on today's challenges. Huysmans (2006) employs and critiques the securitization perspective of the Copenhagen School in his analysis of 'Fear, Migration and Asylum in the EU', and several post-9/11 volumes cover the topic of security and migration (e.g., Guild and van Selm 2005; Givens *et al.* 2009). Loescher *et al.* (2008) provide a useful overview of the state of the international refugee regime and the organization mandated to oversee it, the UNHCR. A good overview of the state of research on the relationship between environmental change and migration can be found in the Foresight report *Migration and Global Environmental Change* (2011).

## Chapter 13

# Climate Change and the Politics of the Global Environment

*NEIL CARTER*

The environment is commonly regarded as a matter of 'low politics', a second-order problem in comparison with the substantive concerns of war and peace, or 'high politics' (Mearsheimer 2001). Environmental issues have steadily risen up the international political agenda since first coming to prominence at the 1972 Stockholm United Nations Conference on the Human Environment. There have been numerous cycles of interest in the environment when various issues, including acid rain, deforestation, ozone depletion and biodiversity loss, have experienced brief moments in the limelight. However, in recent years one issue – climate change – has risen far above all the others to become the dominant concern of global environmental politics. Climate change diplomacy has become increasingly intense: the negotiation of the Kyoto Protocol resulted in major political ructions that caused a genuine rift between the US and the European Union (EU), while the annual ritual of the UN climate change conference regularly generates public spats between governments. International efforts to conclude a post-Kyoto deal have made climate change a major item at several G8 summits, starting at Gleneagles in 2005, and the issue first made it onto the agenda of the UN Security Council in 2007. It would appear, therefore, that climate change has ascended to the realm of high politics.

This chapter will examine climate change as an issue in global politics. It will focus on efforts to negotiate an effective climate change regime, assessing the roles of the US and the EU, tensions between developed and developing countries and the ongoing challenges of overcoming territorial conceptions of sovereignty (see Mansbach, this volume). The discussion will demonstrate the extraordinary complexity that characterizes climate change: it is a transboundary issue that needs international solutions but is beset by major collective action problems. It requires governments (and businesses and citizens) to set aside national interests and short-term political horizons to support policies that may have high short-term costs but deliver indefinable long-term benefits.

## Climate change

There is overwhelming agreement among the world's leading scientists that human-induced climate change is happening and that a failure to limit greenhouse gas (GHG) emissions will have catastrophic consequences for the planet and life as we know it (IPCC 2007). Global warming will result in rising sea levels, melting glaciers, increased desertification, the destruction of coral reefs and the extinction of hundreds of species. Hundreds of millions of people will face food shortages, flooding and reduced access to drinking water; many will become environmental refugees.

There is a natural 'greenhouse effect', whereby various atmospheric gases keep the earth's temperature high enough to sustain life. These gases allow radiation from the sun to pass through but then absorb radiation reflected back from the earth's surface, trapping heat in the atmosphere. Without the natural greenhouse effect it is estimated that the average global temperature would be about 33C lower. However, there is consensus among the world's leading scientists that human activities have strengthened the greenhouse effect by increasing the concentration of these GHGs in the atmosphere, notably by burning fossil fuels, deforestation, raising livestock and growing rice. Since the Industrial Revolution, concentrations of the main GHG, carbon dioxide ($CO_2$) have increased by almost 40 per cent, from 280 parts per million (ppm) to around 390 ppm in 2010 (UNEP 2011: 16). The concentration of all the main GHGs is rising rapidly by around 2.5 ppm annually. On current trends, a doubling of pre-industrial GHG concentrations to at least 580 ppm is expected by mid-century, rising to 800–900 ppm by 2100 (Stern 2009: 25). (Total GHGs are measured in $CO_2$ equivalent, or $CO_2e$, which is the aggregation of non-$CO_2$ GHGs with $CO_2$, weighted to reflect their respective contributions to the change in net radiation at the upper troposphere.)

The earth's average temperature has risen by 0.7C since 1900 and is predicted to rise by anything between 1.1C and 6.4C by 2100 (IPCC 2007: 13). It is widely agreed that any temperature increase in excess of 2C is potentially very dangerous (although the view that 1.5C is the maximum 'safe' increase is gaining ground). To have a likely (i.e., more than 66 per cent probability) chance of staying within 2C it is estimated that the world will need to be producing no more than 44 gigatonnes (Gt) $CO_2e$ per annum by 2020. Yet in 2009 world emissions were 49.5 $GtCO_2e$ (UNEP 2011: 15). Many countries have promised to reduce their GHG emissions, but even if they all implemented their current commitments to the maximum extent then emissions in 2020 would still be 50 $GtCO_2e$ – and in the more likely event that these commitments are not fully implemented it could rise to 55 $GtCO_2e$. So the 'emissions gap' in 2020 could be anything between 6 $GtCO_2e$ and 11 $GtCO_2e$ (UNEP 2011: 8), which would indicate that the world is on course for a rise, not of 2C, but in the potentially catastrophic range of between 3C and 5C. Moreover, by 2050, since cumulative emissions determine the global temperature increase, to have a 'likely' chance of complying with the 2C target total GHG emissions need to be about 46 per cent lower than their 1990 level, or about 53 per cent lower than their 2005 level (UNEP 2011: 9).

Climate change has become an increasingly salient issue in international politics for several reasons. First, the dramatic scientific message has finally been accepted by the political elites in most countries, strengthened by growing evidence that the effects of climate change are already observable. Second, the Stern Review, published in the UK (Stern 2007), demonstrated that climate change will have serious economic consequences if the world does not act, as the overall costs and risks of climate change will be equivalent to losing at least 5 per cent of global GDP each year, forever (Stern 2007: xv). Thus Stern provided a powerful economic case in terms immediately understandable to political and business elites. In particular, he communicated the need for radical measures in the short term – the next 10 to 15 years – by identifying how rapidly the economic costs of inaction will increase, the longer the mitigation efforts are delayed. Third, public concern about climate change has escalated, with growing pressure on governments to act. Finally, with the Kyoto Protocol running its course in 2012, there has been a huge and continuing international effort to negotiate a legally binding replacement treaty. Although the 2009 Copenhagen climate conference seems to have derailed that process the 2011 Durban conference appears to have got it back on track with all participants agreeing to work towards a new legal regime to succeed Kyoto.

## Climate change: a distinctive issue in world politics?

Climate change, like other global environmental issues, has several distinctive features that make it a very complex and challenging problem. In particular, it is an example of Hardin's (1968) parable of the 'tragedy of the commons', whereby individuals and communities over-exploit common environmental resources and continue to do so even when they know it is damaging their long-term interests. The global atmospheric commons is a 'sink' into which the waste pollutants generated by the consumption of fossil fuels are dumped. Individual actors have an interest in exploiting the commons to the maximum, because they gain the full benefits from their actions (e.g., someone driving to work or an electricity supplier burning coal to generate electricity), while the costs – climate change – are shared by everyone else on the planet. That is the 'tragedy': rational individual actions produce collectively irrational outcomes. The challenge is to intervene to stop that seemingly inexorable process. Yet there is no incentive for individuals to change their behaviour because they will lose the benefits of exploiting the common sink while others free-ride on their altruistic efforts.

Climate change is a global problem, both because every country has contributed to it and because everyone will suffer the consequences. Crucially, however, some countries have contributed more than others, and some will suffer more. In particular, the rich developed countries historically have generated far more GHG emissions than the developing world and, with some exceptions, they continue to do so. But it is quite clear that the worst effects of climate change will fall on the latter, partly because most are located in tropical and sub-tropical zones where the negative impact will be greatest, but also because their weak infrastructures limit their capacity to adapt to these changes. Climate change also brings new divisions: for example, countries with extensive low-lying coastal areas and small island states will be particularly threatened by rising sea levels and storm damage, although again some richer countries (e.g., The Netherlands) are better equipped to deal with these threats than poorer countries (e.g., Bangladesh).

Climate change poses some serious threats to traditional territorial notions of state sovereignty and to the state-centric focus of academic International Relations. Climate change is a transboundary problem that does not respect national borders; it can only be effectively addressed through concerted action by national governments, businesses and citizens across the world to reduce their GHG emissions. If one country takes action to reduce its carbon emissions, it cannot exclude others from benefiting, so how can it persuade other countries to make reductions when they could just free-ride on the efforts of others? The doctrine of national sovereignty means that there is no international authority equivalent to a national government – no global government – with the power to force every country to conform. Moreover, the growth in GHGs is not the result of individual states pursuing particular policies or deliberate aggressive acts; rather it is an unintended by-product of the everyday social and economic activities of organizations and individuals. One implication is that solutions cannot be delivered by state actors alone: they also require a host of non-state actors – non-governmental organizations (NGOs), businesses, individual citizens – to change their everyday behaviour.

Yet, in other respects, climate change has reinforced the importance of the state because international mitigation efforts have involved cooperation between states. It is states that sign up to international treaties and national governments that have the responsibility to ensure that their emission reduction targets are met. While those targets cannot be delivered without the active involvement of non-state actors, ironically, the extent of the emission reductions required will increasingly force national governments to intervene extensively and creatively in the activities of businesses and the lifestyles of citizens (Giddens 2011).

Another important feature of climate change is the centrality of scientific knowledge and the uncertainty that surrounds it. Without science we would not know about climate change and we obviously depend on scientists to tell us about the nature of the threat, the need for action, the viability of alternative solutions and the kind of adaptation measures required. One of the distinctive contributions characterizing global environmental politics has been the emergence of transnational networks of scientists who are sufficiently moved about the urgency of a problem to act as an 'epistemic community' promoting international action to address climate change (Haas 1990). Their capacity to influence the political process rests on their ability to persuade others that their knowledge is valid and sufficiently important to require a policy response. However, science is contested and the development of climate change science has been characterized by many uncertainties. Despite the strong scientific consensus that temperatures are rising and that global warming is largely due to human activities, the persistence of a handful of dissenting voices – albeit rarely the leading scientific experts in the field – is still exploited by political sceptics to impede the progress of climate change policy. This sceptical discourse has been much more influential in the US, where it was actively mobilized in support of President George W. Bush's repudiation of the Kyoto Protocol, than in Europe. That said, the 'Climategate' controversy, when over 1,000 private emails and documents written by climate scientists were stolen from the University of East Anglia in the UK and published immediately before the 2009 Copenhagen climate conference, did briefly shake public opinion. Although claims by climate sceptics that the emails undermined the evidence supporting global warming were debunked by three separate inquiries, the emails did reveal that the scientists had engaged in some poor academic practices.

Lastly, traditional realist accounts usually dismiss climate change as a security threat. However, there is the genuine possibility of conflict between states over access to water sources, especially in the Middle East, or from the mass migration of environmental refugees in search of food across an international border (Homer-Dixon 1999). Moreover, an alternative critical approach to security suggests that climate change poses a different kind of security threat. The conventional militaristic language that defines security threats nationalistically as coming from other states should, it is argued, be replaced by the recognition that climate change is transboundary and requires international cooperative solutions that address its root causes, rather than the symptoms (Dalby 2009; Deudney 2006; Lacy 2005).

## Developing a climate change regime

The scientific consensus on climate change emerged slowly during the 1980s and 1990s. A key role was played by the Intergovernmental Panel on Climate Change (IPCC) formed in 1988. Its first report, published in 1990, confirming the scientific consensus that human activities were contributing to climate change and calling for immediate policy action to reduce carbon emissions, contributed significantly to the political momentum that resulted in the United Nations Framework Convention on Climate Change (UNFCCC) agreed at the 1992 Rio Earth Summit. The main objective of the UNFCCC was to stabilize GHG concentrations at levels that should mitigate climate change. It identified a set of operating principles: precaution, cooperation, sustainability and equity. In particular, it established the principle of 'common but differentiated responsibilities' as the basis of equitable burden sharing. Thus developed countries were expected to take the lead in combating climate change and to transfer financial and technological resources to developing countries to help them address the problem. But the UNFCCC set no firm targets; developed countries were simply given the 'voluntary goal' of returning GHG emissions to 1990 levels. Nevertheless, the Rio treaty represented an important achievement, especially given the opposition of the US to any binding commitments, but it was clear that its worthy principles quickly needed to be turned into something more concrete.

A new institutional framework was established to continue negotiations aimed at strengthening the nascent climate change regime. The first Conference of the Parties to the UNFCCC (COP-1) in Berlin in 1995 agreed the 'Berlin mandate' which recognized the need to work towards a protocol that set targets and strengthened commitments to reduce GHG emissions. Eventually, the Kyoto Protocol, hammered out over 10 days of intense negotiations in December 1997 (COP-3), agreed legally binding targets for developed countries (Annex 1). Together these targets aimed at an overall reduction in the basket of the six main GHGs of 5.2 per cent of 1990 levels for the 5-year period 2008–12. However, subsequent efforts to firm up the details agreed at Kyoto floundered, and in 2001 the newly elected President Bush repudiated the Kyoto Protocol. As the US was then responsible for over 20 per cent of global GHG emissions, this decision prompted a major crisis because the Protocol could not enter into force until it had been ratified by 55 countries and by countries which together were responsible for at least 55 per cent of the GHG emissions of the developed Annex 1 countries. Frenzied diplomatic activity to bring other prevaricating developed countries into the process eventually persuaded Japan and Russia to sign the binding agreement, with the latter winning additional concessions through hard bargaining, allowing the Kyoto Protocol finally to enter into force in 2005. The US and Australia were the only major developed countries not to ratify it, although Australia subsequently did so in 2008. By 2012, 191 countries (plus the EU) had ratified the Kyoto Protocol.

Proponents of the Kyoto Protocol regarded it as a major breakthrough in international climate change politics. The primary achievement of the Protocol was to bind most of the developed countries to emissions reductions on business-as-usual levels. This agreement represented the practical application of the principle of 'common but differentiated responsibilities', which underpinned the recognition by developed nations that: (1) they were responsible for the largest share of historical and current GHG emissions; (2) the per capita emissions of developing countries were far smaller; and (3) emissions in developing countries needed to continue to grow to meet essential social and development needs.

This principle informed the decision to set emission reduction targets for the 31 Annex 1 countries that differed in recognition of the capacity of different countries to make cuts. Key targets included 8 per cent for the EU, 7 per cent for the US, 6 per cent for Canada and Japan, zero for Russia, while Australian emissions could increase by 8 per cent. The overall EU 8 per cent target acted as a 'bubble' within which member states had targets that ranged from reductions of 21 per cent for Denmark and Germany, and 12.5 per cent for the UK, zero for France and Finland, to an increase of 27 per cent for Portugal. To secure the support of Russia and other eastern European states, these net emission targets could be achieved by offsetting carbon sinks, such as afforestation projects, against actual GHG emissions. The Protocol also introduced three measures – the so-called Kyoto mechanisms – to enable countries to implement their Kyoto targets:

1. An international emissions trading regime allowing industrialized countries to buy and sell emission credits among themselves.
2. A Joint Implementation procedure enabling industrialized countries to implement projects that reduce emissions or remove carbon in another Annex 1 country in exchange for emission reduction credits.

3.  A Clean Development Mechanism permitting developed countries to finance
    emissions reduction projects in developing countries and receive credit for
    doing so.

The Protocol also established the institutional mechanisms for future negotiations
and regime strengthening.

Critics point out that even if the overall Kyoto abatement target were to be
achieved, it would do no more than scratch the surface of the problem. In short, the
inexorable rise of global GHG emissions would continue unchecked. The compro-
mises needed to secure agreement at Kyoto meant that the targets were too timid,
and the option of sequestering $CO_2$ into carbon sinks weakened them further. The
Protocol was also characterized by two key tensions: the refusal of the US to ratify
it and the absence of any requirement that developing countries, particularly large
rapidly industrializing countries such as China and India, should reduce their emissions. While the first of these, the absence of the US, was a clear failure of the
regime-building process, the second was a positive demonstration by developed
countries of the 'common but differentiated responsibilities' principle. However,
both issues represent unresolved – and interlinked – tensions that dogged the
Kyoto negotiations and continue to hamper efforts to strengthen the climate
change regime.

The reluctance of the US to embrace the Kyoto process reflects wider divisions
among developed countries regarding their willingness to make firm commitments. Under President G. W. Bush resistance coalesced around the US, along
with others in the JUSCANZ (Japan, US, Canada, Australia and New Zealand)
'Umbrella Group'. Clearly, as the then world's largest producer of GHG emissions
(until China recently overtook it), the inclusion of the US in any regime is vital to
its success. Yet, while the EU and some other industrialized nations pressed for
quantified targets throughout the climate change negotiations, the US government
has always dragged its feet. President George H. W. Bush was reluctant to sign the
Framework Convention at Rio and the Clinton-Gore administration then blocked
agreement on targets or timetables at Berlin. Before eventually accepting a 7 per
cent reduction target at Kyoto, Gore won significant concessions, including the
introduction of an emissions trading system, while the main sticking point when
subsequent negotiations broke down at the Hague COP-6 in 2000 was the insistence of the US government that it be allowed to offset its emissions against its
forest sinks.

The resistance of the US demonstrates the importance of the political economy
of climate change politics. Disagreements between developed countries can be
attributed in large part to differences in energy resources and the structure of the
energy industry (Patterson 1996). Countries that rely on fossil fuels for export
income, such as Middle Eastern oil-producing states, and those with large energy
resources, including the US, have been most resistant to cuts. The latter has an
abundance of fossil fuel energy: it is a major oil, gas and coal producer. The
American 'gas-guzzler' culture of cheap, available energy generates strong
domestic resistance to any interference with oil prices. The economic and political

costs of implementing emission cuts are therefore seen as higher in the US than elsewhere, and because climate change has lower salience in America than across the Atlantic, the US government believes the costs of adapting to climate change (rather than mitigating it) are affordable. Furthermore, American politicians have been subjected to strong pressure from a powerful domestic industrial lobby, particularly motor and energy interests (which bankrolled President G. W. Bush's presidential campaigns), to obstruct the regime-building process (Lisowski 2002). Consequently, the Bush administration played the role of veto state with some aplomb, doing its best to reframe the climate change debate on its own terms. For example, in the face of growing scientific consensus about climate change, the US government exploited remaining uncertainties, and it tried to persuade Russian President Putin not to ratify the Kyoto Protocol. Later, as it became harder even for Bush to continue denying climate change was a problem, he shifted tack by launching the Asia-Pacific Partnership on Clean Development and Climate, a 2005 initiative with Australia, China, India, Japan and South Korea to find voluntary ways of reducing emissions by accelerating 'the development and deployment of clean energy technologies'. It was, transparently, an attempt to undermine the Kyoto Protocol.

However, there was a gradual shift in climate change politics within the US as the public mood, which linked events such as Hurricane Katrina with climate change, became more sympathetic to environmental issues. Initially, this shift was a bottom-up process that gathered momentum in the face of federal intransigence from the Bush White House. For example, three separate regional cap-and-trade systems now exist across North America, including the Regional Greenhouse Gas Initiative involving nine north-eastern states (C2ES 2012). The election of President Obama brought the possibility of a transformation in the US role in climate change diplomacy, with potentially significant implications for the negotiation of an effective post-Kyoto treaty. Obama made his differences from Bush on climate change a key feature of his election campaign and entered office declaring that 'We will make it clear to the world that America is ready to lead. To protect our climate and our collective security, we must call together a truly global coalition' (Obama 2009). Obama quickly launched a tranche of initiatives including a green economic stimulus package, investment in renewable technologies and an Energy Bill that would introduce federal targets to reduce GHG emissions and a cap-and-trade scheme. Yet, significantly, the familiar oil and gas lobby mobilized its considerable resources in opposition to the Bill and ensured that after receiving approval in the House of Representatives in 2009 it never even came to a vote in the Senate. Rather than confront Congress with further legislation, Obama subsequently adopted a less obtrusive approach, seeking to achieve domestic emissions reductions by enforcing existing regulations and imposing tougher pollution standards.

The US's abrogation of leadership on climate change left a vacuum that the EU has been eager to fill. Throughout the 1990s, the EU pushed for stringent international emission reduction commitments. At Kyoto, although it failed to win the kind of tough cuts it wanted, the EU still accepted the highest reduction target, which may have helped persuade other countries to accept more ambitious cuts than initially intended. By 'playing hardball', the US had a more profound impact than the EU on the architecture of the Protocol because it was able to win concessions on the flexibility mechanisms such as carbon sinks and the use of emission trading (Oberthür and Kelly 2008: 36). However, when Bush repudiated the treaty, the EU stepped up to the mark impressively. The EU's decision to 'go it alone' by pressing ahead without the US, illustrated by its telling diplomatic interventions at subsequent climate conferences and its eventual success in delivering Russian ratification, effectively saved the Protocol and demonstrated the EU's resolve as an actor in international politics (Vogler 2011; Wurzel and Connelly 2011).

Subsequently, the EU has sustained this leadership role. It set up the world's first international carbon emissions trading system (ETS) in 2005. In March 2007, EU heads of state reasserted the EU's long-standing commitment to hold mean global temperature increases to 2C above pre-industrial levels and promised to cut EU $CO_2$ emissions by 20 per cent of 1990 levels by 2020, increasing this to 30 per cent if other developed countries were to agree to a new post-Kyoto treaty. To give substance to its 20 per cent reduction commitment, in 2008 the EU agreed a climate change package consisting of six pieces of legislation aimed at delivering the required emission reductions across the energy, business and transport sectors in the 27 member states. The EU has limited 'hard' political and economic powers to force other countries to cut emissions, so it has effectively employed 'softer' forms of leadership such as 'leadership by example', diplomacy, persuasion and argument (Oberthür and Kelly 2008; Wurzel and Connelly 2011).

Why has the EU embraced, with some alacrity, this leadership role, when it might have just let Kyoto wither and die, thereby avoiding the considerable compliance costs of reducing emissions? Several factors, relating both to the specific challenge of climate change and to the wider role of the EU as an international actor, explain this decision. Many European governments – at least those in the old EU15 – regard climate change as a grave threat. Most EU member states are heavily dependent on imported energy and, in the absence of an American-style gas-guzzling culture, governments therefore have a stronger balance-of-payments incentive to cut carbon emissions and reduce imports of fossil fuels. Growing concerns about the security of energy supplies, particularly after massive increases in oil and gas prices around 2005 and the increasing dependency on Russian gas, have brought a new focus on policies aimed at improving energy efficiency and developing renewable energy sources (Oberthür and Kelly 2008). In addition, Bush's repudiation of Kyoto gave European leaders an opportunity to enhance the nascent reputation of the EU as a serious, unified player in global politics, and to strengthen its position *vis-à-vis* the US. Ideology and personality have played their part. Between 1998 and 2005 Germany was governed by a 'red–green' coalition in which Joschka Fischer was an influential Green Foreign Secretary, backed for a while by the presence of Green Party ministers in Belgium, Finland, France and Italy. In the UK Prime Minister Tony Blair embraced the cause of climate change mitigation with enthusiasm and was personally convinced by the arguments, but he also saw it as a way of distancing himself from Bush at a time when he was the subject of strong domestic criticism over the Iraq War. The European Commission, backed by the European Parliament, has played a crucial role because it has recognized the need for the new policy measures, such as the ETS and the 2008 climate change package, both to ensure that member states met their Kyoto commitments and to enable the EU to lead by example in the negotiation of a post-Kyoto treaty (Schreurs and Tiberghien 2007). The EU institutions, alongside German Chancellor Merkel and French President Sarkozy, believed that following the failure to establish an EU constitution in 2005, climate change offered a popular means of reinvigorating and legitimizing European integration because it required genuinely 'European' solutions. Yet the EU's capacity for progressive leadership has encountered increasing internal challenges, partly because of the ongoing financial and economic crises within the Union and partly from its enlargement to 27, which has brought in a bloc of eastern European states, such as Poland, that are dependent on fossil fuels and tend to regard climate mitigation measures as damaging to economic growth.

The continued willingness of the EU to assume a leadership role is crucial if the second long-running tension – between developed and developing countries – is to be resolved. The Kyoto Protocol demonstrated that most developed countries accepted responsibility for taking the initiative in making cuts. Clearly, at least in the medium term, they must continue to make the lion's share of reductions because they have been responsible for around 70 per cent of GHG emissions since 1950, even though developed countries contain only about 1 billion of the global population of 7 billion people alive today (Stern 2009: 23). Developed countries also have far higher per capita emissions. Moreover, they have the resources to invest in the necessary shift to a low-carbon economy.

But it is also clear that any effective climate change regime must, sooner rather than later, bring the rapid growth of emissions in developing countries under control. The developing world will soon be the source of most emissions. Global GHG emissions are currently split roughly 50/50 between developed (and transition) countries (Annex 1) and the rest of the world. Several of the largest developing countries, including China, Iran and India, now rank in the top ten for the *absolute* level of $CO_2e$ emissions, although their per capita emissions remain below those of the developed world. China, for example, has seen its GHG emissions grow by around 70 per cent since 1990, due to its rapid economic growth and heavy dependency on coal for its energy supply, to become the largest emitting country in the world, with well over 20 per cent of global GHG emissions. It is projected that China will contribute 33 per cent of global emissions by 2030 assuming it continues its development path of energy-intensive rapid economic expansion (Garnaut 2008: ch. 3). With population growth concentrated in the developing world and the per capita growth of emissions rapidly escalating as poorer countries industrialize, then (on business-as-usual projections) the developing world might be responsible for as much as 80 per cent of global emissions by 2050.

The principles of 'common but differentiated responsibilities', equity and sustainability are open to many different interpretations. Thus a major stumbling block for the US throughout the Kyoto negotiations was the absence of any firm commitment by developing countries to reduce their emissions. The US government was mindful of the 1997 Byrd–Hagel resolution to the US Senate that opposed the Kyoto Protocol on the grounds that it excluded developing countries and would harm the competitiveness of US industry. That concern has been exacerbated by the continued rapid growth of China, which is now a major competitor.

However, the major developing countries, such as China and India, demand that they should not have any targets imposed on them while they remain so far behind the developed world. In particular, they point out that their per capita emissions are much lower than in developed countries: for example, in 2009 $CO_2$ per capita emissions in the US were over twelve times higher than in India and around three times higher than in China (IEA 2011a: 97–8). As long as this gross inequality within the international system remains, it will be very difficult to persuade developing countries to take significant action to control their emissions. As the Indian climate change envoy to COP-15 observed, 'Western countries are hypocritical and must sacrifice some luxuries before asking developing countries to cut greenhouse gas emissions' (Nelson 2009). It is important to recognize that China and India are not – as some in the North have suggested – irresponsibly ignoring the problem of climate change. China, for example, is very conscious of its dependency on coal-fired electricity generation and there is a strong lobby within the political elite pushing for a strategic switch towards a low-carbon economy. China has ambitious targets to reduce energy intensity, notably by improving energy efficiency, it is rapidly developing renewable sources of energy and is preparing a trial of emissions trading (Reuters 2011). India, too, has ambitious plans for a massive expansion of solar energy. Any serious efforts to reduce emissions will depend heavily upon the transfer of financial and technological resources from rich countries to developing nations to fund the introduction of clean technologies, renewable sources of energy and so on. But, in practice, developed countries have been unwilling to put their hands in their pockets, and big private corporations are reluctant to relinquish control of technologies without economic or financial compensation (e.g., access to markets).

One widely touted solution to the equity problem is the notion of 'contraction and convergence', which aims for per capita parity at a 'safe level' of 2.0 tonnes of $CO_2$ by 2050. Most developing countries are currently below that figure while high-income countries are far above it. So developed countries must cut rapidly and substantially to 2.0 tonnes $CO_2$ per capita, while the former should be allowed to expand until, say, 2030 or 2040, but then be required to cut back to reach parity by 2050 (Schreuder 2009: 60). But even this radical proposal ignores another feature of the globalized economy, which is that a large proportion of the goods manufactured in industrializing countries such as China, Mexico and South Korea are exported to and consumed in the developed world, although these 'embedded emissions' are not allocated to them in official UNFCCC data.

Other commentators see market-based mechanisms as the key both to the overall problem of emissions reductions and to the North–South divide (Stern 2009; Tickell 2008). One hugely significant outcome of the Kyoto Protocol has been the development of 'carbon commodification', whereby carbon reductions have been turned into commodities that can be traded in the market. Global carbon markets were worth US$142 billion in 2011, up from US$31 billion in 2006, although registering their first decline in five years (World Bank 2011c: 9). Despite recent market instability, carbon trading has grown impressively to establish itself as a new commodity.

The carbon market is dominated by the EU ETS, which in 2011 accounted for 84 per cent of its value and 97 per cent if the secondary offsetting markets are included (World Bank 2011c: 9). The EU was initially unenthusiastic about the American insistence on the inclusion of emissions trading in the Kyoto Protocol, but when it adopted the mantle of climate change leader at the turn of the century, the EU turned to emissions trading as a means of ensuring that member states would be able to meet existing and future emission reduction targets. The ETS, launched in 2005, is a carbon trading scheme based upon the principles of cap-and-trade that allocates energy-intensive installations a number of carbon permits that can then be traded. The scheme helps overcome the 'free-rider' problem by requiring all large European organizations – currently around 11,000 sites are included – to join the ETS. By guaranteeing the scheme will remain in place businesses have the long-term security to justify investing in cleaner technologies plus the financial incentive to cut emissions so that they can sell surplus emissions permits for a profit in the new carbon market. The ETS has had many teething problems. Phase 1 (2005–7) and Phase 2 (2008–12) have seen the overall cap set too high and a huge oversupply of permits (which were mostly issued free, enabling some businesses to make huge profits from them), which resulted in the price of carbon falling to a level so low that it was an ineffective incentive to reduce emissions. Overall, Phase 1 had little, if any, impact on GHG emissions, and Phase 2 effected only a small real reduction in emissions (Sandbag 2011). Phase 3 (2013–20) centralizes the allocation of permits, with a larger proportion to be auctioned, and it is extended to include aviation, but the problems of oversupply and the low carbon price are unlikely to go away.

Another important Kyoto innovation was the Clean Development Mechanism (CDM), which is the only part of the Protocol that provides an active role for developing countries to reduce their emissions. The CDM permits developed countries to finance emissions reduction projects in developing countries in return for credits that count towards their Kyoto targets. An additional incentive for Annex 1 countries is that it may be cheaper to achieve emission reductions in developing countries than domestically. The attraction for developing countries is that CDM may facilitate technology transfer and attract new foreign investment to projects that deliver sustainable development.

The CDM took off at a rapid rate after the Protocol entered into force in 2005, boosted by the EU's decision to allow CDM credits to be traded within the ETS. By 2012, there were well over 3,000 registered CDM projects, which were estimated to deliver an average of 500 million Certified Emissions Reductions (one CER is equivalent to 1 tonne of $CO_2e$) amounting to a total of over 2 billion tonnes of emissions reductions by 2012 (UNFCCC 2012). The assumption underpinning

CDM is that all reductions in GHGs are equally good for climate change mitigation, whether they occur in the US or Mali. However, there are political costs if developed countries are perceived as using CDM as an easy option to avoid having to rein in the consumerist lifestyles of their own citizens. In short, it will fuel the familiar refrain from the South that developing countries cannot be expected to take actions that might harm them if the rich North is unwilling to accept some pain too.

The CDM has also had its problems (Tickell 2008). For example, there is a concern about the extent to which a CDM investment generates 'additionality', or simply finances a project that would have happened anyway. Many CDM schemes are intended to produce short-term, low-cost GHG reductions, such as an end-of-pipe methane gas capture scheme, rather than a more capital-intensive renewable energy scheme that might have a longer lead-in time before it generates emission reduction benefits. With over 80 per cent of CDM projects located in China and India they have not spread benefits broadly across many of the poorest nations. Whilst in many respects CDM has been a success, it needs to be reformed if it is to generate the volume of transfers of technology and financial investment from rich to poor countries that will be essential to resolve North–South tensions (Stern 2009), and it must have the long-term certainty that a new legally binding international climate treaty to replace the Kyoto Protocol could deliver.

## The future of climate change politics

International climate diplomacy has followed a very bumpy and winding road towards a post-Kyoto treaty. Once Kyoto was ratified the annual climate conferences were geared to securing agreement for a new treaty at the Copenhagen COP-15 meeting in December 2009, but the event was beset by conflict. When it looked as though no agreement in any shape or form was likely, President Obama intervened to broker the non-binding Copenhagen Accord, a flimsy document which seemed to mark the beginning of the end for a legally based treaty. The Accord introduced a new concept of 'pledge and review' in which countries adopted voluntary national commitments with little monitoring and no sanctions. On a positive note COP-15 marked the return to the fold of the US. It also heralded the emergence of the BASIC coalition of Brazil, India, China and South Africa – large, powerful industrializing countries that together generate over 30 per cent of global $CO_2$ emissions. Significantly, Obama's method of securing agreement was through a series of bilateral meetings with the BASIC group members, which marginalized the previously influential EU and undermined the democratic, but increasingly unwieldy, consensus-building UNFCCC bargaining process (Christoff 2010). The reinforcement of the pledge and review process the following year at Cancun and the failure of major emitters to offer sufficiently large reduction commitments suggested that prospects for a formal treaty were bleak. Yet the Durban COP-17 in 2011 surprisingly agreed to work towards a new legal regime.

Durban demonstrated that climate politics are very dynamic and rapidly changing. We should no longer characterize climate diplomacy along a simple
North–South fault-line. The two groups that dominated Copenhagen were again
expected to shape the outcome of the COP-17 conference: the developed states led
by the US and Canada, and the BASIC group, speaking for the developing world.
The first group was implacably opposed to a legal treaty without the involvement
of the major developing nations; the latter seemed equally unwilling to agree to
legally binding emission reduction targets. But then a new configuration cutting
across the developed–developing country divide entered the fray. The so-called
'Cartagena Dialogue' – the EU, small island states and least developed countries,
plus other progressive states – collectively agreed a set of common positions and
put a new deal on the table calling for the continuation of the Kyoto Protocol and
negotiations for a legally binding treaty. This proposal split the BASIC group:
Brazil was unhappy about siding with the US and its allies, South Africa wanted a
positive outcome on its home turf and then China became the deal-maker, helping
to win over a reluctant India (Jacobs 2011). Eventually all 194 countries supported
the plan for a new treaty to be agreed by 2015, to come into force in 2020, with the
Kyoto Protocol continuing to operate until then. After being humiliated in its own
backyard at Copenhagen the EU re-established itself as an important player,
having won the trust of many of the poorest countries. But Durban emphasized that
China is now a central actor in international climate politics, and one that seems
slowly to be taking up the challenge in a positive way.

Of course, there is still a long way to go and the new deal could yet be derailed;
indeed, just days after the Durban conference Canada struck a profoundly negative
note by announcing it was withdrawing from Kyoto Protocol. Familiar challenges
remain: pushing legislation through the US Congress will be a major problem for
any future President. India was a very unwilling signatory. And climate change
mitigation policies are often unpopular. Thus while China and the US were
supporting the proposed treaty at Durban they were also challenging the legality of
the EU's decision to include aviation emissions within the EU ETS from 2013,
which would affect all airlines flying into the EU. And the challenge of persuading
the developing world to embrace a development trajectory based on the low-
carbon economy is yet to be won.

Yet the pressures for a new treaty are not going to disappear. The scientific
evidence underpinning climate change, notwithstanding the best efforts of the
climate sceptics, gets steadily stronger. The economic case for (rapid) action has
slowly permeated the boardrooms of many major corporations. Several traditional
realist concerns are also important. The energy security case for climate action has
been strengthened by global fluctuations in oil and gas prices that have strengthened the case for a shift to a low-carbon economy, as indicated by the inclusion of
significant climate change measures in the fiscal stimulus packages introduced
during 2008–9 in China, France, South Korea, the US and elsewhere. Moreover, as
the damage we have already done becomes increasingly evident, humankind will
have to deal with the impact of climate change. The challenge of adaptation raises
both new and old difficulties. Although there is a fear in some circles that focusing

on adaptation will shift the emphasis away from mitigation, the costs of adaptation will be unavoidable, high and unevenly distributed with developing countries suffering first and being less able to deal with the challenges.

Whatever deal eventually replaces Kyoto, it is important not to assume that regime formation and implementation represent everything there is to say about global climate change politics. There are numerous multilateral and bilateral agreements that exist alongside – albeit often inspired by – the Kyoto process. Transnational climate change governance has taken off rapidly in recent years (Bulkeley and Newell 2010). The carbon market has grown exponentially, with the EU ETS gradually being supplemented by new or planned emissions trading systems in the US, Canada, Australia, South Korea, New Zealand and elsewhere. Beyond that, a myriad of public–private partnerships, private, voluntary and individual initiatives are flourishing (Patterson 2009: 150–1). In short, climate change governance has a momentum of its own that might be hampered, but not undermined by a failure in the overarching international regime process.

## Guide to further reading

Several books offer lively introductions to international climate change politics (Giddens 2011; Schreuder 2009; Stern 2009; Tickell 2008). It is important to grasp the stark reality of climate change science (IPCC 2007) and the complex relationship between science and policy (Hulme 2009). The Stern Report (Stern 2007) is essential reading to grasp the economic case for global action on climate change. The academic journals *Climate Policy*, *Environmental Politics* and *Global Environmental Politics* are a rich source of reading on all aspects of climate change politics and policy. Political philosophers have also engaged constructively with the ethical issues raised by North–South issues and equitable burden sharing (Garvey 2008). There is a growing literature on climate change and environmental security (Dalby 2009; Lacy 2005). It is also useful to locate climate change in the wider literature on international environmental politics and policy (Carter 2007; Clapp and Dauvergne 2011).

# Chapter 14

# Energy Security and World Politics

*AMELIA HADFIELD*

Energy security is an unwieldy but fascinating topic. For the private sector, securing energy has long been a competitive business arena involving the mining and sale of fossil fuels. The business has periods of long-term price stability interspersed by sudden shocks. For politicians, achieving energy security has come to dominate virtually every agenda, dictating both public and foreign policy; some see it as something the state should do itself while others as something the market supplies in collaboration with the state. For climate change activists, long-term reliance on oil and gas presents both a challenge and an opportunity. For the media, energy either sits quietly on the sidelines or makes front-page news due to accidents (Fukushima, Japan, March 2011; BP Deepwater Horizon, Gulf of Mexico, April 2010), resource-driven conflicts (Nigerian and Russian pipelines) or international summits that attempt to tackle environment, energy and climate change (Copenhagen, December 2009).

Studying energy security means engaging with three distinct scholarly traditions. First, the narrative of 20th-century energy security represents a compressed history of the major dynamics of war, peace, trade, security and prosperity that have shaped the relations between developed and developing states in East–West and North–South variants for roughly a century. Second, debates about energy security are a microcosm of the dominant themes of *realpolitik*, neoliberalism and governance that now categorize the majority of state-to-state relations. Third, debates about energy security illustrate the different perspectives on how best to manage the three-way relationship between the state, markets and international politics: are statist, market-led, or institutionalized governance structures best fitted to allocate the production and distribution of energy resources?

This chapter introduces readers to all three traditions. It does so first by presenting the key features of post-Second World War energy history to demonstrate some of the major trends of energy security. It then introduces readers to the main 'personalities' of energy security, the consumer and producers, both commercial and sovereign, whose uneasy interplay constitutes both the broad contours and myriad details of contemporary energy security. The chapter concludes with an overview of energy governance as the most recent idea associated with attempts by states to manage their energy security concerns.

## What is energy security?

[T]here is a strong disconnect between the publicly stated policies, coming from officials and experts in net energy producing and consuming countries alike, in praise of international cooperation, collective security, free markets, fair distribution of resources and commitment to sustainable growth and the welfare of future generations, and the reality on the ground, characterized by volatile energy prices, rising geopolitical instability, suppliers using strong-arm tactics against consumers while consumers beat their chests about energy self-sufficiency and boost their military capabilities to ensure their access to energy. If everybody agrees on the bedrock principles of an effective global economic system why do we face today the gravest risks to our energy supply? (Luft and Korin 2009: 335)

Energy security is a composite term, associating *national security* needs with the use of various natural resources for the consumption of *energy*. Energy powers states, underwrites society, constitutes markets, shapes trade and investment patterns, sets hierarchies and generally provides a standard of living that differs drastically for individuals, based on their physical access to available energy supply. In short, energy is the fuel of the world.

The modern state needs a reliable stream of natural resources including water, oil, gas, coal, biomass, uranium, solar and wind power to generate energy. We in turn rely heavily on both energy resources and energy outputs to satisfy our economic, social, political and biological needs. We use energy as a private customer and rely on it as a citizen of our state. Those in developed Western states have of late become reliant on plentiful and cheap forms of energy. This reliance, however, comes at a price; not only do we expect energy to continue to be easy and cheap to acquire, states and markets alike have become uniquely vulnerable to supply shortages, price spikes, market downturns and upturns, accidents, natural disasters and even terrorism, all of which constitute a very wide-ranging sphere of real and perceived threat.

The unique geopolitical and market conditions under which each state operates in the global energy system determines its conceptualization of energy security. No state's requirements are identical; hence energy security can be explained in countless ways. However, there are some fundamental differences that enable a categorization that the reader can use as a rule of thumb. Net energy *producer states* seek 'security of demand' for their natural resources, that is, a reliable market purchasing their energy assets at the highest price for as long as possible, principally because their state budget and economic development is dependent on the revenues derived from the export of energy. Net energy *consumer states*, however, require predictable, shock-free 'security of supply' of energy resources at affordable prices to power their economic growth. Both producers and consumers together require 'security of transit', that is, the security of the transportation of the energy, whether a state, water route or form of infrastructure (e.g., pipeline or grid). There are even states, known as transit states, for whom energy security refers to the security of revenue derived from transit fees earned from the distribution of energy over their territory.

All three types of energy players share the need for market stability. Ensuring a stable market environment is conditional upon finding the right balance in the complex web of interdependencies that characterizes the interplay between all energy actors. This is a highly delicate task, not least because of the diverging ways in which states operate in the global energy market. Consumers and producers can exist as private market entities (international energy companies such as ExxonMobil) and sovereign entities (national energy companies, such as Norway's state-owned Statoil). This makes energy security simultaneously a commercial issue about the trade of energy as a commodity *and* a political issue orienting the public and foreign policies of states. Both components come together in the concept of *energy interdependence,* i.e., the framework that captures both statist ambitions and market-led aspirations of contemporary energy actors around the world.

In simple terms, when energy trade is reliable energy relations are commonly thought of as something best left to markets and firms but when threats are encountered it becomes the business of the state. From ordered structures of supply and demand to protracted policy disputes and even outright conflict between states or societies, there are a number of trends that have emerged to characterize the world of 20th- and 21st-century energy security. Conventional resources, for instance, have moved from a 'paradigm of plenty' to an 'endgame era' for fossil fuels, although there is considerable debate as to the timing of that end. Technological advances in exploration and production (E&P), such as 3D seismic mapping and horizontal drilling, have revealed a range of new potential hydrocarbon reserves and have opened up access in places where extreme conditions, both on and off shore, have been prohibitive in the past, such as the Arctic, ultra-deep water and high-pressure high-temperature wells. These are prolonging the life of fossil fuels, but are dependent on high oil prices to remain economically viable. High prices, however, are a key feature. The 2008 global downturn, increasing difficulty of access, enormous upswings of demand and anxieties about the capacity of the system to cushion shocks have seen oil and gas prices rise steadily in the first decade of the 21st century. Energy security is also complicated by concerns over rising $CO_2$ levels, itself a direct cause of changes in the world's climate. Although the heightened sense of urgency to diversify away from fossil fuels has fostered promising technological advances in the development of energy alternatives, the transition to a more sustainable global economy will be time-consuming, entailing immense financial costs. The result is that today energy security has three main dimensions: commercial (competition), governmental (security) and environmental (mandated $CO_2$ reduction).

# Contemporary energy history: snapshots

## The Second World War

Global and regional conflicts illustrate a dominant trend: states are thirsty for energy, and this dictates their foreign policy. During the Second World War, both Allied and Axis forces relied heavily on availability of oil, frequently shifting their policy to accommodate the search for new sources. The Allied 'Oil Campaign' attempted to reduce Axis synthetic oil production, forcing Germany to launch new fronts in North Africa and Russia. Especially memorable was Operation Chastise (1943) in which Britain's Royal Air Force carried out aerial bombardments of two major German dams: the Möhne and Edersee. Then, as now, dams were crucial strategic targets, providing hydro-electric power and pure water for steel manufacturing, inland waterway transport and drinking water. Both dams were breached, causing severe flooding of the Ruhr and Eder valleys and undermining Ruhr armaments production (Max 2008). With an estimated 85 per cent of Allied wartime oil exported from the United States (depleting 33 per cent of its reserves), US post-war oil policy was to swiftly replenish its reserves, and to adopt a policy that has remained in place for more than 50 years: secure a diversified oil supply (Randall 2005).

## The Arab oil embargo

The response to the October 1973 decision by the US to re-supply the Israeli military during the Yom Kippur War was a swift oil embargo by the Organization of Arab Petroleum Exporting Countries (OAPEC). Global oil prices skyrocketed until the political settlement between Israel and Syria in March 1974 (Hammes and Wills 2005). From a market perspective, high oil prices, disruptions, inflation and recession appeared to be the new reality; politically, US Middle East policy was irrevocably linked to oil. Energy security, as a form of leverage over world oil prices, had been neatly demonstrated by OPEC (the Organization of Petroleum Exporting Countries) to be an effective foreign policy weapon. Oil itself had been proven a necessary prerequisite for a stable global economy. Consumer/OECD (Organisation for Economic Co-operation and Development) states responded by forming the International Energy Agency (IEA) as an organized buyers' market (to parallel the producer market of OPEC), and commencing with new hydrocarbon exploration, including the North Sea (Yergin 2008).

## 1979 crisis

1979 was a turbulent year for oil. The ousting of the Shah by Ayatollah Khomeini in the Iranian Revolution severely disrupted the Iranian oil sector, with production greatly curtailed and exports suspended. President Carter placed an embargo on Iranian imports as a political response, which further drove up prices. In December, Carter responded to the Soviet Union's invasion of Afghanistan with a trade embargo on the US. In January 1980, in his State of the Union address, Carter declared that the US would respond militarily to any interference with US oil interests in the Gulf:

> Let our position be absolutely clear. An attempt by any outside force to gain control of the Persian Gulf region will be regarded as an assault on the vital interests of the United States of America, and such an assault will be repelled by any means necessary, including military force. (American Presidency Project: www.presidency.ucsb.edu)

Known as the 'Carter Doctrine', the statement was intended to deter attempts at hegemony in the Gulf by the Soviet Union; it institutionalized energy as a strategic foreign policy issue, and oil as a strategic commodity.

## 1980s oil glut

Thanks to an economic slowdown in industrialized states and widespread efforts at energy conservation, global oil supplies faced the opposite problem the following decade: a serious surplus of crude oil, with prices falling in 1986 to a low of US$10 per barrel. The concept of an oil glut was variously explained by OPEC increases in oil price, a temporary surplus in global markets, overproduction and declining domestic consumption (Hershey 1989).

## The 2003 invasion of Iraq

After the first Gulf War (1990), in which Iraq invaded Kuwait primarily to annex Kuwaiti oil fields, the Gulf once again rose to prominence as the crucible of global and US energy security anxieties. Operation Desert Storm did not deter Saddam Hussein and in a flurry of confusing reasons largely associated with the 9/11 al-Qaeda attack, unverifiable but compelling assertions about weapons of mass destruction held by Iraq and the legal ambiguities of UN Resolution 1441, the US intervened again in 2003 (IISS 2010). One of the first tasks undertaken by US and coalition troops from Britain, Poland and Australia was an air and amphibious attack on the Al-Faw peninsula with the goal of securing its oil fields and ports, along with oil fields in southern Iraq and offshore oil platforms. The upshot of the 2003 invasion was undeniable proof that, despite allegations to the contrary, the Carter Doctrine appeared alive and well, reinforced when in 2009 oil contracts were awarded by Iraq to oil companies in coalition states. The US invasion also destroyed the delicate diplomatic unity of the European Union, intensely divided between supporters and opponents of the US invasion, who were strongly influenced by their diverging opinions of its energy-driven motivation.

## The economic crisis and the Copenhagen summit

The 2008 economic crisis revealed a web of globalized interdependencies, including energy markets and consumer and producer states. While the recession pushed down energy demand, oil prices remained relatively stable thanks to Asian growth and controlled production from OPEC. In addition to retooling their various banking and monetary sectors, OECD states have also focused on the environmental as well as financial cost of fossil fuel dependence. Yet despite aggressive energy diplomacy from increasingly nationalized producer states like Russia and Venezuela and reluctance for climate change burden sharing by both BRICS and developing states, the world's largest climate change summit in Copenhagen (2009) produced only a loose Accord to rein in $CO_2$ output where possible, not going far enough to prevent future environmental damage (http://unfccc.int/resource/docs/2009/cop15/eng/l07.pdf).

## Energy actors and interests

Not every energy actor falls neatly into the producers/net consumers category. Both the US and Russia, for instance, are large importers and exporters. Private companies and states operate in very different circumstances, with varying perspectives on the need for security, their place in the global economy, the right balance between imported and exported natural resources, and the need to consider alternative types and locations of energy. Equally, however, there are great similarities in how producer and consumer states and companies define themselves, and in their strategic requirements. This section briefly explores the 'critical mass' of energy policies held in common by producer, consumer and transit actors. Whilst international energy companies remain a key feature, this section takes a decidedly geopolitical perspective, acknowledging that because national energy companies control roughly 88 per cent of global hydrocarbon assets, they are, for now, the leading players in contemporary energy security.

As suggested, energy security has a twofold meaning, depending on one's geopolitical and market context. For producers like Saudi Arabia, Qatar, Venezuela, Nigeria and Russia, energy security means a reliable and secure demand for their hydrocarbon products, via a stable energy market. Nationally owned energy companies, or states that hold majority shares in domestic energy companies, can generally be placed in the statist camp. Producers, for the most part, have a particular geopolitical view of the use of their natural resources conditioned by the market forces which make those resources viable exports, a view that dominated from the post-Second World War era until the end of the Cold War. This perspective gave way to the rise of a consumer ethos in which markets were deemed to be the correct mechanism by which prices and capacity should be determined. This viewpoint held sway for much of the 1990s, espoused by consumers, for whom energy security means reliable supply for affordable prices via a stable energy market. Now, however, two things have happened.

First, there has been a serious rise in revanchist energy statism in notable producer states like Russia, Venezuela, Saudi Arabia and the UAE. Second, the idea of energy governance has emerged as a new paradigm to capture the intrinsically interdependent nature of security of supply and demand, of statist and market components. As explored in the final section, energy governance addresses both the neoliberal market principles that typify much contemporary energy trade and the dominant role of states in politicizing, or even monopolizing, energy policy-making. For some states, energy security remains firmly entrenched in the private sector, and a matter of business; for others, energy assets represent a strategic commodity and are a matter for state policy (both domestic and foreign). The geopolitical/market themes that drive this understanding are explored from producer and consumer points of view in the following sections and then touched on again from the perspective of governance in the final section.

## Energy producers

Producer states use a number of strategies, to varying extents, to pursue their specific blend of energy security. The primary objective of energy security is the steady flow of high fossil fuel export revenues to drive economic growth, providing political leverage both at home and abroad.

### *Nationalized energy*

Resource nationalism can be defined as the 'efforts by resource-rich nations to assert (or re-assert) political and economic control of their energy and mining sectors from foreign and private interests to domestic and state-controlled companies'. (Bremmer and Johnston 2009). In recent decades there have been several waves of energy sector nationalization in producing countries. The motivation for resource nationalism is both economic and political. The export revenues for hydrocarbons are generally considerable, even when prices are low. Well-managed export revenues underwrite the financial stability of the state, and allow it to write off its foreign debts, build up reserve accounts and invest in various domestic and international sectors. Examples here include the United States, Canada, Norway and Britain, which all possess liberalized upstream sectors, with independent operators. For other states, however, including Russia, Venezuela and Nigeria, with less well-managed energy sectors, there is a far more limited trickle-down effect from the sale of hydrocarbons into the economy and society of producer states. These states run the risk of succumbing to the 'resource curse', and becoming entirely reliant upon the 'rent' generated by hydrocarbon sales, but doing very little to secure future prosperity and stability. Keeping the energy sector in national hands (that is, owned by the state), rather than in private hands, virtually guarantees a permanent income for the state, allowing it to fund domestic subsidies, as well as re-invest in its own energy infrastructure, or (more recently) to plough funds into developing alternative energy resources. States like Russia, made rich by nationalized energy sectors, are politically powerful, and there is a strong temptation to underwrite economic clout with political muscle by using energy as a foreign policy weapon against importer or transit states, as seen in spats with Belarus and Georgia. Using energy as a tool of foreign policy is nothing new; indeed, a large number of importer states (particularly those in Europe) have historically been well aware of its use and abuse but have only recently configured this into their foreign policy relations with producer states.

For consumer states, the consequences of resource nationalism can be an inability to determine the true foreign policy motives of its suppliers. Investors are also faced with extreme unpredictability regarding their foreign direct investment (FDI) in producer states. For producer states, the problems of resource nationalism may in the long run outweigh the benefits. With no real competition within or between national and private (domestic or international producers) comes a lack of operational efficiency and a lacklustre attitude to attracting investment, or reinvesting profits in either upstream (exploration) or downstream (refining, commercial sale) energy infrastructure. This may undermine both quality and quantity of supply, reducing not only the ability of a producer state to be seen as a reliable supplier, but more broadly to contribute positively to spare production capacity. Uncertain estimates and fluctuating volumes in turn create an increasingly tight market with high price volatility, unable to cushion disruptions, also known as 'supply and demand shocks' in the global flow of energy (Johnston 2010).

Whether state governments or private companies are the right actors to govern the exploration, exploitation and sale of hydrocarbons is a matter of debate. Certainly private companies have a better track record of reinvesting to stay ahead of fierce competition, whilst states have less incentive to govern efficiently and effectively. Many energy-producing states or 'petro-states' like Nigeria, Russia and Venezuela have succumbed in some way to a crippling over-reliance of their national budgets upon hydrocarbon exports (usually anything beyond 45 per cent of GDP), known as the 'resource curse'. This refers to the paradoxical experience of countries with an abundance of natural resources, mainly minerals and fossil fuels, underperforming economically when compared to countries lacking in natural resources. Unfortunately, having kept the doors shut in the past, either diplomatically or commercially, when supply and demand circumstances change, and the need for foreign technology and expertise to sustain and increase E&P re-emerges, international energy companies are understandably reluctant to re-invest, particularly if the host state has a previous history of unilaterally seizing assets (Bremmer and Johnston 2009).

## Institutional frameworks for producer cooperation: OPEC

As a result of the uneasy interdependence of producers and consumers, the need for an overarching institutional affiliation among these groups has emerged. Producers need to ensure they work together to set prices based on production capacity and reserves. Consumers need to ensure they remain as integrated in this market as possible, reducing their vulnerability to supply disruptions by acting in concert where possible. The irony behind the producer cartel of OPEC is that it was created in response to the cartel-like actions of consumers eager to exploit untapped hydrocarbon resources. In 1951, Iran nationalized its oil company (controlled at the time by the Anglo-Iranian Oil Company); in response the US State Department suggested that keeping Iranian oil production in the market would be best accomplished by a consortium of major oil companies. The 'Consortium for Iran' was made up of the 'Seven Sisters': Anglo-Persian Oil Company (now BP), Gulf Oil (acquired by Chevron), Royal Dutch Shell, Standard Oil of California (Socal now Chevron), Standard Oil of New Jersey (Esso, now ExxonMobil), Standard Oil Co. of New York (Socony, now ExxonMobil) and Texaco (acquired by Chevron). The Seven Sisters was a buyers' cartel which leveraged their substantial purchasing power over a variety of producers in developing states. In 1960, however, they were challenged by the rise of OPEC, an intergovernmental organization of 12 oil-producing countries.

Several developments have gradually chipped away at OPEC's market influence. These include internal tensions about the right mechanisms by which to control the price of oil, and discoveries of oil reserves in Canada, the North Sea, the Gulf of Mexico and Alaska. However, OPEC's biggest current weaknesses are Russia and the CIS (Commonwealth of Independent States) exporting widely (if not always reliably); shale gas discoveries in the US; unconventional oil and gas in Canada and Venezuela; and concerns that OPEC's spare capacity (primarily their excess pumping capacity) was far tighter than suggested. As production quotas for individual OPEC members are tied to their proven reserves, there is an incentive for tweaking the numbers or obscuring the decline of oil fields. Saudi Arabia is said to inject salt water into oil fields, thereby increasing pressure and forcing the oil to the surface. Extraction rates can artificially be kept at the level of normal performance, while in fact there is rapid decline. This, however, obscures the peak moment of the well, causing a sudden termination of extraction, compared to a more gradual depletion with normal techniques. The extent to which Saudi Arabia makes use of this technique is unknown, but it certainly puts its spare reserve capacity in doubt. Although OPEC controlled 77.2 per cent of global oil reserves in 2010, and as such is essential for global oil supply with its 41.5 per cent share in global production in that same year (BP 2011), their actual power to influence global oil prices has decreased over the years.

## The producer diversification two-step

The problem for producer states of having to rely on a small number of consumers is twofold. First, any disruption in the consumption of a particular consumer, also known as 'demand shocks', negatively impacts on the revenue flows derived from exporting the hydrocarbons. Consolidation of domestic power becomes problematic for states that are overly reliant on hydrocarbon export revenues, as many of the methods often used (e.g., domestic energy subsidy schemes, or extensive police and secret service organization) are only possible with a steady flow of revenues. Second, dependence on specific consumers limits foreign policy options related to that specific consumer, because there is a relation of mutual dependence.

Russia has traditionally been dependent on oil and natural gas exports to Europe. The EU, however, has been rattling its sabres about the need to diversify away from fossil fuels altogether, and away from reliance on Russian gas in particular. Unsurprisingly, this strains producer–consumer relations, and pushes Russia

*Table 14.1*   Russian oil and natural gas
            pipelines

| | |
|---|---|
| EU–Russia energy imports: | |
| – Natural gas | 32.2% |
| – Crude oil | 33.1% |
| – Hard coal | 34.2% |
| | |
| EU–Russia share of total trade: | |
| – Imports | 9.8% |
| – Exports | 6% |
| | |
| Russia–EU share of total trade: | |
| – Imports | 45.5% |
| – Exports | 46.1% |

*Source*: Directorate General for Trade of the European
Commission, Bilateral Relations EU-Russia (see http:/
trade.ec.europa.eu/doclib/docs/2006/september/tradoc_
113440.pdf).

to consider diversification of both market (from West to East) and of routes to the
market. Consolidating existing relationships is key for Russia, but if that market
proves unreliable (e.g., EU carbon reduction strategies could see a drop in
consumption which would hit Russian revenues), then Russian energy interests,
unsurprisingly, may shift to large markets in the East. However, this plan is
dependent on the substantial investments needed for the construction of pipelines
to China, Japan and South Korea. Some are in the process of being built: in 2006
for example, Transneft, Russia's state-owned pipeline company, began building
the Eastern Siberia–Pacific Ocean oil pipeline (ESPO), bringing oil from East
Siberia to the Chinese market. Plans have been made to build a pipeline for gas,
parallel to the oil pipeline (Perovic and Orttung 2009). (See Table 14.1.)

## Domestic and foreign investment

To maintain and, if possible, enhance energy production levels, continued investment in E&P is indispensable. However, in many countries with nationalized
energy sectors this investment is often lacking. In the case of Venezuela, an OPEC
member, the extensive social programmes developed by President Chávez
require huge amounts of money, but at the same time new E&P also has to be
stimulated. With 15.3 per cent of proven total world oil reserves, about 211 billion
barrels of oil, Venezuela ranked second in the world in 2010. However, its share
of world production was only 3.2 per cent, compared to 4.3 per cent in 2000 and
3.6 per cent in 2005 (BP 2011). Most of its oil fields are mature, meaning that their
production capacity is diminishing. These fields require substantial investments
to maintain current production levels. Venezuela's future oil production depends

on the development of the extra-heavy oil found in the Orinoco Belt in the centre of the country. While Western IOCs (international oil companies) have largely been forced to leave the country, NOCs (national oil companies) from politically friendly nations are increasing their stakes in Venezuela's oil production. Among others, China's state-run companies CNPC, Sinopec and CNOOC are expected to play a vital role in the E&P of heavy crude oil from the Orinoco Belt (Tissot 2009).

## Third World producer problems

The 2008 economic crisis has amplified the vulnerability of national economies overly reliant on hydrocarbon export revenues. Algeria is a case in point. A significant producer and exporter of hydrocarbons, it has the tenth largest natural gas reserves in the world and is the sixth largest exporter, also ranking sixteenth in oil reserves. Oil and gas make up the bulk of its exports, accounting for approximately 95 per cent of total export earnings and 60 per cent of budget revenues (CIA 2012). But complications loom in the future. As is the case with many energy exporting countries in the developing world, it has a fast-growing population, causing a rapid rise in domestic energy demand and consequently reducing export capacity. Combined with urbanization and continued economic growth, reliance on hydrocarbon exports is unsustainable, even in the short run (Stambouli 2011).

On the other hand, Algeria has enormous potential for renewable energy resources (RES), particularly solar and wind power. The Sahara desert covers about 86 per cent of its territory and has some of the highest solar radiation levels in the world (Stambouli 2011). Several national and international projects are in progress to develop solar and wind energy capacity. In 2011 a solar thermal power plant built by a consortium of Algerian and Spanish companies came onstream in Hassi R'mal. Future projects include the country's first wind park in Adrar, and the initiative of the Desertec Foundation, a consortium of German companies which aims to create an extensive network of wind and solar power farms in North Africa and the Middle East over the next 40 years. This network of power plants should provide about two-thirds of the region's energy demand and 15 per cent of that of the EU by 2050.

## Unconventional oil and gas

The energy newcomers consist of 'uncon' types of oil and gas. While troublesome to extract, unconventional gas (including shale gas, tight gas and coalbed methane) has the same properties as conventional gas and is much more widely dispersed than regular natural gas. 'Uncon' E&P has been made viable as a result of continuing high prices and the share of unconventional gas in global production is projected to rise from 13 per cent in 2009 to 22 per cent in 2035 (IEA 2011b). Furthermore, gas-consuming countries that discover 'uncon' will likely be able to reduce their dependence on traditional hydrocarbons. This, however, will have a significant effect on long-term security of demand for countries producing conventional gas.

Two technological developments have made accessing 'uncon' more economically attractive: horizontal drilling, and hydraulic fracturing of stone formations or 'fracking'. The US has pioneered shale gas E&P since the 1980s, and the steady rise of shale gas in its energy mix is predicted by the 2012 IEA *Annual Energy Outlook* to comprise an impressive 49 per cent of total US natural gas production in 2035 (from 23 per cent in 2010). Far more strategically, shale may allow the US to shift gear completely, becoming an overall net exporter of natural gas by 2021. However, uncertain environmental consequences such as water contamination, methane emissions and earthquakes, as well as the lack of clear regulatory frameworks even in developed states, make the necessary private investment difficult. These uncertainties have caused some states, such as France and Bulgaria, to place a moratorium on fracking. Others, like Poland and Ukraine (both of whom are highly dependent on Russian natural gas imports) have well-established exploration efforts. If environmental concerns and regulatory obstacles can be overcome, the overall profile of gas in the world will shift significantly (Deutch 2011). Reassuringly, high prices also make E&P for 'uncon' oil economically attractive. Oil sands are very thick forms of petroleum (known as bitumen) with which certain mixtures of clay, sand and water are saturated, and are found in large quantities in Russia, Kazakhstan and Canada, which has the world's most extensive commercial oil sands industry. However, the extraction of oil sands is an enormous operation causing substantial damage to the environment, including surface mining and extensive bodies of contaminated water, whilst the refining process itself produces higher $CO_2$ emissions than conventional oil (forcing Canada to leave the Kyoto Protocol in 2011). Yet these negative externalities are not included in the price. As a result, the profits are private while the environmental costs remain public.

## Energy consumers

### *The consumer diversification quickstep*

As illustrated above, diversification is as crucial for consumers as for producers. The US is a case in point. For decades the US political establishment has proclaimed the need to become 'energy independent'. One of the arguments used is the need to reduce dependence on supplier states with unstable political regimes (such as Iraq, Iran, Libya and Venezuela) in favour of 'compliant' exporters like Saudi Arabia and Kuwait. Although the US is the third largest oil producer, it was also responsible for more than one-fifth of global oil consumption in 2010 (BP 2011), importing 49 per cent of the oil it consumed in that year. The top five oil import locations are Canada (25 per cent), Saudi Arabia (12 per cent), Nigeria (11 per cent), Venezuela (10 per cent) and Mexico (9 per cent) (EIA 2011). After 9/11, dependence on Gulf oil (17 per cent total oil imports) came to be seen as highly unsatisfactory and the US has sought to further diversify its oil supplier portfolio, choosing West Africa as one of the primary regions, especially Nigeria. Yet a slightly different view of the numbers suggests, for example, that 51 per cent of US oil supply is domestic, and 37 per cent of its imports are from 'safe' (Canada) and 'reliable' suppliers (Saudi Arabia). With 88 per cent of its supply safe, coupled with strong growth of domestic shale oil, the US may have political rather than strictly commercial reasons for staking a claim in 'energy hotspots' around the world.

Turning to the EU, the majority of gas received by the EU is from Russia (primarily delivered via pipelines running through the Ukraine and Belarus). The EU's demand for gas is expected to grow substantially in the coming decades as a result of the increased share of gas in its primary energy mix (Perovic and Orttung 2009). This has caused anxieties about Russian reliability as an energy partner. Is Russia indeed an unreliable producer partner? The EU will not admit to so undiplomatic a suggestion, despite recurrent problems with deliveries of Russian gas through Ukraine and Belarus (the infamous 'gas spats' of 2006, 2009 and 2012), and Russia's much-vaunted Asian diversification strategies. The knock-on effect is that the EU has identified diversification as one route to improved energy security, specifically via the ill-fated Nabucco pipeline. This pipeline, organized by a consortium of European and US companies, would create a new Southern energy corridor, bringing Caspian gas from Azerbaijan directly to the south-eastern quarter of the European energy market. From Russia's perspective, the Nabucco pipeline could seriously diminish its stake in EU's natural gas imports. However, its main asset is the sheer fragmentation of the EU member states on the question of how (or even why) to diversify away from Russia. The European Commission has for almost a decade called for a common energy strategy; yet EU member states continue to strike long-term gas contracts with Russia bilaterally, some of which directly undermine the proposed Nabucco non-Russian pipeline project.

The lack of coherence among EU member states forms an important obstacle to the successful implementation of this strategy, and Russia has made swift and persistent use of it. Indeed, March 2012 reports from the online energy sector think tank *European Energy Review* (Riley 2012) suggest that although the European Commission 'has thrown its weight behind the famous mega-pipeline project Nabucco', including plans by Energy Commissioner Oettinger to establish a collective gas purchasing consortium, the Caspian Development Corporation, there is still stasis. The same can be said of the Southern Gas Corridor proposal to import non-Russian sources of gas from Central Asia to Europe via Turkey (www.europeanenergyreview.eu). Despite being key foreign policy features of the EU–Russia landscape, bargaining chips for negotiating security of supply, neither plan appears viable at this point. Diversification is thus paradoxically both a method by which to alleviate energy insecurity, and an effective way of guaranteeing it.

## Transforming the energy mix

Another strategy adopted by consumer states is diversification of the energy mix. To mitigate dependence on conventional energy resources and the supply risks entailed in their distribution, as well as diminishing $CO_2$ emissions, states have sought alternatives to the usual energy resource suspects (see Figure 14.1). In light of the first motivation, high oil prices and technical innovation have made the E&P of unconventional oil and gas reserves economically attractive. At the same time, continued developments in the biofuels and renewable energy sources (RES) sectors have created opportunities for further diversification of the energy resource portfolio. Examples of the latter can be found in the generation of electricity through biomass, hydro, solar, wind, tidal wave and geothermal sources.

Most contentious is nuclear power. At the end of 2010 there were 441 operational nuclear power reactors dispersed over 30 countries, generating 13 per cent of the world's electricity. The US, France and Japan contribute the most with 104, 58, and 54 reactors respectively (IEA 2011b). Nuclear energy has been popular for several reasons: it enables energy importing countries to become less dependent on the supply of natural resources, thereby increasing their energy security; it has low carbon emissions; and it is commercially viable (while construction costs are significant, operating costs are relatively low). Opponents, however, refer to the risks of waste and associated risks of nuclear weapon proliferation, terrorist attacks on nuclear plants, and deadly nuclear accidents, such as the Chernobyl disaster (1986) and the nuclear catastrophe in Fukushima, Japan (2011). As a direct result of Fukushima, and an indirect result of other concerns, several states, most notably Germany, announced either moratoria or phase-outs. Despite 23 per cent

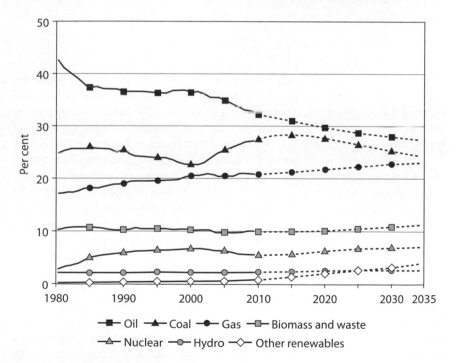

*Figure 14.1*   Global energy mix in new policies scenario

*Source*: International Energy Agency (2011b).

of its total electricity generation being derived from nuclear power as of 2010 (IEA 2011b), Germany aims to have its plants offline before 2022. Other EU states like France, and to a lesser extent Britain, have more firmly rooted nuclear traditions and a stake in maintaining or even expanding the current framework. The outcome confirms the EU as ever agnostic about the use of nuclear power in its energy mix.

### New consumers

China's energy security is in many respects different from that of large OECD consumer nations. China only became a net importer of oil in 1993. In 2010 its reserves accounted for a mere 1.1 per cent of the world's conventional oil reserves and 1.5 per cent of the world's natural gas reserves. At the same time, it was responsible for a 10.6 per cent share of total crude oil consumption in 2010, an increase of more than 90 per cent compared to 2000. Whilst its share of total natural gas consumption was only 3.4 per cent, this signalled an increase of 21.8 per cent over the previous year (BP 2011). With these figures in mind, combined with the average GDP growth rate of 10 per cent in the last decade, the focal point of China's energy security is the need to secure sufficient energy and raw materials to keep up with its rapidly expanding economy. Long-term access to resources is vital for its domestic economic development (Newmeyer 2009).

## Climate change narratives

Climate change presents considerable uncertainty about the use of fossil fuels over the medium to long term. However, the impact of fossil fuels on environmental security is very certain indeed: the longer the use, the worse off the world. Switching energy types is arguably the best way forward, with the objective of mainstreaming alternatives and renewable, complemented by reduced domestic demand as well as large-scale energy efficiency initiatives. Can these new 'green' methods bring about better energy security? If security is basic reliance on a commodity to the extent that it becomes strategic, then the gradual diminution of the commodity (either in terms of availability or access) imposes very real threats on consumers and producers alike. Reducing energy consumption can increase the energy security of consumers and producers alike, reducing their reliance on non-renewable energies. The use of smart grids and meters is a good example of the technology curve driving policy ambitions.

Some states, however, want to go much further. A long-standing ambition of the EU for instance, is the creation and completion of an internal electricity and gas market. In the EU's most recent energy strategy (EU 2010) the creation of a pan-European energy market is considered one of the five pillars on which the successful pursuit of its energy security depends. This entails the integration of the physical gas and electricity distribution infrastructure, and the harmonization of regulatory frameworks existing in national energy markets. Connecting the power grids of member states is a *sine qua non* for the economic viability of RES. The

European super-grid envisages a network of high-voltage direct current (HVDC) power lines linking the energy systems of countries in Europe and those in North Africa and the Middle East. The problem of intermittence can thus be solved, with surplus energy flowing wherever it is needed. Without grid connection, cross-border energy trade from RES is not possible. Combined with the harmonization of national energy regulation, and the 'unbundling' of vertically integrated energy companies, RES can start to compete with conventional energy sources, a necessary prerequisite for reaching the EU's 2050 climate goals.

The institutional requirements for such ambitions, however, are heavy indeed. Combining intergovernmental entities and inter-institutional frameworks of public and private energy actors and agencies, the EU itself and a number of states are heading steadily towards the idea of a new energy policy paradigm. This breaks new ground, not only in terms of new energy *actors*, but also the *content* of energy policy (producing something of an energy security, environmental protection and climate change nexus), as well as new processes of governance which go beyond traditional definitions of statist *realpolitik* and market-led neoliberal dynamics.

## Energy security governance

Energy security has been illustrated above as an uneasy blend of commercial and strategic concerns, an intersection of public and private, business and geopolitics. Every era has seen increased geopolitical friction as a result of strife over energy sources; yet regulatory, legal, commercial and diplomatic solutions have also been found which have contributed to enhancing the multi-tiered nature of global energy security to the point where its inherent interdependence is its greatest strength. Thus volatile moves by one actor produce waves that have a material impact on everyone else, but which can ultimately be absorbed by the depth of the structure. The better energy trade is managed, the more likely that competition, however fierce, will have a beneficial rather than corrosive effect upon sellers and buyers alike.

This final section looks briefly at the role of energy governance as a benign or beneficial force in sorting out the increasingly complex energy terrain of the 21st century. The terrain itself is composed of ordered and unregulated dynamics, and between statist and market-led principles. In what way can governance carve a third path between politicized geopolitical statist identities and market-led identities underwritten by neoliberal market principles? How can governance accommodate both fiercely pro-market identities (e.g., the UK) on the basis of liberalization, privatization and deregulation of competition, and vehemently statist identities (e.g., Russia) on the basis of exclusively national use of sovereign assets, usually by centralized governments, as well as the difference between structured and unstructured responses to energy challenges?

Between statist and market-oriented management approaches lies the concept of governance (Youngs 2009): government-regulated market forces defining the contours and content of energy trade and investment. Helpful heuristic devices by which to understand these three approaches are the associated energy identities of producer, consumer and governance entities. A *governance entity*, briefly put, is a break from the dual orthodoxy of state- or market-led energy security, and – with a broader purview of the intrinsically cross-border, interdependent nature of energy as a nexus linking markets, states, societies and the environment – places the management of such issues in intergovernmental (or even supranational) forums and institutions. Governance thus attempts to capture the intrinsically multi-faceted nature of energy security by effectively de-politicizing energy issues and broadening the surface area of the policy to allow new actors new modes of delivery in an interdependent fashion on new and old policy objectives.

Governance actors include institutions like the IEA, which can help correct market failure via their emergency response mechanisms designed to cushion price shocks. IEA members are required to have mandatory volumes of Strategic Petroleum Reserves (SPR). Within Europe, governance is more developed for gas, and it is thus a regional form of governance, rather than a truly global example. Short-term supply risks in Europe can be addressed via gas storage and interconnectors, which could provide a buffer against Russia–Ukraine transit spats. Institution-driven governance goes beyond infrastructure responses to market supports, starting with more stringent requirements on the publication and transparency of states' reserve and production capacities to prevent rampant market speculation and price volatility. Data gathering by OPEC, IEA and the most recent Joint Oil Data Initiative (JODI) is a governance response to this problem, all geared essentially at reducing the asymmetry of information and ultimately reducing transaction costs. Most effective are the codified rules and norms of energy governance, in which the World Trade Organization, NAFTA (North American Free Trade Agreement) and the Energy Charter Treaty have variously set standards for energy trade. The plethora of bilateral and multilateral investment regimes cobwebbed beneath these institutions all lay out an emerging body of rules for trade and investment in energy goods and services (both traditional and alternative). Rule setting is also a hallmark of the EU's own ethos, and at the global level can be seen in its climate change guise as the emerging system to regulate GHG (greenhouse gas) emissions within the United Nations Framework Convention on Climate Change (UNFCCC), or through the ETS.

The danger, of course, is that if far too many actors and processes become involved, the nexus itself becomes overloaded in terms of just how many facets of energy it can capture, states resent attempts to edge out sovereign interests, and this generates a geopolitical backlash. Recent European examples illustrate the challenge of lining up traditional statist models of guarantees, subsidies and vertically integrated monopolies (both EU and non-EU) against national and private actors who feel energy trade should be nothing less than the 'pure expression of market forces', reliant solely on the market's invisible hand (Victor *et al.* 2006: 322). The other danger, of course, is that governance exists institutionally but has no effect either in law or policy; it looks good, in other words, but is functionally futile. The stakes, however, have never been higher, so public and/or private attempts at rewriting the energy rule book are urgently needed.

## Guide to further reading

For an accessible introduction to the characteristics of the global energy system and energy security, see Müller-Kraenner, S., *Energy Security* (2008). A more comprehensive and more technical introduction can be found in Pascual, C. and Elkind, J., *Energy Security: Economics, Politics, Strategies, and Implications* (2009). Yergin, D., *The Prize: The Epic Quest for Oil, Money and Power* (1991) gives a historical overview of the global petroleum sector. 'The New Seven Sisters: Oil and Gas Giants Dwarf Western Rivals' by Carola Hoyos in the *Financial Times* (2007) adds to the picture the rise of national oil companies (www.ft.com/ intl/indepth/7sisters). The following books research the energy conceptualization of particular countries: Youngs, R., *Energy Security: Europe's New Foreign Policy Challenge* (2009) gives a comprehensive evaluation of the EU's perspective on energy security, while Kalicki, J. and Goldwyn, D., *Energy and Security: Toward a New Foreign Policy Strategy* (2005) does the same for the US. However, these perspectives need to be seen in the larger context of different actors with different interests. Two further works address the complex network of interdependencies in which they exist: Luft, G. and Korin, A., *Energy Security Challenges for the 21st Century: A Reference Handbook* (2009) and Bahgat, G., *Energy Security: An Interdisciplinary Approach* (2011). In addition one should read Mitchell, C., *The Political Economy of Sustainable Energy: Energy, Climate and the Environment* (2010) to get an understanding of how the common threat of climate change impacts on the energy system and the way actors operate.

## Chapter 15

# Nationalism and Ethnicity

RICHARD W. MANSBACH

Observers of world politics regard ours as the epoch of globalization in which peoples organized in territorial states are becoming ever more interconnected by and enmeshed in global political, economic, cultural and knowledge networks that reduce local autonomy and link the fates of people geographically remote from one another. Globalization deterritorializes and denationalizes state functions. Its advocates believe that as globalization thickens, it will be accompanied by cosmopolitan identities in which individuals view themselves as members of a single global community. But is globalization reversible? Continuing global economic and financial crises make this an urgent question.

In some respects, globalization is antithetical to localization, in which individuals identify with disparate and exclusive communities that evaluate their well-being relative to 'outsiders'. Among the most significant 'local' communities are nations and ethnic communities, and 'nationalism' is the ideology that places these communities at the acme of human loyalties. Globalization advocates believe that nationalism is waning, but, in fact, nationalism remains a powerful though changing force and an ideology with great appeal in both the developing and developed worlds. Its persistence reveals an intensification of identity politics in which individuals and groups assess goals and policies on the basis of 'who they are' (Ferguson and Mansbach, 2004).

To some extent, the revival of nationalism is a reaction to the homogenizing impact of globalization and the end of the Cold War's ideological bifurcation of global politics. A dramatic resurgence in identity theory is apparent in scholarship as diverse as Huntington's civilizational thesis and the various strands of constructivist thought. National movements reflect the unleashing of old (or forged) identities and memories as reflected in the passionate separatist yearnings that have gripped Bosnian Muslims, Kosovars, Kurds, Tibetans and others

In recent years nationalist fervour has been encouraged and manipulated by political leaders; for example, Russia's Vladimir Putin has used symbols ranging from the canonization of the murdered Tsar Nicholas as part of linking the Russian Orthodox Church to the regime and the restoration of the Soviet national anthem to citing the threat posed by Russia's 'enemies' such as Chechen rebels, American hegemony and Georgian adventurers. For their part, leaders of former Soviet republics like Georgia, Moldova and Latvia, and former Soviet bloc countries have pointed to resurgent Russian power to mobilize nationalist sentiments at home.

Indeed, on every continent national movements are gaining renewed vigour. Today, as in past centuries, nationalism is a companion of political and social upheaval; it was and remains 'a subversive and revolutionary force' (Szporluk 1998: 27).

## What are nations, nationalism and ethnicity?

'Nation' and 'ethnicity' are contested concepts that denote a self-conscious community of people who differentiate themselves from others on the basis of one or more shared and exclusive traits such as language, common history and myths, culture, religion, physical similarity and/or ancestry that justify a common origin. Nations imply a self-conscious ethnic group, and both often refer to peoples united by a putative common ancestry. Although Weber conceded that 'the whole conception of ethnic groups is so complex and so vague that it might be good to abandon it altogether', he defined ethnicities as 'human groups that entertain a subjective belief in their common descent because of similarities of physical type or of custom or both' (Weber, cited in Verkuyten 2005: 74, 75). Ethnicity, then, 'is based on a myth of collective ancestry, which usually carries with it traits that are believed to be innate' (Horowitz 2000: 52). However, as Weber argued, a genuine blood tie is not necessary for a sense of shared ethnicity, and formation of a political community may itself foster ethnic solidarity. Perhaps the only consensual attribute of nations and ethnicities is that adherents share an intangible sense of ownership of the community as a whole. 'The essence', argues Connor (1993: 70), 'is a psychological bond that joins a people and differentiates it, in the subconscious convictions of its members, from all nonmembers in a most vital way.'

How do nations arise? Some scholars argue that they are primordial, that is, rooted in the mists of antiquity. China's emperors, for example, depicted themselves as heirs to mythical sage kings who were divinely mandated by Heaven. In Japan's case, Shinto proclaimed emperors to be divine and depicted an unbroken dynastic line of over two millennia from a founding sun goddess. Ancient Romans believed that their city had been founded by the twins Romulus and Remus, sons of the god Mars and the priestess Rhea Silvia, who, according to legend, were suckled by a she-wolf. This myth was altered when the Roman Republic was transformed into an empire by Augustus, who commissioned the poet Virgil to write the *Aeneid* to legitimize imperial Rome and, by inventing Trojan ancestry, to differentiate Romans from Greeks (Balsdon 1979: 30).

In contrast to the primordial perspective is the view that nations are constructed by those who see themselves as having a common fate. Although this view is associated with contemporary constructivists, it dates back to Ernest Renan (1994: 17), who in the 19th century answered his question 'what is a nation?' by describing it as 'a soul, a spiritual principle' and adding a voluntary aspect to the primordial conception: 'Only two things, actually, constitute this [a nation's] soul... One is in the past, the other is in the present. One is possession in common of a rich legacy of remembrances; the other is the actual consent, the desire to live together... The existence of a nation is… an everyday plebiscite.' Alluding to Renan, Benedict Anderson (1991: 6–7) described a nation as an 'imagined community': 'It is imagined because the members of even the smallest nation will never know most of their fellow-members, meet them, or even hear of them', and 'it is imagined as a community, because, regardless of the actual inequality and exploitation that may prevail in each, the nation is always conceived as a deep, horizontal comradeship. Ultimately it is this fraternity that makes it possible… for so many millions of people, not so much to kill, as willingly die for such limited imaginings.' Gellner, too, (1983: 7, emphasis in original) emphasizes the subjective basis of nations, arguing that individuals 'are of the same nation if and only if they *recognize* each other as belonging to the same nation' and that such recognition 'turns them into a nation, and not the other shared attributes, whatever they might be, which separate that category from non-members'. For Anderson, nationalism is a historically embedded phenomenon that is linked to modernity. Traditions 'which appear or claim to be old are often quite recent in origin and sometimes invented' (Hobsbawm 1983: 1).

The debate between primordialists and constructivists misses the point that 'identity and memory are virtually the same concept' and that both view as critical 'the role of memory and rhetorics of collective identity in constructing and maintaining the nation-state' (Boyarin 1994: 23, viii). As Smith (1986: 2, 3) observes, 'there can be no identity without memory (albeit selective), no collective purpose without myth', and 'the constituents of these identities and cultures – the myths, memories, symbols and values – can often be adapted to new circumstances by being accorded new meanings and new functions'. Myths, memories and symbols 'represent and reinforce the boundary definition of a nation' (Smith 2001: 8). The debate also misunderstands how history works with novelty to produce identities. In the course of their lives, people recognize only a few of their shared traits as worthy of self-definition, and the behaviour of other communities toward them may promote new traits or the rediscovery of old ones. Which common features will animate individuals is by no means predetermined, since identities are a state of mind. Political actors seeking additional legitimacy may produce new categories of 'others' to provide mirror images for identity groups they seek to lead. To cement in-group unity and attract support, political entrepreneurs may emphasize the psychological distance – the degree of dissimilarity between cognitive frameworks or ways of looking at, assigning meaning to, and coping with the world – between followers and 'others'. Thus, 'the emotional attachment to lineage, ancestry and continuity is shared by both those who have power and those who are deprived of it' (Conversi 2004: 2).

For such reasons, one cannot overestimate the importance of acts of remembering – rituals that reinforce and renew collective myths and memories. Whether memorializing an idealized Battle of the Boyne by Irish Protestants or the Battle of Kosovo by Serb nationalists, almost any (even fictionalized) historical event can be resurrected to challenge authority. Acts of remembering, including national pageants, recollections of ancient wrongs, tribal ceremonies, religious pageants, ethnic parades and even monuments, are part of a contest over the meaning of history. Historical memories sustain old identities and loyalties, thereby linking generations. Religion, literature, dialect, poetry, painting, music and ritual are a few of the ways in which ancient identities are nourished. Any may foster the 'rediscovery' of 'nation' or 'ethnicity' and demands for national autonomy.

'Nations' should be distinguished from 'states'. Some nations are stateless, for example, the Kurds and Palestinians, and many states are multinational. If nations are 'imagined communities' of people, the existence of which is the product of a continuing process of identity formation, states are juridical entities that enjoy territoriality and internationally recognized boundaries. Such recognition entails sovereignty that affirms that the state enjoys legal control over its territory and of people who reside within its boundaries. States are legal equals, implying that they have no right to intervene in one another's domestic affairs. Finally, states have governments that enjoy the authority to act on their behalf. Sovereignty 'lodges a distinctive claim to the rightful exercise of political power over a circumscribed realm' and 'seeks to specify the political authority within a community which has the right to determine the framework of rules, regulations and policies within a given territory and to govern accordingly' (Held *et al.* 1999: 29). Further, as a *legal* concept, state sovereignty is *not* the same as state autonomy (the capacity to act independently) or state power (the actual ability to accomplish objectives), both of which are *empirical* attributes. Indeed, states rarely measure up to the ideal of sovereignty. Many cannot control their borders, do not enjoy authority over much of their territory or segments of their population, and do not even have a functioning government (Krasner 1999).

How are 'state' and 'nation' related? Gellner (1983: 1) argues that nationalism is 'a political principle which holds that the political and the national unit should be congruent'. This was a premise of historical nationalism as it accelerated in the 18th and 19th centuries, which saw the union of the passions and energy of 'nation' with the bureaucratic, fiscal and territorial resources of 'state', thereby producing a polity of unprecedented political, military and economic power – the nation-state.

## The evolution of nationalism: theory and practice

The French Revolution played a major role in the emergence of nation-states by shifting the basis for rulers' legitimacy from what Hall (1999: 133–72) calls 'territorial-sovereign' to 'national-sovereign' identity. Instead, Bobbitt suggests that this polity was a *transition* to the modern nation-state. He argues (2002: 146, 196, 178, emphasis in original) that the French revolutionary and Napoleonic wars ushered in the 'state-nation', defined as 'a state that mobilizes a nation – a national ethnocultural group – to act on behalf of the State' that 'can thus call on the revenues of all society and on the human talent of all persons'. The state-nation 'was not responsible *to* the nation; rather it was responsible *for* the nation', a relationship that the nation-state, according to Bobbit, would reverse. The state-nation was energized by mass conscription, citizen soldiers and standing armies. And, 'the more universal military service became… the more tightly the strands of identity and obligation, welfare and duty, were knitted in a single category of citizenship' (Sheehan 2008: 14). One consequence was the emergence of enormous armies driven by aggressive expansionism in the nation's name.

Bobbitt suggests that the transition from state-nations to nation-states accelerated during the mid-19th century and featured the 1848 revolutions, the Crimean War, and broader suffrage in much of Europe, climaxing in Italian and German unification. Nation-states were legitimized by the principle of national self-determination, whereby the 'nation' was the repository of sovereignty, and 'nation' linked 'state' to 'society'. The doctrine of self-determination, spread globally by Europe's colonizers, would later boomerang and bring an end to the overseas empires of Europe's state-nations (Jackson 1983: 119–26). As Klaebel (2007: 225) observes: 'With the emergence of the idea of national self-determination and later the process of decolonization, "nationalism" entered many communal narratives, suggesting a link between three "objects" of desire: a specific parcel of land, a specific "people" (the community *as* nation) and the apparatus of the sovereign state.' Europe's colonial wars were brutal affairs, and wars among Europeans themselves became total, identity-based conflicts made possible by industrialization. It was during the transition from state-nations to nation-states that subjects became genuine citizens and assumed exclusive allegiance to 'their' states.

At least two forms of nationalism are evident in this sequence: liberal (or benevolent) and historicist (or malignant). According to Mayall (1990: 30), 'liberal' nationalists regarded self-determination as 'a liberal principle' and 'objected to the idea that the cause of freedom and self-determination could be served by the deliberate use of force'. Like the French Jacobins and Napoléon, liberals like Mazzini and Kossuth believed that national identities were crucial to establishing a republican order in Europe based on popular sovereignty. This version of nationalism reached its apogee with the 1848 revolutions, but, after their failure, European nationalism was infected by racial myths and worship of violence.

'Historicist nationalists' took a different view of the role of force and nationalism in global politics. Early in the 19th century, Hegel had already elaborated an organic model of the individual's relation to the nation-state. Napoléon's conquest of Prussia had created mistrust of democracy among Prussian elites, and the destruction of feudal institutions in that country had driven its leaders toward authoritarian solutions built on national loyalty. Eulogizing the Prussian state, Hegel (1969: 619) argued that reason found expression in the collectivity, and that '[m]an must therefore venerate the state as a secular deity'. War, he argued, was a healthy purgative for a nation, allowing citizens to appreciate the triviality of daily existence. Historicist nationalism dominated German unification, especially after 1848. In Bismarck's Prussia, historian Heinrich von Treitschke argued that nations were competitors in a world from which only the strong could emerge whole. Strong nations were, he declared, obliged to extirpate inferior races, as 'the Redskins in America withered before the Basilisk eye of the Palefaces' (cited in Bowle 1964: 359). Like Social Darwinists, Treitschke considered other nations inferior to his own and believed that the greatness of human history 'lies in the perpetual conflict of nations' (cited in Bowle 1964: 353) .

Thus, 'the line can be traced from Hegel's insistence that the conquests of the historical nations contribute to human progress through the frenzied enthusiasm of the belligerents during the early stages of the First World War, to the contemporary scene of freedom fighters engaged in real and imaginary wars of national liberation' (Mayall 1990: 31). After 1848, nationalism gradually became synonymous with exclusion and otherness. No longer were the boundaries between nation-states softened by the cohesion of aristocratic elites. In the cases of liberal and historicist nationalism, elites manipulated similar identities for different ends. Those like Bismarck and Louis Napoléon who manipulated nationalism to reinforce authoritarian power hijacked the ideology for their own ends, and their example has been emulated by modern demagogues from Mussolini to Milosevic. As Etzioni (1992–3: 21) suggests, national self-determination and democracy frequently are adversaries: 'While they long served to destroy empires and force governments to be more responsive to the governed, with rare exceptions self-determination movements now undermine the potential for democratic development in nondemocratic countries and threaten the foundations of democracy in the democratic ones.'

## National self-determination and the nation-state

The idea of 'national self-determination' legitimized the nation-state. National self-determination, which can mean either autonomy for a 'people' within an existing state or a 'people's' ownership of its own state, was very much in the air in the second half of the 19th century, especially as it applied to multinational empires such as Austria-Hungary. Referring to the Versailles Conference, American President Woodrow Wilson (2006: 415) declared in 1919 that '[t]here was not a man at the table who did not admit the sacredness of the right to self-determination, the sacredness of the right of any body of people to say that they would not continue to live under the Government that they were then living under'. Wilson's Secretary of State Robert Lansing was aghast at the prospect. 'Will it not breed discontent, disorder and rebellion?' he asked. 'The phrase', he continued, 'is simply loaded with dynamite. It will raise hopes which can never be realized. It will, I fear, cost thousands of lives' (cited in Binder and Crossette 1993: A1).

In recent decades, nationalism and national self-determination have become sources of localization, eroding collective identities of states, and challenging global governance. In the 1950s and 1960s, nationalism and national self-determination – enshrined in the UN Charter, Article 1(2) – were ideological bases of decolonization. Today, nationalism is, as Rosenau (2003: 107) argues, 'a form of exclusionary localism' because 'it emphasizes boundaries and the distinction between us and them, with the result that even in the United States the idea of a melting pot has tended to give way to what some regard as a multicultural regime in which different minorities stress their ethnic and racial ties even as they downplay the relevance of an inclusive identity that links them to the varied groups that reside in their country'. As identities, nationalism and ethnicity are associated with closure and with the thickening of vertical barriers across space. 'Wherever nationalism is highly salient in states today, or wherever nations aspire to become states, exclusionary localism can be readily discerned, with the ethnic cleansing policies of Serbia in the 1990s the most notorious recent example that can be cited in this regard' (Rosenau 2003: 107).

Nationalism no longer automatically reinforces state power. If 19th- and 20th-century statesmen invoked nationalism to unify citizens against foreign foes or to distract public attention from domestic woes, contemporary nationalism increasingly divides states and escapes leaders' control. And, if the 18th and 19th centuries witnessed the wedding of 'nation' and 'state', they have become increasingly divorced since the First World War. There is a growing queue of groups in global politics that want their own state, even if this means the collapse of existing states like the Soviet Union and Yugoslavia, or state failure. In much of the developing world, following the Cold War, ethnic and tribal loyalties threatened the integrity of existing states. Bloody examples in Rwanda, Sri Lanka, Sudan, and elsewhere illustrated how politicians manipulate ethnic divisions. Not only did the USSR split into quarrelling nationalities, but several remain at each other's throats – Armenians and Azeris, Georgians and Ossetians, Russians and Georgians, and Russians and Moldovans. After all, 'seldom do political and ethnic borders coincide' and, when faced with demands for nation self-determination, there is a 'universal tendency of governments to render decisions upon the implicit assumption of the need to preserve the entire political unit' and 'proclaim the right to stamp out rebellion and the duty to prevent secession' (Connor 1993:16).

'If we don't find some way that the different ethnic groups can live together in a country', asked former US Secretary of State Warren Christopher, 'how many countries will we have?' His answer: 'We'll have 5,000 countries rather than the hundred plus we now have' (cited in Binder and Crossette 1993). Since almost any group can claim to be a distinctive 'people', there is a risk of fragmentation of political authority into ever smaller and less viable polities. Far from ending history, the Cold War's end saw an upsurge in civil conflict and tribal violence. Even on the marchlands of Europe and Canada, there are 'ethno-national' groups that contend that their culture has been swallowed up by majorities within nation-states – Spanish Basques and Catalans, French Bretons and Corsicans, Canadians Inuits and Native Americans, Celtic Scots and Welsh, and others.

Nationalism and ethnicity need *not* imperil globalization. People, after all, have multiple identities and are simultaneously members of many polities which may overlap. There is no reason, for example, that one cannot identify oneself as both a Basque or a Scot, and a European. The former identity may be relevant for some issues, and the latter for others. 'Europe' provides economies of scale that would be unavailable to a tiny nation. In this sense, it is rational for members of extensive polities to advocate ethno-national secession from existing states. Ethno-national movements such as those of the Basques in Spain, the Flemish and Walloons in Belgium, or the Bretons in France may reduce the cohesion of 'their' state while deriving greater benefits from globalization. Indeed, although many ethno-national groups still seek autonomy or independence, there was a significant decline in violent ethnic movements by the end of the 1990s. 'By the late 1990s, the most common strategy was not armed conflict but prosaic politics' (Gurr 2000: 53).

Nevertheless, nationalism can still be invoked to resist or dilute the cultural homogenization associated with globalization. Thus, in Asia, as elsewhere, glob-alized culture has been mixed with and modified by efforts to update and assert traditional values and norms. Global culture is, in effect, filtered through local languages and meaning systems that help preserve local cultures, producing a 'typical pattern of hybridization: selective absorption, rejection, and assertion of national identity constructs' (Blum 2007: 74). The result has been simultaneous acceptance and resistance of global culture on the part of local elites bent on anchoring nationalism, preserving power and reinforcing traditional normative structures linked to religion, language, and/or ethnicity.

A greater problem arises if nationalism and ethnicity prove to be Hobbesian categories based on passion rather than reason. Ethnic conflict is frequently intractable and the 'contest for worth and place is the common denominator of ethnic conflict among unranked groups' that are divided 'by a vertical cleavage' (Horowitz 2000: 186, 17). To some extent, whether such conflicts are zero-sum depends on the degree to which national or ethnic cleavages crosscut or reinforce other social cleavages such as economic status. If they reinforce each other, conflicts may prove irreconcilable and even produce state collapse.

## Negative localism: state failure, national diasporas, and national assimilation

Although national and ethnic pride can be healthy individual and collective iden-tities, they can also produce negative localism and, as we have observed, impede globalization. The negative localism associated with nationalism and ethnicity afflicts both the developing and developed worlds and may assume several forms.

### State failure

The failure to build viable and stable states after the retreat of colonialism and the post-Cold War upsurge in violence within and across states in parts of Africa and Asia are frequently associated with national, tribal and ethnic rivalries, revived and manipulated by ambitious politicians seeking political power and loot. In Africa, Europeans imposed states and political boundaries that inhabitants never fully accepted and that divided ethnic groups or enclosed ethnic rivals within the same states. Governments of such states may be in the hands of one of the ethnic contenders, may be deemed illegitimate by members of other ethnic groups, may be unable to exercise authority over a state's territory, may be unable to provide security or essential services to citizens, and frequently confront armed opponents.

Such states 'can no longer reproduce the conditions for their own existence' (Di John 2008:10).

The absence of central authority in countries like Somalia, Afghanistan and the western regions of Pakistan makes them attractive asylums for terrorists, narcotics traffickers and even pirates, and threatens to spread violence and disorder into neighbouring states or across entire regions.

State failure is multi-causal (King and Zheng 2001; Carment 2003). However, although the relationship is complex, ethnic heterogeneity and historical animosities often play a role in state failure. 'The civil wars that characterize failed states', concludes Rothberg (2003: 5), 'usually stem from or have roots in ethnic, religious, linguistic, or other intercommunal enmity.' When combined with poverty and uneven economic development, overpopulation, refugee communities, and environmental stress, state institutions in countries such as Sudan, Ivory Coast, Somalia, Yemen, and Haiti have become badly overburdened. According to *Foreign Policy*'s (2011) Failed States Index, of the twenty 'of the world's most vulnerable countries', fourteen are in Africa (Somalia, Chad, Sudan, Democratic Republic of Congo, Zimbabwe, Central African Republic, Cote d'Ivoire, Guinea, Nigeria, Niger, Kenya, Burundi, Guinea-Bissau and Ethiopia), three are in Asia (Afghanistan, Pakistan and Myanmar), two are in the Middle East (Iraq and Yemen) and one (Haiti) is in the Caribbean. Virtually all are multiethnic societies.

## Ethnic and national assimilation

A second form of negative localism is partly a reaction to globalization. Ethnic xenophobia of resident national groups is a consequence of the large-scale movement of persons as refugees and as migrants across state frontiers combined with the spread of terrorism and unemployment. This is Thomas Friedman's (2000: 35) 'olive tree backlashing against the Lexus', and, for Nederveen Pieterse (2009: 81), it is how cultural interaction produces 'intense and dramatic nostalgia politics, of which ethnic upsurges, ethnicization of nations, and religious revivalism form part'.

Residents argue that migrants do not assimilate into dominant cultures and create economic and social problems for their adopted societies including lower wages, human smuggling, street crime and spiralling welfare costs. The issue of economic migration from poor to rich countries has become a focus of political contention both within and among states. Migration is partly a product of demographic forces. Population growth has ended and in some cases populations are decreasing in wealthy countries owing to factors such as urbanization and greater opportunities for women. Simultaneously, populations are 'greying'. Especially in Europe and Japan the consequences include spiralling costs of health care and social security and a declining tax base with fewer young people to fill jobs, especially lower-paying jobs. By contrast, burgeoning populations in Africa, the Middle East and parts of Asia are producing a surplus of young workers in search of employment and higher wages. 'These movements of people, often from former colonies, whether welcome or not, have created a multiculturalism that is qualitatively different from the diversity of personal difference or lifestyles of historic, territorially based minorities that already characterize some Western European countries' (Modood 1997: 1).

Until recently, Europe was predominantly Christian and Caucasian, but large numbers of Muslims of different nationalities arrived after the Second World War as a result of guest-worker programmes, filling poorly paid jobs that Europeans avoided. Although initially guest workers were only supposed to be temporary residents, many remained and were joined by family members. By 2005, Europe's Muslim population had reached between 15 and 20 million or four to five per cent of Europe's total population, and it may double by 2025 (Leiken 2005: 122). With the exception of Germany, most Muslim immigrants in Europe originated in the country's former colonial territories.

Following the 9/11 terrorist attacks, Europeans grew apprehensive about the growing numbers of Muslims in their midst, even as many of the children and grandchildren of the first generation of Muslim migrants were alienated from Western culture. 'Jihadist networks', writes Robert Leiken (2005: 120), 'span Europe from Poland to Portugal, thanks to the spread of radical Islam among the descendants of guest workers... In smoky coffeehouses in Rotterdam and Copenhagen, makeshift prayer halls in Hamburg and Brussels, Islamic bookstalls in Birmingham and "Londonistan", (Philips 2006) and the prisons of Madrid, Milan, and Marseilles, immigrants or their descendants are volunteering for jihad against the West.'

Polls reveal that almost sixty per cent of Germans believe that Muslim immigration from the Middle East and North Africa is a 'bad thing', although majorities elsewhere continue to regard such immigration as positive (Pew 2006) and 'the vast majority of Europe's 15-20 million Muslims have nothing to do with radical Islamism and are struggling hard to fit in, not opt out' (Giry 2006: 87). Among Europeans and North Americans, fear of Muslim extremism is highest in Russia, Spain and Germany and lowest in Canada, the United States and Poland (Pew 2005). For their part, many Muslim residents in Europe – 51 per cent in Germany, 42 per cent in Britain, 39 per cent in France and 31 per cent in Spain – believe that Europeans are hostile toward them (Pew 2006). In addition, large majorities of European Muslims identify themselves as Muslims first and only secondarily as citizens of their country (Pew 2006). Among Europeans, fear has fuelled xenophobic nationalism and has increased support for right-wing anti-immigrant politicians.

France, long regarded as epitomizing a nation-state with a distinctive secular and national culture, now has the largest proportion of Muslims in its population of any European country and is confronting challenges to its ethnic homogeneity. More than the Americans or British, the French believe that immigrants should assimilate, speaking the local language and adopting local mores. This belief has been challenged by growing communities of North Africans concentrated in the impoverished outskirts of French cities. Controversy surrounds French efforts to foster a secular national culture by banning the wearing of 'conspicuous' religious symbols such as headscarves in French schools, a position that enjoys overwhelming public support.

Unlike France, America's multicultural tradition allows immigrants greater latitude to express their identities, but even in the United States, there is growing nationalist concern about the assimilation of the country's Mexican immigrant community. This sentiment is controversially represented by Harvard's Samuel Huntington who argues that Hispanic immigrants are not assimilating into American society. Americans, Huntington argues (2005: xvi), define their national identity to include 'the English language; Christianity; religious commitment; English concepts of the rule of law, the responsibility of rulers, and the rights of individuals; and dissenting Protestant values of individualism, the work ethic, and the belief that humans have the ability and the duty to create a heaven on earth, "a city on the hill". In his view, Hispanics are establishing insulated cultural islands, and their sheer number in the United States threatens to undermine America's culture. Huntington's provocative claim rests on the assertion that Hispanics do not assimilate into American society as did earlier waves of immigrants from Europe. The result, he contends (2005: 221; see also Hanson 2003: 20), will be 'a culturally bifurcated Anglo-Hispanic society with two national languages'.

In addition to sheer numbers, other factors, Huntington argues, make Mexican immigration unique, including the fact that Mexico is America's neighbour, thereby permitting continuous movement back and forth across the border, the high concentration of Mexicans in particular localities like Los Angeles, the high proportion who enter the country illegally, the persistence of the immigration northward, and Mexico's historical claim to American territory. Huntington argues that the barriers to Hispanic assimilation include failure to learn English, poor education levels, low income, and low naturalization and intermarriage rates. The density of links across the US–Mexican border, Huntington (2005: 247) contends, 'could produce a consolidation of the Mexican-dominant areas into an autonomous, culturally and linguistically distinct, economically self-reliant bloc within the United States'.

Huntington's analysis is an extension of his view that we are entering an era of clashing civilizations (Huntington 1996). He is a nationalist whose views are those of one who fears that relentless globalization will undermine existing national cultures and perhaps even national independence. To his critics, Huntington is a xenophobic nationalist, whose belief that American culture is rooted in Anglo-Protestant tradition is false and whose fears are overheated. To his supporters, he summarizes the resentment towards a global tidal wave that threatens national identities, boundaries, and traditional values. Some of Huntington's critics contend that Hispanics do, in fact, assimilate in the same way that their predecessors did. Others argue that his version of American culture has been made obsolete by generations of immigrants and that he does not understand how the United States has repeatedly integrated waves of immigrants into a culture that reflects them all.

Nederveen Pieterse (2009: 42–8) regards Huntington's thesis as one of three cultural paradigms, the others being 'McDonaldization' and 'Hybridization'. He regards Huntington's 'clash of civilizations' as a romantic vision that assumes cultures are closed; its 'fallacy is the reification of the local, sidelining the interplay between the local and the global' (2009: 47). By contrast, 'McDonaldization' assumes cultural homogenization owing to diffusion from a hegemonic core via transnational economic enterprises that produces convergence in states' economic policies, a trend that Armstrong (2000: 372) fears 'could produce the marginalization of local cultures within their own borders', thereby threatening the community's survival. Finally, hybridization entails a mixing of cultural traits 'that resolves the tension... between the local and the global' (Nederveen Pieterse 2009: 57).

## Neomercantilism

Globalization is generally seen to have gone farthest and be least subject to reversal in the economic realm. Cerny (1996: 124–5) writes of the 'competition state', arguing that '[the key to the new role of the state lies in the way that economic competition is changing in the world'.

> [S]tate structures today are being transformed into more and more market-oriented and even market-based organizations themselves, fundamentally altering the way that public and private goods are provided... [W]e may be witnessing the transmutation of the state from a civil association into a more limited form of enterprise association... operating within a wider market and institutional environment. This is not merely a change in degree, but a change in kind.

'The functions of the state', Cerny (2003: 65) maintains, 'although central in structural terms, are becoming increasingly fragmented, privatized and devolved.' Thus, the 'ongoing division of labor ("globalization")' places states 'under ever-increasing pressure, and with it sovereignty-based IR theory' (Osiander 2001: 283). Cerny's competition state is similar to Bobbitt's (2002: 211) 'market-state'. 'Whereas the nation-state, with its mass free public education, universal franchise, and social security policies promised to guarantee the welfare of the nation, the market-state promises instead to maximize the opportunity of the people and thus tends to privatize many state activities and to make voting and representative government less influential and more responsive to the market.'

Globalization notwithstanding, economic nationalism or neomercantilism has not disappeared. Mercantilism's normative assumption is that economic policy should advance *state* power, especially military power, rather than benefit individuals or the world economy as a whole. Like nationalists of all stripes, mercantilists evaluate policy in terms of the *relative* rather than *absolute* benefit it affords nations in comparison to one another, seek to strengthen their states' boundaries, and encourage their independence from outsiders. To this end, mercantilists 'seek to make the international economy fit with the patterns of fragmentation in the political system by reducing the scope of the global market. They emphasize the integrity of the national economy and the primacy of state goals (military, welfare, societal). They advocate protection as a way of preserving integrity, but may be attracted to the construction of their own economy dominating at the centre' (Buzan 2008: 252). In encouraging economic independence and discouraging economic interdependence and transnational links, protecting 'domestic' industries from foreign competition, and assisting 'national champions', even at the expense of foreign rivals, neomercanilists undermine the basic premise of those who support globalization – that the free movement of goods and services globally without being hindered by political boundaries benefits everyone. In this respect, economic nationalism has merged with political and cultural nationalism. 'There are', as Rupert (2000: 17) observes, 'sectors of the anti-liberalization movement which explicitly rejected free trade in favor of a more assertive nationalism, and which continue to organize against globalization in any form.'

All major trading states have developed sophisticated non-tariff barriers to free trade, such as America's 'antidumping' policies that ostensibly aim to 'ensure competition by punishing foreign firms that sell their products at "unfair" prices in US markets' but that has become 'little more than an excuse for special interests to shield themselves from competition' (Mankiw and Swagel 2005: 107).

Perhaps the most striking evidence of economic nationalism is the failure of the Doha Round of global trade talks that began in 2001. In Doha, it was agreed that negotiations would focus on freeing trade in agriculture and services, both contentious issues in global trade, with an eye toward reaching agreement by 2005. Unfortunately, none of the three impediments identified by Bergsten (2005: 1) as preventing agreement, which requires WTO consensus, has been overcome: 'massive current account imbalances and currency misalignments pushing policy in dangerously protectionist directions in both the United States and Europe; the strong and growing anti-globalization sentiments that stalemate virtually every trade debate on both sides of the Atlantic and elsewhere; and the absence of a compelling reason for the political leaders of the chief holdout countries to make the necessary concessions to reach an agreement'. The 'most contentious issue' at Doha involved agricultural subsidies in the developed world that prevent developing countries from selling their products overseas (Panagariya 2005: 4). Efforts to reach agreement collapsed in July 2006 as the United States and the European Union failed to agree over agricultural subsidies and, in response, developing countries like Brazil refused to open their markets to developed countries' manufactured goods and services. This outcome threatens 'long-term damage to the notion of multilateralism' (Sutherland 2005: 1).

Additional evidence of economic nationalism emerged with dramatic increases in grain and commodity prices in 2008. Confronted with domestic unrest, countries as varied as Ukraine, Argentina, Pakistan, India and China reacted by imposing export taxes and export bans on grains and fertilizers, thereby intensifying food shortages elsewhere, especially in East Africa. Russia imposed a similar export ban two years later.

Finally, in the United States opposition to concluding bilateral trade agreements with countries such as Colombia and South Korea, along with unwillingness to make hard decisions that would rescue the Doha Round, suggest that Washington may no longer be prepared to exercise leadership in maintaining a liberal economic system. Without the hegemon to lead, economic liberalism will surely slow and perhaps even be reversed in some respects.

## Conclusion: nationalism in the near future

State failure, demands that migrant communities assimilate, and neomercantilist policies are only some of the manifestations of surging national and ethnic sentiments. Whatever one's view of Huntington, his nationalist impulse is widely shared in the United States and Europe, especially since 9/11. It is reflected in the fence along America's border with Mexico, the tightening of immigration controls in the European Union, and public skepticism toward Doha, NAFTA and other trade agreements in the United States.

A more important factor in accelerating and reinforcing nationalism is the lengthy financial and economic crises that began with America's toxic sub-prime mortgage market and that were spread around the world by the transnational links among banks, corporations and states. Globalization, it seems, not only spreads wealth but also impoverishment. Globally, the response to these crises was intially massive state intervention in the form of aid to banks and corporations, greater regulation of capital flows and financial enterprises, and deficit spending. 'The ideology of the dictatorship of the market', declared French President Nicholas Sarkozy (cited in *Fortune Watch* 2008) in October 2008 'is dead. 'Historians will one day see that this crisis marks the real start of the 21st century', a century which will see the 'return of politics' in managing national economies that will prove to be 'an intellectual and moral revolution'.

Whether or not President Sarkozy is correct, multilateralism has already been a casualty, a fact perhaps most clearly reflected in the inability of the European Union to respond cooperatively to the threat of sovereign debt default by Greece, Portugal, Ireland and Italy. Moreover, previous eras of intense interdependence have ended when confronted with political and economic turmoil. Indeed, as Niall Ferguson (2005: 66) reminds us, the 'last age of globalization' with its 'relatively free trade, limited restrictions on migrations, and hardly any regulation of capital flows' that characterized the late 19th and early 20th centuries abruptly ended in the First World War in 'economic warfare' and 'postwar protectionism' and collapsed during the Great Depression. As in the 1930s, the near future is likely to see national and regional efforts to curb the effects of globalized financial and economic distress at the expense of international and transnational cooperation or to assuage resulting discontent by brandishing nationalist symbols and threatening political and economic adventurism overseas. In the face of stubborn unemployment, domestic resentment against immigrants who would appear to compete with citizens for jobs is likely to intensify and to strengthen xenophobic and nationalist political parties that seek to 'regain control' of national borders already seen to be threatened by terrorism and transnational crime. Finally, the profound geopolitical cleavages that threaten violence in the Middle East, South Asia and Africa are likely to persist, along with the identity conflicts – ethnic, tribal, and religious –

that accompany them. Although globalization will persist and, in some respects, may deepen, national and ethnic identities and loyalties retain a powerful and widespread ideological appeal and will repeatedly emerge in reaction to globalizing tendencies.

## Guide to further reading

Several analyses provide an understanding of the historical origins and conceptual variants of nationalism and ethnicity (Gellner 1983; Connor 1993, 1996; Calhoun 2007; Smith 2001; Gagnon *et al.* 2011). There are also excellent works concerning the evolution of nationalism in relation to the state (Bobbitt 2002) and the specific attributes of ethnicity (Verkuyten 2005). These can be extended to analyses of contemporary nationalism and ethnicity and their relationship to globalization (Rosenau 2003; Blum 2007) and their role as one among various competing identities (Ferguson and Mansbach 2004). There are also recent works dealing with nationalism, ethnicity and conflict (Taras and Ganguly 2009; Di John 2008), and the problem of assimilating national and ethnic minorities who have migrated for economic and political reasons, often to the developed world (Modood 1997; Huntington 2005; Leiken 2005; Philips 2006). Valuable analyses are also available on economic nationalism (Bergsten 2005; Tonelson 2006).

# Chapter 16

# Gendering World Politics in the 21st Century

## RAHEL KUNZ AND MARIANNE H. MARCHAND

For many people, gender and international relations is primarily about *women* in an international context. Gender, however, means a good deal more than this. It can be defined as 'socially constructed roles, behaviours, activities and attributes that a given society considers appropriate for women and men [as well as boys and girls]' (Council of Europe 2011). The first feminists in the discipline of International Relations (IR) asked an important question: 'Where are the women?', criticizing the conventional focus on male-dominated institutions and powerful men, and highlighting the under- and mis-representation of women in world politics and their relations to powerful men.

When the concept of gender was first introduced it was contrasted with sex, which is defined as the biological difference between men and women. But more recent studies suggest that the differences between gender and sex are not so clear-cut and that the (biological) bodies of men and women or girls and boys are also socially constructed. This can be observed when, on the birth of a baby, one of the first questions asked is whether it is a girl or boy, thus making parents and medical staff declare its sex which in certain cases, such as those of hermaphrodites, can be ambiguous. Moreover, as young girls and boys we are taught about the performativity of our bodies, in terms of how to act, what to wear, and so on (Butler 1990; Peterson and Runyan 2010). In other words, gender is about men, women, boys and girls as well as masculinities and femininities and the social construction of these identities. Moreover, gender also intersects with class, ethnicity, race, nationality, age and sexuality to produce specific forms of masculinities and femininities and a web of gender and other inequalities.

The central themes of this chapter are how world politics is gendered, how gender operates at different levels and in different contexts, and why the concept of gender is of importance for our understanding of world politics in the 21st century. To pursue a gender analysis of world politics we will use the analytical approach of relational thinking. Such an approach assumes that gender operates at different inter-connected levels and that one needs to analyze these dimensions and their connections in order to fully understand or analyze the gendered nature of world politics. According to Spike Peterson, relational thinking encompasses three dimensions. One deals with an ideological dimension through the representations of social practices and processes and their relative value in society. This implies that activities are distinguished as masculine or feminine; and at the same time, practices considered masculine are seen as more important than feminine practices. The second dimension is oriented towards the gendered nature of social relations, particularly those practices, institutions and structures which are connected to social reproduction. Finally, the third dimension deals with the social construction of male and female bodies, that is, with the way in which identity and a sense of subjectivity are constructed (Peterson 2003; see also Marchand and Runyan 2000; 2011). In sum, relational thinking allows us to introduce gendered subjectivities and subjects in our analysis of world politics; it reveals the gendered representations and valorizations of world politics' social realities; and it recognizes gendered power relations and how they intersect with other unequal power relations.

In the remainder of the chapter we provide a gendered analysis of a selection of relevant issues in 21st-century world politics, using the analytical framework of relational thinking. The second section examines how feminist analyses have shaped research on conflict and security in IR and provides a gender analysis of two current issues within the field of security studies: 'violent women' and security sector reform (SSR). The third section addresses the gender dimensions of labour, focusing particularly on migrant and domestic workers, as well as on the gender dimensions of factory workers in export processing zones. The conclusion provides a short summary of the relevance of gender in 21st-century world politics.

## Gender matters in International Relations

This section outlines feminist contributions to the analysis of conflict and security in IR and provides a gender analysis of two current issues in the field of security: the increasing mediatization of 'violent women' and the emerging field of security sector reform (SSR). Using an analytical framework based on relational thinking, we argue that paying attention to gender issues allows for more comprehensive and accurate understanding of conflict and security issues.

### Feminist security studies

A discipline born out of war, IR has been prominently concerned with understanding conflict and researching security. Traditionally, gender has rarely been considered relevant to the analysis of conflict and security. Yet, since the 1980s, a rich feminist literature on the gender dimensions and implications of conflict and international security has challenged this view. The two strands of this literature demonstrate that gender is intrinsic to both the concepts and the politics of conflict and security, and analyses ways in which femininities and masculinities are constructed and reproduced in conflict and security practices.

First, feminist theorists have explored the roles that women and gender play in conflict and conflict resolution (Elshtain 1987; Moser and Clark 2001; Goldstein 2003). They argue that women have always been part of conflicts, both as victims and as perpetrators of violence, and gender has always been central to the ways in which conflicts are recounted and analysed. Thus, for example, Goldstein (2003) reveals that women and girls have always been associated with armed forces and Armed Non-State Actors (ANSAs), and have taken on both support and combat roles. Even though women's representation in the armed forces is currently rather small – it ranges from 0.4 per cent in Bolivia and 0.8 per cent in Colombia to 14 per cent in the US (RESDAL 2010: 56) – reform aimed at increasing women's participation in armed forces is ongoing in many countries. Women and girls also constitute up to 30 to 40 per cent of the membership of some ANSAs (Goldstein 2003: 81–3): for example, they made up nearly a third of Sandinista troops in Nicaragua during the 1980s and about half the fighting force of the Liberation Tigers of Tamil Eelam (LTTE) (Goldstein 2003: 81–3). Enloe (1990) has demonstrated the key role women play as prostitutes in US military bases around the world.

Second, feminist research has highlighted the gender bias inherent in the concept of security as it has traditionally been understood, urging for a reconceptualization (Enloe 1983; Tickner 1992; Steans 2006). Moving beyond statist conceptions, feminists have broadened the notion of security into a more multi-level and multi-dimensional concept that allows expansion of the security agenda beyond the high politics of military security to include insecurities linked to poverty, environmental change or domestic violence (Tickner 1992). Feminist approaches to security problematize the state as 'protector' and guarantor of security. They have also shifted the referent object of security from the state to the individual or the community level and have been crucial to the opening up of debate about human security more broadly (see Newman, this volume). Recent feminist scholarship has also asked 'the man question', that is, using notions of gender to look at male and female subjectivities, to 'interrogate the constituted subject of man and his varied masculinities in order to offer an alternative, gendered exposé of the study and practice of international politics' (Parpart and Zalewski 2008: 1). Research on violent masculinities analyses the role that they play in justifying and perpetuating conflict, and how they influence peace negotiations. In sum, feminists argue that 'gender is conceptually, empirically and normatively essential to studying international security' in order to produce accurate and rigorous scholarship (Sjoberg 2010: 2). Most recently, two issues have become the focus of feminist scholarship: the increasing mediatization of 'violent women' and the emerging field of security sector reform.

## Violent women

The increasing focus on women and gender issues in conflict has had the unfortunate effect of portraying women mostly as victims (of sexual violence), or as ideal peace negotiators, based on gendered stereotypes of women as inherently peaceful and innocent. Violence therefore remains commonly associated with masculinity and peace with femininity, with the result, for example, that the term 'combatant' often automatically refers to men and boys, thus contributing to the exclusion of women, girls and gender issues. Accounts that do consider gender and women's and girls' roles in armed conflict tend to focus on the exposure of women and girls to sexual violence and other conflict-related vulnerabilities (Card 1996). Consequently, women and girls have often been portrayed as victims and denied agency. With these gendered stereotypes in mind, we prefer to overlook female fighters, since non-fighting civilian women and girls correspond more closely to the ideal of peace-loving women (Specht and Attree 2006: 226).

Feminists have reacted by becoming interested in 'violent women' who, variously, participate in armed conflict, fight in rebel groups, take hostages, carry out suicide attacks and abuse prisoners (Alison 2004; Parashar 2009; Sjoberg and Gentry 2007). The main interest is in studying 'women's violence in global politics with the aim of determining what their actions mean both for global political perceptions of women's characteristics and for feminist theories of women's roles in international relations' (Sjoberg and Gentry 2007: 3). For example, research has analyzed the gendered mediatization of female suicide bombers in Chechnya or the widely reported case of Lynndie England in connection with Abu Ghraib prisoner abuse. Female presence in ANSAs and their direct participation in violent acts challenge our idealized notions of women and femininity, according to which they are 'beautiful souls' – innocent and naturally reluctant to fight (Sjoberg 2010: 54). Faced with the seemingly paradoxical situation of women and girls as perpetrators of violence, observers typically portray these women and girls as 'mothers, monsters or whores' (Sjoberg and Gentry 2007). What these narratives have in common is their tendency to sexualize women's violence and portray violent women as victims, rather than perpetrators, deceived by violent men, rather than acting out of their own will, thus minimizing their agency.

As part of the increasing attention paid to 'violent women', there is a growing literature on female combatants in ANSAs that analyses why women and girls join ANSAs, the roles they play and how they experience their participation, and explores the implications of their activities for conflict and post-conflict situations (Alison 2004; Parashar 2009). The fact that women take up armed struggle contradicts the stereotypical notion that women are naturally more peaceful than men and breaks with the victimization discourse. This might explain why, despite the international community's growing awareness of the prevalence of women and girls associated with ANSAs, they are often ignored in conflict analyses and excluded from peace negotiations, post-conflict reconstruction and demobilization (DDR) processes (Dietrich Ortega 2009). These processes often mainly aim at men, based on the gendered assumption that depicts men as the actors of war and as the key security risk in post-conflict situations (MacKenzie 2009). Moreover, given the social stigma, female combatants have many incentives to 'invisibilize' themselves in post-conflict situations. Hence, not only is representing women as victims analytically problematic, but it can also have adverse policy implications.

This illustrates the key role that gender stereotypes play in determining policies and assessing their implications, and shows how gender matters not only as an analytical tool, but also in terms of addressing the impact of specific policies.

In sum, the dominant discourse of existing peace and conflict research, as well as among practitioners in the field of international security, portrays women and girls as victims or particularly vulnerable groups that need assistance and protection, or as inherently peaceful and thus potential partners for peace-building initiatives. These gendered representations are intimately linked to gendered practices and processes, such as humanitarian assistance, conflict resolution, peace-building initiatives and DDR programmes. In the process, these narratives and practices produce gendered identities, opposing the female victim to the male protector, and casting women as mothers, monsters or whores. Yet, 'violent women' act to challenge these narratives and practices, refusing to conform to dominant gendered identities.

## Gender and security sector reform

The field of security sector reform (SSR) emerged in the 1990s in the context of the increased linking of security and development issues in the post-Cold War period. SSR aims to 'create a secure environment that is conducive to development, poverty reduction, good governance and, in particular, the growth of democratic states and institutions based on the rule of law' (GFNSSR 2007: 4). The most widely endorsed definition of SSR is that of the United Nations: 'Security sector reform describes a process of assessment, review and implementation as well as monitoring and evaluation led by national authorities that has as its goal the enhancement of effective and accountable security of the State and its peoples without discrimination and with full respect for human rights and the rule of law' (United Nations 2008: 6). Over time, SSR has gained importance, as illustrated in the increasing involvement of key international actors such as the Organisation for Economic Cooperation and Development (OECD), the European Union or the World Bank, and has attracted considerable donor funding (Schnabel and Farr 2012: 4).

SSR has been criticized as being a top-down, state-based and Eurocentric project. These criticisms refer to two main areas: its definition of (in)security and the referent object of security, and its definition of security providers. First, SSR practice has tended to focus on security as national security, the state being its key referent object (Baker and Scheye 2007: 505). Such an understanding of security tends to be expert-led and 'one size fits all', and its conception of security needs is top-down, with a focus on state and institution building. SSR theory and practice have also been accused of being largely donor-driven (Luckham 2009: 2). And as with other seemingly gender-neutral fields and issues, feminists have been quick to challenge SSR over its lack of inclusion of women and gender issues and to point out the gendered dimensions and implications of SSR discourse and practice. Key gender critiques of SSR include: the lack of equitable participation in security needs assessment, decision making and provision; insufficient focus on meeting the different security and justice needs of women, men, girls and boys; and the failure to transform institutional culture, including cultures of violent masculinities (Kunz and Valasek 2012: 127).

Hence, a gender focus allows us to introduce gendered subjectivities and subjects into the analysis and practice of SSR and to highlight gendered representations and practices. SSR has been criticized for perpetuating women's underrepresentation in security decision making and security sector institutions (SSIs) (Naraghi-Anderlini 2008: 105–6). As a result, feminists highlight the need for women to join SSIs, including combat roles in the military, in order to become full citizens and security providers rather than the stereotypical victim needing protection (Carter 1998: 33–4). In response, security sector actors have often implemented initiatives to increase the number of female security sector personnel. Yet, these initiatives have been criticized for equating gender sensitivity with numerical representation and for ignoring the fact that simply including more female personnel in institutions imbued with sexism may endanger or co-opt women rather than transform those institutions. In addition, arguments of 'operational effectiveness' used to promote female participation have been critiqued for essentialism and instrumentalization.

A gender analysis argues against uncritically advocating women's participation in security discourses and practices without an analysis of existing gendered power dynamics (Bendix 2009). Indeed, rampant corruption, impunity, human rights violations and misogyny pervade many institutions undergoing SSR processes – especially the armed forces, police and border guards. Forms of militarized, violent masculinities are institutionally cultivated in the name of military conduct and group loyalty, resulting in discriminatory institutional policies, structures and practices, including high rates of sexual harassment and exploitation. Despite the urgent need for SSR initiatives to address misogynistic and xenophobic institutional cultures, '[e]ven in post-conflict situations, security sector reform processes do not necessarily lead to any questioning of militarism, or of the cultures of masculinities sustained within military institutions' (Clarke 2008: 63). As in the field of development, feminist critiques of SSR also challenge the simplistic categories of 'women' and 'men', and note that in addition to gender, other factors influence security access and agency, such as ethnicity, class, sexual orientation, location, religion and ability.

Feminists have also challenged the existing priorities and concerns of the study of world politics. In the field of security, feminists have pushed to broaden the agenda to include gender-sensitive understandings of security and the addressing of genderspecific security needs. Thus, for example, feminists are critical of the way in which SSR in Mexico has been framed in a way that does not allow specific gendered forms of violence to be taken into account, such as the *feminicidios* (the murder of hundreds of women) in Ciudad Juárez since 1993. Instead, these gender-specific crimes have been subsumed and concealed in recent years under the larger umbrella of security concerns, making it difficult to address their gender-specific needs.

Hence, critics have called for a fundamental shift in SSR discourse and practice. Rather than starting with the objective of building effective and accountable SSIs, the point of departure should be the diverse security and justice needs of people. This allows gendered subjects to be brought into the abstract story of SSR: men, women, boys and girls who have different security and justice needs based upon a wide range of social, cultural, political and economic factors. Feminists have come to the conclusion that current SSR initiatives that prioritize institution building over the identification of and response to justice and security needs have important gender-specific implications. Analysis shows how the seemingly neutral concepts and institutions of security and SSR are based on gendered assumptions, and how the practice of SSR reproduces gendered narratives and violent masculinities. As a result, SSR tends to ignore or marginalize women's and girls' specific security needs.

## Gender matters in International Political Economy

For the last twenty years or so, the global political economy has seen profound transformations, which tend to be captured by the catch-all term of globalization. Analyzing globalization from a gender perspective allows us to show how it is gendered in multiple ways by bringing together ideational, material and 'bodily' dimensions. To begin with, as Marchand and Runyan argue, it is better to conceptualize the process of globalization as a global restructuring because it alludes to the breaking down of an old order and the construction or creation of a new one (2011: 7; see also Marchand 1996: 577). Such a conceptualization suggests that global restructuring is made up of a set of processes that are multi-dimensional, do not necessarily occur at the same speed, and may be disconnected (Marchand and Runyan 2011: 7). In other words, global restructuring (or globalization) is 'messy' and has to be analyzed in concrete situations in order to understand its complexities and contradictions.

For many, neoliberalism is a key feature of contemporary globalization or global restructuring, engendering not only shifts in economic policies but also setting the stage for changes in the subjectivities and identities of people. Neoliberal policies have effected a shift in boundaries between public and private spheres, resulting, among other things, in a re-privatization of reproductive tasks that had become part of welfare state provision. Examples include the re-privatization of childcare and other kinds of care work.

But, as Charlotte Hooper suggests, neoliberal globalization also provides the context for changing subjectivities, in particular the emergence of a new Anglo-American hegemonic masculinity, which she calls 'frontier masculinity' (2000: 70). This 'hegemonic masculinity is being reconfigured in the image of a less formal, less patriarchal but more technocratic masculine elite with the whole globe as its playground' (Hooper 2000: 70). Kimberly Chang and L.H.M. Ling, in turn, suggest that globalization is to be seen as a dualistic process consisting of Global Restructuring 1, or techno-muscular capitalism, and Global Restructuring 2, or a regime of labour intimacy (Chang and Ling 2000: 27–42). Different groups inhabit both spheres. The dominant realm of techno-muscular capitalism is inhabited by

Hooper's technocratic masculine elite, while the sphere of labour intimacy's regime is feminized and provides a home for, in particular, migrant women, working as domestics and nannies. Saskia Sassen supports this conceptualization in her work on global cities, which she defines as 'strategic sites for the specialized servicing, financing and management of global economic processes' (Sassen 2002: 94). In Sassen's words:

> These cities are also sites for the incorporation of large numbers of women and immigrants in activities that service the strategic sectors; but this is a mode of incorporation that renders these workers invisible, therewith breaking the connection between being workers in leading industries and the opportunity to become – as has been historically the case in industrialized economies – a 'labor aristocracy' or its contemporary equivalent. In this sense 'women and immigrants' emerge as the systemic equivalent of the off-shore proletariat. (2002: 94)

These different spheres of the global political economy are not only related to different subjectivities but are also valorized in different ways. For instance, domains that are connected to hegemonic masculine subjectivities, such as the global financial sector, tend to be seen as representing power and being more significant than, for instance, the feminized and racialized service sector of cleaning or care work, which often remains invisible.

In the next section we will take a closer look at a different aspect of neoliberal globalization or global restructuring. This deals with the changes in production and the global division of labour, and is about export processing zones (EPZs), also known as *maquiladoras* in Mexico and Central America.

## Export processing zones or maquiladoras

Global restructuring is not only a reflection of profound transformations, but in turn is also generating changes in society. For instance, production has undergone major changes since the 1970s. As O'Brien and Williams suggest, the global production structure has undergone two important changes:

> The first has been the globalization of production. There has been proliferation of corporate activity and business networks around the world. The second major development has been the change in underlying principles of the organization of production and key features of the global production system. (2010: 193)

The increasing global reach of transnational corporations (TNCs) would not have been possible without major transformations in the way goods are produced. Technological changes, such as improvements in communications, information technology and logistics, have enabled firms to outsource part of their operations to other parts of the world. Initially, EPZs played an important role in this, but in more recent years a new form of outsourcing has appeared in the form of call centres. These call centres are located in India, among other countries, and employ many young people with a college education who first need to learn to speak American or British English before being allowed to answer the phones.

Before the 1970s it was possible to identify people's work based on where they lived – geographic location defined one's position in the international division of labour (O'Brien and Williams 2010: 254). With first the internationalization of production in the 1970s and later the globalization of production from the 1990s the old international division of labour was transformed into the new international division of labour (NIDL) and, subsequently, the global division of labour (GDL).

The NIDL has been characterized by an internationalization of production, in which TNCs would move part of their production process abroad in order to save money and thus become more competitive. This is clearly exemplified by EPZs or *maquiladoras*. Since the 1970s TNCs have started to move a significant part of their production offshore in order to save on labour costs and be able to produce in a hospitable or lax regulatory environment, particularly as regards working conditions, and environmental and health and safety issues.

From a gender perspective EPZs or *maquiladoras* are of particular interest because they employ predominantly women. Why is over 80 per cent of the *maquiladora* workforce female? Women are employed because they are stereotyped as having 'nimble fingers', as being more docile than men and thus easier for management to control and, finally, because they can be paid less, as their income is seen as 'a little extra' for the household (see, e.g., Cravey 1998; Sklair 1989; Fernández-Kelly 1983).

Since these EPZs and *maquiladoras* were first introduced there have been important changes. One such change is that from the early 1990s the make-up of the *maquiladora* workforce has changed. Now there are about 65 per cent women and 35 per cent men employed by the *maquiladoras* on the US–Mexico border. Interestingly, however, there is a difference in the number of male and female workers according to the type of *maquiladora* which employs them. Men tend to work for the high-tech sector, for example, in the automotive industry, while women are usually working in older industries such as clothing and electronics assembly (televisions etc.). As María Eugenia de la O Martínez (2006) suggests, a geographic relocation is also occurring, resulting in older and less profitable *maquilas* moving to the southern (and central) states of Mexico. She argues, further, that this relocation is not gender-neutral: the *maquilas* on the northern border are being 're-masculinized' while the ones in the central and southern parts of Mexico tend to employ predominantly female workers. In sum, this shows that gender relations are not static but do undergo transformations according to the needs of the global political economy.

## Conclusion

21st-century world politics is gendered. Gender analyses show gendered dynamics and the gender-specific implications of conflict, peace and security, international institutions, global governance, development and human rights, and global economic and social processes through which gendered identities and inequalities are produced and reproduced. Feminists have also demonstrated how key concepts in International Relations and International Political Economy and their related analytical frameworks – such as security, the state, and production – are gendered. Moreover, they have broadened the IR agenda and challenged the dominant conception of the key concerns of the discipline. Yet, as this chapter illustrates, gender remains more than ever crucial to understanding issues in 21st-century world politics. As Peterson writes:

> gender is hard to see and critique because it orders 'everything' and disrupting that order feels threatening... Yet, however much we are uncomfortable with challenges to gender ordering, we are in the midst of them. Failure to acknowledge and address these challenges both impairs our understanding of the world(s) we live in and sustains relations of domination. (Peterson 1997: 199)

Thus, gender matters both for a better understanding of 21st-century world politics in general, and for analyses of its power relations in particular.

## Guide to further reading

Cynthia Enloe's work (1983, 1990) is among the classics that continue to inspire scholars working on gender in IR/IPE. Peterson and Runyan (2010), Steans (2006), Sylvester (1994) and Whitworth (1997) provide a good general introduction to gender issues in IR and IPE. For an introduction to gender in IR and security studies more particularly, see Tickner (1992). A good overview of current feminist research in security studies can be found in Sjoberg (2010). Cohn's article (1987) is one of the most fascinating feminist analyses of defence intellectuals and nuclear weapons technologies. Peterson (2003) provides an interesting framework for critical gender analysis of IPE. For analyses of the numerous dimensions of gender and globalization, see Marchand and Runyan (2011).

# Chapter 17

# Democracy and Democratic Change

*WILLIAM CASE*

Democracy, though traceable to the ancients, began to cohere in its modern representative form as a way to organize political life during the European Enlightenment. It has spread around the world through what Samuel Huntington (1991) identified as 'waves'. A first wave, beginning during the 19th century and extending into the 20th, enveloped much of Europe. But it lost ground during the 1920s and 1930s amid the rise of totalitarian ideologies. A second wave coincided with the break-up of empires after the Second World War, bringing democracy to Africa and Asia. But during the 1950s and 1960s, it retreated before military coups and modernizing bureaucracies. Beginning in the mid-1970s, though, democracy surged anew, culminating in the third wave.

The third wave of democracy began in Portugal, Spain and Greece and spread swiftly into South America. During the late 1980s, 'people power' in the Philippines also encouraged the 'snowballing' of democracy across South Korea and Taiwan. At the end of the decade, the fall of the Berlin Wall and the end of the Cold War enabled Eastern Europe to democratize, followed by parts of sub-Saharan Africa and Asia. Thus, by the early 1990s, the number of democracies had so increased that for the first time, a majority of the world's countries and people lived under them. By 2006, nearly two-thirds of the world's countries could be classified as democratic (see Diamond 2008: appendix). Only China, Russia, Central Asia and Arab societies seemed to stand as major hold-outs against democracy. In this context, Francis Fukuyama (1992) was moved to proclaim the 'end of history', arguing that with the demise of communism, democracy was now widely recognized as the only legitimate type of regime. Accordingly, during the late 20th and early 21st centuries, democratization arose as a key issue in world politics.

The aim of this chapter is to survey some major aspects of this remarkable reorganization of political life. Where once military governments, single-party systems and personal dictatorships had prevailed, democratic institutions now often stood. The analysis begins by briefly rehearsing two major ways of understanding democracy. It then outlines some of the preconditions for democracy that have been identified, as well as the motivations possessed by different social groups for seeking democratic change. Some obstacles will also be enumerated before turning finally to the transitional pathways along which democratic change takes place.

The chapter also evaluates the extent to which globalization may have shifted decisional power from governments to such a degree that democracy organized at the national level loses relevance. And as power gravitates to multilateral institutions and transnational corporations, are there any prospects for democratizing politics at the global level? In this context, the chapter examines the likelihood of what Diamond (2008: ch. 3) describes as a 'democratic recession'. It finds that while democracy's advances have been tested by some reversals, its prospects may at the same time be brightening. Finally, this chapter considers whether, even if democratic change continues, it will make any real difference in the lives of ordinary citizens?

## What is democracy?

Modern democracy has principally been understood by theorists in two competing ways: substantive and procedural. Substantive democracy refers to conditions of equality between socio-economic classes, ethnic communities, genders and other forms of identity and affiliation, culminating in a literature that finds expression in social, economic and industrial democracy. In this view, policies and programmes that give rise to social equality take precedence over institutions and procedures. By contrast, the notion of procedural democracy puts greater emphasis on civil liberties and competitive elections. In considering which interpretation is more analytically fruitful, Burton *et al.* (1991: 2) remind us that social equality may be a precondition for democracy, or it may follow as a policy outcome, but equality and democracy are not the same thing. Indeed, they contend that the conflation of these two aspects can cause analytic confusion. As one example, they observe that the former German Democratic Republic, in its commitments to social justice, distributed wealth relatively equitably, yet could hardly be considered democratic. Accordingly, most analysts of democracy and democratic change today agree that a procedural understanding is best. Only in the more vexed analysis of democracy's consolidation has an insistence on equality in outcomes returned.

In conceptualizing democracy in procedural ways, O'Donnell and Schmitter's (1986) classic text distinguished between civil liberties and competitive elections. They thus drew upon Robert Dahl's (1971) earlier notion of the liberal and inclusionary elements of what in the real world he elaborated as 'polyarchal democracy'. Civil liberties include free speech, press and assembly, enabling citizens to communicate freely and then organize in pursuit of their interests and causes. Elections, meanwhile, must be free, fair, regularly held and meaningful, enabling governments to be held accountable. These contests are free in that the voting franchise is inclusive. They are fair in that the incumbent government eschews a grossly partisan use of state agencies, facilities and funding, ensuring competitiveness. They are held regularly within fixed time frames, recorded in a constitution. And they are meaningful in that the state apparatus is controlled by elected chief executives and legislators, not cabals of generals, bureaucrats and sundry economic elites nestling unaccountably in 'reserved positions' (Schedler 2006: 41).

## Democratic preconditions and motivations

Democracy requires that participants strike a fine balance between competitiveness and restraint. In a vibrant democracy, political parties, civil society organizations and social movements compete over institutional positions and policy outcomes, though not at all costs. Winners must display tolerance, while losers prepare to compete another day. This 'restrained partisanship' led scholars to canvas the preconditions that might underpin democracy's complex sets of institutions and procedures. These included appropriate historical legacies, past experience with democracy, social structures, developmental levels, institutional designs and cultural outlooks. According to Myron Weiner (1987), specifically British colonial experience, in exposing indigenous elites to the rule of law through new bureaucratic structures and to restrained competitions through elections, amounted to a 'tutelary model' that greatly favoured democracy. But as Diamond (2008: 155) recounts, this model was often countered by a vice-regal tradition, involving 'an ugly, racist system of exploitation and domination that was intrinsic to the very nature of colonial rule'. Thus, although India and Jamaica have internalized enough British common law values and electoral traditions to remain democracies, Pakistan, Burma, Malaysia, Singapore and many African countries that were once part of the Empire have not.

In examining the social structures deemed necessary for democracy, theorists have primarily examined socio-economic classes and ethnicity. In Britain and the United States, where private capital took the lead in fomenting development, capital-owning classes, in seeking to defend their property rights against state predation, sought to strengthen their resistance through elected parliaments. This echoed Barrington Moore's (1966) pithy dictum, 'no bourgeoisie, no democracy'. According to modernization theorists, however, urban middle classes were more crucial. Uplifted by general prosperity and made confident by their business and professional dealings, they sought to extend their independent decision making from their private pursuits to political life. This led them to support political parties and join civil society organizations in ways that enabled them to hold governments accountable. And yet, the historical record equally shows that where these have been dependent upon the state for economic benefits and protection from the lower classes that vastly outnumber them, they can oppose democratic change. This is particularly so in countries that came late to industrialization. One observes the recent actions of middle-class demonstrators in the Philippines and Thailand, cohering respectively in People Power II and the People's Alliance for Democracy (PAD) which, in criticizing populism and poor governance, both succeeded in ousting elected governments, actions funded by business magnates, winked at by the military and sanctioned by the courts. Even students can be unreliable democrats, with Huntington (1991–2: 604) casting them as the 'universal opposition' who stridently criticize any regime in place, whatever its tenor. Accordingly, Eva Bellin (2000), in charting the varying political preferences and behaviours of these classes, has labelled them as, at most, 'contingent democrats'.

In the view of Rueschemeyer *et al.* (1992), then, it is the industrial working class that is the most reliable democratizing agent. Organized into powerful trade unions and seeking the representation in government that can improve labour welfare, workers drive democracy by pressing for democratic concessions from the government and the capital-owning classes, who often collude with one another. However, though the working class might sometimes operate along these lines, it seems just as easily drawn into patterns of top-down populism and corporatism, as well as protectionist strategies, which can equally easily support authoritarian rule. Thus, if organized labour helped to advance democratization in 19th-century Europe, it has since been identified also with the authoritarian rule of Juan Peron in Argentina and Mahmoud Ahmadinejad in Iran. Further, labour is today often disorganized, dispersed throughout global production networks rather than concentrated in specific countries, greatly reducing its effectiveness.

Nor does ethnicity have a straightforward impact on the prospects for democracy. In societies in which multiple ethnic communities reside, Huntington (1984) argued, democracy was stronger due to the dense mosaic of impenetrable ethnic redoubts and cultural baffles that resisted any systematic intrusiveness of state power. The surprising persistence of democracy in India, notwithstanding its low level of development, is often attributed in part to its extraordinary ethnic, linguistic and religious complexity (see, e.g., Kohli 2001). By contrast, Rabushka and Shepsle (1972) argue that ethnic divisions and conflict lead to the breakdown of democracy, citing the cases of Malaysia and Lebanon as evidence. Arend Lijphart (1969) and Benjamin Reilly (2001) have showed how communal peace can be preserved through painstaking constitutional engineering, electoral innovations and power-sharing processes. But where competitiveness is thus reduced in order to apportion state power and positions on a ethnic basis, questions arise over how democratic the regime then is.

A more powerful thesis, then, first proposed by Seymour Martin Lipset (1959), focuses on developmental levels and democratic outcomes. Put simply, it contends that as societies grow richer and better educated, hierarchical statuses and patterns of deference begin to break down, encouraging social groups, especially the middle class, to become more participatory. Usually parsed as modernization theory, this expectation, along with its more contemporary refinements, has been enormously influential. In some studies, even necessary average per capita income levels have been specified. And yet, even though most rich countries are indeed democracies, some, like Singapore and the Gulf states, are not. Rapid economic growth, generating a kind of performance legitimacy, and petroleum exports, generating revenues that empower the state sooner than social forces, can dampen pressures for democratic change, even in rich countries. At the same time, though in a much-cited study, Przeworski *et al.* (1996) argued that democracy is more likely to persist in rich countries than poor ones, we note its lengthy practice in places like India, Botswana and Mali.

Accordingly, the debate over economic development and democracy has grown convoluted. If development's causality is frequently brittle, it may be, then, that directionality cuts the other way. With democracy freeing the participatory impulse of citizens, its liberal elements may carry over into private entrepreneur-ship and innovation, helping fuel economic development. But this argument stands in contrast to the post-war record of industrializing gains in Japan, Korea, Singapore and, in some measure, Taiwan, documented in an immense literature on state-led strategies and industrial policies (e.g., Wade 2003b).

Given the ambiguities that haunt the search for democracy's preconditions, most theorists have abandoned it. To be sure, national wealth often helps. And hyper-nationalism, radical Islamism and state oil revenues do not. But with democracy so often failing to appear in settings where it might be predicted, and in other cases taking root where it would not be, much scrutiny shifted during the third wave to elite-level preferences, bargaining and outright contingency.

## How does democratic change take place?

With structures so indeterminate, democracy theorists like Dankwart Rustow (1970), O'Donnell and Schmitter (1986) and Burton and Higley (1987) shifted attention to national leaders and elites. They addressed the ways in which elites interacted with one another (whether in restrained or warlike ways) and appealed to their followers (either galvanizing or under-mobilizing them), while giving shape to the directionality of structural forces. As O'Donnell and Schmitter (1986: 19) intoned, 'there is no transition whose beginning is not the consequence – direct or indirect – of important divisions within the authoritarian regime itself'.

As comparativists turned to the dynamics of democratization, a vast literature appeared that came informally to be labelled transitology (Schmitter and Karl 1994). Focusing intently on inter-elite relations, a new vocabulary emerged that included hardliners and softliners in the authoritarian coalition and minimalists and maximalists standing in opposition. Further, in tracing the ways in which the coalition unravelled, popular upsurge took place and democratic change unfolded, researchers identified patterns of top-down 'transformation' (as in Spain and Brazil), bottom-up replacement (Portugal, the Philippines and Indonesia) and a more evenly negotiated process that Huntington termed 'transplacement' (South Korea).

In emphasizing contingency, this approach seemed to its detractors to offer no more than description. But some constraining conditions were gradually discovered. Most notably, the pathways by which democratic change took place were tracked back to the distinctive forms of authoritarian rule from which they had emerged. Using a simple typology of military governments, single-party systems and personal dictatorships, comparativists identified military governments as most likely to undertake top-down transformations (Geddes 1999). With generals abhorring the politicization of their institution that so eroded professionalism and corporate élan, they were often keen to cede state power and return to the barracks. Thus, where they could claim some industrializing success while in power, they initiated processes of pre-emptive transformation, then negotiated from a position of strength, giving rise to extensive 'pacting' through which to gain amnesties while retaining control over selected state enterprises and budgets. On this count, Spain's transformation during the mid-1970s, mediated by the prime minister and encouraged by the king, was viewed as paradigmatic (Gunther 1992). But where their records were disastrous, as in Greece and Argentina, humiliated by defeat in war, militaries were pushed from power much more briskly. In these cases, contention arose over any amnesties that had been granted, leading in some cases to generals being jailed.

By contrast, under personal dictatorships, with strongmen having so personalized the state apparatus and most aspects of economic life, they had no counterpart to the barracks to which they might safely retreat. In the case of the Philippines, as Mark Thompson (1995) has documented, President Ferdinand Marcos possessed no refuge outside the state, and hence refused to negotiate any withdrawal from power. Under personal dictatorships, then, it is only through replacement, exemplified by the 'people power' uprising that took place in 1986, that democratic change can take place.

Finally, single-party systems, while often resilient, lack the coercive capacity of militaries. Yet where economic crisis or societal pressures loom large, they may be willing to cede state power. Further, their willingness to do this may be increased by the fact that in contrast to personal dictatorships, they possess party organizations that may find a stake in any democratic regime of multi-party elections that follows. Thus, for some Communist parties in Eastern Europe, as well as the Institutional Revolutionary Party in Mexico and the Kuomintang in Taiwan, the democratization of politics did not amount to the end of the world. It seemed, then, that single-party systems most often underwent democratic change through the process of transplacement described above.

But despite these constraining conditions and identified pathways, the analytic focus on elite-level contingency was increasingly criticized for the modest levels of theorizing that it was able to generate. Accordingly, attention began finally to shift from elites to the institutions and structures in which their statuses were anchored, encouraging new and deeper study of militaries and dominant parties. Moreover, as democracy's third wave began to weaken, comparativists observed that in some cases, military officers had been socialized in ways that enabled them to perpetuate their regimes, once understood as transient, over long periods of time, as in Burma (Kyaw 2009). Single parties too could maintain their dominance for long periods if they effectively controlled patronage, as the United Malays National Organization (UMNO) has done in Malaysia. Transitology, then, while once having been expected to flow logically and seamlessly into the study of democracy's consolidation ('consolidology'), spawned a new subset of inquiry into authoritarian durability.

However, even where transitions to democracy took place and seemed likely to consolidate, scrutiny shifted from elites to the much more varied terrain of civil society. In O'Donnell and Schmitter's early formulation of popular upsurge, a sudden spike in mass-level activism and street protest only took place in the wake of the break-up of the authoritarian coalition. Thus, Diamond (2008: 102) responded that civil society had to be 'resurrected' as a leading causal force. But this, of course, opened the door to new questions. For example, where processes of transformation have unfolded, how were elites so pressured by civil society that they yielded to democratic change? Further, who were the minimalists with whom softliner elites might negotiate in a process of transplacement? And where elites were swept clean away through a process of replacement, how had civil society so thoroughly overcome its problems of collective action? But despite new uncertainties, as recognition grew that the dynamics by which transitions to democracy took place were far wider and more complex than had been believed, new attention was given to civil society. In particular, scholars focused on the ways in which its activists coordinated direct action, increased political education and levels of mobilization, and then, in turning to political society, filled the interstices between opposition parties and politicians in ways enabling them to form more effective front organizations (Weiss 2006).

In addition, while the study of democratic transitions had long been conducted in domestic arenas, new attention was now given to external factors. During democracy's second wave, perhaps the most enduring transitions took place in Germany, Italy and Japan through a process of conquest and imposition by Allied countries. But in the third wave, the democratization of Grenada and Panama through US military action remained vastly overshadowed by the far more numerous and momentous cases in which internal dynamics were weightiest. In almost all cases of democratic transition, then, most attention was given to patterns of inter-elite and elite-mass relations.

But if cases of democratization by imposition were rare during the third wave, other forms of exogenous pressure grew in importance. In particular, during the late 1970s, the United States began to scale back its support for dictators with whom it had allied in waging the Cold War. This new turn in foreign policy aims was taken first during the presidency of Jimmy Carter, and accelerated under Ronald Reagan. Across the developing world, where governments demonstrated greater respect for civil liberties, human rights and electoral contestation, the United States began to dispense developmental aid, principally through its vehicle, the US Agency for International Development (USAID). Governments that resisted were confronted by varying levels of economic sanctions, usually involving trade and investment restrictions. Further, while Germany had long supported party-building programmes in developing countries, it was joined now by some other Western states in undertaking broader campaigns of explicit democracy promotion. To this end, the US Congress formed the National Endowment for Democracy (NED) in 1983 which, together with its various subsidiaries, provided financial support and training for non-governmental organizations (NGOs), political parties, newspaper publications, judiciaries and teams of election monitors. British, Dutch, Scandinavian and Taiwanese organizations have provided much the same. Thus, as elections began to take place in ever more national settings, large numbers of monitors were recruited by these democracy-promoting agencies in order to evaluate freeness and fairness.

As more countries democratized, they seemed to encourage democratic change in other places, helping give impetus to the third wave identified by Huntington.

Through what were variously characterized as demonstration effects and snow-balling, politics were democratized with surprising speed across South America. One notes also the ways in which democracy activists in South Korea had learned from the strategies adopted by their counterparts in the Philippines, bringing pressures to bear that finally disposed the government to bargain. Even more dramatically than in South America, then, the South Korea and Philippines cases showed that political learning could drive democratic change more rapidly than structural forces such as developmental levels and global economic positioning.

However, just as doubts had grown over the importance of preconditions and elite-level preferences for democratization, so too have they begun to mount over the potency of external factors. In their exhaustive study of international 'leverage' and 'linkage', Levitsky and Way (2010) show convincingly that near proximity to the United States and Western Europe encouraged lasting democratic change. But in more distant localities, any such change remains fragile and reversible. Thus, if war-time imposition by the United States succeeded in important cases in several countries after the Second World War, the large-scale investment it made in Iraq has grievously retarded democracy's advance. Indeed, during the last years of the Bush presidency, even the United States retreated from its democratizing mission to a more realist approach to foreign policy-making.

The impact of less coercive forms of democracy promotion has also been disappointing, with efforts to reform institutions and procedures often being either distorted or repulsed by many governments, especially in Russia under Vladimir Putin and in Central Asia under a variety of autocrats (see Carothers 2006). Indeed, election monitoring agencies have grown so fearful of raising the ire of the governments at whose pleasure they operate that they routinely overlook many electoral transgressions, announcing blandly that regardless of any cheating, the government would have been returned to office anyway. To be sure, so egregious was the conduct of the Russian presidential election of 2012, which shifted Putin from the prime ministership to the presidency, that observers grew inclined to speak out. But the government blunted their criticisms by denouncing them as 'frauds' through a series of televised exposés (Barry and Kishkovsky 2012). Further, governments in countries such as Sudan and, until recently, Myanmar, in seeking the international investments and markets that generate the patronage required for their survival, have turned their backs on Western countries that threaten sanctions over undemocratic behaviour, forging ties instead with an uncritical China. What is more, even the snowballing that seemed so decisive across South America has had little effect in regions like Southeast Asia. With the Association of Southeast Asian Nations (ASEAN) bound together by its operating principle of non-interference, people power in the Philippines affected South Korea more than it did ASEAN's members. And if the *reformasi* movement that brought democratic change to Indonesia during the late 1990s was emulated by some civil society organizations in Malaysia, it ultimately amounted to little, with the prime minister during this period, Mahathir Mohamad, warding off pressures on his authoritarian rule. In this context, Thomas Carothers (2002), a leading analyst and practitioner of democracy promotion, pronounced the 'end of the transition paradigm'. Larry

Diamond (2008: 106), in evaluating the impact of international forces more generally, has remained more optimistic, but contends that they can only contribute to democratic change when other internal factors are strongly in its favour.

## Can democracy be globalized?

Debates over democracy and democratization, though enthusiastically conducted by theorists and practitioners, appear in the view of some analysts to be quite misplaced. Put simply, even if democracy has made gains across many countries, it has at this level also grown more irrelevant. To be sure, democratic ideas have spread round the world. But so too have investment capital, production chains, trading networks and regulatory norms. And the price for most countries, particularly in the developing world, that participate in these activities – attracting investors, entering export markets and finding assistance amid economic shocks – is to cede much of their policy autonomy to far-off decision makers, in particular, transnational corporations and multilateral institutions. But even in the Western countries in which the organizations are usually headquartered and to which they might seem beholden, governments have lost much autonomy to globalized entities. Thus, as citizens exercise their civil liberties and vote in elections at the national level, the value of their participation and seeking accountability in this way is diminished in tandem with the capacity of governments to demonstrate responsiveness.

Moreover, in combating the cross-national problems that more globalized activities create, many more international or regional organizations might need to be formed. Analysts have thus noted the need for regulatory agencies whose authority effectively supersedes that of particular governments in order to deal with environmental ills, diseases, international crime and the contagion of financial crises (see, e.g., Drezner 2007). But as multilateral institutions like the International Monetary Fund, the World Bank and the World Trade Organization (WTO) are joined by an array of new regulatory agencies, questions mount over how to maintain popular sovereignty in this new and complex setting.

Organizations and movements of what is sometimes called global civil society have taken up this call, sometimes through direct action, mounting mass protests at the venues where multilateral institutions have met. And in organizing their activities, these elements have been greatly aided by communications technologies that have bolstered civil society at the national level, in particular, the Internet and mobile telephony. In an effort to foster transparency, the WTO has responded by uploading copious amounts of information about its internal workings onto its website. Its officials argue too that they are responsive to the national governments that have selected or vetted them – and that these governments are in turn accountable to their citizens. But plainly, this chain of democratic accountability is too extended and disarticulated to foster any meaningful sense of mass-level participation.

Mechanisms for increasing responsiveness and accountability among multilateral institutions and regional agencies have been recently canvassed. David Held

(1999: 106–7), perhaps the leading scholar on this front, envisions the nation-state withering away, for 'states can no longer be ... the sole centers of legitimate power within their own borders'. To be sure, in this vision, states are diminished, but do not disappear. Rather, they are 'relocated' within an overarching transnational framework of democratic law in which people possess 'multiple citizenships'. Under what Held has called 'cosmopolitan democracy', people retain or even enhance their political participation at the local and national levels on relevant issues. But in responding to today's transnational challenges and institutions, they participate increasingly also in global politics, primarily through global civil society. Held (ibid.: 108) thus lauds the 'new voices' that were heard at the Rio Conference on the Environment, the Beijing Conference on Women and the Cairo Conference on Population Control. He is less clear on how accountability might be obtained through voting and elections, though he cites the representativeness of the United Nations as a 'normative resource' and 'innovative structure which can be built upon'.

But such schemas still strike many as quite utopian. That democracy's viability should wither at the level of nation-states offers no assurance that it will be recovered among international financial institutions and regional agencies. Indeed, for Robert Dahl (1999: 21–3), the size and complexity of even the EU, let alone global institutions, so increases the need for delegation that mechanisms for participation, representativeness and accountability grow unacceptably stretched. He thus sketches a dilemma in which, while 'a world government might be created in order to deal with problems of universal scope ... the opportunities available to the ordinary citizen to participate effectively ... would diminish to the vanishing point'. On this count, Dahl notes too that even in established democracies, citizens are rarely able to influence their government's conduct of foreign affairs. And so, he asks, 'What grounds have we for thinking ... that citizens in different countries engaged in international systems can ever attain the degree of influence and control over decisions that they now exercise within their own countries?' And how might even the 'general good' be determined when democracy is extended across countries and regions, vastly increasing the 'diversity of interest, goals, and values among the people in the unit'. Accordingly, though democracy has made important advances in the world for the past quarter-century, it may now have reached a plateau. It may even be falling into reverse, unable to cope at the global level, while quietly being undermined from within.

## Democratic recession?

In terms of analysis, as well as in its real-world practice, the headiest days of the third wave appear to have passed. Indeed, some of the most insightful work being conducted today involves the study of authoritarian durability mentioned above. To be sure, where democratization has taken place, it has seldom broken down. And even where reversals have occurred, as in Turkey in 1980, Fiji towards the end of the 1980s, Peru in 1992, a number African countries during the 1980s and

1990s, Thailand in 1991 and 2006, Pakistan in 1999, and the Maldives in 2012, at least partial re-democratization has usually followed. Even so, Larry Diamond (2008: ch. 3) argues that during the first decade of the 21st century, the world slipped into democratic recession. It is not just that the pace at which new democracies have been appearing has slowed. More gravely, in many cases where democratic change had been unfolding, it has stalled or even been rolled back, yielding cases of low-quality democracy; or, where it has dropped below critical thresholds, various forms of authoritarian rule have set in (Schedler 2006).

Under what Schedler (2006) conceptualizes as 'electoral authoritarianism', for example, governments regularly hold elections, offering a snapshot of propriety on the day contests are held. But they have truncated civil liberties beforehand, thereby hindering opposition parties from contesting effectively. Opposition parties are permitted to organize, set up headquarters, raise funds, select their own leaders and candidates and then recruit cadres and at least modest constituencies. But they are also prevented from reaching wider audiences by the government's control over most media outlets; they are restricted in circulating their own party publications; and they are barred from organizing mass rallies, even during campaign periods. Opposition members who persist are often targeted with crippling defamation suits, the rescinding of government contracts and bank loans or even arrest. Further, on the electoral dimension, outcomes may be skewed through delineation exercises that involve extreme malapportionment, gerrymandering and distorted forms of multi-member districting. Meanwhile, government candidates may make partisan use of state resources in campaigning, practices winked at by a weak election commission. In these circumstances, opposition parties are able to articulate the grievances of their followers, though only in muted ways. And they are able to win enough legislative seats to gain a toehold in parliament, though never enough to be able to replace the government.

Thus, many governments have borrowed some of the elements of democracy in order substantially to avoid it. Recognizing the legitimacy that democracy has come to attain, they have mostly abandoned the crude military rule, single-party systems and personal dictatorships that once proliferated. They have turned instead to strategies of electoral authoritarianism, gracing their multi-party elections, however distorted, with some legitimating cover. As the long-time prime minister of Malaysia, Mahathir Mohamad, used to say to his critics, 'If you don't like me, defeat me in my district' (quoted in Case 2002: 7). The offer, of course, was disingenuous, for there was little prospect of turning Mahathir's constituents, coddled with patronage, against him. Mexico under the Institutional Revolutionary Party, Russia under Putin, Singapore under the People's Action Party and Cambodia under Hun Sen offer other prominent examples of this regime type, one which is probably the most subtle, yet serious challenge to democracy's deepening.

To be sure, even under conditions of electoral authoritarianism, governments have, in underestimating the intensity of societal discontents, sometimes been 'stunned' by the results of the elections they have held. Diamond (2008) records that one in seven of the governments organizing elections along these lines have eventually lost. Moreover, these defeats can in themselves amount to democratic change, hence producing yet another pathway of transition that has been conceptualized as democratization-by-election (Lindberg 2009). Perhaps the best-known example involves the Philippines, where Marcos's attempt to steal the election triggered popular upsurge and replacement.

But even after democratization takes place in this way, some social groups, especially those based in new urban middle classes, sometimes grow alienated with the democracies that follow. Associating democratic politics with poor governance, economic stagnancy, unfunded populist distributions and diminished personal security, these groups may resort to upsurge again, though this time to oust elected governments. Through street actions that have been variously designated 'rally democracy', 'muscular democracy' and the 'People Power II' noted above (see, e.g., *Time Asia*, 29 January 2001), citizens have forced governments from power in the Philippines, Thailand and at the local level in South America. Moreover, in doing this, they have sometimes won the sanction of disaffected elites in the legislature, the courts and, most crucially, the military. This has done little, however, to bolster the quality or policy performance of democracy.

Thus, as 'reform fatigue' sets in, increasing numbers of citizens may grow more attuned to the 'rationalized' authoritarianism that China, in having perpetuated several decades of rapid industrial expansion, and Russia, vitalized until recently by petroleum and gas exports, are sometimes understood to practice. Fired with economic prowess and nationalist pride, these countries appear to have rediscovered the fact that performance legitimacy can, for as long as it lasts, trump the political legitimacy generated by low-quality democracies.

The standing of democracy has also declined in tandem with that of the United States, its foremost advocate on the international scene. It is deeply ironic that during the presidency of George Bush, a tenure marked by a sharp increase in democratizing commitments, the valuation of democracy around the world was eroded by the ineptitude with which these ambitions were pursued. Most signally, in response to the authoritarianism across Arab societies that appeared pervasive and the rise of religious terrorism, US policymakers came to define democratization in national security terms. But with the invasion of Iraq marking an escalation from strategies of benign democracy promotion to democracy-by-imposition, the United States elicited quite unintended consequences. Put simply, as the mayhem in Iraq worsened, the United States found its political and military prestige diminished, while the very authoritarianism and terrorism that it had hoped to roll back gained momentum. In this context, the United States became more authoritarian itself, weakening civil liberties at home while engaging overseas in detention without trial, 'extraordinary rendition' and interrogation techniques amounting to torture. And its change in attitude seemed hastened too by the fact that where democratic change had taken place in the Middle East, the elections then held in settings like Lebanon and Gaza were often won by Islamist elements.

Further, in Iran, the reformist Green movement was prevent from participating in the March 2012 parliamentary election, enabling the Principalists, supporters of the supreme leader, Ayatollah Ali Khameini, to win an overwhelming majority.

And suitably empowered, Khameini, having tired of his rivalry with Ahmadeinejad and 'the messy unpredictability of presidential races', has prepared simply to eliminate the presidential office (MacFarquhar 2012). Hence, the fillip given to democracy at the end of the Cold War appeared soon to dissipate amid new kinds of international conflict.

Even so, ambiguity, rather than any clear recessionary trend, prevails. The long-standing military government of Myanmar, after conducting a sham election in November 2010, appeared thereafter to grow more committed to change, unleashing a surprising, if tightly calibrated, process of transformation. Most notably, through a by-election held in April 2012, Aung San Suu Kyi, a long-time symbol of dignified resistance, was able to claim a place in the People's Assembly. She was joined by members of her newly re-registered National League for Democracy, winning 43 of the 44 seats that the party contested. What is more, the willingness of Myanmar's government, led by President Thein Sein, to countenance such change was partly attributed to economic sanctions that had been imposed, effectively barring any usage of the US dollar for trading or investment (Popham 2012). Myanmar's over-reliance on investment from China seemed also to contribute to the government's change of heart, again highlighting the ways in which international factors can bear on democratic outcomes.

Further, in 2011, a string of longstanding and seemingly resolute authoritarian regimes, amounting to personal dictatorships, began suddenly to dissolve across North Africa and the Middle East in what came collectively to be hailed as the 'Arab Spring'. True to transitology's expectations, dynamics involved bottom-up processes of replacement, with strongmen deposed through popular uprisings in Tunisia, Egypt, Libya and Yemen. To be sure, however remarkable these changes and vocal the international acclaim they received, it remains uncertain whether the fall of dictators will culminate in any fourth wave of democracy. And what progress was made across the region was soon eclipsed by prolonged and bloody civil warring in Syria.

But among the Arab Spring countries, Tunisia has made clear headway. Through mass-level protest heralded as the Jasmine Revolution, Tunisia's dictator, Zine al-Abidine Ben Ali, was forced into exile in early 2011. And at the end of the year, the country's first free elections were held since its gaining independence from France 55 years earlier. A new Constituent Assembly was then formed, which in turn elected a prime minister, Hamadi Jebali, from the largest party, the Islamist, but moderate Ennahda. A new president was also elected. Some time after the constitution has been completed, new elections for the assembly and all executive positions will then be held, probably in early 2013. Observing the widespread agreement among major parties on democratic procedures, underpinned by the 'twin tolerations', that is, an acceptance by secular parties of Muslim religious activities, matched by an acceptance by Muslim parties of secular political institutions, Alfred Stepan (2012: 92) has concluded that Tunisia has featured some of the most 'effective consensus-building...in the history of "crafted" democratic transitions'. Accordingly, in bucking the democratic recession, Tunisia's democratizing prospects appear to be brightening today.

Stepan is far less confident about neighbouring Egypt. Though the country's dictator, Hosni Mubarak, was deposed shortly after Ben Ali in Tunisia, military leaders, gathered in the Supreme Council of the Armed Forces, stepped swiftly into the breach, sidelining civilian parties and politicians. At the same time, by far the largest party, the Muslim Brotherhood, seemed unsure about its democratic commitments (Kirkpatrick 2012). The 'twin tolerations', then, crucial to the progress of democracy in the Middle East and North Africa, have remained scarce in Egypt. Thus, shortly before elections were held in June 2012, the military issued a 'constitutional declaration' which would strip the presidential office of most power. The election was won by the former leader of the Islamic Brotherhood, Mohamed Morsi. And for some months afterward, Morsi seemed to accede to the military's supremacy. However, in August, he abruptly renounced the constitutional declaration, then retired the defence minister, Field Marshal Tantawi, regarded as the symbol of the military's political ambitions, as well as the army chief of staff and the chiefs of the navy and air force. In one fell swoop, Morsi thus gained new influence over the panel tasked with writing Egypt's new constitution, as well as new powers over legislation. It remains uncertain, of course, how the military might finally react. Unclear, too, is whether Morsi, backed by the Muslim Brotherhood, might finally resort to executive abuses.

## Does democracy make a difference?

Even where democratic change has taken place, avoiding the pitfalls of globalization and the setbacks inherent to recession, questions are regularly raised over whether it makes any difference in ordinary people's lives. On one level, democracy's worth seems clear. In respecting the civil liberties of individuals and social groups, while registering the choices of citizens through elections, democracy allows for what is commonly cast as popular sovereignty, therein raising human dignity in ways that authoritarian regimes cannot. It is striking, for example, to find that in democratic Brazil today, residents of *favelas* who were once routinely evicted under military governments to make way for development projects, are able to resist relocation today by officials seeking to build urban venues for the 2016 Olympics and football's World Cup. By appealing to the courts and an often sympathetic media, mounting public protests, and mobilizing through Twitter accounts, working-class citizens have protected their communities in ways that their counterparts in Bejing never could as the groundwork was rapidly laid for the Olympics in 2008 (Romero 2012). More broadly, in its respect for due process and human rights, democracy spares citizens the arbitrary detention and extrajudicial killings that so frequently characterize coercive authoritarian rule.

Democracy may in concrete ways advance human security too. On this score, Amartya Sen has argued that under democracy, the planning disasters that result in widespread famine, for example, are far less likely to occur, owing to the feedback loops that readily communicate to governments information about shortages and mass-level discontent (see Diamond 2008: 28). Further, at the global level, democracy may contribute to more ordinary security. Although the relationship is hardly ironclad, the record suggests strongly that countries that are democratic, in their liberal commitments and belief systems, are less likely to wage war against one another than are authoritarian states. In this context, an academic subfield of democratic peace theory has flourished. Accordingly, there appear to be good reasons for large majorities of citizens, when responding to surveys administered in many dozens of societies, regularly declaring their preference for democracy over authoritarian rule.

And yet, in the real world, democracy too often lags behind these ideals. As one example, during the prime ministership of Thaksin Shinawatra in Thailand, though the government was popularly elected, press freedoms were truncated through harassment of journalists and ever more concentrated patterns of media ownership. Human rights were also seriously violated through the killings of alleged drug traffickers and Muslim separatists, actions taken by security forces that were welcomed by large numbers of Thai citizens. Additionally, democratic change has done less to moderate corrupt practices than to decentralize them, with payments and vote-buying fanning out now from the national leader, his or her family members and cronies, top bureaucrats and generals to the political party leaders, legislators on multiple tiers and the ordinary voters that democracy has empowered. Indeed, Ross McLeod, in writing about the dispersion of corrupt practices across Indonesia today, refers to Suharto's period of authoritarian rule as a 'better class of corruption'. Little is achieved either in terms of redressing income disparities, with studies long having demonstrated that social inequality remains impervious to democratic change (eg., Jackman 1974).

Democracy theorists responded, then, with a new research agenda on consolidation, trying to weave notions of regime longevity and policy performance into their conceptualization. Lengthy investigation was thus conducted into requisite elite-level attitudes, supportive mass-level outlooks and appropriate institutional design, generating prolonged debate over the merits of presidential and parliamentary systems (see, e.g., Linz 1990; Stepan and Skach 1993). But with theorists unable to reach consensus over what consolidation involved, much less over which sets of factors would most favour it, these debates were gradually abandoned. In their wake, a more focused agenda has set in addressing democracy's quality. In recognizing that the records of democracies vary greatly, theorists now examine a variety of dimensions, including rule of law, popular participation, representativeness, policy responsiveness and accountability (e.g., *Journal of Democracy* 2004). They have even begun to rank different democracies through 'audits', identifying abuses that have, in some cases, grown so great that they have been reclassified as undemocratic. For example, politics in the Philippines, the incubator of people power, have been reassessed by Freedom House (2009) as 'partly free'. And yet, though an evaluative framework has been taking shape, doubts persist over whether it will be able to show how these different dimensions affect each other, whether in mutually reinforcing or negating ways, or even to specify the clear thresholds necessary for measurement. In this context, with disillusion mounting over procedural democracy's limited social impact and even capacity for clear measurement, scholarly interest in substantive understandings of democracy may soon reawaken.

## Guide to further reading

The literature on how democracy is best understood is voluminous. The classic text is Joseph Schumpeter's (1943) *Capitalism, Socialism and Democracy*; but see also 'What Democracy is … And is Not' by Philippe Schmitter and Terry Lynn Karl (1991) and the introductory text by Jean Grugel (2002). The debate over democracy's preconditions, once vibrant, has long since waned. But a concise cataloguing of factors is provided in *Politics in Developing Countries: Comparing Experiences with Democracy* edited by Diamond *et al.* (1990). For a more recent and highly mathematicized exploration of preconditions, see Jan Teorell (2010), *Determinants of Democratization: Explaining Regime Change in the World, 1972-2006*. With analysis moving next to the dynamics of democratic transitions, attention shifted initially from structural forces to voluntarist calculations. Strong expressions in this genre include Dankwart Rustow (1970), O'Donnell and Schmitter (1986) and Burton *et al.* (1991). But probably the key overview of transitional processes is given in Samuel Huntington's (1991) *The Third Wave*. See also the fine collection of essays by Guillermo O'Donnell (1999). For an early analysis of civil society and democracy, see John Keane's (1988) *Democracy and Civil Society*. The literature on democratic consolidation, whether understood in terms of institutions, elite and mass-level attitudes, or the emergence of civil society, has also grown vast, even as the term lost currency precisely because of its multiple meanings and unclear causal directions. But Larry Diamond (1999) offers a comprehensive overview. And his (2008) more recent *Spirit of Democracy* addresses the new uncertainties over democracy's prospects. See also Thomas Carothers (2002), whose groundbreaking 'The End of the Transition Paradigm' addresses the limits on quality that bedevil so many new democracies. By contrast, David Held's work, in particular, *Democracy and the Global Order: From Modern State to Cosmopolitan Governance* (1995), assesses the possibilities for internationalizing democracy and strengthening its relevance in a more globalized polity and economy.

# Chapter 18

# International Law, Justice and World Politics

*AIDAN HEHIR*

Following the September 11 attacks, US President George W. Bush is alleged to have declared, 'I don't care what the international lawyers say; we are going to kick some ass' (Clarke 2004: 24). In a similar vein he later stated, 'We don't really need the United Nations' approval to act…When it comes to our security, we don't need anyone's permission' (White 2004: 660). While the 'Bush doctrine' and the 'war on terror' are today widely regarded as ideologically extreme visions of the US's role in the world, the sentiments expressed by Bush are not unique to his administration. In 1999 at a meeting with his US counterparts, UK Foreign Secretary Robin Cook expressed reservations as to the legality of using force against the Federal Republic of Yugoslavia, noting that the UK's legal advisers had warned that any strike would be illegal. In response, US Secretary of State Madeleine Albright stated bluntly, 'get new lawyers' (Sampford 2003: 85). Perhaps more infamously, the UK Attorney General Lord Goldsmith has similarly been accused of crafting legal advice to meet the political demands of the Blair government prior to the invasion of Iraq in 2003 (Sands 2006: 196–200). Indeed, the prevalence of this *à la carte* approach to international law led Richard Falk to wonder whether Kant's dismissal of international lawyers as 'miserable consolers' willing to degrade the law to appease the powerful remains accurate (2004: 39).

There are myriad examples of the wilful disregard of international law and the cynical utilization of its tenets, and it is perhaps no surprise that many claim that international law is essentially irrelevant, a conceit which obscures 'the real world' (Walzer 2006: xx–xxi). With the end of the Cold War, however, international law became one of the dominant issues on the political agenda. Debates on the key issues in the post-Cold War era – such as humanitarian intervention and the 'war on terror' – have focused to a large degree on legality. Additionally, the high-profile trials of, for example, Slobodan Milosevic and Charles Taylor, and the establishment of the International Criminal Court (ICC) have added a punitive dimension to international law which was arguably previously lacking. These changes have been accompanied by a new optimism as to law's role and future efficacy.

This chapter begins with an overview of the debate on the role of international law, concentrating in particular on those arguments which advance a positive view of law's efficacy. The following section examines the contemporary era and the various developments which led to a marked upsurge in optimism as to the future of international law generally, and the United Nations (UN) in particular. Next, I engage with the tension between law and morality which gained currency in the late 1990s, leading to much division especially with respect to the invasion of Iraq in 2003. The final section assesses the future of international law and the various outstanding dilemmas which continue to impact on its efficacy.

## The role of international law

International law has long been considered by many as comprising no more than lofty words and declarations which statesmen 'cheerfully subscribe to considering that such is their vagueness...the mere act of subscribing to them carries with it no danger of having one's freedom of action sufficiently impaired' (Kennan 1985: 207). There is certainly no doubt that the prevailing view within the discipline of International Relations (IR) throughout the Cold War was that international law, including the institutions that regulate it, was of limited utility, its role consigned to peripheral areas such as communication and trade with limited relevance for international security. No-one seriously disputed, or disputes, the existence of international law, or indeed that many of the key precepts – such as the impermissibility of the aggressive use of force – are rational and laudable; rather, the idea that law is of limited utility stems from the belief that the relative distribution of power alone determines state behaviour. Adherence to law, therefore, is deemed to stem from a coincidence between national interests and law rather than the independent constraining influence exercised by the law.

The history of the 20th century certainly provides ample grounds for justifying the view that international law's role, particularly on the 'big' security issues, has been minimal. The laws established by the League of Nations very obviously failed to prevent aggression in the 1930s; Haile Selassie's speech to the League's Assembly in June 1936 following Ethiopia's invasion by Italy constitutes a damning excoriation of the utility of the law and the realities of power. Even after the establishment of the UN the prohibition on the aggressive use of force (or threatened use) contained in Article 2.4 of its Charter does not seem to have greatly inconvenienced the Soviet Union or the United States during the Cold War – or indeed many other less powerful states – nor can it be said that violations of international law were punished in anything amounting to a consistent or efficient manner. For many, the 2003 invasion of Iraq – described as illegal by no less than the UN Secretary General Kofi Annan (Kreiger 2006: 386) – represented a contemporary continuation of this disdain for international law both because of the violation itself and the fact that the US and its allies were not subsequently punished (Bowring 2008: 1; Chomsky 2011).

Nonetheless, many have countered that, accepting the many violations that have occurred since 1945, international law and the UN *have* played a constructive and important role in international relations. There are broadly two arguments made to advance this view: first, that law *has* influenced the behaviour of states, and second, that international law is not analogous to domestic law and thus must be judged according to different indices of effectiveness. Each is discussed in turn below.

## Evidence of law's influence

Many contend that international law *is* respected in the vast majority of cases. Indicatively Peter Malanczuk argues, 'Spectacular cases of violation of international law, which attract the attention of the media more than regular conduct, are exceptional and should not be confused with the ordinary course of business between states' (2006: 6). If international law was as insignificant as is often suggested, the world – particularly the modern globalized world – would simply grind to a halt. This is in large part because law facilitates rather than merely proscribes and, crucially, reflects collective norms which states have an interest in upholding. Law should be seen, then, not as an external imposition on states but rather as an enabler, a means by which shared interests can be realized (Koskenniemi 2006: 65). Contemporary international law has its origins in the various conferences held amongst the Allies between 1943 and 1945 which led to the establishment of the UN, an organization which, by definition, reflects the interests of states. Given these origins, it stands to reason that law – a reflection of collective interests – is on the whole respected, albeit with the occasional 'spectacular violation'.

Of course, the fact that states routinely adhere to the majority of international laws does not necessarily negate the argument that international law's role is limited; many still contend that law's role *is* limited with respect to the ostensibly more important issues of international security and justice. Yet, while there have been myriad examples of law's failings since the new legal framework was established in 1945, comparatively, it is claimed, the contemporary era constitutes an improvement. Prior to the many legal developments which occurred in the 20th century – chief among them the establishment of the UN – the international system was more disorderly, as there were far less restrictions on using force; state behaviour was 'regulated' more obviously by the relative distribution of power and the more malleable, and inherently subjective, natural law (Bellamy 2004: 141). The UN is, in this vein, credited by some with playing a key causal role in the prevention of a major war between any of the modern great powers since 1945, a significant achievement in the context of catastrophic wars which occurred in the first half of the 20th century (Chesterman and Byers 2003).

Additionally, Sir Arthur Watts (2001) points to the fact that 'virtually without exception states seek always to offer a legal justification for their actions'. Illustratively, even Saddam Hussein claimed that his invasion of Kuwait in 1990 was legal. This trend, Watts argues, is of great significance as it 'demonstrates the value attached by states to compliance with international law' (2001: 7). Why, indeed, would states claim that their actions were/are legal if the legality was irrelevant? While Bush's bellicose 'I don't care what the international lawyers say...'

statement quoted at the beginning of this chapter seems to suggest a dismissal of law's importance, it is noteworthy that the US and the UK have continued to claim that the invasion of Iraq *was* legal. The inquiry into the Iraq War – commonly referred to as the Chilcott Inquiry – established by the British government in 2009 has spent years and millions of pounds seeking to establish the legality of the decision to invade Iraq. Key actors involved in the decision in 2003 – most notably former Prime Minister Tony Blair – have testified to robustly defend the legality of the invasion. If international law was irrelevant, why, one might well ask, would they bother?

## An alternative conception of international law

Aside from these empirical arguments which challenge the narrative that international law has not had a direct influence on international security, there is a separate defence of international law which is based on an alternative conception of international law. Those who criticize international law often do so by comparing it unfavourably with domestic law; this, it is claimed, is simply a flawed comparison (Henkin 1990: 250). Domestic legal systems benefit from the obviously hierarchical configuration within states and the coercive organs of the state, namely the police and the military. These features facilitate compliance, enforcement and punishment by virtue of their coercive power, real and latent. International law is, however, horizontal in nature with states acting as both subjects and architects of the law. The enforcement of these laws is further compromised by the absence of any international force comparable to the domestic police and army. By virtue of these profound differences, international law should be judged on whether it can 'facilitate the interaction between these legal equals (states) rather than control or compel them in imitation of the control and compulsion that national law exerts over its subjects' (Dixon 2007: 2). This, indeed, leads to a particular justification – and indeed explanation – for international law's efficacy, namely that while the formal mechanisms for enforcing international law are weak and highly politicized, the existence of treaties and rules has an effect on state action as it creates a delineated framework for legitimization. No state, or statesman, wishes to be seen to violate international law, lest they be perceived more generally as a pariah; action, therefore, is designed to cohere with the prevailing legal framework, even by the most powerful states (Cassese 2005: 155). International law, therefore, ensures that those who profess to recognize it become, as Luke Glanville argues, 'rhetorically entrapped' and thus, regardless of their military or economic power, they are compelled to behave in ways which are occasionally inconvenient (2011: 471). Thus, David Armstrong and Theo Farrell argue that an 'alternative way of thinking about international law might be as a site of legitimation for state action'. Rather than international law and its institutions constituting something analogous to the domestic, they argue:

> it might be more useful to view them as political spaces where states engage in normatively bounded deliberation about legitimate action. These sites are

normatively bounded in the sense that state reasoning, deliberation and action is constituted and constrained by pre-existing norms that shape social identities and situations. (Armstrong and Farrell 2005: 7).

The norms prevalent in these 'political spaces' do overtly challenge, albeit occasionally, the influence of raw power. The constraint ostensibly exercised by these pre-existing norms is, however, almost by definition imperceptible and thus often unrecognized. Instances of inconvenient compliance with international law are in essence invisible and go unreported. When, indeed, do we actually see states desist from taking certain action because to do so would be illegal?

In practice this realm where international law influences practice has grown and evolved. Andrew Hurrell argues that the evolutionary trajectory of international law has been characterized by a 'shift away from a system in which international law was made by the strong for the strong…towards a system in which norm creation becomes an increasingly complex and pluralist process' (2005: 18). The establishment of the ICC, for example, arguably constitutes an example of the tempering of power. The ICC – almost inconceivable twenty-five years ago – was born from initiatives undertaken by states from the developing world acting within the constitutionally egalitarian UN General Assembly against often extremely aggressive opposition from the modern great powers; the US in particular sought – ultimately unsuccessfully – to block the court's establishment (Weller 2002). While Russia, China and the US have yet to ratify the Rome Statute, the ICC exists and the UN Security Council has twice referred cases to the court – Darfur (Sudan) in 2005 and Libya in 2011 – despite the negative stance adopted by these three permanent members of the Council. These defences of international law undoubtedly gained momentum after the end of the Cold War, and the new more positive assessment of law's role is undoubtedly from the result of many contemporary developments. The following section assess this new era.

## The age of enforcement?

The implosion of the Soviet Union led to an upsurge in optimism as to the future capacity of the UN to regulate inter-state relations (Barnett 2010: 21). The end of the Cold War, it was hoped, ensured that the paralysis which had restricted the ability of the Security Council to take collective action was no more. In particular, many argued, and indeed assumed, that the laws on human rights could finally become more than just hortatory declarations; we had, according to Geoffrey Robertson, entered 'the age of enforcement' (2000: xvii).

Despite the Cold War, the number of human rights treaties prohibiting states from treating citizens in certain ways increased dramatically after 1945 (Landman 2005: 14). Of course, there was a jarring disjuncture between these laws and the actual practice of states. The vast majority of human rights treaties lacked effective means of enforcment, while compliance was largely a matter of self-validation (Armstrong *et al.* 2007: 15–8). In the post-Cold War era, however, human rights have become one of the dominant concerns in international relations and often top the Security Council's agenda. During the 1990s the Security Council dramatically revised its understanding of its power to act under Chapter VII of the Charter; these provisions enable the Council to become involved in the domestic affairs of states – including through military intervention – if a situation is deemed to constitute a 'threat to international peace and security'. The scope of this provision was stretched in a number of cases – such as Iraq in 1991, Somalia in 1992 and Haiti in 1994 – to include intra-state humanitarian crises. This creative use of existing international law constituted a profound change in the practice of the Security Council; Antonio Cassese, indeed, described this 'new ethos' as akin to a 'Copernican revolution' (2005: 333). The collective action sanctioned by the Security Council against Libya in March 2011 was heralded by many as an archetypal example of robust measures being taken to enforce international human rights law and a continuation of a more general post-Cold War trend characterized by a move away from indifference (Weiss 2011).

That the Security Council has engaged in a new phase of activism cannot be denied; whether this reflects the greater influence of international law is, however, far less clear. Simon Chesterman, for example, has noted that whenever the Security Council has sanctioned action under Chapter VII, key national interests of one or more of the permanent five members (P5) have been involved and were ultimately the causal factor in the decision to take action; as a consequence the Council's record has been erratic and a function of a coincidence between national interest and human suffering (Chesterman 2003: 165). This was most evident in 1994 when the Security Council sanctioned the collective use of force against the military junta in Haiti but failed to act as robustly in response to the manifestly graver situation in Rwanda where the genocide claimed some 800,000 lives. The erratic enforcement of international law is a function of fact that while the Security Council may *choose* to act, it is under no obligation to do so; the Council's powers are discretionary in nature even with respect to responding to cases of genocide (Milanovic 2006: 571). The Security Council's new pro-active stance – largely a consequence of pressure from the US, the UK and France – has not, therefore, been universally welcomed; indeed for many states in the developing world the UN's shift from guardian of sovereignty to supporter of intervention was viewed in decidedly negative terms (Roberts 2006: 71). The prohibition on external interference has been routinely championed by states in the developing world that see sovereignty as, in the words of the former African Union President Abdelaziz Bouteflika, 'our final defense against the rules of an unjust world' (Weiss 2007: 16). The fact that the ICC has focused overwhelmingly on crimes committed in Africa by Africans has similarly led to a charge that the law is biased. Sceptics also point to the fact that the key architects behind the invasion of Iraq have yet to be charged, while allies of the West – such as Israel and Saudi Arabia – have escaped the censure imposed on others – such as Libya and the former Yugoslavia – for similar crimes.

While statesmen have arguably increasingly referred to international law in justifying the actions they have taken, there remains a disjuncture between rhetoric and practice; law has, some allege, become a means of adding a veneer of legitimacy to action rather than an independent constraint (Glennon 2008: 162; Hurd 2007: 129). While Western states have often sought Security Council approval for their actions, they have demonstrated a willingness to ignore the Council when necessary, as evidenced by the 1999 intervention in Kosovo and the 2003 invasion of Iraq. Indeed, at its fiftieth anniversary conference in April 1999 NATO declared, 'Even though all NATO member states undoubtedly would prefer to act with such mandates [from the Security Council] they must not limit themselves to acting only when such a mandate can be agreed' (Caplan 2000: 31).

This selective adherence to, and enforcement of, international law has come as no surprise, however, to those who have always maintained that international law (and indeed domestic law) reflects the interests of the powerful (Bull 2002: 53; Koskenniemi 2001: 166; Orford 2009). The powers of the P5 members of the Security Council certainly compromise any normative ideal that post-1945 all states are now equal; this arrangement in fact, Gerry Simpson argues, constitutes a form of 'legalised hegemony' (2004: 68). The justification for the extraordinary powers afforded to the P5 remain largely the same today; order can only be maintained if the most powerful states are constitutionally recognized as the arbiters of disputes and judges of laws' applicability in any given situation (Bourantonis 2007: 6). This means, of course, that the international legal system – in contrast to the norm domestically – is characterized by an explicit union between politics and law. The P5 thus constitutes, according to Nigel White, 'a realist core in an institutionalist framework – a political core in a legal regime' (2004: 666). The Security Council's reaction to the crisis in Syria in 2011–12 arguably constitutes an obvious contemporary example of the influence of power on the application of law, with China and especially Russia accused of shielding their ally from appropriate external censure. Of course, China and Russia are not unique in blocking action that the majority of Security Council support; the US has used the veto more than any other state in the post-Cold War era and in January 2011 was the only state to oppose – and therefore veto – a resolution condemning Israel. This naked politicization of law enforcement has led some to argue in favour of an alternative framework based on 'justice' and 'natural law'.

## Law or justice?

Interestingly, one of the features of the contemporary debates about international law has been the attempt by Western states to unilaterally alter the laws and norms governing the use of force. With respect to both humanitarian intervention and the 'war on terror', Western states have championed more permissive regulations, though on the condition that these powers are restricted to democracies (Falk 2005: 37; Simpson 2004: 71). This has been reflected within academia in the debate between 'restrictionists' and 'counter-restrictionists' with the latter supporting the idea of a more conditional legal regime (Bellamy 2007: 158).

It has been argued that the legitimacy of Security Council decision making is compromised by the fact that two of the P5 – Russia and China – have poor human rights records and weak democratic credentials. Indicatively Alex Bellamy asked, 'Why should undemocratic states with poor human rights records prevent a group of democratic states from protecting people in foreign countries?' (2002: 212). The need to react quickly and effectively to humanitarian crises led to the emergence of a view that the laws governing the use of force and the organs established to sanction this use, could at times be legitimately subverted, as otherwise law would be 'an obscenity' (Robertson 2000: 428). NATO's intervention in Kosovo in 1999 illustrated this disposition; following the intervention the Independent International Commission on Kosovo concluded that NATO's action was 'illegal but legitimate' (2000: 4). This disconnect between legitimacy and legality illustrated for many the flaws with the existing legal system. The intervention emboldened those who argued that the democratic credentials of Western states and their inherent concern for human rights justified their occasional subversion of the ostensible anachronistic legal order established in 1945 in favour of moral norms or 'natural law' (Onuf 2003; Nardin 2003: 19; Walzer 2006: xx–xxi). The September 11 attacks added a new rationale as the apocalyptic threat posed by global terrorism supposedly demanded new, more permissive, rules to protect not just the West but the world from destruction (Gow 2005:119). Democratic states should, it was claimed, be empowered with exceptional rights and competencies; the unique confluence between power and political and ethical legitimacy ostensibly characteristic of the unipolar era necessitated a new legal system more concerned with justice and human rights than order and state sovereignty, and more reflective of the prevailing distribution of power (Elshtain 2003; Buchanan and Keohane 2004; Ikenberry and Slaughter 2006). This was, some argued, the attempted 'rehierarchization' of the international system into 'liberal' and 'illiberal' states (Reus-Smit, 2005). While the Bush administration's stance often appeared to be an aberration, others argued this overt attempt to reorder the rules could be situated in a trajectory which pre-dated President Bush and reflected a more general Western consensus (Byers and Chesterman 2003: 190; White 2004: 660). Somewhat paradoxically, therefore, in the contemporary era Western democracies became a threat to the international legal system by virtue of their desire to promote and achieve 'international justice' (Armstrong *et al.* 2007: 175).

This is not necessarily as surprising as it may first appear; history suggests that dominant powers invariably seek to manipulate the prevailing norms and laws to suit their agenda. As noted by Martti Koskenniemi, 'an empire is never an advocate of an international law that can seem only an obstacle to its ambitions' (2001: 34). Given the 'triumph' of liberal democracy at the end of the Cold War, it stands to reason that these newly dominant states would seek to alter the law to suit their agenda. The 2003 invasion of Iraq arguably demonstrated the perils of unilateral determinations of what should be done and certainly discredited the argument that democratic states could be trusted with exceptional rights. This 'multiple assault on the foundations and rules of the existing UN-centred world order' (Thakur and Singh Sidhu 2006: pp. 3–4) highlighted the dangers inherent in privileging moral norms over positive law. While acting morally may be an attractive alternative to obeying the law in certain situations – the anti-apartheid movement in South

Africa being the obvious example – the advantage of law is its (relative) clarity and capacity in the longer term to 'reduce complexity' (Malanczuk 2006: 7). Flawed though the legal system may be, the alternative is arguably worse; writing in the 17th century, Samuel von Pufendorf cautioned against regulating force through moral norms, stating '…any man might make war upon any man upon such a pleasure' (Nardin 2003: 16). Indeed, according to Alex Bellamy, 'Positive international law…derived as a response to the endemic abuse of natural law' (2004: p. 141), and thus moves to reintroduce morality or natural law as the dominant framework for regulating state behaviour are seen by many as constituting a regression.

While the challenge to international law posed by the Bush administration and the more general clamour for 'benevolent imperialism' (Cooper 2004; Ferguson 2004) was arguably resisted, this contemporary struggle illustrates a greater tension between law and morality that has been evident for centuries and is likely to continue in some form so long as humans debate justice. While the popular image of international law tends to be of rigidity and torpor, it efficacy is determined by its capacity to respond to – and reflect – shifts in moral norms. There is much evidence to support the idea that international law, despite its many limitations, *has* evolved in recent times, particularly with respect to human rights (Byers 2005b). This is explored in the following section.

## The contemporary efficacy of international law

While for some the invasion of Iraq demonstrated the weakness of international law – and the US's disdain for its tenets – others have presented a more positive appraisal. The very fact that both the US and the UK sought Security Council authorization and argued so vehemently that the laws governing the use of force had to change, arguably demonstrated the continued importance of international law even in an era of unipolarity (Hurrell 2005: 18). That the Security Council refused to accede to the US's demands likewise arguably evidenced the capacity of the existing institutions to resist pressure; the attempt to reorder the rules ultimately failed (Byers 2005). In recent years the emphasis on changing the rules has arguably waned and the election of Barack Obama in 2008 was heralded by many as evidence of a more measured disposition within the US. Nonetheless, while Obama's Presidency has not been characterized by the bitter international division wrought by his predecessor, the balance sheet is not wholly positive: while the US sought (and received) UN support for the intervention in Libya, Obama has been criticized for not closing the detention centre at Guantanamo Bay, his extensive use of unmanned drones to carry out targeted assassinations, and his failure to sign up to the ICC. The US, therefore, has not fully submitted to the law, though given its power and the vocal (and powerful) constituency within the US which opposes US adherence to international law as an article of faith, this is hardly a likely scenario.

Aside from the US disposition towards international law, there remain many crises which appear to highlight international law's glaring limitations in the face of power: the UN Charter's commitment to 'reaffirm faith in fundamental human rights, in the dignity and worth of the human person, in the equal rights of men and women and of nations large and small' continues to fail the Palestinians, Chechens, Kurds, Tamils, the opposition groups in Syria and Bahrain and many others. Indeed, in 2001, reflecting on the litany of intra-state massacres since 1945, the Secretary General of the UN, Kofi Annan, described the 1948 Genocide Convention as a 'dead letter' (Annan 2001). Given that since Annan's damning indictment the world has witnessed state-sponsored brutality in Darfur, Sri Lanka and Syria to name but three, the international response to mass atrocities can hardly be said to have markedly improved. The slaughter of innocent civilians by their own state constitutes one of the more obviously illegitimate and emotive acts under international law's purview and so long as the legal proscriptions against such crimes are ignored – by both perpetrators and observers – the credibility of international law will be diminished. The ICC has in recent years come under increasing criticism for its failure to look beyond Africa and a seemingly politically motivated determination to ignore Western criminality (Branch 2011). The global arms trade continues to constitute something of a legal penumbra, due in no small part to the fact that (paradoxically) the P5 are among its chief beneficiaries (Amnesty 2012). Indeed, the power of the P5 remains one of the most obvious, and most lamented, flaws in the current system. The increasingly outdated P5 constitute an unrepresentative group of states, and in recent times Brazil, India, Germany, South Africa and Japan have been touted as deserving of inclusion. Aside from the identity of the veto-wielding powers, the very existence of a group within the legal system with disproportionate power and driven by disparate political agendas – namely the P5 – has been cited by many as untenable (Hehir 2012; Weiss 2009).

There is little doubt but that power continues to influence the application and influence of international law. While all states are formally legal equals, as Colin Warbrick notes, 'The actual capacity of a state to influence the law making processes or to obtain compliance with its legal rights is in large measure proportionate to the resources available to the state' (2006: 223). This fact has to temper any appraisal of international law's role but it should not induce fatalism. The nature of the international legal system established in 1945 is, as Hans Kelsen observed, 'primitive' (1945: 338). Crucially, however, Kelsen considered this to be a developmental stage rather than an immutable reality. In judging international law's influence in the contemporary era, therefore, we should be mindful of the evolution which preceded it. If we compare law's role in international relations in 1945 to that of 2012 can we identify progress? While we may certainly identify many high-profile instances in the contemporary era where law failed to influence events positively, there are many other examples of international law's new vitality. As an illustration, was it conceivable in 1945 that the government of the UK would be prevented from deporting a foreigner suspected of terrorism by a European court based in Strasbourg, as was the case with respect to Abu Qatada in 2012? Could we have imagined that former heads of state such as Slobadon Milosevic and Charles Taylor would be tried by international courts? That a court such as the ICC would come into existence? Was it conceivable during the dark days of the Cold War that the Security Council would sanction a collective military intervention against a regime because it was violating its people's human rights, as was the case with respect to Libya in 2011? Since 1991 the agenda of the Security Council and public debates on the issues of the day more generally, have been to an unprecedented extent concerned with issues of legality and what constitutes lawful behaviour for states both in terms of their internal and external affairs. While this in itself is not evidence of law's pre-eminence it is certainly illustrative of law's new vitality and a potential harbinger of a more mature international legal order.

## Conclusion

The debate in world politics as to international law's influence is likely to continue for some time and doubtless many will remain wedded to the belief that law is what the powerful states do. For others less convinced of international law's redundancy, the challenge is to determine whether we can identify law operating in international relations in ways distinguishable from self-interest and coincidence. Obviously states obey those laws which benefit them monetarily or otherwise, and occasionally states frame their action as being driven by a determination to abide by the law when really this was/is a secondary concern. International law's merit must be measured, however, by its independent capacity to influence state behaviour even when states would rather behave otherwise. As Koskenniemi writes:

> The point of law is to give rise to standards that are no longer merely 'proposed' or 'useful' or 'good', and which therefore can be deviated from if one happens to share a deviating notion of what in fact is useful and good. (2006: 69)

At present it is surely doubtful whether Koskenniemi's criteria can be said to apply to powerful states at the very least. The logic of Koskenniemi's criteria, of course, is arguably a means by which deviations from international law are discouraged by more than just the fear of shame; in essence through coercive means analogous to the domestic police and army.

Such developments are clearly inconceivable in the short term though we should be mindful of the great strides taken in the past 100 years. A feature of modern times has been what Sir Arthur Watts describes as a 'judicial climate change', namely a 'greater willingness on the part of the international community to impose strong judicial structures on itself' (2001: 14). Increasingly states have turned to international law as at the very least the forum for their disputes and the framework for delineating legitimate action. These notable features of contemporary international relations constitute evidence for some of law's 'resurgence' (Milanovic 2006: 554). Of course not everyone agrees; where some see progress others see the subversion of law by the powerful and the degradation of the international legal order (Bowring 2008; Orford 2009). Yet, as Charlesworth and

Kennedy concede, 'international lawyers specialize in crises...We always feel as though there is something peculiarly challenging and significant about this moment in international law' (2009: 405), and thus the fear expressed in many quarters may well be the norm rather than unique to the contemporary era.

Imperfect though international law manifestly is, it is worth concluding with two observations that should at least be considered when reflecting on international law's utility. Given recent events and the prominence today afforded to both the ICC and the Security Council in particular, it is surely no longer tenable to dismiss international law entircly; rather it is better to seek to determine its significance, however limited. As Malanczuk wrote, 'the role of international law in international relations has always been limited, but it is rarely insignificant' (2006: 4). Finally, beyond the empirical, it is worth recalling Koskenniemi's observation that international law 'exists as a promise of justice and thus as encouragement for political transformation' (2006: 69). Unless we adhere to the tenets of anarchism we must agree with the basic premise that the normative goal of law – domestic *and* international – is to enable peaceful societal interaction and protect personal freedom, and that it is thus of definite benefit to humankind. Frustration with the existing international legal system should, therefore, compel the observer to suggest alternatives rather than induce fatalism as a world without law is surely a grim prospect.

## Guide to further reading

There are a number of excellent textbooks outlining the nature of international law which go beyond narrow technical details (Cassese 2005; Malanczuk 2006; Dixon 2007). Many canonical historical figures have written extensively on law's normative rationale, including Thomas Aquinas, Hugo Grotius, Jeremy Bentham, Thomas Hobbes, Samuel Pufendorf and Emmerich de Vattel, but for more succinct commentaries see Watts (2001) and Koskenniemi (2006). For more on the relationship between International Relations and international law see Chesterman (2003), Simpson (2004), Armstrong *et al.* (2005), Hurd (2007), Armstrong *et al.* (2007), Orford (2009) and Hehir *et al.* (2011).

## Chapter 19

# Media and World Politics

PETER VAN ONSELEN

Any examination of the role of the media in the modern globalized world requires an understanding of the economic, political and social circumstances which impact on the media. Regulations exist in all societies, in some more than most. Rules governing the media play an important role in the way in which the media engages with communities at the local level, as well as the capacity or otherwise for foreign media to be absorbed in nations which do not enjoy relative media freedoms. There are a wide variety of media forms, from large multinational corporations right down to citizen journalists operating out of basements. The rise of new media has facilitated this diversity during the past decade. This chapter will unpack the significance of the media in modern world politics, taking a particular look at new media and their role in transforming journalism in the reporting of international events. This will include a look at the rise of Twitter, You Tube, Facebook and various other social media sites, and the impact that they have had on events such as the Arab Spring.

Electronic and digital capabilities allow the media to operate as the connective tissue in the international community in a way that it was unable to in past generations. But we need to be sure not to overstate the significance of changes any more than we must avoid trying to understand change itself. Equally, the impact of a more connected global community via greater access to new media is not necessarily always a good thing. Local communities may be losing their identity because of their exposure to more powerful cultures and institutions abroad.

Understanding the role of the media on the global stage also requires a knowledge of the domestic pressures media organizations face, partly because of the forms of new media threatening traditional business models. To understand the ways in which the media have changed and will continue to change as actors in the global community, we must understand the pressures within states on media organizations, and how those pressures are impacting on the practice of journalism. This chapter will address three key questions: In what ways can the role of the media in the international system be examined? What impact, if any, do the modern media have on policy decision making? How have media theories been changed because of the rise of new media?

## The media and international politics

There are two distinct ways of examining the role of the media in the international system: as a tool of the state and as actors in their own right. Historically, the media have been used both in times of war and peace to promote the power of the nation-state on the global stage. This possibility is most commonly associated with the increasingly influential notion of 'soft power' (Nye 2004). In *Manufacturing Consent* (1988) Edward Herman and Noam Chomsky argued that the corporate nature of commercial media made them susceptible to governmental influence because of the media's need to access power. More recently, the so-called 'CNN effect' has seen the media operate within the foreign policy process as actors in their own right. However, since the events of 9/11 the media have been increasingly viewed by some scholars as being actively involved in the promotion of 'Western' values (Kellner 2004). Rather than being an independent force, traditional media are again seen by some critics as a tool of the state, a possibility highlighted in the controversy over the 'embedding' of reporters during the war in Iraq (Pfau *et al.* 2005). More broadly, some commentators think the media are complicit in promoting a set of homogeneous 'global' values, threatening local identities in the process (see, for example, Morely and Robins 1995; Albrow 1996; Terry 2007; Castells 2009).

There is no denying that the new media of the 21st century have complicated relations within civil society by giving citizens and politicians greater direct access to one another (Margolis and Moreno-Riano 2009). The rise of 'citizen journalism' is supported by the Internet and the many social networking sites that operate within it, both empowering ordinary citizens and challenging the traditional media. We are still coming to terms with exactly how significant the impact of new media will be on foreign policy considerations of states and the reporting of international news. Not only has new technology allowed citizens within states to organize more effectively, it has blurred national boundaries, having an impact on foreign and domestic policy settings in the process. The rise of the Internet and the various social media platforms it accommodates does not have much respect for nation-state boundaries.

The ability of the media to transpose international events into people's homes in real time was never more on display than during the terrorist attacks on September 11. The global audience watching the planes crash into the World Trade Center had a better idea of what was transpiring than did the people right in the middle of it (Paterson and Sreberney 2005: 3). The Internet was used by millions of people to access up-to-date information at the time and to upload photos and details of the events in the aftermath.

Nevertheless, most scholars agree that international news reporting is inadequate (Paterson and Sreberny 2005). A study by the international Council for Human Rights found that media coverage focuses on civil and political rights to the detriment of coverage of cultural and economic rights. It also concluded that media coverage of developing nations is superficial and biased, leaving audiences inadequately briefed about the issues contributing to the events being covered. A further issue for coverage of international events is the challenge of competing with other programming, such as sports, entertainment and even domestic politics. Paterson and Sreberny (2004) claim that reporting of international events now suffers from what they call 'rooftop journalism', or the reporting of events from afar, making it more difficult to communicate what is happening to the audience.

In recent years social media have provided a layer of local content to help offset this trend, but without traditional media investing in journalists on the ground to evaluate what is presented via social media, it is difficult to verify events, which leads to the risk of misreporting.

## The 'CNN effect' and Al Jazeera

The concept of the 'CNN effect' emerged in the 1990s when governments were increasingly intervening in domestic conflicts on humanitarian grounds. The media came to be seen as larger than the state – representative of multinational organizations without traditional ties to individual countries. Foreign policy makers worried that the new 24/7 news coverage which had such a profound impact on citizens, courtesy of the images beamed directly into their living rooms, was not beholden to the same nationalistic interests as the governments prosecuting wars.

Further, the CNN effect was a problem for policymakers because it has both a capacity to create public support for intervention in international trouble spots, and an equal ability to turn citizens off foreign policy engagements soon after they have started. It is the emotive effect of images on viewing audiences and the ability of the broadcast media to quickly and easily transmit them that can impact on government decision making. The CNN effect marked a shift from the media being used as a tool of government to promote an agenda, to becoming independent actors with the capacity to mobilize opinion and thus impact on government decision making. It is therefore seen as empowering the media, at least certain sections of the media, possibly at the expense of government. But scholars question the applicability of the CNN effect in the post-9/11 world, and some scholars question whether the so-called CNN effect was ever as powerful as claimed (see Gilboa 2005 and Robinson 2005).

Unfiltered, or largely unfiltered, images can provoke highly emotive reactions in the general public, pressuring politicians to act (perhaps prematurely), which in turn has a profound impact on policy decision making. Foreign policy – once the preserve of elite decision makers – is opened up to the will of the general public in a way not previously seen, courtesy of the CNN effect. Scholars are divided on whether or not that is a good thing. Those in favour of the change to a more active media say that the humanitarian interventions which follow are in line with the role democratic governments should play in international affairs. Others suggest that it is an over-extension of the role of the Fourth Estate with knock-on effects for foreign policy.

If the CNN effect has seen some transfer from passive to active engagement by the media in international affairs, the role of social media has further punctured the old structure of the media as a tool of propaganda, opening up access to information in hot spots journalists have not always managed to access.

But whatever the impact of the so-called CNN effect on the reporting of news internationally and domestically, the role of the non-Western news agency Al Jazeera has caused Western policymakers more concern. Al Jazeera started broadcasting in 1996 following a US$140 million funding allocation by the Emir of Qatar, Sheikh Hamad bin Khalifa al-Thani. Because of the pro-Palestinian nature of Al Jazeera's reporting of the Arab–Israeli conflict, it has been seen by some as an anti-Western news organization with a reach facilitated by the rising capacity of broadcast and digital media to access a wider audience. It was important in countering Western broadcasts into the Middle East, as well as offering opinions from the Middle East for Western audiences.

However, Al Jazeera has also been a thorn in the side of some Arab leaders because of its preparedness to raise sensitive issues such as the rights of women and the administrative competence of national governments in the region. When former Egyptian President Hosni Mubarak visited Al Jazeera's headquarters in Qatar he commented: 'all this trouble from a matchbook like this'. Such is the power of a cable news network with the reach of Al Jazeera (Seib 2004: 7). The network was allowed to remain in Taliban-controlled Afghanistan after Western journalists were ordered to leave, and its global brand recognition increased as it started broadcasting leaked video footage of Osama bin Laden.

As a news organization Al Jazeera has been less susceptible to the 'soft power' influence of government than other media interests have been. But Al Jazeera has not only challenged Western government influence over the media. Coupled with the rise of new media via the Internet, Al Jazeera has played a transformative role in the way international news is reported and distilled to the public (Seib 2004).

## 'New' new media and global affairs

'New media' is a rather broad concept which largely focuses on the role of on-demand content digitally supplied to the public. While the Internet and the use of blogs and various forms of social media are often identified as the primary realm of new media, the use of digital technology to provide varying forms of content – often interactive – through more traditional broadcast forms of media also falls within the definition (Bainbridge and Tynan 2008).

While commercial Internet service providers emerged in the 1990s, the 21st century has ushered in the true rise of the Internet. Google has become a major source for people to access information. Blogs have risen in prominence as have social networking sites such as Facebook. These aspects of the Internet allow citizens to post information and have it widely distributed in ways that were previously unavailable, largely without editorial constraints. Broadband technologies have helped overcome the frustrations of endlessly buffering video content, ushering in sites such as You Tube and giving the public more access points for the distribution of information. According to Flew (2008), we must understand new forms of media according to the extent to which they may alter our society.

As a consequence of the rise of 'new' new media, traditional media organizations have been forced to embrace the change. Newspapers have promoted their own websites and digital content has required the media to update the public with new information at a pace not previously seen (Allan 2006). Digital convergence is seen by major print providers as the future. Even Rupert Murdoch – a long-time advocate for the printing presses – told the Leveson Inquiry in 2012 that print media would need to transition fully to digitally provided content in ten years, perhaps even in five years. This has already put significant pressures on fewer and fewer journalists to produce content more and more quickly. What the future holds is anyone's guess. So far, major print providers have been unable to make the online business model for converting their operations to digital economically viable in any meaningful way.

However, that is only one part of the story. News reporting is no longer restricted to those who have the financial capability to engage in mass printing or purchase broadcasting rights. The Internet has created a more inter-connected global news environment, more accessible to citizens, forcing changes to the nature of political reporting by journalists in the process. While journalists operating in traditional media environments are under increasing pressures, the blogosphere has opened up access to content and given rise to more choices for consumers of news (see, for example, various chapters in Dale 2010). This has certainly 'internationalized' the news.

In recent years the rise of 'new' new media has revolutionized the role of the media in political debate. Where once traditional forms of media – print and broadcast – were seen as agents of the state or private enterprise, 'new' new media have opened up the potential of 'citizen journalism' where the traditional filters which once existed have changed (Hirst 2010: 10–11). This is a potentially radical shift of control of information, empowering citizens in a way not seen previously. Twitter, for example, often sees politicians interacting directly with citizens, keeping them connected with constituents even when they are not on the campaign hustings.

Importantly, younger generations have shown a clear preference for the 'new' new media of the Internet and the increasing ways it allows access to information. In his 2005 address to the annual meeting of the American Society of Newspaper Editors in Washington, Rupert Murdoch spoke of the 'fast developing reality' that the newspaper business must confront. 'I wasn't weaned on the web, nor coddled on a computer,' he said, contrasting that with his two younger daughters who are 'digital natives' (Murdoch, 2005). He thus noted that the younger generation was likely to turn to the Internet for news.

Central to Murdoch's view – supported by survey research – that younger generations are shunning newspapers for the web is that they do so not only because they have been brought up in a digital world, but also because they do not like the 'command and control' nature of traditional media. That is, editors commanding what is newsworthy and controlling its distribution. Young people, according to Murdoch, do not 'want to rely on a god-like figure from above to tell them what's important'. They would rather receive news on demand, or as Murdoch put it, they want 'control over their media instead of being controlled by it'.

Whether the traditional media, and even the new media which predate the 21st century, can respond to this changing sentiment in today's youth remains to be seen. Online information can be updated, is interactive, can be easily corrected (and its inaccuracies exposed) and is far more widely distributable than information has ever been before. The traditional media are making efforts to interact with media audiences. Blogging on newspaper websites is a growth area. Broadcast news programmes increasingly read out emails and display Twitter messages in an effort to interact with viewers. But none of these attempts to turn modern media into a two-way process have the immediate impact of the Internet in empowering citizen journalism. The Internet and the social media sites that it supports have opened up a whole new set of considerations when examining the role of the media in the modern globalized world.

## New media in action: Wikileaks

Founded in 2006, but only rising to prominence since 2010, Wikileaks has been described as a transformational form of new media. It has also led some scholars to question whether the way in which it operates can truly be described as media, rather than simply a repository for information. The website publishes raw data in the name of free speech, but this in itself raises interesting questions about the role of Wikileaks in the media landscape. In most countries free speech is not an absolute right, but is often tempered by a public interest test as a form of civil protection.

The *New York Times* reported in December 2010 that the Wikileaks website had been adjusted to proclaim itself a 'news organization'; the website states that its purpose is 'to bring important news and information to the public'. Initially, it did so as a user-editable website, or wiki, but it has gradually shifted away from user edits and no longer allows them. However, volunteer workers operating in a decentralized international sphere are the backbone of the Wikileaks website, giving it a citizen journalism feel.

Wikileaks has released many documents which have become front page news items in major newspapers across the world. In October and November 2010, it worked with media organizations to release redacted US State Department diplomatic cables. These included nearly 400,000 documents which chronicled deaths in the Iraqi conflict. Prior to this Wikileaks had published gun-sight footage from Iraq, for example, which showed journalists being killed, a release which came to be known as 'the Collateral Murder video'. There were many other examples which brought the efforts of the organization into direct conflict with national governments right around the world.

What does it say about Wikileaks that it chooses to use traditional media to distribute its raw material? Was it because it needed to access the resources of traditional media to filter what information it had and to then ensure it was distributed widely enough? Even traffic to the Wikileaks website would have no doubt been driven by the reports on that information contained in newspapers across the world. Or did the decision makers at Wikileaks determine that the legal protection afforded by being published in traditional media was important? For Wikileaks to be considered as a branch of journalism does it need to include news impact analysis and filter the information it distributes? These are important questions with no clear consensus as to the answers.

The traditional media largely views Wikileaks as a source. The US State Department has described its founder Julian Assange as a 'political actor'. Assange even declared an interest in running for the Australian Senate. Wikileaks has its own Facebook page with nearly two million 'fans'. Whatever is the most accurate classification of Wikileaks' role in journalism, its place in the new media cycle of the 21st century, or its status as a political actor, it has clearly had a significant impact on the media and the political landscape in a short space of time.

## New media in action: the Arab Spring

The role of the Internet in the Arab Spring highlights the truly revolutionary impact of the Internet and its capacity to transform political struggle (Stepanova 2011). The Arab Spring, which started in Tunisia and spread across many states in the Middle East, led to the overthrow of longstanding oppressive regimes. While the aftermath has been messy, and its long-term impact uncertain, there is no denying the role social media played in both marshalling support for the various uprisings and communicating what was going on to the rest of the world while it was happening. Even academics such as Anderson (2011), who questions how revolutionary the use of new media really was during the uprisings, acknowledges that it at least played a facilitating role, as old media did in previous examples of uprisings: 'The Egyptian Facebook campaigners are the modern incarnation of Arab nationalist networks whose broadsheets disseminated strategies for civil disobedience throughout the region in the years after World War I' (Anderson 2011: 2).

Claims about the importance of social media for the Arab Spring vary from it being the main factor in the spread of calls for change, to a more subdued recognition of its value as a tool within the wider process. There is evidence that Facebook in particular was used by many in the Middle Eastern uprisings to arrange protests (York 2011). You Tube was an important mechanism for uploading images of the violence to raise international awareness. Because a disproportionate number of activists during the Arab Spring were disillusioned youth seeking a greater say in the running of the states they lived in and more economic opportunities, they brought a 'tech-savvy' approach to their protests.

In Egypt the speed with which protestors followed the events in Tunisia can at least partially be attributed to the mobilizing effects of social networking sites. The protests were started via a Facebook campaign run by the opposition, known as 'April 6 Youth Movement' (Stepanova 2011: 1). The unprecedented steps taken by the government to shut down online communications during the uprisings failed because of the accessibility and abundance of information communication technology in the 21st century. As Stepanova highlights, the attempted crackdowns 'spurred new technology solutions, such as utilizing routers / path diversity methods, IP proxy servers, and Google's voice-to-Twitter applications' (2011: 2).

The Dubai School of Government has conducted research showing that social media usage in the Arab world more than doubled during the Arab Spring (Mourtada and Salem 2011). As far back as February 2010 Egypt had more than 17 million Internet users. This fits with the uprisings as largely youth-driven movements. Social media are tools more frequently used by younger people, which is in line with younger people's interest in the Internet as the preferred source for accessing news over more traditional media.

On 7 November 2011 US Secretary of State Hillary Clinton said: 'Democracies make for stronger and stabler partners. They trade more, innovate more, and fight less…for all these reasons…opening political systems, societies, and economies is not simply a matter of idealism. It is a strategic necessity.' Clinton was talking about what she hoped would be the positive fallout of the Arab Spring (Clinton 2011). While the aftermath has seen less desirable outcomes for Western leaders, including, for example, the electoral success of religious Islamic parties in some states, the hope remains that freer societies will stem from the uprisings, and in that social media have played a significant role.

## State power and media theory

New debates are emerging about an old phenomenon: the closeness of the media to political decision making. While the traditional media are in the spotlight in this respect, especially in Britain, there are wider issues with respect to the way in which the media more generally interact with politics. Governments arm themselves with communications specialists to 'spin' their messages. The print media seek to re-establish their relevance by breaking stories, which can result in sensationalism. Broadcast media continue to provide a much more shallow level of analysis. And online accounts of political events, especially so-called citizen journalism, suffer from questions over the accuracy and anonymity of how they operate.

Former head of Britain's Government Information Service, Bernard Ingram, presented an insider's view of the growth of communications professionals inside governments (2003). He nominated 11 September 2001, when a departmental media adviser in Britain reacted to the attacks on New York and Washington by emailing colleagues that 'it's now a very good day to get out anything we want to bury' as the nadir of the spin merchants and their obsession with government advantage. Ingram believes that the British public has come to expect to be 'conned' by government communications, to the detriment of politics and the operation of government. This has significant implications for the way governments can prosecute their foreign policy as well as achieve domestic outcomes.

Whereas the media were once seen as tools of the state – for the purposes of propaganda both domestically and abroad – today they are often seen as actors in themselves. The post-Cold War era has seen governments responding to calls for 'humanitarian intervention' in domestic conflicts courtesy of the media's ability to transmit images directly into people's living rooms. More recently new media have shed an often unwelcome light on the internal politics of non-democratic states, however much domestic governments might try and block the freedoms of the Internet. There has also been a backlash in favour of humanitarian interventions in the post-9/11 world, partly as a consequence of the information the media have communicated. But as McQuail (2000) notes, we should be aware that media theory has been developed with a 'western bias' generated by the largely Western construct of the mass media.

Two forms of state engagement with the media are 'soft power' and 'public diplomacy', sometimes interchangeable concepts. In media studies 'soft power' can refer to states using the media to promote their interests domestically or abroad. 'Public diplomacy' refers to the ways in which the state interacts with the media to manage its self-image (see Carruthers 2005). For example, media management by the state includes press releases, private briefings and even engagement on social media sites such as Twitter and Facebook. Using the web to advertise what state agencies do and are trying to achieve is a relatively new and growing phenomenon.

The aim of public relations (PR) is to garner favourable media coverage of the client organization by exploiting opportunities in the free media, as noted through press releases and conferences and through contacts with journalists and editors (Turner 2002). This is the public diplomacy governments engage in through the media when briefing journalists, issuing media releases and courting the Fourth Estate in a bid to push a 'soft diplomacy' line. PR professionals tend to exclude advertising from their methods, since getting the media to carry your message for nothing is both cheaper and more effective. While government and political party communications strategies tend to integrate advertising and PR methods domestically, that approach is not as easily available when pushing foreign policy objectives.

Whereas it was at one time not as necessary to engage with mass populations to 'sell' state activities on the international stage, the reach of the media in modern times demands that states present their case to an increasingly sceptical public audience. The mass societies of the modern world – certainly in developed states – require the political class to respond to popular opinion more than ever before.

The need for the state to consider how to use or influence the media towards its policy objectives has come about because of media power. The significance of the mass media has been recognized since the rise of the printing presses in the 19th century and increased during the course of the 20th century with the development of the broadcast media and the subsequent breakdown of class and social cleavages which had previously limited people's willingness to consider new political positions on issues of public policy.

Jay Blumler (2001) has highlighted the impact of social and political change in Western democracies on political communication. Blumler and Kavanagh (1999) have written about what they term the 'third age' of media communication in politics, defined by an abundance of media requiring an understanding of the fragmented and diverse nature of the listening and reading audience. This third age follows previous more rigid periods of political communication. The first age – broadly in the 1940s and 1950s – was a period of deep partisanship and strong political institutions with a simple mass media. The second age was dominated by network television, which saw a limited number of gatekeepers controlling an expanded section of the population newly exposed to political communications. The public was seen as largely passive when observing politicians, and the political parties focused their attention on television rather than newspapers.

The increased social and geographical mobility of modern societies has challenged the traditional frameworks through which citizens once approached politics. According to Movius (2010), globalization has profoundly influenced traditional media theory. Where previously political leanings framed in childhood were merely adjusted in adulthood, rarely radically transformed, today's individualist society (at least in many Western nations) means that citizens are more open to the media's political influence, even if filters such as increased levels of education now exist (Muhlmann 2010). This, combined with the penetration of the modern media, has the potential to increase the media's influence over politics in addition to its more active role in international affairs.

## The evolving media as custodians of democracy?

What role the media plays in encouraging (or discouraging) political discourse and engagement is one of the most important questions when evaluating its role in civil society. The media's role is to foster debate, act as a check on governments and on abuses of power more widely, make democracy more accessible to the public and, arguably, redistribute political influence. The changing nature of the media is interesting when assessing the way it achieves these sometimes competing goals. If we look at a country like China, the media are unable to fulfill these goals because of state restrictions. China restricts the freedom of information on the Internet, has limited the power of Google to deliver uninhibited searches and imposed strict conditions on News Corporation's entry into China via its satellite service Star Asia (Dover 2008). Limiting Western influence as it might impinge on local customs and culture is often used as the reason behind such state intervention in a free media. But the non-democratic nature of China is clearly a factor as well.

Dover (2008) notes that soon after News Corporation acquired Star Asia, comments made by Rupert Murdoch in a speech promoting the benefits of satellite television may have undermined News Corporation's efforts to penetrate the Chinese market. Murdoch declared that 'satellite broadcasting makes it possible for information hungry residents of many closed societies to bypass state controlled television channels'. According to Dover, Chinese officials reacted badly to such comments – unsurprisingly given the country's non-democratic nature.

There are several problems with the notion that the media will always provide open discourse in democratic societies. Firstly, the media may omit information that the public should be aware of when forming views on subject matter. Second, the quality of debate may be reduced because of the profit motive element of commercial media. And finally, debate risks being skewed by the media towards issues that they (whatever 'they' constitutes) support. The critique is encapsulated in the notion of the media as 'gatekeepers', coupled with the idea that they represent the privileged exercising power over the less powerful.

When it comes to international reporting, this effect has led to suggestions that the media are selective in their reporting of international events, in some instances because of 'emotional fatigue' over images being broadcast. New forms of social media can be seen as challenging this process, by improving global access to information, and by helping remove (for better or worse) the journalist as gatekeeper to the distribution of information.

While the World Wide Web should ensure that globally significant stories receive attention courtesy of the sheer volume of input from various sources combined together, what might the decline in print media mean for local stories that do not have wider implications but do have important micro-effects communities should know about? This issue conjoins fears some scholars have about the ability of media to penetrate smaller communities without regard for their local identity (see, for example, Nie and Hillygus 2002).

## Political and public policy reliance on the media

Right across the democratic world politicians rarely get the chance to communicate directly with the electorates they serve. For all the talk of 'worn-out shoe leather', representatives find it difficult to do more than communicate directly with a small fraction of the electorate. The greater the seniority of the politician, generally the more vast the constituency for which they become responsible, and in turn the more remote they can become from it. This makes political leaders all the more reliant on the media, which can deliver political messages to a wider audience (Fogarty and Wolak 2009). Equally, at the state actor level, governments in communicating with domestic and international audiences are reliant on the media, whether the role of the media is as a partner in communicating a message via 'soft diplomacy', or as an 'actor' governments must engage with.

Journalists covering politics are uniquely placed to gain access to the political class. Media coverage of political decision making is vital to how the community reacts to decisions made. Even in the age of rising forms of new media the traditional relationship between the journalists covering the news and the policymakers legislating the parameters of the debate is important. This is not to underestimate the ways in which new media are transforming the relationship between politicians and citizens. You Tube, for example, can be a two-way street. Whilst it gives citizens opportunities to become participants in the political debate, thereby further democratizing politics, it is also an easy repository for political messaging, allowing spin doctors to bypass journalists and upload information directly without the interpreting filter of the media. This is the new media equivalent of state-owned broadcasters which have traditionally been used to push political messages abroad, albeit without the attendant restrictions on alternative voices.

The media therefore act as an important filter of information, even in an age where social media are sometimes opening up direct lines of communication between governments, representatives and citizens. Traditionally it has been diffi- cult to overstate the extent to which the media can influence the perceptions of, and attitudes toward politics that citizens in individual nations have. When the printing presses dominated, this involved confronting or even challenging the authority of political elites on behalf of ordinary people (readers). Newspaper editors often saw themselves as playing a complementary role to that of political oppositions: hold- ing governments to account. Many still do today. It was this construct which saw the terminology of the 'fourth estate' take hold (Schultz 1998). However, this role has raised significant questions, in terms of the rise of an elite media acting as gate- keepers to information and decision makers of what constitutes 'news', factors which conjoin with the new active media participating in international affairs.

The rise of broadcast media in the 20th century widened the public's access to information, but it did so by simplifying the message and increasingly does so today as a form of 'infotainment' (Anderson 2004). This presents new challenges for politicians the world over. In the 20th century, the use of broadcast media in times of war became an important tool for the state. During the First and Second World Wars radio and television news were used as a form of propaganda to advance the cause of states both domestically and abroad. By the time of the Vietnam War the role of the broadcast media as actors capable of influencing public opinion against the efforts of government became a point academics openly debated (see Kellner 1992).

More recent conflicts such as the first Gulf War and new millennium wars in Iraq and Afghanistan have seen a renewed tightening of control over wartime reporting. New media, however, have made it more difficult for governments to control mainstream reporting, but much of what passes as content over the Internet is unsubstantiated and often difficult to verify. In terms of day-to-day reporting, the importance of image and delivery has become as significant as the message being delivered, perhaps even more so. But the potential pay-off is a more broadly informed citizenry, even if elements of the public policy debate can be 'dumbed down' at times.

Even now, in an age of rising new media which facilitates so-called 'citizen journalism', filters remain. For all the opportunities social media provide to bypass the journalist as gatekeeper or the spin doctors of politicians, these longstanding roles remain. Twitter provides an opportunity for journalists to quickly interpret comments made by politicians at media conferences. The 24-hour news cycle phenomenon of news channels covering press conferences by politicians in full includes analysis of what was said immediately afterwards, and often every hour on the hour after that, until events move the cycle onto the next issue.

Notwithstanding the rise of new media, in most democratic countries the free media continue to come up against well-armed PR teams within governments (Errington and van Onselen 2007). And in under-developed states the role of government continues to interfere with a free media. The foreign media often only superficially understand the issues locals are grappling with. Technology in the digital space has opened up new possibilities, but barriers do still remain.

In many Western countries the number of PR specialists spinning government lines now far outweighs the number of journalists covering stories. The ongoing decline of the press continues to widen this gap. This imbalance has a range of potential impacts. One of them is the notion of a permanent campaign (Ornstein and Mann 2000), which impacts on the way politicians approach policy development during their time in office, including in foreign affairs. No longer do parties contesting office only gear up for the campaign in the weeks and months before polling day – what has been termed the formal campaign period. Modern professional politics demands permanent campaigning in what has become a PR state, which in turns means new media have become an important battleground for that contest. British Prime Minister David Cameron, appearing at the Leveson Inquiry, highlighted that this is a serious issue for the body politic to consider.

The need for political leaders to communicate with the public is central to political messaging. Even authoritarian rulers are forced to use media to deliver their messages, although when doing so they have a control over the media not seen in democratic regimes, turning the art of spin into propaganda delivery. The rise of new media has given citizens a better way of organizing resistance to repressive regimes, as well as garnering international attention and support when doing so. As previously noted, the 2011 Arab Spring was a good example. The Wikileaks website provides a fascinating example of a new form of media which has divided experts on the extent to which what the site does can be categorized as 'journalism'. In other cases, such as China, however, the new media have not only been suppressed by the state but often support authoritarian rule (Stockmann and Gallagher 2011).

So the media remain a powerful bridge between politicians and the public, but the nature of just how the modern media operate, and how they are likely to function in the coming years, is uncertain, changing and contested. The (somewhat) clean lines which existed between politicians and the Fourth Estate in years past have been blurred by the rise of citizen journalism and new media, and continue to be challenged by the professionalization of politics.

## Conclusion

The role of the media is a key issue in world politics. This is readily apparent in the use of new media to articulate issues right around the world. The Arab Spring in 2011 was a turning point for social media, highlighting the impact they can have for social and political change. The ability of the Wikileaks website to attract information which was readily distributed to traditional media outlets for further synthesis and publication highlighted that new and old media can work together in the public interest of open access to information. Yet still there is resistance, wrapped up in concerns about the use of the media to promote Western values.

The opportunities of the role of the media in modern politics are certainly matched by the challenges. An information age which is seeing more people informed appears to be thinning the spread of information. The dangers of this equate to a 'dumbing down' of debate. Academics and professionals alike have expressed concerns over where all this leads us. 'Infotainment' media may be able to attract greater audiences to the political sphere and appear to be more attractive to younger generations than old-fashioned news and current affairs programming. But are those drawn to 'infotainment' programmes joining the discussion to be part of a meaningful civic discourse?

Civil society thrives on citizen engagement, which proponents of the changing media landscape tell us is the most significant opportunity the Internet affords – active rather than passive engagement. And social networking sites like Facebook, Twitter and You Tube bypass gatekeepers, allowing even the most amateur citizen journalist to be heard. But is that necessarily a good thing? The anonymity of the Internet might seem like a good thing when an activist in an oppressive nation seeks to draw attention to their plight. But what about when it is used to lower the tone of debate in otherwise secure democracies?

The changes that are occurring in the international media landscape are far from over. The digital revolution is ongoing and how it will redistribute media power and influence remains unclear. There are certainly examples of its capacity to empower populations in authoritarian regimes, and in democratic nations to give outsiders a platform to express themselves, which they previously did not. But where all of this is leading remains unclear, and what impact it might ultimately have on political decision making is also uncertain. What we do know is that the media's impact on political discourse within nations and between them is changing, as is the very definition of what the media might incorporate. This is no small change, given the central role the media have always played, both as a defender of democracy and a lightning rod to help achieve it.

## Guide to further reading

In *Online News: Journalism and the Internet*, Stuart Allan (2006) provides an introduction to new sources of online news and the factors that have underpinned their development. A range of recent case studies are used to illustrate these issues. For useful introductory texts on the 'mediasphere' and the media more generally see Bainbridge *et al.* (2008) *Media and Journalism* and Flew (2008) *New Media: An Introduction*. Christians *et al.* (2009) look at the role of the media in democratic societies and the philosophical underpinnings that suggest what journalism ought to be in *Normative Theories of the Media: Journalism in Democratic Societies*. The potential implications of the Internet in particular and its relationship to democratic theory are considered in Margolis and Moreno-Riano (2009) *The Prospect of Internet Democracy*.

# Chapter 20

# After Neoliberalism: Varieties of Capitalism in World Politics

*MARK BEESON*

For the last couple of years the international economy has been characterized by growing levels of volatility and uncertainty. Since the global financial crisis (GFC) erupted in 2008, international money markets, political leaders and popular commentary have been variously distinguished by grim determination, a sense of rising panic and incredulity. In such circumstances, it is understandable that our attention is focused on the remarkable levels of volatility that have shaken the world's increasingly influential money markets and the day-to-day efforts of policymakers as they struggle to get to grips with a crisis that looks more serious than anything we have seen since the 1930s. Some of the most important and apparently secure elements of the international system are seemingly much more fragile than we might have thought. The future of the European Union, for example, is much more uncertain than seemed possible a couple of years ago. Likewise, the position of the United States as the dominant, stabilizing bedrock of the international system is far less assured than it was a few years ago when many commentators were predicting a period of 'unipolarity' and continuing American hegemony (Wohlforth 1999). Now, by contrast, the US economy is associated primarily with a destabilizing weakness that is compounded by an increasingly dysfunctional domestic political system (Beeson and Broome 2010).

These developments are shocking and largely unforeseen – especially by an economics profession that was still wedded to the idea that markets are inherently efficient and that they should be as free as possible of government 'interference' (see Colander *et al.* 2009). How times change. In the aftermath of the GFC, governments around the world found themselves having to bail out banks that had indulged in speculative – even predatory – practices that were poorly understood and badly overseen, and which ultimately led to economic chaos. Many of the debts that were incurred by a poorly regulated financial sector were taken over by governments, creating the preconditions for the sovereign debt crisis that shows no signs of abating at the time of writing. For those with long memories or a sense of history there is something unsurprising and frustrating about such developments. After all, it was the reckless actions of a poorly regulated banking sector that did more than anything else to cause the Great Depression of the 1930s (Kindleberger 1973). It is not necessary to dwell on the appalling political and social consequences of this earlier economic crisis to recognize that there is something to be said for effective regulation and for attempting to learn the lessons of history (Reinhart and Rogoff 2009).

Although we cannot be certain what the long-term consequences of the current economic turmoil will be, one thing seems reasonably clear in the short term, at least: 'neoliberalism', or the economic paradigm that championed free markets, minimal regulation, economic liberalization and a limited role for the state, is not the force it was. On the contrary, even unabashed admirers of market forces, such as former Chairman of the Federal Reserve, Alan Greenspan, have been forced to admit that there may be 'flaws' in the economic system that dominated both the US and the wider international system for decades. This masterpiece of understatement reminds us of two important things: first, what J.K. Galbraith famously called the 'conventional wisdom' can change. In other words, today's orthodoxy can become tomorrow's heresy and vice versa. Second, although it was dominant in the so-called Anglo-American economies in the US, Canada, Britain and Australasia, even in its heyday neoliberalism did not sweep all before it. On the contrary, in many parts of the world it was either resisted or adopted in a half-hearted fashion. Even though capitalism may have become the default social system, it manifested itself in significantly different ways in various parts of the world. In the aftermath of the GFC, when the US and the UK were the initial epicentres of the crisis, the neoliberal model looked far less attractive that it had done. Indeed, the GFC is something of a misnomer as some parts of the world – most notably an East Asian region led by a rising China – were initially largely unaffected (Breslin 2011). As a consequence, many governments around the world are looking with renewed interest at economic models that are at odds with the American experience, but which hold out the prospect of an alternative route to economic development.

At a time when capitalism appears to be experiencing one of its all too frequent crises, it is important to understand its general principles and the significantly different ways it has manifested itself across the world. Drawing on the 'varieties of capitalism' literature, which has usefully highlighted the institutional and organizational diversity of contemporary economic forms, this chapter provides an overview of capitalist development in some of its more important incarnations. The key point that emerges from this discussion is that the international system generally and economic activity more particularly are inherently dynamic and may currently be at an important historical turning point. While we may not be able to predict how this process will play itself out, we can, at least, try to identify the forces in play.

## Capitalism in context

There is nothing 'natural' or inevitable about the way economic systems are organized. Indeed, the entire history of the 20th century was profoundly shaped by a major ideological – and sometimes military – contest between the capitalist and socialist states about the best ways of organizing economic activity (Arrighi 1994). As we all know, the capitalists under the leadership of the United States won the Cold War and the rest, as they say, is history. And yet the legacy of this period lingers on, and the apparent triumph of capitalism, or at least of *liberal* capitalism, is far from assured as a result of recent events. Even before the recent crisis, one of the largest economies in the world – the Peoples' Republic of China – was still notionally 'communist'. While genuine socialists may be something of an endangered species in China these days, the general point holds: there are fundamental and enduring institutionalized differences in the way economies are organized and these reflect specific historical circumstances and developmental experiences of the countries involved (Haggard 2004).

Clearly, however, ideological contestation is no longer such an important factor in determining how economic systems are organized, and this helps to explain why market-oriented economic systems seem so 'natural' and uncontested (Gamble 2009). And yet we cannot understand the continuing uniformity *or* diversity of economic systems unless we recognize the impact that long-running geopolitical confrontation has had on economic development and what we now think of as 'globalization' (see Cerny, this volume). After the Second World War when the US assumed a 'hegemonic' or dominant position in the international system and effectively assumed the leadership of the Western world, American policymakers had the chance to create a new international economic order which broadly reflected their norms and interests (Latham 1997). Crucially, however, there were limits to how far they could impose their preferred economic vision. Not only were some countries outside the capitalist camp, but some of the US's closest allies, such as Japan, persisted with a very different form of capitalism which became something of a model for much of East Asia (Beeson 2007). Even in the US's 'backyard', many Latin American economies adopted policies of import substitution and self-reliance in an effort to promote economic development.

Western Europe also developed quite distinctive economic structures, styles of labour relations and social welfare systems, despite benefiting significantly from US aid and investment in the post-war period (Albert 1993; Esping-Anderson 1990). Significantly, the degree of international economic integration was much less than it is now – partly because of the limited role played by money markets and cross-border finance, partly because of the underdeveloped nature of multinational corporations, and partly because that was the way national governments wanted it. In what Ruggie (1982) famously called the 'compromise of embedded liberalism', individual governments retained a good deal of policy autonomy, something that tended to entrench national differences. There was also a general enthusiasm for the sort of policy approach developed by the influential British economist, John Maynard Keynes, who advocated a significant role for the state in overcoming the crises to which capitalism by its very nature is occasionally prone (Hall 1989).

For twenty years or so, what has been described as the 'golden age of capitalism' saw unprecedented levels of economic development, not just in Europe, but in East Asia too. The multilateral economic institutions established under

American auspices (see Higgott, this volume) seemed to function well and offer the prospect of continuing growth and stability. However, a number of factors began to undermine the old regime and pave the way for the eventual turn to neoliberal ideas.

## The rise of neoliberalism

By the end of the 1960s, Keynesian policies seemed unable to address an emerging series of problems. Economic growth began to decline and unemployment rose. Even more alarmingly, inflation continued to rise despite growing unemployment – an unexpected development that was dubbed 'stagflation'. This was bad enough in itself, but during the 1970s a series of economic 'shocks' further destabilized the global economy. Perhaps the most decisive blow to the old order, though, were the problems experienced by the US, the hegemonic power of the era and, according to one influential school of thought, a vital source of stability for the overall international economic system (Kindleberger 1973).

But the US was increasingly unable – or unwilling – to play the role of system stabilizer that the old order established at Bretton Woods was based upon and needed for its survival (Beeson and Broome 2010). True, some of the institutions remained outwardly the same, but the role played by organizations such as the International Monetary Fund (IMF) was radically transformed as the US unilaterally decided to break with the old order of managed exchange rates. This period ushered in the contemporary system of predominantly 'floating' exchange rates, triggering an explosion in cross-border financial transactions and the rapid growth of money markets as financial institutions sought to profit from the new system. While it may ultimately have been states that oversaw and effectively authorized this massive growth in the size and importance of private sector activities, the net effect was to sharply increase the power of market forces generally and financial capital in particular (Helleiner 1994).

Important as these changes in the underlying structures of the global economy were, of equal if not greater significance in the longer term were changes in the dominant economic discourse or ideology. Two figures loom large in this transformation from Keynesian to monetarist ideas, as the emerging economic paradigm came to be called. Former US president Ronald Reagan and British prime minister Margaret Thatcher did more than anyone to popularize economic ideas that had hitherto been marginal. The apparent failure of Keynesianism may have provided the crisis which many observers think is a prerequisite for major, paradigm-shifting institutional change, but it is also important to recognize how active supporters of the free market and monetarism were in promoting the new order (Cockett 1994).

Monetarism was a radical economic position which argued that inflation – one of the key problems of the 1970s – was ultimately caused by the money supply. Pioneered primarily by the prominent American economist Milton Friedman, monetarism essentially claimed that governments were to blame for inflation because they printed too much money. For a while, at least, monetarism gave a veneer of intellectual credibility to a wider array of economic, political and social initiatives that would ultimately be subsumed under the broad rubric of neoliberalism. The new economic ideas were reinforced by similar changes in the study and practice of politics, as 'public choice theory' with its inherent suspicion of governments and political processes became increasingly influential (Blyth 2002). The central precepts of the emerging neoliberal paradigm were in part a renewed emphasis on an older tradition of liberal ideas dating back to Adam Smith, which emphasized the efficacy of market forces and individual self-interest. But what was distinctive and ultimately transformative about neoliberalism was not just a faith in the rationality and entrepreneurial self-interest of individuals, but a political agenda to bring such potential benefits to fruition.

Much of this policy paradigm is now so familiar that younger readers may find it difficult to believe that things were not ever thus. But they were different, and in many places they still are. At the centre of the policy paradigm that became synonymous with Margaret Thatcher's reformist government (which was anything but conservative), was a programme of privatization and deregulation. Formerly publicly owned utilities like water, gas and the railways were sold off in line with the idea that the market is the best allocator of resources and provider of services; the government's role is simply to act in cases of 'market failure', such as defence or the police. Now, however, even security has become increasingly privatized in ways that seemed inconceivable only a decade ago (Mandel 2001).

In reality, however, the 'retreat of the state' has been rather overstated as the state still accounts for a good deal of economic activity and social provision – especially since many governments have chosen to bail out the financial sector. Even more fundamentally, the degree of deregulation is generally equally overstated as it is simply not possible for capitalism of any sort to survive without some form of legal system, regulatory regime and political order. For all the talk about globalization, there are some things that – thus far, at least – only states can do (see Cerny, this volume).

## Capitalism in practice

There are a number of levels at which we can look at different forms of political economy. We can, for example, look at the reactions of different states to the pressures of 'globalization' as Philip Cerny does in Chapter 3. Alternatively, we can look at the historical development and internal constituent parts of different nationally based systems to try and understand how they differ, and why such differences persist despite the apparently universal pressures associated with globalization. One useful concept in this context is 'path dependency'. Simply put, path dependency suggests that the present and the future are shaped by the past, and in the absence of powerful systemic shocks, are likely to continue reflecting institutionalized, routine modes of interaction (Pierson 2000). This is a potentially important idea if we want to explain the persistence of different patterns of development and organization. At the very least, we need to recognize that contemporary states and societies begin from very different starting points and may have profoundly differ-ent levels of 'state capacity' and consequent abilities to implement policies – even where policymakers appear to subscribe to broadly similar ideas (see Polidano 2000). Indeed, it is clear that there remain significant variations not only in policy outcomes across nations but also in the economic visions that inform them.

Even if we accept that the state still plays an important role in determining economic outcomes, there are still very different ways of embedding states in the societies of which they are such an important part. Here the 'varieties of capital-ism' literature provides a comparative snapshot of the different ways capitalism has been institutionalized, as well as a way of conceptualizing its component parts. One very broad brush distinction made by many observers is between 'liberal market economies', such as those found in places like Britain, the US and Australia (the Anglo-American economies), which are hierarchical and based on competi-tive markets, and 'coordinated market economies', which make more use of non-market relationships and socially embedded networks to organize economic activities (Hall and Soskice 2001). Coordinated market economies are associated with countries such as Germany and especially Japan, where some of the most basic and important institutions of a capitalist economy – relations between the banking and business sectors, for example – have been organized quite differently over long periods of time (Zysman 1983).

Despite Japan's current economic problems, for many years it attracted much attention for the astounding rapidity and depth of its industrial expansion, and the distinctiveness of its corporate structures, financial system and labour relations. And yet, it is clear that much has gone wrong in Japan's political practices and economic outcomes – especially when compared to its earlier formidable develop-mental performance. As a consequence of domestic political failures and sustained external pressure for reform, Japan finds itself in the worst of all possible worlds – neither an effective coordinated economy, nor a reformed liberal model (Vogel 2006). Nevertheless, we need to recognize that Japan and many other parts of East Asia retain very different institutional arrangements within their economies, and that these are unlikely to be easily swept away where they enjoy continuing support from politically powerful domestic actors (Lincoln 2001).

For some observers, the difference in the constituent parts of coordinated market economies, where firms may have had close relationships with banks, other firms and even affiliated trade unions for many years, meant that these collective forms of coordination and cooperation were simply incompatible with the neoliberal model (Hollingsworth and Boyer 1997: 24). But it is clear that some of the close links between corporate and financial capital that were such a distinc-tive feature of the Japanese and German models have begun to unravel and are not as decisive or distinctive as they once were (Katz 1998; Streeck 1997). There is consequently a good deal of debate about the prospects for 'convergence', or the possibility that the international diffusion of ideas about public policy 'best prac-tice' will encourage countries to adopt increasingly similar strategies (Dobbin *et al*. 2007; Simmons and Elkins 2004). However, it is also evident that, even in an era of greater transnational economic interaction and political cooperation, not all countries share the same ideational frameworks or assumptions about the way the world works, or about the best ways of responding to global pressures (Drezner 2001).

The possible existence of different economic perspectives becomes especially important at a time when some observers feel that 'the economic credibility of the West has been undermined by the crisis' that has so profoundly affected the US in particular (Altman 2009: 10); this will plainly have major implications for the convergence debate. But even before this most recent crisis, many felt that the model championed by the US and the international financial institutions (IFIs), such as the IMF and the World Bank, was neither appropriate nor useful for countries in very different circumstances and phases of development. On the one hand, it was apparent that every country that had ever successfully industrialized had done so by employing precisely the sorts of 'interventionist' policies that have been being actively discouraged by the IFIs (Chang 2002). Without state assistance – even protection – industries were unlikely to develop, much less thrive in a world dominated by the established Western economies. On the other hand, one of the big comparative lessons of the East Asian and Latin American experiences was that the latter had failed to adopt specific 'industry policies' as effectively or fully as the East Asians had (Rodrik 2007). In other words, there was, and perhaps still is, a role for government intervention in helping to promote development and the sort of institutional environment within which economic growth might occur. This was not, however, a view shared in much of the West or the IFIs.

## The Washington consensus and its critics

Despite a growing recognition that their internal structures and subordinate positions in the global economy meant that many impoverished economies were simply unable to take advantage of the supposed opportunities offered by a liberal economic order (see Kiely, this volume), the IFIs have largely continued to advocate further economic liberalization (Wade 2010). A growing number of critics have drawn attention to the World Bank's and the IMF's failure to relieve poverty and their role in promoting policies closely associated with the interests of the developed rather than the developing world (Peet 2003). Despite this, the IFIs have demonstrated a continuing adherence to a set of policies that have come to be known as the 'Washington consensus'.

Originally coined by the American economist John Williamson (1994), the Washington consensus describes what Williamson called the 'common core of wisdom embraced by all serious economists'. The following were, Williamson and other 'serious', mainstream economists thought, self-evidently the best policies for both developed and developing economies:

- fiscal discipline;
- redirection of public expenditure towards basic education, primary health care and infrastructure;
- tax reform;

- interest rate liberalization;
- competitive exchange rate;
- trade liberalization;
- liberalization of foreign direct investment (FDI) flows;
- privatization;
- secure property rights.

While it may be hard to disagree with spending on health and education, other issues are far more controversial, especially given their potential impact on developing economies. The dangers of premature capital account opening had been demonstrated graphically in the East Asian crisis of the late 1990s, while the benefits of free trade were even more moot – something that helps to explain the continuing resistance to their universal adoption in Asia to this day (Beeson and Islam 2005). As Reinert (2007: 119) points out, in a world characterized by radically different levels of economic development and power, 'asymmetric free trade will lead to the poor nation specializing in being poor, while the rich nation will specialize in being rich. To benefit from free trade, the poor nation must first rid itself of its international specialization in being poor. For 500 years this has not happened anywhere without heavy market intervention.'

In the face of growing criticism the World Bank in particular has attempted to modify the impact, if not always the underlying ideological thrust, of some of its policies. The so-called 'post-Washington consensus' marks a significant concession on the Bank's part that markets may not always be perfect and that states may actually have an important role to play in the developmental process (Fine 2003; World Bank 1997). But the IFIs have generally persisted in seeing development as an essentially technocratic project and failed to recognize the inherently political nature of economic activity and reform – something that a belated interest in social safety nets and the need for greater local 'ownership' of the entire process could not disguise (see Higgott, this volume; Higgott 2000).

The suspicion remained that the IFIs were either, at best, under the spell of an especially powerful economic discourse or, at worst, simply the obliging hand-maidens of American foreign policy. As radical scholars have never tired of pointing out, even if many nations have benefited from the institutional order created at Bretton Woods, the principal beneficiaries have been American-based economic entities and consumers, and the geopolitical agenda of the US itself (Arrighi 1994; Harvey 2003; Panitch and Gindin 2004). That, after all, was the point of being the dominant power: the US, like Britain before it, was able to shape the international system to reflect and further what it took to be in its national interest (Agnew 2005).

Now, however, things are looking rather different. Not only are there renewed doubts about the durability of the Anglo-American model of capitalism, but other countries are beginning, explicitly or implicitly, to challenge the dominance of neoliberalism and American hegemony more generally.

## Competing capitalisms

There have always been different types of capitalism. What has attracted attention most recently, however, is the rapid rise to economic prominence of a number of economies whose leaders are not especially enamoured of neoliberalism or the Washington consensus, and who are far from liberal in their political beliefs and practices. Indeed, it has become fashionable to talk about the emergence of 'illiberal' political regimes, which may be ostensibly democratic, but which do not promote political liberty (Zakaria 2003). Of course, there have always been non-democratic regimes, too, even if the concept of illiberal democracies is rather new and distinctive. But the rise of illiberal political regimes has attracted increased attention for a number of reasons. First, only a few years ago, some were predicting that liberal democracy would become the dominant paradigm the world over, because it was thought to be most compatible with a global economy and modern political sensibilities (Fukuyama 1992). Although such views may seem wildly optimistic now, there was a good deal of apparently compelling evidence about the seemingly inexorable spread of democratic practices (Huntington 1991).

As we now know, of course, the end of the Cold War did not bring about a process of political convergence or the end of ideological contestation. On the contrary, some believe that globalization has actually intensified cultural or even civilizational fault lines, making the development of common social, political and economic practices even less likely (Barber 2001; Huntington 1996). Although many of these claims are controversial and highly contested, it is clear that the world is characterized by enduring differences in some of its most basic organizational principles and even sources of identity, which some claim account for differential economic outcomes (Mahbubani 2008). In such circumstances, the possibility that different forms of capitalism might also endure becomes more plausible. What has given this idea even more credibility, however, has been the problems afflicting neoliberal capitalism in the US, and the – until recently, at least – apparently inexorable rise of new centres of economic and political power outside the established 'core' economies.

As Nick Bisley explains in Chapter 2, the last few years have seen a remarkable transformation in the established international pecking order. Although some of the 'new' centres of power in China and Russia have, in fact, long been major players in international affairs, it is striking that countries such as Venezuela are enthusiastically championing values and economic models that are markedly at odds with what has until recently been the relatively unchallenged neoliberal orthodoxy. Even in the Middle East, where the US has some important notional allies, rapidly expanding oil revenues have meant that a number of countries that have been relatively minor players in international affairs have suddenly found themselves enjoying greater influence (Kimmit 2008). The reason for this is simple: rapid industrialization, rising living standards and all the associated benefits of globalization have – paradoxically enough – caused a dramatic spike in the price of raw materials, energy and resources, and this has thrust the likes of Russia back into the centre of global power politics (Gat 2007).

The recent economic crisis not only provided a demonstration of just how volatile resource prices can be, it also served to remind us that competition for finite resources and especially energy looks likely to be one of the defining issues of the 21st century. What makes the behaviour of a 'state capitalist' like China so significant is that it is responding to the challenge of energy provision, not by relying on the market, but by using its own expanding foreign exchange reserves to make strategic investments. The rise of so-called 'sovereign wealth funds' is perhaps the most striking example of the changing economic order and the desire that some states have to take a much more direct role in how national wealth is invested (Gawdat 2008). Such 'neo-mercantilist' strategies are fundamentally at odds with the neoliberal orthodoxy that has become so influential over the last few decades.

In former times we might have expected the US to use its influence over the IFIs to encourage or coerce other states into adopting more orthodox economic policy. Now, however, with its own economic prospects under a cloud and its reputation for effective economic management seriously tarnished, its influence has been markedly diminished. Indeed, one of the most noteworthy features of the financial crisis was the Chinese government lecturing the Americans on the unsustainable and irresponsible nature of their economic policies (Edgecliffe-Johnson 2009) – a criticism to which America's reliance on continuing inflows of Chinese money leaves them badly exposed. Despite the recent economic crisis, therefore, it would seem that – all other things being equal – China might eventually become an alternative economic growth engine and saviour of the world economy, an idea that is especially appealing to the distressed economies of Europe (Anderlini and Zhang 2011). Equally importantly, China could also provide an alternative, non-neoliberal vision of how the world could be organized.

## The Beijing consensus

If China can continue its remarkable economic expansion – a big 'if' given the impact of the recent crisis and the profound environmental constraints that are emerging as a consequence of breakneck industrialization and population growth (see Beeson 2009) – then it will overtake the US as the world's largest economy within the next couple of decades. This would be important enough in itself as it marks an epochal shift in the prevailing balance of material power and influence in the international system. However, what makes this especially significant in the context of a discussion of competing forms of capitalist organization is that China has achieved this historically unparalleled transformation via a very different form of state capitalism. The label that has come to be attached to this model of development is 'the Beijing consensus'. The term was coined by Joshua Cooper Ramo, a former editor of *Time* magazine, to describe the highly pragmatic approach to policy-making that developed in China.

As with the Washington consensus, the Beijing consensus is something of a caricature, but it does capture something essential about capitalism in China that is dramatically different from its counterparts in the West. It could hardly be otherwise. After all, China remains notionally a communist country, and its historical experience imparts a very different pattern of path dependency, one which makes radical change difficult. It was the initial embrace of capitalism inaugurated by Deng Xiaoping and the effective repudiation of socialism it brought in its wake that marked the really big change. This was a profound transformation of world historical significance as it did, indeed, seem to mark the end of serious paradigmatic competition to capitalism as the primary global form of economic organization. It is important to remember that until relatively recently, those who embarked upon what was derisively known as the 'capitalist road' were seen as dangerous counter-revolutionaries who had sold out to the West. Since the 1970s, however, there has been steady incremental change toward a market economy and away from the old model of central planning (Naughton 2007).

Deng's famous aphorism – it doesn't matter whether a cat is black or white as long as it catches mice – perfectly captures the spirit of pragmatism that infused his own thinking and which is central to the Beijing consensus. Ramo (2004: 4) suggests that the Beijing consensus is 'defined by a ruthless willingness to innovate and experiment, by a lively defense of national borders and interests, and by the increasingly thoughtful accumulation of tools of asymmetric power projection'. There is a pragmatic commitment to do whatever seems to work – as long as it does nothing to undermine the sovereignty of the nation or the pre-eminent position of the extant political elite. In other words, the Beijing consensus is about maintaining political control and authority, whilst simultaneously allowing a pragmatic, but still limited, expansion of the role of the private sector (Huang 2008). However, it is also important to recognize that China's expanding capitalist class has shown little interest in pressing for the political reform of a system from which it benefits, and with which it is closely connected (Tsai 2007). In other words, there is nothing inevitable or pre-ordained about the relationship between political authority and economic development, and no reason to suppose that China's development will replicate the earlier historical experiences of Europe, America or even Japan (Beeson 2012).

The failure of the capitalist class – thus far, at least – to push for political liberalism is quite at odds with the European experience and contrary to the expectations of much Western political theory. While this is plainly a challenge for Western scholars, there is a more immediate and practical consequence of China's distinctive pattern of development: China is serving as something of a role model for other countries, especially those that dislike the intrusive and politically difficult demands of the Washington consensus (Zhao 2010). For many extant political elites, China's experience suggests it is possible to have political development without political reform. China's own increasingly sophisticated diplomacy, when combined with its growing importance as a trade partner and source of investment, is giving a surprising degree of ideational influence to its model at the expense of the rather discredited Anglo-American alternative (Lampton 2008). It is also clear that China's form of 'state capitalism' serves an equally important *political* purpose. As Ian Bremmer (2010: 52) points out, 'state capitalists see markets primarily as a tool that serves national interests, or at least those of ruling elites, rather than as an engine of opportunity for the individual'.

While we might expect a former communist country with high levels of state ownership and involvement in the economy to continue having very different, structurally embedded patterns of organization, what is novel about China's position is that first, it may eclipse the US as the world's largest economic power, and second, it offers an alternative developmental paradigm for those countries unimpressed by the Washington consensus. Given such an environment, we might expect to see the persistence, rather than the end, of differences between capitalist systems. Such a possibility has become even more likely as a consequence of the current crisis, which has seen the future of the European Union called into question. Whatever one thinks about the European project, it represents the most ambitious attempt thus far to politically engineer a process of policy convergence and economic coordination across national boundaries in very different national contexts. That this experiment could fail would not only be a major blow to the standing of 'the West' and its models of political and economic development, it would also increase the material importance and ideational influence of alternatives.

## Concluding remarks

At a time when the international political economy is in the middle of the worst economic crisis since the Great Depression, it would be foolhardy to try and predict what might happen to individual economies, much less the international system more generally. It is possible, however, to make a few observations about what we already know and the possible lessons of history – even if we seem to be incapable of learning from them. The first point to make is that much will depend on what happens to the American and Chinese economies. As far as the US is concerned, its admirers would argue that we've been here before: in the 1980s, many predicted that the US would be overtaken by Japan (yes, Japan) as the American economy became less competitive. And yet, as we now know, the US bounced back in the 1990s to such an extent that some thought its ascendancy was likely to continue indefinitely and its power could be used to reshape the world. Ironically, this hubris encouraged American policymakers to embark on ruinously expensive, strategically disastrous adventures in Iraq and Afghanistan, undermining not only America's geopolitical position, but its economy as well. The current state of America's domestic politics offers little encouragement that its policymakers will be able to engineer a 1990s-style recovery anytime soon. On the contrary, its indebtedness to and reliance on China in particular may become an increasingly important and neuralgic public policy issue in the future – and a measure of its continuing decline. However policymakers in America respond to its problems, the sort of neoliberal paradigm that the US has historically advocated – if not always practised – looks discredited and incapable of turning its fortunes around.

China, by contrast, is seen as the great hope of the world. This is not to say that other countries are necessarily about to adopt Chinese-style economic or political practices, but the Chinese economy is seen as one of the few potential engines of growth in an otherwise moribund, crisis-ridden global economy. Although there is no certainty that China will be able to play this role given its own developmental, environmental and political problems, it is a remarkable state of affairs, nonetheless. Only three or four decades ago, China was an impoverished largely agrarian economy on the periphery of international economic activity; now it is an increasingly central actor in both the production of 'real' goods and services and – via its symbiotic relationship with the US – in the financial sector, too. There are signs that Chinese policymakers want to translate this growing economic weight into political leverage and begin to exercise the sort of influence over the international system that the US did when at the height of its hegemonic powers. Quite what the world will look like if and when this happens is unclear, but it is safe to say that it will be rather different from the neoliberal order that has played such an influential role over the last thirty years or so.

## Guide to further reading

Ian Bremmer's (2010) book provides an excellent and provocative introduction to the development of state capitalism and the challenge it presents to the existing international order. Ha-joon Chang's (2002) book puts development in historical perspective and explains why the state has always played an important developmental role. The paper by Hall and Soskice (2001) offers a very useful and seminal contribution to the varieties of capitalism debate. Ramo's (2004) book on the Beijing consensus has the great merit of being short and provocative. My own (Beeson 2009) article on Sino-US relations provides an overview of the 'hegemonic transition literature' as well as an analysis of the prospects for China supplanting the US.

# Chapter 21

# Conclusion: Paradoxes, Problems, Prospects

MARK BEESON AND NICK BISLEY

The contributors to this collection have covered a lot of ground. The intention of this final chapter is not to try and distill the substance of earlier chapters, but to consider a number of their main implications, which are complex and often contradictory. Indeed it is quite reasonable for the reader of the book to come away from this experience feeling somewhat overwhelmed by the range of important issues that command the attention of students in 21st-century world politics. Equally, we should recognize that it is not only students who are confronted by the degree of complexity: policymakers face the same daunting array of complex and intertwined issues. There is currently a vast and growing range of issues that states are expected to address; these issues are rarely discrete and cut across traditional divisions between foreign and domestic policy (Rosenau 1997). Moreover the transnational quality of so many issues means that, although expectations for state action remain high, the problems to be managed by policymakers resist the efforts of even the most capable and affluent states. From climate change to population movement, financial crises to infectious diseases, states have increasingly to collaborate with others to defend their interests (Keohane and Victor 2011). Yet even if states can act collectively – and international inaction on climate change is a sobering reminder that this is by no means a given – these actions can be of limited impact due to the increasingly disparate and diffuse nature of power in the international system.

## Caveats and caution

When thinking about the contemporary world, it is hard not to consider China. China's rise may not have changed everything, but its dramatic re-emergence at the centre of world politics throws familiar issues into newly sharp relief. For example, China's leaders have, over the last few decades at least, enjoyed greater 'performance legitimacy' than their counterparts in Europe and North America (Zhu 2011). It is not just the West that is dazzled by the performance of the Chinese economy; so, too, are the Chinese themselves. In the People's Republic of China, as well as the other BRICs, and many of 'the rest', successful development is still something of a novelty and expectations are often being met. There are growing concerns about rising inequality and endemic corruption, graphically illustrated by the ousting of Bo Xilai in early 2012, and the toll being taken of the natural environment by growing numbers of affluent consumers is frankly alarming. But for many of the world's aspirant poor such problems may not appear to be quite as pressing as they are for readers in the wealthy developed world. It is worth remembering that anyone with access to a book such as this and the ability to critically engage with its contents is still a member of a very fortunate minority of the world's population, as Ray Kiely (Chapter 11) reminded us.

This reflects a first broader caveat: the way we define or indeed think about the major problems or issues in world politics depends to a great extent on who we are and where we find ourselves. The sense we have of the importance of any particular issue will depend on whether we are male or female, black or white, rich or poor, repressed or empowered. At one level this is fairly obvious, yet it is worth reiterating because our understanding of the world is fundamentally bound up with our location, identity and opportunities in life. This brings us to a larger point. Unless you are a believer in one of the more fundamentalist religious doctrines that claim to be able to explain existence by reference to some transcendent reality unavailable to the rest of us, or an admirer of a rather unfashionable 'grand narrative', such as Marxism, then we have to accept that there is no objective position from which to make judgments about the sorts of issues that have been discussed in this book (Rorty 1991). Trying to understand issues or indeed to make policy, in other words, inevitably reflects particular ways of thinking about the world and inevitably advantages some interests over others.

The inescapably political and inherently unequal nature of social existence matters for a number of reasons. First, even the most 'technical' of issues are not immune either from politicization or from the possibility that their attempted resolution will reflect a particular set of values and advantage a particular set of interests. Climate change, as Neil Carter (Chapter 13) reminded us, is not simply a 'scientific' issue which requires a technical fix. Indeed, even though there is almost universal agreement amongst the expert scientific community about the physical science of a changing climate, the adoption of appropriate responses has thus far has proven to be extremely challenging in political terms. In many ways the primary reason for this is that enacting such policies would impose significant costs on groups who are currently very influential. Climate change is thus representative of many pressing political issues, in that efforts to address it inevitably produce winners and losers and the latter, unsurprisingly, tend to resist change.

The politicization of knowledge is a distinctive, but rather surprising aspect of modern life (Haas 1990; Foucault 1980). After all, the very existence of this book and its assorted essays is a vivid reminder of the fact that none of us can claim sufficient understanding of the panoply of issues that demand attention and analysis, especially in such a large and complex international system. The extent, variety and specialization of knowledge simply precludes universal comprehension at the expected level of expertise – hence collective endeavours of the sort you currently have in your hands. But even if we accept the necessity and perhaps even the advantages of an intellectual division of labour, it does not mean that we will necessarily agree with or like its consequences. The other striking feature of contemporary policy-making and politics is just how contested and even polarized it has become in many developed states. The United States is, perhaps, the most consequential and surprising example of this in the contemporary system. Whether the United States is in the process of inescapable long-term decline is one of the most important questions of the early 21st century (Layne 2012; Krauthammer 2009). Perhaps the most illustrative example of this is the impasse within the American political system over how to manage the massive US budget deficit. The inability of the most powerful country on the planet to adopt sensible measures to deal with problems of its own making powerfully highlights America's current difficulties.

Things were not supposed to be this way. Just over twenty years ago, some thought history – understood as a long-term process of ideological and philosophical struggle – had come to an end (Fukuyama 1992). Liberal democratic capitalism had beaten all comers and was thought to be the only viable path for sophisticated societies. All that remained was for those unfortunate enough to be caught up in history's ongoing struggles to be brought in from the cold. The end of the 20th century seemed to denote the beginning and not the end of a long period of American global dominance, what some have called a condition of global unipolarity (Wohlforth 1999). We now know, of course, that such visions of continuing American authority and the inexorable spread of 'Western' values were a beguiling mirage. America and much of the West is experiencing its worst economic downturn in over seventy years. The political systems of many states seem incapable of coping with these developments. At the global level the institutions established by the Western powers seem equally ill-equipped to deal with contemporary challenges (Mittelman 2010). One of the more remarkable consequences of the global financial crisis in Europe has been the effective suspension of democratic processes and the appointment of unelected governments of technocrats in Italy and Greece. While this may prove a temporary aberration, the fact that it has happened at all is an indictment of the political class in both countries and their ability to deal with long-term problems of economic management 'in the national interest'. These very significant problems in the ostensibly 'victorious' social models of the West stand in marked contrast to the currently successful, but decidedly illiberal, ways of organizing politics and economics in many of the rising powers, as Nick Bisley (Chapter 2) pointed out.

While interesting in and of itself, such circumstances make developing accurate accounts of large-scale social processes particularly challenging. While not even technical 'scientific' knowledge is immune from the problem of politicization and intellectual contamination, things are even more contested and uncertain in the social sciences. Somewhat ironically, economics – the discipline that has most assiduously tried to reproduce the methodologies and credibility of the natural sciences – has arguably suffered most from a collapse in confidence about its ability to understand, much less address, contemporary economic problems (Colander 2011; Krugman 2009). Successive financial crises, and the economics profession's role in creating rather than ameliorating them, have caused significant damage to the 'dismal science's standing. While some may think that this is no bad thing, it adds to the crisis of legitimacy that pervades the international financial institutions which attempt to manage the global economy and maintain international security. Not only are there doubts about the ability of institutions such as the International Monetary Fund or the United Nations to actually solve problems, but their undemocratic nature raises questions about their mandates and authority to do so (Streeck 2011).

This is a distinctive feature of the modern world and arguably part of a more general loss of confidence in expertise, or the idea that specialists know best and can be relied upon to apply their knowledge to effectively resolve complex problems. It is now painfully apparent, as Timothy Sinclair (Chapter 6) pointed out, that there have been a number of major regulatory failures in the management of the international financial system in particular. In part this was generated by a naïve faith in 'the market' to bring about the best of all possible worlds as the inherent dynamism of the capitalist system is unleashed. Recent crises have provided a sobering reminder of a lesson we might have hoped was learned during the Great Depression: economic systems are the sum of complex social relations which need careful regulation if they are not to be captured by powerful vested interests (Baker 2010). Far from becoming redundant, the state, as Philip Cerny (Chapter 3) reminded us, remains a powerful, pivotally important force, even in an era characterized by ostensibly global forces.

## Contested global governance

It is important to stress how surprising and counter-intuitive all this is. Many argue that there is something essentially superior about the way economic and political activities have evolved in what have been described as the West's 'open access orders' (North *et al.* 2009). Not only is it unclear whether the populations of some Western countries have quite the same degree of confidence in the inclusive, merit-based, lawful, open and equal nature of their societies that inspire such optimism among many liberals, but there are now powerful and successful alternatives to the hitherto dominant Western model. These unreconstructed states with their patronage networks, close links between politics and economics, and neo-mercantilist economic strategies may yet prove to be archaic throwbacks that are incompatible with 'globalization'. Alternatively, they may come to redefine what we think globalization actually is. Greater economic integration may indeed be one of globalization's defining characteristics, but it is not clear that liberal democracy, free trade and a limited role for the state are necessarily part of the equation. Even in the West the clear separation between politics and economics has frequently been a pious aspiration rather than an empirical reality – as the powerful nexus between Washington and Wall Street reminds us (Hacker and Pierson 2010). In other parts of the world, it is not even necessary to maintain this fiction.

Again, China is the most consequential manifestation of this possibility. Not everyone is enamoured of China's authoritarian politics, or its style of state-led economic development, of course. But China's growing weight in the international system, the remarkable success of its own national development story, and the recurring problems associated with 'neoliberal' capitalism, mean that illiberal forms of economics and politics are no longer seen as serious outliers from the international norm, nor are they without their admirers and champions (Jacques 2009). One of the more interesting questions for students of international politics is whether, if China's rise continues, we will see a concomitant shift in the values and interests which the various institutions of international relations advance and protect. If the institutional setting of post-Second World War world politics privileged Western interests and Western values, then it would not be at all surprising that Western decline may open the door for a new set of ideational underpinnings of the global order. Equally, it may generate new ways of thinking about how international affairs operate.

It is no coincidence that some of the most influential theories about international relations have emerged from the United States. The US is not simply the most powerful country in the world, but for many observers – especially American ones – the US is what former Secretary of State Madeleine Albright famously described as an 'indispensable nation'. Many of the most influential schools of thought in international relations have explicitly or implicitly reflected the assumption that there was something essential, and possibly beneficial, about the historical role played by the US in underpinning the post-war international order (Ikenberry 2004). Our point here is not to make the sorts of boilerplate criticisms of US hegemony that have become staples of anti-Americanism. While there are valid criticisms to be made about the economic inequalities and self-serving concentrations of power that have continued to characterize the international system, the period of American hegemony has also been associated with the greatest economic transformation in the history of the planet. True, much of the transformation that has occurred in East Asia in particular has happened largely as a consequence of the efforts of the indigenous populations themselves, rather than the altruism or actions of the US or the agencies of international development. And yet one of the great ironies of history is that the US and some of the key institutions it was instrumental in creating, such as the World Trade Organization, have played a pivotal role in allowing, even encouraging 'communist China' to become the world's second largest economy (Hsueh 2011). As a consequence, one very important question about any future world order in which China and other rising powers play a larger part, is whether any international system they help determine will offer similar 'paths from the periphery' for other aspirant rising powers.

## The end of the old order?

Whatever one may think about the overall impact of 'American hegemony' it allowed, even encouraged, some states to develop economically. Indeed, it is important to remember that at the core of American grand strategy during the Cold

War was a desire to save capitalism from what had looked like a formidable 'socialist' alternative. Everyone – apart from North Korea, perhaps – seems to have come around to the idea that capitalism is a better path to economic development than central planning, or the type of central planning they went in for in the Soviet Union, at least. State-led capitalist economic development of the sort practised in East Asia, and now emulated elsewhere, is a very different matter, though (Bremmer 2010). Not only has it generally been highly successful, but it is winning new admirers in other parts of the world. The question is whether something like this developmental model might be universally adopted.

At the height of the Cold War, the stakes could hardly have been higher. In existentially fraught circumstances, the US was able and willing to provide systemic stability, to be a market of last resort, and provide a host of other staples of benign hegemony that are invoked by admirers of America's historical role (Kagan 1998). Equally importantly, the US was also willing to compel compliance with, and undermine opposition to, the liberal order that was institutionalized at Bretton Woods. The question now is what role these institutions will play in a new world order in which power is distributed among a larger group of states, in which there is greater uncertainty and contestation about the sorts of policies and values these institutions ought to promote, and where there is no existential threat uniting them.

A number of observers have begun to ask whether we are in the midst of a period of 'hegemonic transition', in which a declining US is replaced by a rapidly rising China (Beeson 2009; Chan 2008). For some, this process will inevitably lead to instability and even actual conflict as a fundamental, materially based transformation of the underlying structures of the international system brings about a new distribution of power (Mearsheimer 2001). While we do not accept the implicit determinism in these sorts of claims, the idea that the US is in a process of relative decline, and that this will have major consequences for the way the international system operates, seems increasingly uncontroversial to us. When seen in the long sweep of history, there is absolutely nothing unusual or surprising about changes in the relative standing of various empires, civilizations or – in our time – states. What is proving difficult for some observers to accept is that this could be happening to the US. What is less clear-cut are the implications of this relative decline for global order. Some argue that the liberal order that America established is institutionally robust, is able to be adjusted and would be very difficult and expensive to overturn (Ikenberry 2011). From this point of view American decline will not necessarily mean an end to the current international rules of the road. Yet others feel that the American-dominated order was made possible precisely because of the disproportionate cost borne by the US. Whether in underwriting the international monetary order after the Second World War or providing the military balance in East Asia, the US has supplied very considerable public goods over a long period of time. Its relative decline may well reduce its inclination or even its ability to provide these goods and as such the foundations of the current order may well crumble (Ferguson 2010).

Should we be concerned at this turn of events? As we have suggested, much depends on who 'we' are. Plainly there are advantages that accrue to the most powerful country on earth, not least of which is the ability to 'live beyond one's means' in a way no other country can (Cohen and DeLong 2010). In extremis, the US can simply print more dollars to pay its bills and shift the burden of adjustment onto the rest of the international system – a not unprecedented outcome in recent history (Beeson and Broome 2010; Reinhart and Rogoff 2009). Given the temptations that accrue to hegemons, one question we might want to ask is whether we actually want or even need a dominant power in the international system any more. After all, recent experience of hegemonic dominance has produced some very dubious outcomes, as the conflict in Iraq and the recent global financial crisis remind us. Indeed, the most recent economic crisis was made in America and largely confined (thus far, at least) to Europe and the US itself. Likewise, the successful strategic intervention in Libya was one in which the US took a back seat. The global order may well be changing in ways that make the kind of role played by great or hegemonic powers in the past redundant (Buzan 2011).

The evidence in support of claims about the 'needs' of the international system and the inevitability of hegemonic dominance is unpersuasive. These are large, complex arguments and we cannot do justice to them here, but by way of conclusion, let us offer some reasons for thinking that there is nothing inevitable about the way the international system is likely to develop, and suggest that there might be other ways of organizing and conceptualizing the international system.

## The future isn't what it used to be

First, we do not have many examples of hegemonic rule or illustrations of the way any transition to a new order or period of hegemonic rule might occur. The shift from British to American dominance was punctuated by the Great Depression and two world wars. More importantly, perhaps, American hegemony was shaped by the imperatives of the Cold War – a unique set of historical, ideological, social and above all, strategic circumstances that it is difficult to imagine being repeated in quite the same way. Whatever happens in the future, there is no reason to suppose it will replicate the experience of the 20th century or indeed of the century that preceded it. This has never happened before; why should it now?

Second, although the debate about the impact and extent of 'globalization' remains inconclusive, it is not unreasonable to claim that the world really has become a very different place from the one that existed in the first half of the 20th century when the preconditions for the last epochal shift in the international system and the ascendancy of the US were being established. The shift from British to American dominance occurred in a wildly different demographic, technological and normative context. Globalization sceptics are right to emphasize that previous societies in history have experienced very deep forms of economic interconnection, but that these remain radically different from the kind of linkages that exist in today's world.

We should certainly be careful not to expect that the very existence of economic interdependence will make war unthinkable in the way some have predicted from time to time. And yet it is difficult to believe that the 'benefits' of war or organized violence more generally are understood in quite the same way. If the political leaders who blundered into the First World War had had the remotest idea of the devastation and carnage they were about to unleash, it is difficult to imagine that they would have gone about it in quite the same way. Moreover, few states around the world subscribe to the kind of thinking about war as a source of national honour and pride that was commonplace in the 19th and early 20th centuries. Any remaining doubts about the destructive potential of war were reinforced by the Second World War and the advent of nuclear weapons. Warfare really is too dangerous to contemplate between the major powers and this is undoubtedly one of the contributing causes to the remarkable decline in the amount and role of organized violence in the modern world. Attitudes to the use of force by states have changed, as have many of those in the populations that constitute them (Pinker 2011).

The general point to make, then, is that the basic parameters within which international political life – and social life more generally – is conducted look rather different from the way they did when the era of American hegemony began. The necessity for cooperation between powers that are less asymmetrical, and in which the need for trans-border solutions to collective action problems grows by the day, is certainly a challenge, but perhaps an opportunity, too. Indeed, the passing of American dominance may not be the destabilizing catastrophe some fear. There have been historical examples where the major powers actually worked more or less 'in concert' to achieve collective outcomes – 19th-century Europe being the quintessential case in point. There is no reason to believe such a system could not be feasible again. It is also possible that the plethora of regional and issue-specific institutions that have become such a prominent feature of the contemporary international system may play an increasingly effective role in managing international affairs.

None of these remarks are meant to minimize the formidable problems that we collectively confront. The 'we' in this case is the human species. It now makes sense to describe the era we inhabit as the 'anthropocene', one characterized by the discernible impact our kind is having on the rest of the natural environment (Zalasiewicz *et al*. 2010). This is a new, unprecedented development with which many scholars of traditional international relations, not to mention policymakers, are finding it difficult to come to terms. As Edward Newman (Chapter 10) reminds us, definitions of security are not what they were. Yet this, too, may be cause for modest celebration; it may even be an indication of 'progress' in human affairs.

It is, of course, rather unfashionable to talk about progress, but here is a final paradox: while some contemplate the 'fifth extinction' and the collapse of human civilization, others point to remarkable, historically unprecedented indicators of human progress and development: millions have been lifted out of grinding poverty; literacy rates continue to rise; growing numbers of women have been emancipated; democracy continues to spread (albeit with local characteristics and the occasional reversal); life expectancy continues to increase; and violence and war continue to decline. These look to us like clear, measurable indicators of 'progress', even if they have often come at some cost to the natural environment. The challenge is to ensure that the indicators of progress continue to point in the right direction, and that they can be made to do so without irrevocably damaging the natural environment in the process. Understanding the nature of the issues is a good place to start.

# References

Abrahamian, E. (2003) 'The Media, Huntington, and September 11', *Third World Quarterly* 24 (3): 529–44.

Adamson, F.B. (2005) 'Globalisation, Transnational Political Mobilisation, and Networks of Violence', *Cambridge Review of International Affairs*, 18 (1): 31–49.

Adler, Emanuel (1997) 'Imagined (Security) Communities: Cognitive Regions in International Relations', *Millennium*, 26 (2): 249–77.

Agnew, J. (2005) *Hegemony: The New Shape of Global Power* (Philadelphia, PA: Temple University Press).

Ahlers, D. (2006) 'News Consumption and the New Electronic Media', *The International Journal of Press / Politics*, 11(1).

Akerlof, G.A. and R.J. Shiller (2009) *Animal Spirits: How Human Psychology Drives the Economy and Why it Matters for Global Capitalism* (Princeton, NJ: Princeton University Press).

Albert, M. (1993) *Capitalism vs. Capitalism* (New York: Four Walls Eight Windows).

Albrow, M. (1996) *The Global Age* (Cambridge: Polity).

Aleksashenko, S. (2012) 'Russia's Economic Agenda to 2020', *International Affairs*, 88 (1): 31–48.

Ali, T. (2002) *The Clash of Fundamentalisms: Crusades, Jihads and Modernity* (London: Verso).

Alison, M. (2004) 'Women as Agents of Political Violence: Gendering Security', *Security Dialogue*, 35:4.

Allan, S. (2006) *Online News: Journalism and the Internet* (Open University Press).

Altman, R.C. (2009) 'The Great Crash, 2008: A Geopolitical Setback for the West', *Foreign Affairs*, 88 (1): 2–14.

al-Zawahiri A. (2005) English translation of a letter from Ayman al-Zawahiri to Abu Musab al-Zarqawi, <http://www.weeklystandard.com/Content/Public/Articles/ 000/000/006.

Amnesty International (2012) 'No Arms for Atrocities or Abuses: Commit to an Effective Arms Trade Treaty', 23 January. Available online, http://www.amnesty.org/en/ campaigns/control-arms/reports/no-arms-for-atrocities.

Anderlini, J. and Zhang, L. (2011) 'Wen Sets Preconditions to help Europe', *Financial Times,* 14 September.

Anderson, B. (1991) *Imagined Communities* (London: Verso).

Anderson, B. (2004) *News Flash: Journalism, Infotainment, and the Bottom-line Business of Broadcast News* (San Francisco, CA: Jossey-Bass).

Anderson, D. (1998) 'David Mitrani (1888–1975): An Appreciation of his Life and Work', *Review of International Studies*, 24 (3): 577–92.

Anderson, K (2010) 'Predators Over Pakistan', The Weekly Standard, March 8. 15 ( 24).

Anderson, L. (2011) 'Demystifying the Arab Spring', *Foreign Affairs*, 90 (3): 2–7.

Annan, K. (1999) 'Annual Report of the Secretary-General to the United Nations General Assembly', 20 September, available at: http://www.un.org/News/Press/docs/1999/ 19990920.sgsm7136.html.

Annan, K (2001) 'Message Honouring Raphael Lemkin', UN Press Release SG/SM/7842, 13 June. Available online, http://www.un.org/News/Press/docs/2001/sgsm7842.doc. htm.

Archibugi, D. (2000) 'Cosmopolitan Democracy', *New Left Review*, 4: 137–50.

Archibugi, D. (2008). *The Global Commonwealth of Citizens: Toward Cosmopolitan Democracy* (Princeton, NJ: Princeton University Press).

Archibugi, D., Balduini, S. and Donati, M. (2000) 'The United Nations as an Agency of Global Democracy', in B. Holden (ed.) *Global Democracy* (London: Routledge).

Arend, A. and Beck, P. (1993)*International Law and the Use of Force: Beyond the UN Charter Paradigm* (London: Routledge).

Arends, B (2011) 'IMF Bombshell: Age of America Nears End', *MarketWatch.com* 15 April.

Armijo, L. (ed.) (2002) *Debating the Global Financial Architecture* (New York, NY: New York State University).

Armstrong, D., Lloyd, L. and Redmond, J. (2004) *International Organisation in World Politics* (Basingstoke: Palgrave Macmillan).

Armstrong, D. and Farrell, T. (2005) 'Introduction', in D. Armstrong, T. Farrell and B. Maiguashca (eds) *Force and Legitimacy in World Politics* (Cambridge: Cambridge University Press).

Armstrong, D., Farrell, T. and Lambert, H. (2007) *International Law and International Relations* (Cambridge: Cambridge University Press).

Armstrong, K. (2000) *The Battle for God* (New York, NY: Alfred A. Knopf).

Armstrong, S. (2000) 'Magazines, Cultural Policy and Globalization: The Forced Retreat of the States', *Canadian Public Policy,* 26(3) (September): 369–85.

Arrighi, G. (1994) *The Long Twentieth Century: Money, Power, and the Origins of Our Times* (London: Verso).

Arthur, M. (2008) *Dambusters: A Landmark Oral History* (London: Virgin Books).

Australian Government (2012) *Convergence Review*, Final Report. <http://www.dbcde. gov.au/__data/assets/pdf_file/0007/147733 Convergence_Review_ Final_Report.pdf>

Aylwin-Foster N. (2005) 'Changing the Army for Counterinsurgency Operations', *Military Review*, Nov/Dec.

Badie, B. and Birnbaum, P. (1983) *The Sociology of the State* (Chicago, IL: University of Chicago Press).

Baev, P. and Øverland, I., (2010) 'The South Stream versus Nabucco Pipeline Race: Geopolitical and Economic (Ir)rationales and Political Stakes in Mega-project', *International Affairs,* 86 (5): 1075–90.

Bahgat, G. (2011) *Energy Security: An Interdisciplinary Approach* (New York, NY: John Wiley).

Bainbridge, J. and Tynan, L. (2008) 'The New Media Environment', in J. Bainbridge, N. Goc and L. Tynan (eds), *Media and Journalism* (Oxford: Oxford University Press).

Baker, A. (2010) 'Restraining Regulatory Capture? Anglo-America, Crisis Politics and Trajectories of Change in Global Financial Governance', *International Affairs,* 86(3): 647–63.

Baker, B. and Scheye, E. (2007) 'Multi-layered Justice and Security Delivery in Post-conflict and Fragile States', *Conflict, Security and Development,* 7 (4).

Baker, D. (2009) *Plunder and Blunder: The Rise and Fall of the Bubble Economy.* (Sausalito, CA: PoliPoint Press).

Balachandra, P., Ravindranath, D. and Ravindranatha, N. (2010) 'Energy Efficiency in India: Assessing the Policy Regimes and their Impacts', *Energy Policy,* 38 : 6428–38.

Baldwin, R. (2006) Multilateralising Regionalism: Spaghetti Bowls as Building Blocs on the Path to Global Free Trade', *The World Economy*, 29 (11): 1451–518.

Baldwin, R., Evenett, S. and Low, P. (2007) 'Beyond Tariffs: Multilaterising Deeper RTA Commitments', *Multilateralizing Regionalism Conference*, Geneva, 10–12 September 2007, at www.wto.org/english/tratope/regione/consep07e/ Baldwin_evenett_low_e. pdf.

Balsdon, J. (1979) *Romans and Aliens* (Chapel Hill, NC: University of North Carolina Press).

Balzacq, T. (ed.) (2010) *Securitization Theory: How Security Problems Emerge and Dissolve* (London: Routledge).

Bank of England (2008) *Financial Stability Report*, April (London).

Barber, B. (2001) *Jihad vs. McWorld,* (New York, NY: Ballantine Books).

Barkawi, T. (2004) 'On the Pedagogy of "Small Wars"', *International Affairs,* 80 (1): 19–37.

Barker, E. (ed.) (1962) *Social Contract: Essays by Locke, Hume and Rousseau* (New York, NY: Oxford University Press).

Barma, N., Ratner, E. and Weber, S. (2007) 'A World without the West', *The National Interest,* Jul/Aug: 23–30.

Barnett, M. (2010) *The International Humanitarian Order* (London: Routledge).

Barry, E. and Kishkovsky, S. (2012) 'Russian Turnout Includes Thousands of Eager Election Observers', *New York Times,* 4 March, at http://www.nytimes.com/2012/03/05/world/europe/russian-vote-draws-thousands-of-election-observers.html?pagewanted= all.

Bass, G. (2008) *Freedom's Battle: Humanitarian Intervention in the Nineteenth Century* (London: Knopf).

Beckley, M. (2012) 'China's Century? Why America's Edge will Endure', *International Security* 36(3): 41–78.

Beeson, M. (2007) *Regionalism and Globalization in East Asia: Politics, Security, and Economic Development* (Basingstoke: Palgrave Macmillan).

Beeson, M. (2009) 'Hegemonic Transition in East Asia? The Dynamics of Chinese and American Power', *Review of International Studies,* 35(01): 95–112.

Beeson, M. (2012) 'Democracy, Development, and Authoritarianism', in M. Beeson. and R. Stubbs (eds), *The Routledge Handbook of Asian Regionalism* (London: Routledge): 236–47.

Beeson, M. and Bell, S. (2009) 'The G-20 and International Economic Governance: Hegemony, Collectivism, or Both?' *Global Governance,* 15 (1): 67–86.

Beeson, M. and Broome, A. (2010) 'Hegemonic instability and East Asia: Contradictions, crises and US power', *Globalizations,* 7(4): 479–95.

Beeson, M. and Higgott, R. (2005) 'Hegemony, institutionalism and US foreign policy: theory and practice in comparative historical perspective', *Third World Quarterly,* 26 (7): 1173–88.

Beeson, M. and Islam, I. (2005) 'Neo-liberalism and East Asia: Resisting the Washington Consensus', *Journal of Development Studies* 41 (2): 197–219.

Bell, C. (2007) *The End of the Vasco da Gama Era: The Next Landscape of World Politics,* Lowy Institute Paper No. 21 (Sydney: Lowy Institute for International Policy).

Bellamy, A.J. (2002) *Kosovo and International Society* (Basingstoke: Palgrave Macmillan).

Bellamy, A. (2004) 'Ethics and Intervention; The "Humanitarian Exception" and the Problem of Abuse in the Case of Iraq', *Journal of Peace Research,* 41/2: 131–47.

Bellamy, A. (2005) 'Is the War on Terror Just?', *International Relations,* 19 (3) : 275–96.

Bellamy, A. (2007) *Just Wars: From Cicero to Iraq* (Cambridge: Polity).

Bellamy, A. (2009a) 'Humanitarian Intervention' in M. Dunn Cavelty and V. Mauer (eds), *The Routledge Companion to Security Studies* (London: Routledge).

Bellamy, A. (2009b) 'Humanitarian Intervention', in A. Collins (ed.), *Security Studies* (Oxford: Oxford University Press).

Bellamy, A. (2009c) *Responsibility to Protect: The Global Effort to End Mass Atrocities* (Cambridge: Polity).

Bellamy, A. and M. McDonald (2002) '"The Utility of Human Security": Which Humans? What Security? A Reply to Thomas and Tow', *Security Dialogue*, 33(3).

Bellamy, A. and P.D. Williams (2009) *Understanding Peacekeeping*, 2nd edn (Cambridge; Polity).

Bellamy, A. and P.D. Williams (2011) 'The New Politics of Protection? Côte d'Ivoire, Libya and the Responsibility to Protect', International Affairs, *87: (4)*.

Bellin, E. (2000) 'Contingent Democrats: Industrialists, Labor, and Democratization in Late-developing Countries', *World Politics*, 52(2): 175–205.

Bello, W. (1998) 'East Asia: On the Eve of the Great Transformation?' *Review of International Political Economy,* 5 (3): 424–44.

Bendix, D. (2009) 'A Review of Gender in Security Sector Reform: Bringing Post-colonial and Gender Theory into the Debate', in M. Jacob, D. Bendix and R. Stanley (eds), *Engendering Security Sector Reform: A Workshop Report*, Berlin, 9–31.

Bendix, R. (1964) *Nation-Building and Citizenship* (Garden City, NY: Anchor Books).

Bergsten, C. (2005) 'Rescuing the Doha Round', *Foreign Affairs,* 84(7) (December).

Bergsten, C., Freeman, C., Lardy, N. and Mitchell, D. (2008) *China's Rise: Challenges and Opportunities* (Washington, DC: CSIS and IIE).

Berman, P. (2003) *Terror and Liberalism* (New York, NY: Norton).

Bernanke, B. (2000) *Essays on the Great Depression* (Princeton, NJ: Princeton University Press).

Bhagwati, J. (2004) *In Defence of Globalization* (Oxford: Oxford University Press).

Bhagwati, J. and Patrick, H. (1990) *Aggressive Unilateralism: America's 301 Trade Policy and the World Trading System* (Ann Arbor, MI: Michigan University Press).

Bhalla, S. (2010) 'Raising the Standard: The War on Global Poverty', in S. Anand, P. Segal and J. Stiglitz (eds) (2010) *Debates on the Measurement of Global Poverty* (Oxford: Oxford University Press), pp.115–42.

Bigo, D. (2005) 'From Foreigners to "Abnormal Aliens": How the Faces of the Enemy have Changed Following September the 11th', in E. Guild and J. van Selm (eds), *International Migration and Security: Opportunities and Challenges* (Abingdon: Routledge).

Bilmes, L. and Stiglitz, J. (2008) *The Three Trillion Dollar War: The True Cost of the Iraq Conflict* (New York, NY: Norton).

Binder, D. and Crossette, B. (1993) 'As Ethnic Wars Multiply, US Strives for a Policy', *New York Times,* 7 February, A1, A14.

Bisley, N. (2007) *Rethinking Globalization* (Basingstoke: Palgrave Macmillan).

Bisley, N. (2011), 'Biding and Hiding No Longer: A More Assertive China Rattles the Region', *Global Asia,* 6 (4).

Black J. (2001) *War in the New Century* (London: Continuum).

Black J. (2004) *War and the New Disorder in the 21st Century* (London: Continuum).

Black, J. (2005) 'War and International Relations: A Military-Historical Perspective on Force and Legitimacy', *Review of International Studies,* 31 (Supplement):127–42.

Blair, T. (1999) 'Doctrine of the International Community', speech to the Economic Club of Chicago, Hilton Hotel, Chicago, 22 April.

Blair, T. (2010) *A Journey* (London: Random House).

Blankley, T. (2005) *The West's Last Chance: Will We Win the Clash of Civilizations?* (Washington, DC: Regnery Publishing).

Blum, D. (2007) *National Identity and Globalization: Youth, State, and Society in Post-Soviet Eurasia* (Cambridge: Cambridge University Press).

Blumler, J. (2001) 'The Third Age of Political Communication', *Journal of Public Affairs*, 1 (3): 201–9.

Blumler, J. and Kavanagh, D. (1999) 'The Third Age of Political Communication: Influences and Features', *Political Communication*, 16 (3): 209–30.

Blyth, M. (2002) *Great Transformations: Economic Ideas and Institutional Change in the Twentieth Century* (Cambridge: Cambridge University Press).

Bobbitt, P. (2002) *The Shield of Achilles* (New York, NY: Random House).

Bolton, J. (2007) *Surrender is Not an Option: Defending America at the United Nations and Abroad* (New York, NY: Threshold Editions).

Bond, B. (1996) *The Pursuit of Victory: from Napoleon to Saddam Hussein* (Oxford: Oxford University Press).

Booth, D. (1985) 'Marxism and Development Sociology: Interpreting the Impasse', *World Development* 13(8): 761–87.

Booth, K. (1991) 'Security and Emancipation', *Review of International Studies*, 17(4).

Booth, K. (1997) 'Security and Self: Reflections of a Fallen Realist', in K. Krause and M. Williams (eds), *Critical Security Studies: Concepts and Cases* (London: UCL Press).

Booth, K. (ed.) (2004) *Critical Security Studies and World Politics* (Boulder, CO: Lynne Rienner.

Booth, K. (2005) 'Beyond Critical Security Studies', in K. Booth (ed.), *Critical Security Studies and World Politics* (Boulder, CO: Lynne Rienner).

Bornschier, V. and Chase-Dunn, C. (1985) *Transnational Corporations and Underdevelopment* (London: Greenwood Press).

Bourantonis, D. (2007) *The History and Politics of Security Council Reform* (London: Routledge).

Bowle, J. (1964) *Politics and Opinion in the 19th Century* (New York, NY: Oxford University Press).

Bowles, P. (1997) 'ASEAN, AFTA and the "New Regionalism"', *Pacific Affairs*, 70 (2): 219 34.

Bowring, B. (2008) *The Degradation of the International Legal Order?* (Oxford: Routledge Cavendish).

Boyarin, J. (1994) 'Introduction', in J. Boyarin (ed.), *Remapping Memory: The Politics of Time-Space* (Minneapolis, MN: University of Minnesota Press).

BP (2011) *BP Statistical Review*. Online, available at: http://www.bp.com/statisticalreview [Accessed 2 March 2012].

Bradsher, K. (2009) 'Manufacturing Slump Sends Fear across Asia', *International Herald Tribune,* 22 January.

Braithwaite, J. (2008) *Regulatory Capitalism: How it Works, Ideas for Making It Work Better* (Cheltenham: Edward Elgar).

Braithwaite, J. and Drahos, P. (2000) *Global Business Regulation* (Cambridge: Cambridge University Press).

Bralo, Z. and Morrison, J. (2005) 'Immigrants, Refugees and Racism: Europeans and their Denial' in E. Guild and J. van Selm (eds), *International Migration and Security: Opportunities and Challenges* (London: Routledge).

Branch, A. (2011) *Displacing Human Rights* (Oxford: Oxford University Press).

Bremmer, I. (2010) *The End of the Free Market: Who Wins the War Between States and Corporations?* (New York, NY: Penguin).

Bremmer, I. and Johnston, R. (2009) 'The Rise and Fall of Resource Nationalism', *Survival*, 51 (2) :149–58.

Brenner, N. (2004) *New State Spaces: Urban Governance and the Rescaling of Statehood* (Oxford: Oxford University Press).

Brenner, N., Jessop, B., Jones, M. and MacLeod, G. (eds) (2003) *State/Space: A Reader* *(*Oxford: Blackwell).

Breslin, S. (2009) 'Understanding China's Regional Rise: Interpretations, Identities and Implications', *International Affairs*, 85(4).

Breslin, S. (2011) 'East Asia and the Global/Transatlantic/Western Crisis', *Contemporary Politics,* 17(2): 109–17.

Breslin, S. and Croft, S. (eds) (2012) *Comparative Regional Security Governance* (London: Routledge).

Breslin, S., Higgott, R. and Rosamond, B. (2002) 'Regions in Comparative Perspective', in S. Breslin, C. Hughes, N. Phillips and B. Rosamond (eds) *New Regionalisms in the Global Political Economy: Theories and Cases* (London: Routledge): 1–19.

Bronson, R. (2006) *Thicker than Oil: America's Uneasy Partnership with Saudi Arabia* (Oxford and New York: Oxford University Press).

Brooks, S. and Wohlforth, W. (2002) 'American Primacy in Perspective', *Foreign Affairs,* 81(4): 20–35.

Brown, M. (ed.) (2003) *Grave New World: Security Challenges in the Twenty-First Century* (Washington, DC: Georgetown University Press).

Brownlie, I. (1974) 'Humanitarian Intervention', in J. N. Moore (ed.), *Law and Civil War in the Modern World* (Baltimore, MD: Johns Hopkins University Press), pp. 217–21.

Brundtland Commission (1987) *Our Common Future. The Report of the Brundtland Commission* (Oxford: Oxford University Press).

Bruner, R. and Carr, S. (2007) *The Panic of 1907: Lessons Learned from the Market's Perfect Storm* (New York, NY: Wiley).

Buchanan, A. and Keohane, R. (2004) 'The Preventive Use of Force: A Cosmopolitan Institutional Proposal', *Ethics and International Affairs*, 18(1):1–22.

Buchanan, A. and Keohane, R. (2006) 'The Legitimacy of Global Governance Institutions', *Ethics & International Affairs*, 20 (4): 405–38.

Bulkeley, H. and Newell, P. (2010) *Governing Climate Change* (London: Routledge).

Bull, B. (1999) '"New Regionalism" in Central America', *Third World Quarterly*, 20 (5): 957-70.

Bull, H. (2002) *The Anarchical Society* (Basingstoke: Palgrave Macmillan).

Bumiller, E. (2011) Panetta Says Defeat of Al Qaeda Is 'Within Reach' *New York Times*, 10 July, A11.

Burchell, G., Gordon, C. and Miller, P. (eds) (1991) *The Foucault Effect: Studies in Governmentality* (Chicago, IL: University of Chicago Press).

Burke J. (2011) *The 9/11 Wars* (London: Allen Lane).

Burton, M. and Higley, J. (1987) 'Elite Settlements', *American Sociological Review*, 52(3): 295–307.

Burton, M., Gunther, R. and Higley, J. (1991) 'Introduction: Elite Transformations and Democratic Regimes', in J. Higley and R. Gunther (eds), *Elites and Democratic Consolidation in Latin America and Southern Europe* (Cambridge: Cambridge University Press), pp. 1–37.

Butler, J. (1990) *Gender Trouble: Feminism and the Subversion of Identity* (London: Routledge).

Buzan, B. (1983) *People, States and Fear: The National Security Problem in International Relations* (Brighton: Wheatsheaf).

Buzan, B. (1991) *Peoples, States and Fear* (New York, NY: Columbia University Press).

Buzan, B (2004). 'A Reductionist, Idealistic Notion that Adds Little Analytical Value', *Security Dialogue*, 35(3): 369–70.

Buzan, B. (2008) *People, States and Fear* (New York, NY: Columbia University Press).

Buzan, B. (2011) 'A World Order without Superpowers: Decentred Globalism', *International Relations*, 25(1): 3–25.

Buzan, B. and Hansen, L. (2009) *The Evolution of International Security Studies* (Cambridge: Cambridge University Press).

Buzan, B., Waever, O. and Wilde, J. de (1998) *Security: A New Framework for Analysis* (Boulder, CO: Lynne Rienner).

Byers, M. (2005a) 'High Ground Lost', *Winnipeg Free Press*, 18 September, p. B3.

Byers, M. (2005b) 'Not Yet Havoc: Geopolitical Change and the International Rules on Military Force', in D. Armstrong, T. Farrell and B. Maiguashca (eds) *Force and Legitimacy in World Politics* (Cambridge: Cambridge University Press).

Byers, M. and Chesterman, S. (2003) 'Changing the Rules About Rules? Unilateral Humanitarian Intervention and the Future of International Law', in J. Holzgrefe and R. Keohane (eds), *Humanitarian Intervention: Ethical, Legal and Political Dilemmas* (Cambridge: Cambridge University Press).

C2ES (Center for Climate and Energy Solutions) (2012), http://www.c2es.org/states-regions/regional-climate-initiatives.

Calhoun, C. (2007) *Nations Matter* (New York, NY: Routledge).

Cameron, D. (1991) 'The 1992 Initiative: Causes and Consequences', in A. Sbragia (ed.) *Euro-Politics: Institutions and Policymaking in the New European Community* (Washington, DC: Brookings): 23–74.

Caney, S. (1997) 'Human Rights and the Rights of States: Terry Nardin on Non-Intervention', *International Political Science Review*, 18 (1).

Caplan, R. (2000) 'Humanitarian Intervention: Which Way Forward?', *Ethics and International Affairs*, 14: 23–38.

Caputi R. (2012) 'The Systematic Atrocity of Afghanistan's Occupation', *The Guardian*, 13 March.

Card, C. (1996) 'Rape as a Weapon of War', *Hypathia*, 11(4): 5–18.

Carment, D. (2003) 'Assessing State Failure: Implications for Theory and Policy', *Third World Quarterly*, 24(3): 407–27.

Carothers, T. (2002) 'The End of the Transition Paradigm', *Journal of Democracy*, 13 (1): 5–21.

Carothers, T. (2006) 'The End of the Transition Paradigm', *Journal of Democracy* 13(1): 5–21.

Carruthers, S. (2005) 'Media and Communications Technology', in B. White, R. Little and M. Smith (eds), *Issues in World Politics*, 3rd edn (Basingstoke: Palgrave Macmillan).

Carter, A. (1998) 'Should Women Be Soldiers or Pacifists', in L. Lorentzen and J. Turpin (eds), *The Women and War Reader* (New York, NY: New York University Press), 33–4.

Carter, N. (2007) *The Politics of the Environment: Ideas, Activism, Policy*, 2nd edn (Cambridge: Cambridge University Press).

Case, W. (2002) *Politics in Southeast Asia: Democracy or Less* (Richmond: Curzon).

Cassese, A. (2005) *International Law* (Oxford: Oxford University Press).

Castells, M. (2009) *Communication Power* (Oxford: Oxford University Press).

Castles, S. and Miller, M. (2009) *The Age of Migration: International Population Movements in the Modern World*, 4th edn (Basingstoke: Palgrave Macmillan).

Central Intelligence Agency (2012) *The World Factbook: Algeria* [Online] Available at: http://www.cia.gov/library/publications/the-world-factbook/geos/ag.html. [Accessed 27 February 2012].

Cerny, P. (1990) *The Changing Architecture of Politics: Structure, Agency and the Future of the State* (London: Sage).

Cerny, P. (1996) 'What Next for the State?' in E. Kofman and G. Youngs (eds), *Globalization: Theory and Practice* (London: Pinter), pp. 123–37.

Cerny, P. (2000a) 'Globalization and the Disarticulation of Political Power: Toward a New Middle Ages?', in H. Goverde, P. Cerny, M. Haugaard and H. Lentner (eds), *Power in Contemporary Politics: Theories, Practices, Globalizations* (London: Sage), pp. 170–86.

Cerny, P. (2000b) 'Restructuring the Political Arena: Globalization and the Paradoxes of the Competition State', in R. Germain (ed.), *Globalization and Its Critics: Perspectives from Political Economy* (Basingstoke: Palgrave Macmillan), pp. 117–38.

Cerny, P. (2003) 'Globalization and Other Stories: Paradigmatic Selection in International Politics', in A. Hülsemeyer (ed.) *Globalization in the 21st Century: Convergence or Divergence* (New York, NY: Palgrave Macmillan), pp. 51–66.

Cerny, P. (2006) 'Dilemmas of Operationalizing Hegemony', in M. Haugaard and H. Lentner (eds), H*egemony and Power: Consensus and Coercion in Contemporary Politics* (Lanham, MD: Lexington Books on behalf of the International Political Science Association, Research Committee No. 36 [Political Power]), pp. 67–87.

Cerny, P. (2009a) 'Some Pitfalls of Democratisation: Thoughts on the 2008 *Millennium* Conference', *Millennium: Journal of International Studies*, 37(3) (May): 763–86.

Cerny, P. (2009b) 'The Competition State Today: From Raison d'État to Raison du Monde', Policy *Studies*, 31.1 (2010): 5–21.

Cerny, P. (2010) *Rethinking World Politics: A Theory of Transnational Neopluralism* (New York and Oxford: Oxford University Press).

Cerny, P. (2011) '"Saving Capitalism from the Capitalists?" Financial Regulation after the Crash', *St Antony's International Review*, 7(1) (May): 11–29.

Cerny, P. (2012) 'The New Security Dilemma Revisited', paper presented at the annual convention of the International Studies Association, San Diego, CA. 1–4 April.

Chan, S. (2008) *China, the US, and the Power-Transition Theory* (London: Routledge).

Chandler, D. (2005), 'The Responsibility to Protect: Imposing the Liberal Peace', in A. Bellamy and P. Williams (eds), *Peace Operations and Global Order* (London: Routledge), pp. 59–82.

Chang, H.-J. (2002) *Kicking Away the Ladder: Development Strategy in Historical Perspective* (London: Anthem Books).

Chang, K. and Ling L. (2000) 'Globalization and its Intimate Other: Filipina Domestic Workers in Hong Kong', in M. Marchand and A. Sisson Runyan (eds), *Gender and Global Restructuring: Sightings, Sites and Resistances* (London and New York: Routledge).

Charlesworth, H. and Kennedy, D. (2009) 'Afterword', in A. Orford (ed.), *International Law and its Others* (Cambridge: Cambridge University Press).

Charrier, P (2001) 'ASEAN's Inheritance: the Regionalisation of Southeast Asia', *The Pacific Review*, 14 (3): 331–8.

Chen, L. and Narasimhan, V. (eds) (2003), *Global Health Challenges for Human Security* (Cambridge: Harvard University Press).

Chen, S. and Ravallion, M. (2010) 'China is Poorer than we Thought, but No Less Successful in the Fight Against Global Poverty', in S. Anand, P. Segal and J. Stiglitz (eds), *Debates on the Measurement of Global Poverty* (Oxford: Oxford University Press), pp.327–40.

Chesterman, S. (2003) 'Hard Cases Make Bad Law', in A. Lang (ed.), *Just Intervention* (Washington, DC: Georgetown University Press).

Chesterman, S. (2001) *Just War or Just Peace? Humanitarian Intervention and International Law* (Oxford: Oxford University Press).

Chesterman, S. and Byers, M. (2003) 'Has US Power Destroyed the UN?', *London Review of Books*, 21/9.

China, Government of (2005) 'Position Paper of the People's Republic of China on the United Nations Reforms', 8 June.

China UN Mission (2011) 'Explanation of Vote by Ambassador Li Baodong after Adoption of Security Council Resolution on Libya', Permanent Mission of the PRC to the UN, 17 March http://www.china-un.org/eng/gdxw/t807544.htm, downloaded 24 January 2012.

Chomsky, N. (2003) *Hegemony or Survival: America's Quest for Global Dominance*. (New York, NY: Metropolitan Books).

Chomsky, N. (2011) 'The Skeleton in the Closet', in P. Cunliffe (ed.) *Critical Perspectives on the Responsibility to Protect* (London: Routledge).

Christians, C., Glaser, T., McQuail, D., Nordenstreng, K. and White, R. (2009) Normative Theories of the Media: Journalism in Democratic Societies (Champaign, IL: University of Illinois Press).

Christoff, P. (2010) 'Cold Climate in Copenhagen: China and the United States at COP-15', *Environmental Politics*, 19(4): 637–56.

Chwieroth, J.M. (2007) 'Testing and Measuring the Role of Ideas: The Case of Neo-liberalism in the International Monetary Fund', *International Studies Quarterly,* 51 (1): 5–30.

CIA (2012) *World Factbook* Online edition, http://www.cia.gov/library/publications/the-world-factbook/.

Clapp, J. and Dauvergne, P. (2011) *Paths to a Green World: The Political Economy of the Global Environment*, 2nd edn (Cambridge, MA: MIT Press).

Clarke, R. (2004) *Against All Enemies* (New York, NY: Free Press).

Clarke, Y. (2008) 'Security Sector Reform in Africa: A Lost Opportunity to Deconstruct Militarised Masculinities?' *Feminist Africa*, Issue 10.

Clausewitz, C. von (1976) *On War,* translated by M. Howard and P. Paret (Princeton, NJ: Princeton University Press).

Clinton, H. (2011) Keynote Address at the National Democratic Institute's 2011 Democracy Awards Dinner, 7 November. <http://www.state.gov/secretary/rm/2011/11/176750.htm>

CNN Politics (2011) 'Support for Afghanistan War at all time low', 28 October, http://political ticker.blogs.cnn.com/2011/10/28/cnn-poll-support-for-afghanistan-war-at-all-time-low/

Cockett, R. (1994) *Thinking the Unthinkable: Think-Tanks and the Economic Counter-Revolution 1931-1983* (London: HarperCollins).

Cohen, J. (2006) 'Sovereign Equality vs. Imperial Right: The Battle Over the 'New World Order', *Constellations,* 13 (4): 485–505.

Cohen, S. and DeLong, J. (2010) *The End of Influence: What Happens When Other Countries Have the Money* (New York, NY: Basic Books).

Cohn, C. (1987) 'Sex and Death in the Rational World of Defense Intellectuals', *Signs*, 12 (4): 687–718.

Coker, C. (2001) *Humane Warfare* (London: Routledge).

Coker, C. (2002) *Waging War without Warriors: The Changing Culture of Military Conflict* (Boulder, CO: Lynne Rienner).

Colander, D. (2011) 'How Economists Got It Wrong: A Nuanced Account', *Critical Review: A Journal of Politics and Society,* 23(1): 1–27.

Colander, D., Goldberg, M., Haas, A., Juselius, K., Kirman, A., Lux, T. and Sloth, B. (2009) 'The Financial Crisis and the Systemic Failure of the Economics Profession', *Critical Review: A Journal of Politics and Society,* 21(2): 249–67.

Coleman, W. and Underhill, G. (eds) (1998) *Regionalism and Global Economic Integration: Europe, Asia, and the Americas* (London: Routledge).

Collier, P. (2008) *The Bottom Billion* (Oxford: Oxford University Press).

Collier, P., Elliott, V., Håvard, H., Hoeffler, A., Reynal-Querol, A. and Sambanis, N. (2003) *Breaking the Conflict Trap: Civil War and Development Policy* (Oxford: Oxford University Press for the World Bank).

Collins, A. (2009) *Contemporary Security Studies* (Oxford: Oxford University Press).

Commission of the European Communities (2008) 'Proposal for a Regulation of the European Parliament and of the Council on Credit Rating Agencies', 11 November, Brussels.

Commission on Human Security (2003) *Human Security Now – Report of the Commission on Human Security* (New York, NY: UN Publications).

Connor, W. (1993) *Ethnonationalism* (Princeton, NJ: Princeton University Press).

Congressional Research Service (2011) *The Cost of Iraq, Afghanistan, and Other Global Wars on Terror Operations Since 9/11*, CRS Report for Congress 7-5700 Washington, DC: Congressional Research Service, http://www.fas.org/sgp/crs/natsec/RL33110,pdf.

Conversi, D. (2004) 'Conceptualizing Nationalism: An Introduction to Walker Connor's Work', in D. Conversi (ed.) *Ethnonationalism in the Contemporary World: Walker Connor and the Study of Nationalism* (London: Routledge).

Cooper, A., Hughes, C. and De Lombaerde, P. (eds), (2008) *Regionalisation and Global Governance. The Taming of Globalisation?* (London: Routledge).

Cooper, G. (2008) *The Origin of Financial Crises: Central Banks, Credit Bubbles and the Efficient Market Fallacy* (Basingstoke: Harriman House).

Cooper, R. (2004) *The Breaking of Nations* (Atlantic Books: London).

Cooper, S., Hawkins, D., Jacoby, W. and Nielson, D. (2008) 'Yielding Sovereignty to International Institutions: Bringing System Structure Back In', *International Studies Review,* 10(3): 501–24.

Copenhagen Accord (2009) 'Draft Decision CP.15', Fifteenth Session, Copenhagen. [Online] Available at: http://unfccc.int/meetings/copenhagen_dec_2009/items/5262.php.

Cornish, P. (2009) 'The United States and Counterinsurgency: "Political First, Political Last, Political Always"', *International Affairs*, 85(1), January: 79.

Council of Europe (2011) *Convention on Preventing and Combating Violence against Women and Domestic Violence*, Istanbul, http://conventions.coe.int/Treaty/EN/Treaties/Html/210.htm.

Council of Europe (2012) *Lives Lost in the Mediterranean: Who is Responsible?* Report by the Committee on Migration, Refugees and Displaced Persons, 29 March. http://www.assembly.coe.int/CommitteeDocs/2012/20120329_mig_RPT.EN.pdf

Cox, M. (2001) 'Whatever Happened to American Decline? International Relations and the New United States Hegemony', *New Political Economy*, 6(3): 311–40.

Cox, R. (1981) 'Social Forces, States and World Orders: Beyond International Relations Theory', *Millennium*, 10(2): 126–55.

Cravey, A.J. (1998) *Women and Work in Mexico's Maquiladoras* (Lanham, MD: Rowman & Littlefield).

Crenshaw, M. (1981) 'The Causes of Terrorism', *Comparative Politics,* 13 (4): 379–99.

Cronin, A. (2002/03) 'Behind the Curve: Globalization and International Terrorism', *International Security,* 27 (3): 30–58.

Croome, J. (1995) *Reshaping the World Trading System: A History of the Uruguay Round* (Geneva: World Trade Organisation).

Cunningham, S. and Turner, G. (2002) *The Media and Communications in Australia* (Sydney: Allen & Unwin).

Curran, J. and Seaton, J. (2010) *Power without Responsibility: Press, Broadcasting and the Internet in Britain* (London: Routledge).

Dahl, R. (1971) *Polyarchy: Participation and Observation* (New Haven, CT: Yale University Press).

Dahl, R. (1999) 'Can International Organizations be Democratic?', in I. Shapiro and C. Hacker-Cordon (eds), *Democracy's Edges* (Cambridge: Cambridge University Press), pp. 19–36.

Dalby, S. (2009) *Security and Environmental Change* (Cambridge: Polity).

Dale, I. (ed.) (2010) *Guide to Political Blogging in the UK* (London: Total Politics).

Davidson, C. (2009) 'Abu Dhabi's New Economy: Oil, Investment and Domestic Development', *Middle East Policy* 16 (2) : 59–79.

Davison, J. (2011) *What Now For Al Qaeda? Questions Surround Future of Group Behind 9/11*, CBC News, 3 May. Available from http://www.cbc.ca/news/world/story/2011/05/03/f-al-qaeda-after-osama-bin-laden.html.

*Declassified Key Judgements of the National Intelligence Estimate: "Trends in Global Terrorism: Implications for the United States"* April 2006 [cited November 6 2007]. Available from http://www.dni.gov/press_releases/Declassified_NIE_Key_Judgments.pdf.

Deiter, H. and Higgott, R. (2003) 'Exploring Alternative Theories of Economic Regionalism: From Trade to Finance in Asian Co-operation', *Review of International Political Economy*, 10 (3) : 430–54.

De la O Martínez, María Eugenia (2006) 'Geografía Del Trabajo Femenino En Las Maquiladoras De México', *Revista Papeles De Población* , 49: 91–126. Available at http://redalyc.uaemex.mx/src/inicio/ArtPdfRed.jsp?iCve=11204904.

Deng, F. *et al.* (1996) *Sovereignty as Responsibility: Conflict Management in Africa* (Washington, DC: The Brookings Institution).

Deudney, D. (2006) 'Security', in A. Dobson and R. Eckersley (eds) *Political Theory and the Ecological Challenge* (Cambridge: Cambridge University Press), pp. 516–58.

Deutch, J. (2011) 'The Good News About Gas: The Natural Gas Revolution and Its Consequences', *Foreign Affairs*, 90 (1) : 82–93.

Di John, J. (2008) 'Conceptualising the Causes and Consequences of Failed States: A Critical Review of the Literature', *Development as State-Making*, no 25 (January), Crisis States Research Centre [Online] Available at: http://www.dfid.gov.uk/r4d/PDF/Outputs/CrisisStates/wp25.2.pdf.

Diamond, L., Linz, J. and Lipset, S. (eds) (1990) *Politics in Developing Countries: Comparing Experiences with Democracy*, 2nd edn (Boulder, CO: Lynne Rienner).

Diamond, L. (1999) *Developing Democracy: Toward Consolidation* (Baltimore, MD: Johns Hopkins University Press).

Diamond, L. (2008) *The Spirit of Democracy: The Struggle to Build Free Societies Throughout the World* (New York, NY: Times Books).

Dietrich Ortega, L. (2009) *Gendered Patterns of Mobilisation and Recruitment for Political Violence: Lessons Learned from Three Latin American Countries*. (Oxford: CRISE).

Dixon, M. (2007) *Textbook on International Law* (Oxford: Oxford University Press).

Dobbin, F., Simmons, B. and Garrett, G. (2007) 'The Global Diffusion of Public Policies: Social Construction, Coercion, Competition, or Learning?' *Annual Review of Sociology*, 3(3): 449–72.

Dodds, F. and Pippard, T. (2005) *Human and Environmental Security: An Agenda for Change* (London: Earthscan).

Donadio, R. (2011) 'Greece and Italy Ask Technocrats to Find Solution', *New York Times*, 11 November, p.A1F.

Doran, M. (2002) 'Somebody Else's Civil War', *Foreign Affairs,* 81 (1): 22–42.

Dover, B. (2008) *Rupert Murdoch's China Adventures: How the World's Most Powerful Media Mogul Lost a Fortune and Found a Wife* (North Clarendon: Tuttle Publishing).

Doyle, M. and Sambanis, N. (2000), 'International Peacebuilding: A Theoretical and Quantitative Analysis', *American Political Science Review*, 94(4): 779–801.

Drezner, D. (2001) 'Globalization and Policy Convergence', *International Studies Review,* 3 (1): 53–78.

Drezner, D. (2007) *All Politics is Global: Explaining International Regulatory Regimes* (Princeton, NJ: Princeton University Press).

Dupont, A. and Thirlwell, M. (2009) 'The New Era of Food Insecurity', in *Survival*, 51(3): 71–98.

Durch, W. (ed.) (2006) *Twenty-First-Century Peace Operations* (Washington, DC: US Institute of Peace).

*Economist, The* (2012), 'The Proust Index', 25 February.

Edgecliffe-Johnson, A. (2009) 'Wen and Putin Lecture Western Leaders', *Financial Times,* 29 January.

Edwards, M. (2004) *Civil Society* (Oxford: Polity Press).

Elliott, K. and Hufbauer, G. (2002) 'Ambivalent Multilateralism and the Emerging Backlash: The IMF and the WTO', in S. Patrick and F. Shephard (eds) *Multilateralism and US Foreign Policy: Ambivalent Engagement* (Boulder, CO: Lynne Rienner).

Elliott, L. and Breslin, S. (2011) (eds) *Comparative Environmental Regionalism* (London: Routledge).

Elshtain, J. (1987) *Women and War* (Chicago, IL: University of Chicago Press).

Elshtain, J. (2003) 'International Justice as Equal Regard and the Use of Force', *Ethics and International Affairs*, 17(2): 63–75.

Emmott, B. (2008) *Rivals: How the Power Struggle between China, India and Japan will Shape our Next Decade* (London: Allen Lane).

Energy Information Administration (EIA) (2011) 'Oil Crude and Petroleum Products Explained: Oil Imports and Exports.' [Online] Available at: http://www.eia.gov/energy-explained/index.cfm?page=oil_imports. [Accessed 25 February 2012.]

Enloe, C. (1983) *Does Khaki Become You? The Militarization of Women's Lives* (Boston, MA: South End Press).

Enloe, C. (1990) *Bananas, Beaches and Bases: Making Sense of Feminist International Politics* (Berkeley, CA: University of California Press).

Erlanger, S. and Castle, S. (2009) 'Growing Economic Crisis Threatens the Idea of One Europe', *New York Times,* 2 March.

Errington, W. and van Onselen, P. (2007) 'The Democratic State as a Marketing Tool: The Permanent Campaign in Australia', *Journal of Commonwealth & Comparative Politics*, 45 ( 1): 78– 94.

Esping-Anderson, G. (1990) *The Three Worlds of Welfare Capitalism* (Princeton, NJ: Princeton University Press).

Etzioni, A. (1992–3) 'The Evils of Self-determination', *Foreign Policy*, 89 (Summer): 21–35.

EU (2010) *Energy 2020 – A Strategy for Competitive, Sustainable and Security Energy* (Brussels: European Union).

European Commission, Directorate General Trade (2012) 'Russia' (2012) [Online] Available at: http://trade.ec.europa.eu/doclib/docs/2006/september/tradoc_113440.pdf. [Accessed 27 February 2012].

European Parliament (2009) Committee on Economic and Monetary Affairs, 'Draft Report on the Proposal for a Regulation of the European Parliament and of the Council on Credit Rating Agencies' Strasbourg, 13 January.

Evans, G. (2008) *The Responsibility to Protect: Ending Mass Atrocity Crimes Once and for All* (Washington, DC: The Brookings Institution).

Evans, M.G. (2005) *Policy Transfer in Global Perspective* (London: Ashgate).

Falk, R. (1982) *Approach to World Order Studies* (New Brunswick, NJ: Transaction Publishers).

Falk, R. (2003) 'Humanitarian Intervention: A Forum', *Nation*, 14 July.

Falk, R. (2004) 'Humanitarian Intervention After Kosovo', in A. Jokic (ed.), *Lessons of Kosovo* (Ontario: Broadview Press).

Falk, R. (2005) 'Legality and Legitimacy', in D. Armstrong, T. Farrell and B. Maiguashca (eds), *Force and Legitimacy in World Politics* (Cambridge: Cambridge University Press).

Fama, E.F. (1970) 'Efficient Capital Markets: A Review of Theory and Empirical Work', *Journal of Finance*, May.

Fawcett, L. and Hurrell, A. (eds) (1996) *Regionalism in World Politics: Regional Organization and International Order* (Oxford: Oxford University Press).

Fawn, R. (2009) 'Globalising the Regional, Regionalising the Global', Special Issue of *Review of International Studies*, 35(Special Issue).

Feinstein, L. (2007), 'Darfur and Beyond: What is Needed to Prevent Mass Atrocities', Council on Foreign Relations Special Report, Washington, DC.

Ferguson, N. (2004) *Colossus: The Rise and Fall of the American Empire* (London: Allen Lane).

Ferguson, N. (2005) 'Sinking Globalization', *Foreign Affairs*, 84(7) (December): 64–77.

Ferguson, N. (2009) Interview, *The New Statesman*, 2 July.

Ferguson, N. (2010) 'Complexity and Collapse', *Foreign Affairs*, 89(2): 18–32.

Ferguson, Y. and Mansbach, R. (2004) *Remapping Global Politics* (Cambridge: Cambridge University Press).

Fernández-Kelly, M.P. (1983) *For We Are Sold, I and my People: Women and Industry in Mexico's Frontier* (Albany, NY: State University of New York Press).

Fierke, K. (2007) *Critical Approaches to International Security* (Cambridge: Polity).

Fine, B. (2003) 'Neither the Washington nor the Post-Washington Consensus', in B. Fine, C. Lapavitas and J. Pincus (eds), *Development Policy in the Twenty-First Century: Beyond the Washington Consensus* (London: Routledge): 1–27.

Finnemore, M. (2003) *The Purpose of Intervention: Changing Beliefs About the Use of Force* (Ithaca, NY: Cornell University Press).

Fishman, B. (2008) 'Using the Mistakes of al Qaeda's Franchises to Undermine Its Strategies', *The Annals of the American Academy of Political and Social Science* 618 (1): 46–54.

Flew, T. (2008) *New Media: An Introduction*, 3rd edn (Oxford: Oxford University Press).

Fogarty, B. and Wolak, J. (2009) 'The Effects of Media Interpretation for Citizen Evaluations of Politicians' Messages', *American Politics Research*, 37 (1): 129–54.

*Foreign Policy* (2011) 'Failed States: The 2011 Index', *Foreign Policy*, 187 (July/August): 48–9.

Foresight (2011) *Migration and Global Environmental Change: Future Challenges and Opportunities*. Final Report (London: Government Office for Science).

Fortna, V. (2003) 'Inside and Out: Peacekeeping and the Duration of Peace after Civil and Interstate Wars', *International Studies Review*, 5(4): 97–114.

Fortna, V. (2004), 'Does Peacekeeping Keep Peace? International Intervention and the Duration of Peace After Civil War', *International Studies Quarterly*, 48(2): 269–92.

Fortna, V. (2008), *Does Peacekeeping Work? Shaping Belligerents' Choices after Civil War* (Princeton, NJ: Princeton University Press).

*Fortune Watch* (2008) 'New Vow to Fight Global Financial Crisis', 26 October.

Foucault, M. (1980) *Power/Knowledge* (New York, NY: Pantheon Books).

Foucault, M. (2007) *Security, Territory, Population: Lectures at the Collège de France, 1977–1978,* translated by Graham Burchell (London: Palgrave Macmillan; French edition 2004).

Foucault, M. (2008). *The Birth of Biopolitics: Lectures at the Collège de France, 1978–9,* translated by Graham Burchell (London: Palgrave Macmillan; French edition 2004).

Frank, A. (1969) *Capitalism and Underdevelopment in Latin America* (New York, NY: Monthly Review Press).

Frankel, J. (1997) *Regional Trading Blocs and the World Economic System* (Washington, DC: Institute for International Economics).

Freedom House (2009) Freedom in the World 2009: Global Data, at http://freedomhouse. org/uploads/fiw09/FIW09_Tables&GraphsFor Web.pdf.

Friedberg, A. L. (2011) *A Contest for Supremacy: China, American and the Struggle for Mastery in Asia* (New York, NY: W.W. Norton).

Friedman, M. and Schwartz A. (1963) *A Monetary History of the United States, 1857-1960* (Princeton, NJ: Princeton University Press).

Friedman, T.. (2000) *The Lexus and the Oliver Tree: Understanding Globalization*, rev. edn (New York, NY: Farrar, Straus & Giroux).

Fukuyama, F. (1989) 'The End of History?', *The National Interest* 16 (Summer): 3–18.

Fukuyama, F. (1992) *The End of History and the Last Man* (New York, NY: Free Press).

Fukuyama, F. (2004) *State-Building: Governance and World Order in the 21st Century* (Ithaca, NY: Cornell University Press).

Gagnon, A.-G., Lecours, A. and Nootens, G. (eds) (2011) *Contemporary Majority Nationalism* (Montreal: McGill-Queen's University Press).

Galbraith, J.K. (1993) *A Short History of Financial Euphoria* (Harmondsworth: Penguin).

Galbraith, J.K. (1997 [1955]) *The Great Crash 1929* (New York, NY: Mariner).

Gallagher, P. and Stoler, A. (2009) 'Critical Mass as an Alternative Framework for Multilateral Trade Negotiations', *Global Governance*, 15(3): 375–92.

Gallarotti, G. (2000) 'The Advent of the Prosperous Society: The Rise of the Guardian State and Structural Change in the World Economy', *Review of International Political Economy*, 7 (1) (January): 1–52.

Gallarotti, G. (2009) *The Power Curse: Influence and Illusion in World Politics* (Boulder, CO: Lynne Rienner).

Gallie, W.B. (1956) 'Essentially Contested Concepts', *Proceedings of the Aristotelian Society*, 56: 167–98.

Galtung, J. (1980) *The North/South Debate: Technology, Basic Human Needs and the New International Economic Order* (Piscataway, NJ: Transaction Publishers).

Gamble, A. (2009) *The Spectre at the Feast: Capitalist Crisis and the Politics of Recession* (Basingstoke: Palgrave Macmillan).

Gamble, A. and Payne, A. (eds) (1996) *Regionalism and World Order* (London: Macmillan).

Garden, M. (2010) 'Are Predictions of Newspapers' Impending Demise Exaggerated?', *Asia Pacific Media Educator*, 20.

Garnaut, R. (2008) *The Garnaut Climate Change Review* (Cambridge: Cambridge University Press).

Garvey, J. (2008) *The Ethics of Climate Change* (London: Continuum).

Gat, A. (2007) 'The Return of Authoritarian Great Powers', *Foreign Affairs,* 86 (4): 59–69.

Gawdat, B. (2008) 'Sovereign Wealth Funds: Dangers and Opportunities', *International Affairs,* 84(6): 1189–1204.

Geddes, B. (1999) 'What Do We Know About Democratization After Twenty Years?', *Annual Review of Political Science,* 2: 115–44.

Gellner, E. (1983) *Nations and Nationalism* (Ithaca, NY: Cornell University Press).

Gelpi, C., Feaver, P. and Reifler, J. (2005/06) 'Success Matters: Casualty Sensitivity and the War in Iraq', *International Security,* 30(3).

Germain, R. (2010) *Global Politics and Financial Governance* (Basingstoke: Palgrave Macmillan).

Gettleman, J. (2008) 'Somali Pirates Tell Their Side; They want only Money', *The New York Times,* 30 September.

Gibson, I. and Reardon, B. (2007) 'Human Security: Toward Gender Inclusion?' in G. Shani, M. Sato and M. Kamal Pasha (eds), *Protecting Human Security in a Post 9/11 World: Critical and Global Insights* (Basingstoke: Palgrave Macmillan).

Giddens, A. (2011) *The Politics of Climate Change,* 2nd edn (Cambridge: Polity Press).

Gilboa, E. (2005) 'The CNN Effect: The Search for a Communication Theory of International Relations', *Political Communication,* 22 (1): 27–44.

Giles, C. (2009) 'BIS Calls for Global Financial Reforms', *Financial Times,* 29 June.

Gill, S. (2003) *Power and Resistance in the New World Order* (Basingstoke: Palgrave Macmillan).

Giry, S. (2006) 'France and its Muslims', *Foreign Affairs,* 85(5) (September/October): 87–104.

Giustozzi, A. (2009) *Empires of Mud: Wars and Warlords in Afghanistan* (London: Hurst & Co.).

Givens, T., Freeman, G. and Leal, D. (eds) (2009) *Immigration Policy and Security: US, European, and Commonwealth Perspectives* (Abingdon: Routledge).

Glanville, L. (2011) 'Darfur and the Responsibilities of Sovereignty', *International Journal of Human Rights,* 15 (3): 462–80.

Glennon, M. (2008) 'Law, Legitimacy, and Military Intervention', in G. Andreani and P. Hassner (eds), *Justifying War: From Humanitarianism to Counterterrorism* (Basingstoke: Palgrave Macmillan).

Global Facilitation Network for Security Sector Reform (GFNSSR) (2007) *A Beginner's Guide to Security Sector Reform,* University of Birmingham. Available online: http://www.ssrnetwork.net/publications/ssr_beginn.php.

Goldman Sachs (2001) *Building Better Global Economic BRICs* (New York, NY: Goldman Sachs Global Economic Group).

Goldman Sachs (2007) *BRICs and Beyond* (New York, NY: Goldman Sachs Global Economic Group).

Goldstein, J. (2003) *War and Gender* (Cambridge: Cambridge University Press).

Goldstein, J. (2011) *Winning the War on War: The Decline of Armed Conflict Worldwide* (New York: Dutton).

Gordon, P. and Shapiro, J. (2004) *Allies at war: America, Europe, and the crisis over Iraq* (New York, NY: McGraw-Hill).

Gow, J. (2005) *Defending the West* (Cambridge: Polity).

Gowa, J. (1983) *Closing the Gold Window: Domestic Politics and the End of Bretton Woods* (Ithaca, NY: Cornell University Press).

Gray, C. (1999) 'Clausewitz rules, OK? The Future is the Past – with GPS', *Review of International Studies,* 25 (5): 161–82.

Gray, C. (2007) *War, Peace and International Relations: An introduction to Strategic History* (London: Routledge).

Grayson, K. (2008) 'The Biopolitics of Human Security', *Cambridge Review of International Affairs*, 21(3): 383–401.

Grieco, J. (1995) 'The Maastricht Treaty, Economic and Monetary Union and the Neo-Realist Research Programme', *Review of International Studies*, 21(1): 21–40.

Grieco, J. (1999) 'Realism and Regionalism: American Power and German and Japanese Institutional Strategies During and After the Cold War', in E. Kapstein and M. Mastanduno (eds) *Unipolar Politics: Realism and State Strategies After the Cold War* (New York, NY: Columbia University Press), pp. 107–31.

Gries, P. (2005) 'China Eyes the Hegemon', *Orbis: A Journal of World Affairs*, 49 (3): 401–12.

Grimes, S. (2002) 'San Diego-Tijuana: Microregionalism and Metropolitan Spillover', in S. Breslin and G. Hook (eds) *Microregionalism and World Order* (Basingstoke: Palgrave Macmillan), pp. 23–41.

Grimes, W.W. (2009) *Currency and Contest in East Asia: The Great Power Politics of Financial Regionalism* (Ithaca, NY: Cornell University Press).

Grugel, J. (2002) *Democratization: A Critical Introduction* (Basingstoke: Palgrave Macmillan).

Grugel, J. (2006) 'Regionalist Governance and Transnational Collective Action in Latin America', *Economy and Society*, 35(2): 209–31.

Guild, E. and van Selm, J. (eds) (2005) *International Migration and Security: Opportunities and Challenges* (London: Routledge).

Gunaratna, R. (2003) 'Sri Linka: Feeding the Tamil Tigers', in K. Ballentine and J. Sherman (eds), *The Political Economy of Armed Conflict – Beyond Greed and Grievance* (London: Lynne Rienner).

Gunther, R. (1992) 'Spain: The Very Model of the Modern Elite Settlement', in J. Higley and R. Gunther (eds), *Elites and Democratic Consolidation in Latin America and Southern Europe* (Cambridge: Cambridge University Press), pp. 38–80.

Gurr, T. (2000) 'Ethnic Warfare on the Wane', *Foreign Affairs*, 79(3) (May/June): 52–64.

Haas, E. (1958) *The Uniting of Europe* (Stanford, CA: Stanford University Press).

Haas, E. (1975) *The Obsolescence of Regional Integration Theory* (Berkeley, CA: Institute of International Studies Working Paper).

Haas, E. (1990) *When Knowledge is Power: Three Models of International Organizations* (Berkeley, CA: University of California).

Haas, H. de (2005) 'International Migration, Remittances and Development: Myths and Fact', *Global Migration Perspectives No. 30*, April (Geneva: Global Commission of International Migration).

Haas, H. de (2011) 'Mediterranean Migration Futures: Patterns, Drivers and Scenarios', *Global Environmental Change*, September. Available online at: http://www.bis.gov.uk/assets/foresight/docs/migration/drivers/11-1178-dr8b-mediterranean-migration-futures.pdf.

Haas, P. (1990) *Saving the Mediterranean* (New York: Columbia University Press).

Haass, R. (2008) 'The Age of Nonpolarity – What Will Follow US Dominance', *Foreign Affairs,* May/June.

Hacker, J. and Pierson, P. (2010) *Winner-Take-All Politics: How Washington Made the Rich Richer – and Turned Its back on the Middle Class* (New York, NY: Simon & Schuster).

Haggard, S. (2004) 'Institutions and Growth in East Asia', *Studies in Comparative International Development,* 38(4): 53–81.

Hall, P. (1989) *The Political Power of Economic Ideas: Keynesianism Across Nations* (Princeton, NJ: Princeton University Press).

Hall, P. and Soskice, D. (2001) 'An Introduction to the Varieties of Capitalism', in P. Hall and D. Soskice, *Varieties of Capitalism: The Institutional Foundations of Comparative Advantage* (Oxford: Oxford University Press), pp. 1–68.

Hall, R. (1999) *National Collective Identity: Social Constructs and International Systems* (New York, NY: Columbia University Press).

Hall, R. (2007) 'Explaining "Market Authority" and Liberal Stability: Toward a Sociological-Constructivist Synthesis', *Global Society,* 21 (3): 319–42.

Halliday, F. (2009) 'International Relations in a Post-Hegemonic Age', *International Affairs,* 85(1): 37–51.

Hammerstad, A. (2011) 'UNHCR and the Securitization of Forced Migration', in A.Betts and G. Loescher (eds), *Refugees in International Relations* (Oxford: Oxford University Press).

Hammerstad, A. (2012) 'Securitisation from Below: The Relationship between Immigration and Foreign Policy in South Africa's Approach to the Zimbabwe Crisis', *Conflict, Security and Development,* 12 (1).

Hammes, D. and Wills, D. (2005) 'Black Gold: The End of Bretton Woods and the Oil-Price Shocks of the 1970s', *The Independent Review,* IX(4) : 501–11.

Hans, A. and Suhrke, A. (1997) 'Responsibility Sharing', in J. Hathaway (ed.), *Reconceiving International Refugee Law* (The Hague: Kluwer Law International).

Hanson, V. (2002) 'Defending the West', *City Journal,* 25 February.

Hanson, V. (2003) *Mexifornia: A State of Becoming* (San Francisco, CA: Encounter Books).

Hardin, G. (1968) 'The Tragedy of the Commons', *Science,* 162: 1243–8.

Harmon, C. (2001) 'Five Strategies of Terrorism', *Small Wars & Insurgencies,* 12 (3): 39–66.

Harvey, D. (2003) *The New Imperialism* (Oxford: Oxford University Press).

Harvey, D. (2007) *A Brief History of Neoliberalism* (Oxford: Oxford University Press).

Hegel, G. (1969) 'Philosophy of Law', in W. Ebenstein (ed.), *Great Political Thinkers,* 4th edn (New York, NY: Holt, Rinehart & Winston).

Hehir, A. (2012) *The Responsibility to Protect* (Basingstoke: Palgrave Macmillan).

Hehir, A., Kuhrt, N. and Mumford A. (eds) (2011) *International Law, Security and Ethics: Policy Challenges in the Post-9/11 world* (London: Routledge).

Held, D. (1995) *Democracy and the Global Order: From the Modern State to Cosmopolitan Governance* (Cambridge: Polity Press).

Held, D. (1999) 'The Transformation of Political Community: Rethinking Democracy in the Context of Globalization', in I. Shapiro and C. Hacker-Cordon (eds), *Democracy's Edges* (Cambridge: Cambridge University Press), pp. 84–111.

Held, D. (2002) 'Law of States, Law of Peoples: Three Models of Sovereignty', *Legal Theory,* 8 (1): 1–44.

Held, D. (2005) *Democracy and the Global Order: From the Modern State to Cosmopolitan Democracy* (Cambridge: Polity).

Held, D. and Kaya, A. (eds) (2007) *Global Inequality* (Cambridge: Polity).

Held, D. and McGrew, A. (eds) (2007) *Globalization Theory* (Cambridge: Polity Press).

Held, D., McGrew, A., Goldblatt, D. and Perraton, J. (1999) *Global Transformations: Politics, Economics and Culture* (Stanford, CA: Stanford University

Helleiner, E. (1994) *States and the Reemergence of Global Finance,* (Ithaca, NY: Cornell University Press).

Helleiner, E., S. Pagliari and H. Zimmerman (eds) (2010) *Global Finance in Crisis* (London: Routledge).

Henkin, L. (1990) 'Compliance with International Law in an Inter-State System', *Académie de droit international, Recueil des cours 1989* (Dordrecht: Martinus Nijhoff).

Henry, L. (2007) 'The ASEAN Way and Community Integration: Two Different Models of Regionalism', *European Law Journal*, 13 (6): 857–79.

Herd, G. and Akerman, E. (2002) 'Russian Strategic Realignment and the Post-Post Cold War Era?', *Security Dialogue* , 33 (3): 357–72.

Herman, E. and Chomsky, N. (1988) *Manufacturing Consent: The Political* Economy of the Mass Media (New York, NY: Pantheon Books).

Herrmann, R., Tetlock, P. and Diascro, M. (2001) 'How Americans Think about Trade: Reconciling Conflicts among Money, Power, and Principles', *International Studies Quarterly,* 45 (2): 191–218.

Hershey, RD. (1989) 'Worrying Anew Over Oil Imports' [Online] *The New York Times.* [Accessed 26 April 2008].

Hettne, B., Sapir, A. and Sunkel O. (eds) (1999) *Globalism and the New Regionalism* (New York, NY: St. Martin's Press).

Heupel, M. (2008) 'Combining Hierarchical and Soft Modes of Governance: The UN Security Council's Approach to Terrorism and Weapons of Mass Destruction Proliferation After 9/11', *Cooperation and Conflict*, 43 (7):7–29.

Higgott, R. (2000) 'Contested Globalization: The Changing Context and Normative Challenges', *Review of International Studies,* 26: 131–53.

Higgott, R. (2005) 'Old and New Economic Multilateralism: the WTO, IMF and the G20', in J. English, R. Thakur and A. Fenton Cooper (eds) *A Leaders 20 Summit: Why, How, Who and When?* (Tokyo: United Nations University Press.)

Higgott, R. (2006) 'International Political Institutions', in R. Rhodes, S. Binder and B. Rockman (eds), *The Oxford Handbook of Political Institutions* (Oxford: Oxford University Press).

Hill, C. (1994) 'Europe's International Role', in S. Bulmer and A. Scott (eds), *Economic and Political Integration In Europe: Internal Dynamics and Global Context* (Oxford: Blackwell), pp. 103–26.

Hinsley, F. (1966) *Sovereignty* (London: Watts).

Hirst, M. (2011) *News 2.0: Can Journalism Survive the Internet?* (London: Allen & Unwin).

Hirst, P. and Thompson, G. (1999) *Globalization in Question*, 2nd edn (Oxford: Polity Press).

Hobsbawm, E. (1983) 'Introduction: Inventing traditions', in E. Hobsbawm and T. Ranger (eds), *The Invention of Tradition* (Cambridge: Cambridge University Press).

Hoekman, B. and Kostecki, M. (2001) *The Political Economy of the World Trading System* (Oxford: Oxford University Press).

Hoffman, B. (1998) *Inside Terrorism* (New York, NY: Columbia University Press).

Hoffman, B. (2002) 'Defining Terrorism', in R. Howard and R. Sawyer (eds), *Terrorism and Counter-terrorism: Understanding the New Security Environment* (New York, NY: McGraw-Hill).

Hollingsworth, J. and Boyer, R. (1997) 'Coordination of Economic Actors and Social Systems of Production', in J. Hollingsworth and R. Boyer, *Contemporary Capitalism: The Embeddedness of Institutions* (Cambridge: Cambridge University Press), pp.1–47.

Homer-Dixon, T. (1999) *The Environment, Scarcity and Violence* (Princeton, NJ: Princeton University Press).

Homer-Dixon, T. (2006) *The Upside of Down: Catastophe, Creativity and the Renewal of Civilization* (Washington, DC: Island Press).

Hooper, C. (2000) 'Masculinities in Transition: The Case of Globalization', in M. Marchand and A. Sisson Runyan (eds), *Gender and Global Restructuring: Sightings, Sites and Resistances* (London and New York: Routledge).

Horowitz, D. (2000) *Ethnic Groups in Conflict*, 2nd edn (Berkeley, CA: University of California Press).

Hosaka, T. (2010) 'China Surpasses Japan as World's No. 2 Economy', *Washington Post,* 16 August.

Hoyos, C. (2007) 'The new Seven Sisters: oil and gas giants dwarf Western rivals', *Financial Times* 27 March http://www.ft.com/intl/cms/s/2/471ae1b8-d001-11db-94cd-000b5df10621.html#axzz2Ec1T3hre

Hsueh, R. (2011) *China's Regulatory State: A New Strategy for Globalization,* (Ithaca, NY: Cornell University Press).

Hu, X. (2004) 'China to Quadruple GDP by 2020 to $4 trillion', *China Daily,* 26 April.

Huang, E., Davison, K., Shreve, S., Davis, T., Bettendorf, E. and Nair, A. (2006) 'Facing the Challenges of Convergence: Media Professionals' Concerns of Working Across Media Platforms', *Convergence*, 12 (1): 83–98.

Huang, Y. (2008) *Capitalism with Chinese Characteristics: Entrepreneurship and the State* (Cambridge: Cambridge University Press).

Hudson, L., Owens, C. and Flannes, M. (2011) 'Drone Warfare: Blowback From the New American Way of War', *Middle East Policy,* XVIII (3):122–32.

Hulme, M. (2009) *Why We Disagree about Climate Change* (Cambridge: Cambridge University Press).

Human Rights Watch (2012) 'Hidden Emergency: Migrant Deaths in the Mediterranean', *News Release*, 16 August. Accessed at: http://www.hrw.org/news/2012/08/16/hidden-emergency.

Huntington, S. (1984) 'Will More Countries Become Democratic?', *Political Science Quarterly,* 99(2): 193–218.

Huntington, S. (1991) *The Third Wave: Democratization in the Late Twentieth Century* (Norman, OK: University of Oklahoma Press).

Huntington, S. (1991–92) 'How Countries Democratize', Political Science Quarterly, 106(4) (Winter): 579–616.

Huntington, S. (1996) *The Clash of Civilizations and the Remaking of World Order* (New York, NY: Simon & Schuster).

Huntington, S. (2005) *Who Are We? The Challenges to America's National Identity* (New York, NY: Simon & Schuster).

Hurd, I. (1999) 'Legitimacy and Authority in International Politics', *International Organization,* 53 (2): 379–408.

Hurd, I. (2007) *After Anarchy* (Princeton NJ: Princeton University Press).

Hurrell, A. (1995) 'Explaining the Resurgence of Regionalism in World Politics', *Review of International Studies,* 21(4): 331–58.

Hurrell, A. (2005) 'Legitimacy and the Use of Force: Can the Circle be Squared?', in D. Armstrong, T. Farrell and B. Maiguashca (eds), *Force and Legitimacy in World Politics* (Cambridge: Cambridge University Press).

Hurrell, A. (2007) *On Global Order: Power, Values and the Constitution of International Society* (Oxford: Oxford University Press).

Hutchinson, J. and Smith, A. (eds) (1994) *Nationalism* (New York, NY: Oxford University Press).

Hutchinson, J. and Smith, A. (eds) (1996) *Ethnicity* (Oxford: Oxford University Press).

Huysmans, J. (2006) *The Politics of Insecurity: Fear Migration and Asylum in the EU* (Abingdon: Routledge).

Huysmans, J. and Buonfino, A. (2008) 'Politics of Exception and Unease: Immigration, Asylum and Terrorism in Parliamentary Debates in the UK', *Political Studies*, 56 (4), December: 766–88.

Ibrahim, M. (2005) 'The Securitization of Migration: A Racial Discourse', *International Migration* ,43 (5): 163–87.

Ignatieff, M. (1993) *Blood and Belonging Journeys into the New Nationalism* (New York, NY: Vintage).

Ignatieff, M. (1998) *The Warrior's Honor; Ethnic War and the Modern Conscience* (New York, NY: Vintage).

Ignatieff, M. (2001) *Virtual War: Kosovo and Beyond* (London: Picador).

IISS (2010) *The Military Balance 2010* (London: Routledge).

IISS (2012) *The Military Balance 2012* (London: Routledge for IISS).

Ikenberry, G. (2001) *After Victory: Institutions, Strategic restraint, and the Rebuilding of Order After Major Wars* (Princeton. NJ: Princeton University Press).

Ikenberry, G. (2004) 'Liberalism and Empire: Logics of Order in the American Unipolar Age', *Review of International Studies,* 30 (4): 609–30.

Ikenberry, G. (2011) *Liberal Leviathan: The Origins, Crisis, and Transformation of the American World Order* (Princeton: Princeton University Press).

Ikenberry, G. and Slaughter, A. (2006) 'Forging A World of Liberty under Law: US National Security in the 21st Century', *The Princeton Project Papers*, 27 September.

Ikenberry, G. and Wright, T. (2008) *Rising Powers and Global Institutions* (Washington, DC: The Century Foundation Press).

Independent Commission on Disarmament and Security Issues (1982) *Common Security: A Blueprint for Survival* (New York, NY: Simon and Schuster).

Independent International Commission on Kosovo (2000) *Kosovo Report* (Oxford: Oxford University Press).

Ingram, B. (2003) *The Wages of Spin* (London: John Murray).

Intergovernmental Panel on Climate Change (IPCC) (2007) *Climate Change 2007: The Physical Science Basis. Summary for Policymakers. Contribution of Working Group I to the Fourth Assessment Report of the IPCC* (Geneva: IPCC).

International Commission on Intervention and State Sovereignty (ICISS 2001) *The Responsibility to Protect* (Ottawa: IDRC).

International Energy Agency (IEA) (2008) *Russian Energy at a Glance 2007* (Paris: OECD/IEA, 2008): http://www.eia.doe.gov/emeu/cabs/Russia/images/Russian%20Energy%20at%20a%20Glance%202007.pdf [accessed 5 March 2009].

International Energy Agency (IEA) (2011a) *$CO_2$ Emissions from Fuel Combustion: Highlights*, (Paris: IEA). http://iea.org/co2highlights/co2highlights.pdf.

International Energy Agency (IEA) (2011b) *World Energy Outlook 2011,* Figure 2.7: Shares of energy sources in world primary energy demand in the New Policies Scenario. [Online] Available at: http://www.iea.org/weo/docs/weo2011/key_graphs.pdf. [Accessed 20 February 2012.]

International Energy Agency (IEA) (2012) *World Energy Outlook* (Paris: International Energy Agency).

International Monetary Fund (2010) *World Economic Outlook, 2010* (Washington, DC: IMF).

International Monetary Fund (2011) 'About the IMF > History > Societal change for Eastern Europe and Asian Upheaval (1990-2004)', *www.imf.org*, at http://www.imf.org/external/about/histcomm.htm. [Accessed March 2012.]

International Organisation for Migration (IOM) (2008) *World Migration 2008: Managing Labour Mobility in the Evolving Global Economy* (Geneva: IOM).

International Organisation for Migration (IOM) (2011) *World Migration 2011: Communicating Effectively about Migration* (Geneva: IOM).

Jackman, R. (1974) 'Political Democracy and Social Equality: A Comparative Analysis', *American Sociological Review,* 39 (1): 29–45.

Jackson, R. (1983) 'The Weight of Ideas in Decolonization: Normative Change in International Relations', in J. Goldstein and R. Keohane (eds), *Ideas and Foreign Policy: Beliefs, Institutions and Political Change* (Ithaca, NY: Cornell University Press), pp. 119–26.

Jackson, R. (2002) *The Global Covenant: Human Conduct in a World of States* (Oxford: Oxford University Press).

Jacobs, M. (2011) 'What Durban Revealed about Climate's Shifting Allegiances', *Inside Story,* 14 December, http://inside.org.au/what-durban-revealed/

Jacques, M. (2009) *When China Rules the World: The Rise of the Middle Kingdom and the End of the Western World* (London: Allen Lane).

James, A. (1986) *Sovereign Statehood: The Basis of International Society* (London: Allen & Unwin).

Jayasuriya, K. (ed.) (2004) *Governing the Asia Pacific: Beyond the New Regionalism* (Basingstoke: Palgrave Macmillan).

Jensen, R. (2004) 'Daggers, Rifles and Dynamite: Anarchist Terrorism in Nineteenth Century Europe', *Terrorism and Political Violence,* 16 (1): 116–53.

Jervis, R. (1999) 'Realism, Neoliberalism, and Cooperation: Understanding the Debate', *International Security,* 24(1): 42–63.

Johnson, C. (2002) *Blowback – The Costs and Consequences of American Empire* (London: Little, Brown).

Johnston, A. (2007) *Social States: China in International Institutions, 1980 – 2000* (Princeton, NJ: Princeton University Press).

Johnston, C. (2004) *The Sorrows of Empire: Militarism, Secrecy and the End of the Republic* (New York, NY: Holt).

Johnston, P. (2010) 'The security impact of oil nationalization: Alternate Futures Scenarios', *Journal of Strategic Security,* III (4) : 1–26.

Johnstone, S. and Mazo, J. (2011) 'Global Warming and the Arab Spring', *Survival,* 53(2): 11–17.

Jones, R.W (1999) Security, Strategy and Critical Theory (Boulder, CO: Lynne Rienner).

*Journal of Democracy* (2004) 'The Quality of Democracy', *Journal of Democracy,* 15(4): 20–125.

Kagan, R. (1998) 'The Benevolent Empire', *Foreign Policy,* 111: 24–35.

Kagan, R. (2003) *Paradise and Power America and Europe in the New World Order* (New York, NY: Knopf).

Kaldor, M. (2012) *New Wars Organized Violence in a Global Era,* 2nd edn (Cambridge: Polity).

Kaplan, R. (2012) *Monsoon: The Indian Ocean and the Future of American Power* (New York, NY: Random House).

Katz, R. (1998) *Japan: The System That Soured* (Armonk, NY: M.E. Sharpe).

Katzenstein, P. (2002) 'Regionalism in Asia', in S. Breslin, C. Hughes, N. Phillips and B. Rosamond (eds), *New Regionalisms in the Global Political Economy: Theories and Cases* (London: Routledge), pp.104–18.

Kaul, I., Grunberg, I. and Stern, M. (eds) (1999) *Global Public Goods: International Cooperation in the 21st Century* (New York: Oxford University Press).

Keane, J. (1991) *The Media and Democracy* (Polity Press).

Keane, J. (1998) *Democracy and Civil Society* (London: Verso).

Keane, J. (2003) *Global Civil Society?* (Cambridge: Cambridge University Press).

Keidel, A. (2007) 'The Limits of a Smaller, Poorer China', *Financial Times*, 13 November.

Kellner, D. (1992) The Persian Gulf TV War (Boulder, CO: Westview).

Kellner, D. (2004) '9/11, Spectacles of Terror, and Media Manipulation: A Critique of Jihadist and Bush Media Politics', *Critical Discourse Studies*, 1 (1): 41–64.

Kelsen, H. (1945) *General Theory of Law and State* (Cambridge, MA: Harvard University Press).

Kenen, P. (2001) *The International Financial Architecture: What's New? What's Missing?* (Washington, DC: Institute for International Economics).

Kennan, G. (1985) 'Morality and Foreign Policy', *Foreign Affairs*, 64(2): 205–18.

Kennedy, P. (1987) *The Rise and Fall of the Great Powers: Economic Change and Military Conflict from 1500 to 2000* (New York, NY: Random House).

Keohane, R. (1988) 'International Institutions: Two Approaches', *International Studies Quarterly*, 32 (4): 379–96.

Keohane, R. (1990) 'Multilateralism: An Agenda for Research', *International Journal*, XLV (4): 731–64.

Keohane, R. (2005) 'The Contingent Legitimacy of Multilateralism', Working Paper, No. 9, Warwick University: EU FP6 Network of Excellence on Global Governance, Regionalisation and Regulation: The Role of the EU.

Keohane, R. and Nye, J. (1977) *Power and Interdependence: World Politics in Transition* (Boston, MA: Little, Brown).

Keohane, R. and Nye, J. (1998) 'Power and Interdependence in the Information Age', *Foreign Affairs*, September/October, 77(5).

Keohane, R. and Victor, D. (2011) 'The Regime Complex for Climate Change', *Perspectives on Politics*, 9(01): 7–23.

Keohane, R., Macedo, S. and Moravcsik, A. (2009) 'Democracy-enhancing Multilateralism', *International Organization*, 63 (01): 1–31.

Kepel, G. (2003) 'The Origins and Development of the Jihadist Movement: From Anti-Communism to Terrorism', *Asian Affairs*, XXXIV (II): 91–108.

Kiely, R. (2007a) 'Poverty Reduction through Liberalization, or Intensified Uneven Development? Neo-liberalism and the Myth of Global Convergence', *Review of International Studies*, 33(4): 415–34.

Kiely, R. (2007b) *The New Political Economy of Development* (Basingstoke: Palgrave Macmillan).

Kilcullen, D. (2005) 'Countering Global Insurgency', *Journal of Strategic Studies*, 28 (4): 597–617.

Kilcullen, D. (2009), Testimony before the House Armed Services Committee Hearing on HR 1886, the Pakistan Enduring Assistance and Cooperation Enhancement (PEACE) Act 2009, April.

Kimmitt, R. (2008) 'Public Footprints in Private Markets: Sovereign Wealth Funds and the World Economy', *Foreign Affairs*, 87 (1): 119–30.

Kindleberger, C. (1973) *The World in Depression 1929–1939* (Berkeley, CA: University of California Press).

Kindleberger, C. and Aliber, R. (2011) *Manias, Panics and Crashes: A History of Financial Crises*, 6th edn (Basingstoke: Palgrave Macmillan).

King, G. and C. Murray (2001–2) 'Rethinking Human Security', *Political Science Quarterly*, 116(4): 585–610.

King, G. and Zheng, G. (2001) 'Improving Forecasts of State Failure', *World Politics*, 53(4) (July): 623–58.

Kirkpatrick, D. (2012) 'Keeper of Islamic Flame Rises as Egypt's New Decisive Voice', *New York Times*, 12 March, at http://www.nytimes.com/2012/03/12/world/middleeast/muslim-brotherhood-leader-rises-as-egypts-decisive-voice.html?pagewanted=all.

Klaebel, A. (2007) *Unity and Separation in World Politics: Remapping the Question of International Society* (Copenhagen: Department of Political Science, University of Copenhagen).

Kohli, A. (2001) 'Introduction', in Atul Kohli (ed.) The Success of India's Democracy (Cambridge: Cambridge University Press), pp. 1–20.

Kohli, A. (2004) *State-Directed Development: Political Power and Industrialization in the Global Periphery* (Cambridge: Cambridge University Press).

Kohn, H. (1955) *Nationalism: Its Meaning and History* (Princeton, NJ: Van Nostrand).

Kolko, G. (1988) *Confronting the Third World: United States Foreign Policy* (New York, NY: Pantheon Book).

Koppenfels, A.K. von (2001) 'The Role of Regional Consultative Processes in Managing International Migration' IOM Migration Research Series No. 3 (Geneva: IOM).

Koskenniemi, M. (2001) *The Gentle Civilizer of Nations* (Cambridge: Cambridge University Press).

Koskenniemi, M. (2006) 'What is International Law For?', in M. Evans (ed.) *International Law* (Oxford: Oxford University Press).

Kozul Wright, R. and Rayment, P. (2004) 'Globalization Reloaded: an UNCTAD Perspective', UNCTAD Discussion Papers no.167, pp.1–50.

Krain, M. (2005) 'International Intervention and the Severity of Genocides and Politicides', *International Studies Quarterly*, 49(2): 363–87.

Krasner, S. (1999) *Sovereignty: Organized Hypocrisy* (Princeton, NJ: Princeton University Press).

Krause, K. (2004) 'Is Human Security "More than Just a Good Idea?"', in M. Brzoska and P. J. Croll (eds), *Promoting Security: But How and For Whom? Contributions to BICC's Ten-year Anniversary Conference* BICC Brief 30.

Krause, K. and Williams, M. (1996) 'Broadening the Agenda of Security Studies: Politics and Methods', *Mershon International Studies Review*, 40(2): 229–54.

Krause, K. and Williams, M. (1997) *Critical Security Studies: Concepts and Cases* (Minneapolis, MN: University of Minnesota Press).

Kreiger, D. (2006) 'The War in Iraq as Illegal and Illegitimate', in R. Thakur and W. Sidhu (eds), *The Iraq Crisis and World Order: Structural, Institutional and Normative Challenges* (New York, NY: United Nations University Press).

Kruathammer, C. (2009) 'Decline Is a Choice: The New Liberalism and the End of American Ascendancy', *Weekly Standard,* 15(5).

Krugman, P. (2008) *The Return of Depression Economics and the Crisis of 2008,* 2nd edn (Harmondsworth: Penguin).

Krugman, P. (2009) 'How did Economists get it so Wrong?', *New York Times,* 2 September.

Kubicek, P. (2009) 'The Commonwealth of Independent States: An Example of Failed Regionalism?', *Review of International Studies*, 35, Special Issue: 237–56.

Kühnhardt, L. (ed.) (2008) *Crises in European Integration: Challenges and Responses, 1945–2005* (New York, NY: Berghahn).

Kunz, R. and Valasek, K. (2012) 'Learning from Others' Mistakes: Towards Participatory, Gender-sensitive SSR', in Schnabel, A. and Farr, V. (eds), *Back to the Roots: Security Sector Reform and Development* (Zürich and Berlin: LIT), pp. 115–43.

Kyaw, Y. (2009) 'Setting the Rules for Survival: Why the Burmese Military Regime Survives in an Age of Democratization', *Pacific Review* 22 (3), pp. 271–91.

Lacy, M. (2005) *Security and Climate Change* (London: Routledge).

Lampton, D.M. (2008) *The Three Faces of Chinese Power: Might, Money, and Minds* (Berkeley, CA: University of California Press).

Larosière, J. (2009) *The High-Level Group on Financial Supervision in the EU*, chaired by Jacques de Larosière (Brussels, 25 February 2009), http://ec.europa.eu/internal_market/finances/docs/de_larosiere_report_en.pdf.

Lasswell, H. (1935) *Politics: Who Gets What, When, How* (Chicago, IL: Chicago University Press).

Latham, R. (1997) *The Liberal Moment: Modernity, Security, and the Making of Postwar International Order* (New York, NY: Columbia University Press).

Layne, C. (2012) 'This Time it's Real: The End of Unipolarity and the Pax Americana', *International Studies Quarterly*, 56(1): 203–13.

Leen, M. (2004)*The European Union, HIV/AIDS and Human Security* (Dublin: Dochas).

Leiken, R. (2005) 'Europe's Angry Muslims', *Foreign Affairs*, 84(4) (July/August): 120–35.

Leonard, M. (2005) *Why Europe Will Run the 21st Century* (London: 4th Estate).

Levitsky, S. and Way, L. (2010) *Competitive Authoritarianism: Hybrid Regimes After the Cold War* (Cambridge University Press).

Lijphart, A. (1969) 'Consociational Democracy', World Politics, 21(2) : 207–25.

Lincoln, E. (2001) *Arthritic Japan: The Slow Pace of Economic Reform in Japan*, (Washington, DC: Brookings Institute Press).

Lindberg, S. (2009) *Democratization by Election: A New Mode of Transition* (Baltimore, MD: Johns Hopkins University Press).

Lindberg, T. (2005) 'Protect the People', *Washington Post*, 27 September.

Linz, J. (1990) 'The Perils of Presidentialism', *Journal of Democracy*, 1(1): 51–69.

Lipset, S. (1959) 'Some Social Requisites of Democracy: Economic Development and Political Legitimacy', *American Political Science Review*, 53: 69–105.

Lisowski, M. (2002) 'Playing the Two-Level Game: US President Bush's Decision to Repudiate the Kyoto Protocol', *Environmental Politics*, 11(4): 101–19.

Little, R. (2007) *The Balance of Power in International Relations: Metaphors, Myths and Models* (Cambridge: Cambridge University Press).

Loescher, G. (1993) *Beyond Charity: International Cooperation and the Global Refugee Crises* (Oxford: Oxford University Press).

Loescher, G., Betts, A. and Milner, J. (2008) *The United Nations High Commissioner for Refugees: The Policy and Practice of Refugee Protection in the 21st Century* (London: Routledge).

Lowenheim, O. and Steele, B. (2010) 'Institutions of Violence, Great Power Authority, and the War on Terror', *International Political Science Review*, 31 (1): 23–39.

Luck, E. (2006), *UN Security Council: Practice and Promise* (London: Routledge).

Luckham, R. (2009) 'Introduction: Transforming Security and Development in an Unequal World', *IDS Bulletin*, 40 (2).

Luedtke, A. (2009) 'Fortifying Fortress Europe? The Effect of September 11 on EU Immigration Policy', in T. Givens *et al.* (eds), *Immigration Policy and Security: US, European and Commonwealth Perspectives* (Abingdon: Routledge).

Luft, G. and Korin, A. (eds) (2009) *Energy Security Challenges for the 21st Century: A Reference Handbook* (Santa Barbara, CA: Praeger Security International/ABC Clio).

Lynch, T. and Singh, R. (2008) *After Bush: The Case for Continuity in American Foreign Policy* (Cambridge: Cambridge University Press).

MacFarlane, S. and Khong, Y. (2006) *Human Security and the UN: A Critical History* (Bloomington, IN: Indiana University Press).

MacFarquhar, N. (2012) 'Elections in Iran Favor Ayatollah's Allies, Dealing Blow to President an His Office', *New York Times*, 4 March, at http://www.nytimes.com/2012/03/05/world/middleeast/iran-elections-deal-blow-to-ahmadinejad-and-the-presidency.html?pagewanted=all.

Mack, A. (2004) 'A Signifier of Shared Values', *Security Dialogue*, 35 (3) (2004): 366–7.

Mack, A. (2007) *Global Political Violence: Explaining the Post Cold War Decline*, (New York, NY: International Peace Academy, Coping with Crisis Working Paper).

MacKenzie, M. (2009) 'Empowerment Boom or Bust? Assessing Women's Post-Conflict Empowerment Initiatives', *Cambridge Review of International Affairs*, 22 (2): 199–215.

Maddison, A. (2001) *The World Economy: A Millennial Perspective* (Paris: Development Centre of the OECD).

Mahbubani, K. (2008) *The New Asian Hemisphere: The Irresistible Shift of Global Power to the East* (New York, NY: Public Affairs).

Mahbubani, Kishore (2011) 'Asia has had Enough of Excusing the West', *Financial Times*, 25 January. Available at http://www.ft.com/cms/s/0/44616bb0-28c0-11e0-aa18-00144feab49a.html#ixzz1Cc6DR3o4. [Accessed 26 January 2011.]

Maizels, A., Palaskas, T. and Crowe, T. (1998) 'The Prebisch Singer Hypothesis Revisited', in D. Sapford and J. Chen (eds), *Development Economics and Policy* (London: Palgrave Macmillan), pp. 45–70.

Malanczuk, P. (2006) *Akehurst's Modern Introduction to International Law* (London: Routledge).

Mandel, R. (2001) 'The Privatization of Security', *Armed Forces & Society*, 28 (1): 129–51.

Mankiw, N. and Swagel, P. (2005) 'Antidumping: The Third Rail of Trade Policy', *Foreign Affairs*, 84(4) (July/August): 107–19.

Mann, M. (1993) *The Sources of Social Power: The Rise of Classes and Nation-States, 1760-1914*, Vol. II (Cambridge, Cambridge University Press).

Mansfield, E. and Milner, H. (eds) (1997) *The Political Economy of Regionalism* (New York, NY: Columbia University Press).

Mansfield, E. and Milner, H. (1999) 'The New Wave of Regionalism', *International Organization*, 53 (3): 589–627.

Marchand, M. (1996) 'Reconceptualising "Gender and Development" in an Era of Globalization', *Millennium: Journal of International Studies*, 25 (3), 577–603.

Marchand, M. and Sisson Runyan, A. (eds) (2000) *Gender and Global Restructuring: Sightings, Sites and Resistances* (London: Routledge).

Marchand, M.H. and Sisson Runyan, A. (eds) (2011) 'Introduction: Feminist Sightings of Global Restructuring: Old and New conceptualizations', in M. Marchand and A. Sisson Runyan (eds), *Gender and Global Restructuring: Sightings, Sites and Resistances*, 2nd edn (London and New York: Routledge).

Margolis, M. and Moreno-Riano, G. (2009) *The Prospect of Internet Democracy*, (London: Ashgate).

Martin, L. (2006) 'International Economic Institutions', in R. Rhodes, S. Binder and B. Rockman (eds), *The Oxford Handbook of Political Institutions* (Oxford: Oxford University Press), pp. 613–34.

Marx, K. (1913) *The Eighteenth Brumaire of Louis Bonaparte* (Chicago, IL: Charles Kerr).

Mason, D.S. (2008) *The End of the American Century* (Lanham, MD: Rowman & Littlefield).

Mattli, W. (1999) *The Logic of Regional Integration: Europe and Beyond* (Cambridge: Cambridge University Press).

Max, A. (2008) *Dambusters: A Landmark Oral History* (London: Virgin Books).

Mayall, J. (1990) *Nationalism and International* (Cambridge: Cambridge University Press).

McCarthy R. and Beaumont, P. (2004) 'Civilian Cost of Battle for Falluja Emerges', *The Observer,* Sunday 14 November.

McInnes C. (2002) *Spectator Sport: The West and Contemporary Conflict* (Boulder, CO: Lynne Rienner).

McLuhan, M. (1964) *Understanding Media: The Extensions of Man* (New York: McGraw Hill).

McQuail, D. (2000) 'Some Reflections on the Western Bias of Media Theory', *Asian Journal of Communication,* 10 (2): 1–13.

McSweeney, B. (1999) *Security, Identity, and Interests: A Sociology of International Relations* (Cambridge: Cambridge University Press).

Mearsheimer, J. (2001) *The Tragedy of Great Power Politics* (New York, NY: W.W. Norton).

Mearsheimer, J. (2006) 'China's Unpeaceful Rise', *Current History* (April): 160–2.

Mendelsohn, B. (2009) *Combating Jihadism: American Hegemony and Interstate Cooperation in the War on Terrorism* (Chicago, IL: University of Chicago Press).

Mera, L. (2005) 'Explaining Mercosur's Survival: Strategic Sources of Argentine–Brazilian Convergence', *Journal of Latin American Studies*, 37(1): 109–40.

Meyer, J., Boli, J., Thomas, G. and Ramirez, F. (1997) 'World Society and the Nnation-state', *American Journal of Sociology,* 103 (1): 144–81.

Migdal, J. (1988) *Strong States and Weak States: State-Society Relations and State Capabilities in the Third World* (Princeton, NJ: Princeton University Press).

Mignolo, W. (2005) *The Idea of Latin America* (Oxford: Blackwell).

Migration Watch (2007a) Submission to the House of Lords Select Committee on Economic Affairs on 'The Economic Impact of Immigration' (London: Migration Watch UK, Economic Briefing Paper 1.18): www.migrationwatchuk.com/Briefingpapers/economic/1_18_submission_to_the_hol.asp.

Migration Watch (2007b) Migration Benefit 'Equal to a Mars Bar a Month'. Press Release (London: Migration Watch UK, 3 January 2007): www.migrationwatchuk.com/press releases/pressreleases.asp?dt=01-January-2007.

Milanovic, B. (2007) 'Globalization and Inequality', in D. Held and A. Kaya (eds), *Global Inequality* (Cambridge: Polity), pp.11–32.

Milanovic, M. (2006) 'State Responsibility for Genocide', *The European Journal of International Law*, 17(3): 553–604.

Minsky, H. (2008) *John Maynard Keynes* (New York, NY: McGraw-Hill).

Mitchell, C. (2010) *The Political Economy of Sustainable Energy: Energy Climate and the Environment* (Basingstoke: Palgrave Macmillan).

Mitrany, D. (1943) *A Working Peace System* (London: Royal Institute for International Affairs).

Mittelman, J. (2010) *Hyperconflict: Globalization and Insecurity* (Stanford, CA: Stanford University Press).

Modood, T. (1997) 'Introduction: The Politics of Multiculturalism in the New Europe', in T. Modood and P. Werbner (eds), *The Politics of Multiculturalism in the New Europe: Racism, Identity and Community* (London: Zed Books).

Moore, B. (1966) *Social Origins of Dictatorship and Democracy: Lord and Peasant in the Making of the Modern World* (Boston, MA: Beacon Press).

Moore, T. (2008) 'Racing to Integrate, or Cooperating to Compete? Liberal and Realist Interpretations of China's New Multilateralism', in Guoguang Wu and H. Lansdowne (eds), *China Turns to Multilateralism: Foreign Policy and Regional Security* (London and New York: Routledge), pp. 35–50.

Moravcsik, A. (1993) 'Preferences and Power in the European Community: A Liberal Intergovernmentalist Approach', *Journal of Common Market Studies*, 31(4): 473–524.

Morely, D. and K. Robins (1995) *Spaces of Identity: Global Media, Electronic Landscapes and Cultural Boundaries* (London: Routledge).

Morris, I. (2010) *Why the West Rules – For Now: The Patterns of History, and What They Reveal About the Future* (New York, NY: Farrar, Straus & Giroux).

Moser, C. and Clark, F. (eds) (2001) *Victims, Perpetrators or Actors? Gender, Armed Conflict and Political Violence* (London and New York: Zed Books).

Mostov, J. (2008) *Soft Borders: Rethinking Sovereignty and Democracy* (Basingstoke: Palgrave Macmillan).

Mourtada, R. and Salem, F. (2011) 'Arab Social Media Report: Civil Movements: The Impact of Facebook and Twitter, Vol. 1 (2)' <http://www.dsg.ae/en/WhoWeAre/WhoDescription.aspx?ProfileID=202>.

Mousseau, M. (2002/3) 'Market Civilization and its Clash with Terror', *International Security,* 27 (3): 5–29.

Mousseau, M. (2009) 'The Social Market Roots of Democratic Peace', *International Security* 33(4): 52–86.

Movius, L. (2010) 'Cultural Globalisation and Challenges to Traditional Communication Theories', Journal of Media and Communication, 2(1): 6–18.

Moyo, D. (2009) *Dead Aid: Why Aid Is Not Working and How There Is a Better Way for Africa* (New York, NY: Farrar, Straus & Giroux).

MPI (Migration Policy Institute) (2007) 'Foreign-Born Population and Foreign Born as Percentage of the Total US Population, 1850 to 2007', MPI Data Hub: Migration Facts, Stats and Maps. www.migrationinformation.org/datahub/charts/final.fb.shtml (accessed 22 April 2009).

Mueller J. (1995) *Quiet Cataclysm Reflections on the Recent Transformation of World Politics* (London: HarperCollins).

Muhlmann, G. (2010) *Journalism for Democracy* (Cambridge: Polity Press).

Müller-Kraenner, S. (2008) *Energy Security* (London: Earthscan).

Munkler H. (2005) *The New Wars* (Cambridge: Polity).

Murdoch, R. (2005) 'Speech by Rupert Murdoch to the American Society of Newspaper Editors', 13 April. <http://www.newscorp.com/news/news_247.html>

Muttitt, G. (2011) *Fuel on the Fire: Oil and Politics in Occupied Iraq* (London: Bodley Head).

Myers, N. (2002) 'Environmental Refugees: A Growing Phenomenon of the 21st century', *Philosophical Transactions of the Royal Society B*, 357(1420): 609–613.

Myers, N. and Kent J. (1995) *Environmental Exodus: An Emergent Crisis in the Global Arena* (Washington, DC: The Climate Institute).

Naim, M. (2009) 'Minilateralism: The Magic Number to Get Real International Action', *Foreign Policy*, 173, July/August, available online at: http://www.foreignpolicy.com/articles/2009/06/18/minilateralism

Najam, A. (2003) *Environment, Development and Human Security: Perspectives from South Asia* (Lanham, MD: University Press of America).

Naraghi-Anderlini, Sanam (2008) 'Gender Perspectives and Women as Stakeholders: Broadening Local Ownership of SSR', *Local Ownership and Security Sector Reform,* 2008: 105–26.

Nardin, T. (2003) 'The Moral Basis of Humanitarian Intervention', in A. Lang (ed.), *Just Intervention* (Washington, DC: Georgetown University Press).

Narliker, A. (2005) *The World Trade Organisation: A Very Short Introduction* (Oxford: Oxford University Press).

National Intelligence Council (NIC) (2008) *Global Trends 2025: A Transformed World* (Washington, DC: National Intelligence Council).

National Intelligence Estimate (2006) *Declassified Key Judgements of the National Intelligence Estimate: 'Trends in Global Terrorism: Implications for the United States'* April 2006 *[cited November 6 2007]*. Available from http://www.dni.gov/press_releases/Declassified_NIE_Key_Judgments.pdf.

Naughton, B. (2007) *The Chinese Economy: Transitions and Growth* (Cambridge, MA: MIT Press).

Nederveen, P. (2009) *Globalization and Culture: Global Mélange* (Lanham, MD: Rowan & Littlefield).

Nelson, D. (2009) 'Sacrifice your Luxuries, India tells the West' *The Age*, 7 August.

*New York Times* (2011) '9/11 The Reckoning', 8 September.

Newman, E. (2001) 'Human Security and Constructivism', *International Studies Perspectives*, 2 (3): 239–51.

Newman, E. (2010) 'Critical Human Security Studies', *Review of International Studies*, 36 (1): 77–94.

Newmeyer, J. (2009) 'Chinese Energy Security and the Chinese Regime', in D. Moran and J. Russell(eds), *Energy Security and Global Politics: The Militarization of Resource Management* (New York, NY: Routledge Global Security Studies).

Nichols, T. (2005) 'Anarchy and Order in the New Age of Prevention', *World Policy Journal,* 22 (3):1–23.

Nie, N. and Hillygus, D. (2002) 'The Impact of Internet Use on Sociability: Time-Diary Findings', *IT & Society,* 1 (1): 1–20.

Nordbeck, R. (2011) 'Pan-European Environmental Cooperation: Achievements and Limitations of the "Environment for Europe" Process', in L. Elliott and S. Breslin (eds), *Comparative Environmental Regionalism* (London: Routledge), pp. 37–55.

North, D., Wallis, J. and Weingast, B. (2009) 'Violence and the Rise of Open-Access Orders', *Journal of Democracy,* 20(1): 55–68.

Nye, D. (1999) *Consuming Power: A Social History of American Energies* (Boston, MA: MIT Press).

Nye, J. (2004) *Soft Power: The Means to Success in World Politics* (New York, NY: Public Affairs).

Oakeshott, M. (1976) 'On Misunderstanding Human Conduct: A Reply to My Critics', *Political Theory*, 4 (2) (August): 353–67.

Obama, B. (2009) 'From Peril to Progress', White House address, 26 January, at http://www.whitehouse.gov/blog_post/Fromperiltoprogress/.

Oberthür, S. and Roche Kelly, C. (2008) 'European Union Leadership in International Climate Policy: Achievements and Challenges', *The International Spectator*, 43(3): 35–50.

O'Brien, R., Goetz, A.M., Scholte, J.A. and Williams, M. (2000) *Contesting Global Governance: Multilateral Economic Institutions and Global Social Movement,* (Cambridge: Cambridge University Press).

O'Brien, R. and Willams, M. (2010) *Global Political Economy*, 3rd edn (Basingstoke: Palgrave Macmillan).

O'Donnell, G. and Schmitter, P. (1986) *Transitions from Authoritarian Rule: Tentative Conclusions about Uncertain Democracies* (Baltimore, MD: Johns Hopkins University Press).

O'Donnell, G. (1999) *Counterpoints: Selected Essays on Authoritarianism and Democracy* (Notre Dame: University of Notre Dame Press).

OECD/DAC (2007) *Handbook on Security System Reform* (Paris: OECD).

O'Hanlon, M. (2010) 'The US Mission in Afghanistan Beyond 2011', *Foreign Affairs*, September/October.

Ohmae, K. (1990) *The Borderless World: Power and Strategy in the Interlinked Economy* (New York, NY: Harper Business).

Ohmae, K. (1995) *The End of the Nation-State: the Rise of Regional Economies* (New York, NY: Simon & Schuster).

Olcott, M.B. (2005) 'The Great Powers in Central Asia', *Current History,* 104 (684): 331–5.

O'Neill, J. (2011) *The Growth Map: Economic Opportunity in the BRICs and Beyond* (New York, NY: Portfolio).

ONS (Office for National Statistics) (2005) *Focus on People and Migration 2005* (London: ONS).

ONS (Office for National Statistics) (2009) *Populations Trends*, no. 135 (London: ONS, Spring 2009).

ONS (Office for National Statistics) (2011) 'Migration Statistics Quarterly Report November 2011', Statistical Bulletin (London: ONS, 24 November).

Onuf, N. (2003) 'Normative Frameworks for Humanitarian Intervention', in A. Lang (ed.), *Just Intervention* (Washington, DC: Georgetown University Press).

Orford, A. (2009) 'A Jurisprudence of the Limit', in A. Orford (ed.), *International Law and its Others* (Cambridge: Cambridge University Press).

Ornstein, N. and Mann, T. (eds) (2000) *The Permanent Campaign and Its Future* (Washington, DC: AEI Press).

Osborne, D. and Gaebler, T. (1992) *Reinventing Government: How the Entrepreneurial Spirit is Transforming the Public Sector, from Schoolhouse to Statehouse, City Hall to the Pentagon* (Reading, MA: Addison-Wesley).

Osiander, A. (2001) 'Sovereignty, International Relations, and the Westphalian Myth', *International Organization*, 55(2) (Spring): 251–87.

Ostrom, V., Tiebout, C. and Warren, R. (1961) 'The Organization of Government in Metropolitan Areas: A Theoretical Inquiry', *American Political Science Review*, 55 (3) (September): 831–42.

O'Sullivan, J. (2011) 'A Game of Catch Up: Special Report on the World Economy', *The Economist*, 15 September.

Ougaard, M. and Higgott, R. (2002) (eds) *Towards a Global Polity?* (London: Routledge).

Owen, T. (2004) 'Human Security – Conflict, Critique and Consensus: Colloquium Remarks and a Proposal for a Threshold-Based Definition', *Security Dialogue,* 35(3): 373–87.

Panagiriya, A. (1999) 'The Regionalism Debate: An Overview', *The World Economy*, 22 (4): 477–511.

Panagariya, A. (2005) 'Liberalizing Agriculture', *Foreign Affairs,* 84(7) (December). [Online] Available at: http://www.foreignaffairs.org/20051201faessay84706/arvind-panagariya/liberalizing-agriculture.html.

Panagariya, A. (2008) *India: The Emerging Giant* (Oxford: Oxford University Press).

Panitch, L. and Gindin, S. (2004) 'Finance and American Empire', in L. Panitch and C. Leys (eds), *The Socialist Register: The Empire Reloaded* (London: Merlin Press), pp. 46–80.

Pape, R. (2009) 'Empire Falls', *The National Interest,* Jan/Feb: 21–34.

Parashar, S. (2009) 'Feminist International Relations and Women Militants: Case Studies from Sri Lanka and Kashmir', *Cambridge Review of International Affairs*, 22 (2): 235–56.

Parekh, B. (1997) 'Rethinking Humanitarian Intervention', *International Political Science Review*, 18 (1).

Parpart, J. and Zalewski, M. (eds) (2008) *Rethinking the Man Question* (London: Zed Books).

Partnoy, F. (2006) 'How and Why Credit Rating Agencies Are Not Like Other Gatekeepers', in Y. Fuchita and R. Litan (eds), *Financial Gatekeepers: Can They Protect Investors?* (Washington, DC: Brookings).

Pascual, C. and Elkind, J. (2009) *Energy Security: Economics, Politics, Strategies, and Implications* (Washington, DC: Brookings).

Paterson, C. and Sreberny, A. (eds) (2005) International News in the 21st Century (Bloomington, IN: Indiana University Press).

Patterson, M. (1996) *Global Warming and Global Politics* (London: Routledge).

Patterson, M. (2009) 'Post-Hegemonic Climate Politics', *British Journal of Politics and International Relations*, 11(1): 140–58.

Peet, R. (2003) *Unholy Trinity: The IMF, World Bank and WTO* (London: Zed Books).

Perovic, J. and Orttung, R. (2009) 'Russia's Role for Global Energy Security', in A. Wenger, R. Orttung and J. Perovic(eds)., *Energy and the Transformation of International Relations* (Oxford: Oxford University Press).

Peterson, V. (1997) 'Whose Crisis? Early and Post-modern Masculinism', in S. Gill. and J. Mittelman. (eds), *Innovation and Transformation in International Studies* (Cambridge: Cambridge University Press), pp. 185–201.

Peterson, V. (2003) *A Critical Rewriting of Global Political Economy: Integrating Reproductive, Productive and Virtual Economies* (London: Routledge).

Peterson, V. and Sisson Runyan, A. (2010) *Global Gender Issues in the New Millennium*, 3rd edn (Boulder, CO: Westview Press).

Pew Global Attitudes Project (2005) 'Islamic Extremism: Common Concern for Muslim and Western Publics' (14 July) [Online] Available at: http://pewglobal.org/2005/07/14/islamic-extremism-common-concern-for-muslim-and-western-publics/.

Pew Global Attitudes Project (2006) 'Muslims in Europe: Economic Worries Top Concerns About Religious and Cultural Identity' (6 June ) [Online] Available at: http://pewglobal.org/2006/07/06/muslims-in-europe-economic-worries-top-concerns-about-religious-and-cultural-identity/.

Pfau, M., Haigh, M., Logsdon, L., Perrine, C., Baldwin, J., Breitenfeldt, R. and Cesar, J. (2005) 'Embedded Reporting During the Invasion and Occupation of Iraq: How the Embedding of Journalists Affects Television News Reports', *Journal of Broadcasting & Electronic Media*, 49(4): 468–487.

Phillips, A. (2009) 'How Al Qaeda Lost Iraq', *Australian Journal of International Affairs*, 63 (1): 64–84.

Phillips, A. (2010) 'The Protestant Ethic and the Spirit of Jihadism-Transnational Religious Insurgencies and the Transformation of International Orders', *Review of International Studies*, 36 (02): 257–80.

Phillips, A. (2012) 'Horsemen of the Apocalypse? Jihadist Strategy and Nuclear Instability in South Asia', *International Politics*, forthcoming.

Phillips, M. (2006) *Londonistan* (New York, NY: Encounter Books).

Pierson, P. (2000) 'Increasing Returns, Path Dependence, and the Study of Politics', *American Political Science Review* 94 (2): 251–67.

Pijl, K. van der (1998) *Transnational Classes and International Relations* (London: Routledge).

Pinker, S. (2011) *The Better Angels of Our Nature: The Decline of Violence in History and Its Causes* (London and New York: Allen Lane/Penguin).

Plender, J. (2008) 'The Return of the State: How Government Is Back at the Heart of Economic Life', *Financial Times,* 22 August.

Podhoretz, N. (2007) *World War IV: The Long Struggle against Islamofascism,* 1st edn (New York, NY: Doubleday).

Pogge, T. (2002) *World Poverty and Human Rights: Cosmopolitan responsibilities and Reforms* (Malden, MA: Blackwell).

Polanyi, K. (1957 [1944]) *The Great Transformation: The Political and Economic Origins of Our Time* (Boston, MA: Beacon).

Polidano, C. (2000) 'Measuring Public Sector Capacity', *World Development* ,28 (5): 805–22.

Pollard, N., Latorre, M. and Sriskandarajah, D. (2008) *Floodgates or Turnstiles: Post-EU Enlagement Migration Flows to (and from) the UK* (London: IPPR).

Popham, P. (2012) 'Keep Up the Pressure on Myanmar's Generals', *New York Times*, 5 March, at http://www.nytimes.com/2012/03/06/opinion/keep-up-the-pressure-on-myanmars-generals.html.

Power, S. (2002) 'Raising the Cost of Genocide', *Dissent*, 49(2): 69–77.

Prebisch, R. (1959) 'Commercial Policy in the Underdeveloped Countries', *American Economic Review,* 44: 251–73.

Przeworski, A., Alvarez, M., Cheibub, J.-A. and Limongi, F. (1996) 'What Makes Democracies Endure?', *Journal of Democracy* 7(1) : 39–55.

Putnam, R. (1988) 'Diplomacy and Domestic Policy: The Logic of Two-Level Games', *International Organization*, 42(3) (Summer): 427–60.

Rabushka, A. and Shepsle, K. (1972) *Politics in Plural Societies* (Stanford, CA: Stanford University Press).

Radio Free Europe Radio Liberty (2012) 'Drones – Who Makes Them and Who Has Them?', 21 March.

Ramo, J. (2004) *The Beijing Consensus* (London: The Foreign Policy Centre).

Ramsey, P. (2002) *The Just War: Force and Political Responsibility* (Lanham, MD: Rowman & Littlefield).

Randall, S. (2005) *US Foreign Oil Policy since World War I – For Profits and Security,* 2nd edn (McGill-Queen's University Press).

Rapoport, D.C. (2001) 'The Fourth Wave: September 11 in the History of Terrorism', *Current History,* 100 (650): 419–24.

Read, R. (2004) 'The Implications of Globalization and Regionalism for the Economic Growth of Small Island States', *World Development,* 32(2): 365–478.

Record, J. (2004) *Dark victory: America's Second War against Iraq* (Annapolis, MD: Naval Institute Press).

Reddy, S. and Pogge, T. (2002) 'How Not to Count the Poor', www.socialanalysis.org.

Reddy, S. and Pogge, T. (2003) 'Unknown: The Extent, Distribution and Trend of Global Income Poverty', http://www.columbia.edu/~sr793/povpop.pdf.

Reid, T. (2005) *United States of Europe: The Superpower No-One Talks About* (Harmondsworth: Penguin).

Reilly, B. (2001) Democracy in Divided Societies: Electoral Engineering for Conflict Management (Cambridge: Cambridge University Press).

Reinert, E. (2007) *How Rich Countries Got Rich...and Why Poor Countries Stay Poor,* (New York, NY: Carroll & Graf).

Reinhart, C. and Rogoff, K. (2009) *This Time Is Different: Eight Centuries of Financial Folly* (Princeton, NJ: Princeton University Press).

Renan, E. (1994) 'Qu'est-ce qu'une nation?', in J. Hutchinson and A. Smith (eds), *Nationalism* (New York, NY: Oxford University Press).

RESDAL (2010) *Women in the Armed and Police Forces: Resolution 1325 and Peace Operations in Latin America (*Buenos Aires: Red de Seguridad y Defensa de América Latina).

Rethel, L. and Sinclair, T. (2012) *The Problem with Banks* (London: Zed Books).

Reus-Smit, C. (2005) 'Liberal Hierarchy and the Licence to Use Force', *Review of International Studies*, 31 Supplement, pp. 71–92.

Reuters (2011) 'China Planning Emissions Trading in 6 Regions', 11 April, http://www.reuters.com/article/2011/04/11/us-china-carbon-trading-idUSTRE73 A1UY20110411.

Ricks, T. (2009) *The Gamble: General Petraeus and the American Military Adventure in Iraq* (New York, NY: Penguin).

Riley, A. (2012) 'There is life for the Southern Corridor after Nabucco', *European Energy Review* March, http://www.europeanenergyreview.eu.site.pagina.php?id=3580.

Roberts, A. (1993) 'Humanitarian War: Military Intervention and Human Rights', *International Affairs*, 69 (3).

Roberts, A. (1998) 'More Refugees, Less Asylum: A Regime in Transformation', *Journal of Refugee Studies*, 11 (4).

Roberts, A. (2006) 'The United Nations and Humanitarian Intervention', in J. Welsh (ed.), *Humanitarian Intervention and International Relations* (Oxford: Oxford University Press).

Roberts, D. (2008) *Human Insecurity: Global Structures of Violence* (London: Zed Books).

Robertson, G. (2000) *Crimes Against Humanity* (Harmondsworth: Penguin).

Robinson, P. (1999) 'The CNN Effect: Can the News Media Drive Foreign Policy?', *Review of International Studies,* 25: 301–9.

Robinson, P. (2005) 'The CNN Effect Revisited', *Critical Studies in Media Communication,* 22 (4): 344–9.

Rodrik, D. (2001) *The Global Governance of Trade as if Development Really Mattered* (Geneva: United Nations Development Programme).

Rodrik, D. (2006) 'Goodbye Washington Consensus? Hello Washington Confusion? A Review of the World Bank's Economic Growth in the 1990s: Learning from a Decade of Reform', *Journal of Economic Literature,* 44 (4): 973–87.

Rodrik, D. (2007) *One Economics, Many Recipes: Globalization, Institutions, and Economic Growth* (Princeton, NJ: Princeton University Press).

Roe, P. (2008) 'The "Value" of Positive Security', *Review of International Studies*, 34:4: 777–94.

Romero, S. (2012) 'Slum Dwellers are Defying Brazil's Grand Design for Olympics', *New York Times*, 4 March, at http://www.nytimes.com/2012/03/05/world/americas/brazil-faces-obstacles-in-preparations-for-rio-olympics.html?pagewanted=all.

Rorty, R. (1991) *Objectivity, Relativism, and Truth* (Cambridge: Cambridge University Press).

Rosamond, B. (2000) *Theories of European Integration* (Basingstoke: Palgrave Macmillan).

Rosamond, B. (2007) 'The Political Sciences of European Integration: Disciplinary History and EU Studies', in K. Jørgensen, M. Pollack and B. Rosamond (eds), *The Handbook of European Union Politics* (London: Sage), pp. 7–30.

Rosand, E. (2003) 'Security Council Resolution 1373, The Counter-Terrorism Committee, and the Fight Against Terrorism', *American Journal of International Law,* 97 (2): 333–41.

Rose, N. (1993) 'Government, Authority and Expertise in Advanced Liberalism', *Economy and Society,* 22 (3): 283–99.

Rosecrance, R. (ed.) (1976) *America as an Ordinary Country: US Foreign Policy and the Future* (Ithaca, NY: Cornell University Press).

Rosen, J. (1996) *Getting the Connections Right: Public Journalism and the Troubles of the Press* (New York, NY: 20th Century Fund).

Rosenau, J. (1992) 'Governance, Order, and Change in World Politics', in J. Rosenau and E.-O. Czempiel, *Governance Without Government: Order and Change in World Politics* (Cambridge: Cambridge University Press), pp. 1–29.

Rosenau, J. (1997) *Along the Domestic-Foreign Frontier: Exploring Governance in a Turbulent World* (Cambridge: Cambridge University Press).

Rosenau, J. (2003) *Distant Proximities: Dynamics beyond Globalization* (Princeton, NJ: Princeton University Press).

Rosenblum, M. (2009) 'Immigration and U.S. National Interests: Historical Cases and the Contemporary Debate', in T. Givens , G. Freeman and D. Leal (eds), *Immigration Policy and Security: U.S., European, and Commonwealth Perspectives* (Abingdon, Oxon: Routledge).

Ross, G. (1995) *Jacques Delors and European Integration* (New York, NY: Oxford University Press).

Ross, R. (2006) 'Balance of Power Politics and the Rise of China', *Security Studies,* 15(3): 335–95.

Rossi, V. (2003) 'Decoupling Debate Will Return: Emergers Dominate in Long Run', *IEP BN 08/01* (Leuven: Chatham House).

Rostow, W. (1960) *The Stage of Economic Growth* (Cambridge: Cambridge University Press).

Rotberg, R. (ed.) When States Fail: Causes and Consequences (Princeton, NJ: Princeton University Press, 2004),

Rothberg, R. (2003) 'The Failure and Collapse of Nation-States: Breakdown, Prevention, and Repair', in R. Rothberg (ed.), *When States Fail: Causes and Consequences* (Princeton, NJ: Princeton University Press), pp. 1–50.

Roy, O. (2007) *Secularism Confronts Islam* (New York, NY: Columbia University Press).

Roy, R., Denzau, A. and Willett, T. (eds) (2007) *Neoliberalism: National and Regional with Global Ideas* (London: Routledge).

Rueschemeyer, D., Stephens, E. and Stephens, J. (1992) *Capitalist Development and Democracy* (Cambridge: Polity Press).

Ruggie, J. (1982) 'International Regimes, Transactions and Change: Embedded Liberalism in the Postwar Economic Order', *International Organization,* 36 (2): 379–415.

Ruggie, J. (1993) 'Multilateralism: The Anatomy of an Institution', in J. Ruggie, *Multilateralism Matters: The Theory and Praxis of an Institutional Form* (New York, NY: Columbia University Press), pp. 3–47.

Ruggie, J., Katzenstein, P., Keohane, R., and Schmitter, P. (2005) 'Transformations in World Politics: The Intellectual Contributions of E. Haas', *Annual Review of Political Science*, 8: 271–296.

Rummel, R. (1994) *Death by Government* (London: Transaction Press).

Rupert, M. (2000) *Ideologies of Globalization* (London: Routledge).

Rustow, D. (1970) 'Transitions to Democracy: Toward a Dynamic Model', *Comparative Politics* 2(3): 337–63.

Sachs, J. (2008) 'A User's Guide to the Coming Century', *The National Interest,* Jul/Aug: 8–15.

Sampford, C. (2003) 'Get New Lawyers', *Legal Ethics*, 6(1): 85–105.

Sandbag (2011) *Buckle Up: Tighten the Cap and Avoid the Carbon Crash*, July, London, http://www.sandbag.org.uk/annual_review/

Sands, P. (2006) *Lawless World* (Harmondsworth: Penguin).

Sassen, S. (2002) 'Counter-geographies of Globalization: Feminization of Survival', in K. Saunders (ed.), *Feminist Post-Development Thought* (London and New York: Zed Books).

Sassen, S. (2006) *Territory, Authority, Rights* (Princeton, NJ: Princeton University Press).

Sassen, S. (ed.) (2007) *Deciphering the Global: Its Scales, Spaces and Subjects* (London and New York: Routledge).

Schedler, A. (2006) *Electoral Authoritarianism: The Dynamics of Unfree Competition* (Boulder, CO: Lynne Rienner).

Scheuer, M. (2007) *Imperial Hubris: Why the West is Losing the War on Terror* (Washington, DC: Brassey's).

Schiavone, G. (2001) *International Organizations: A Directory and Dictionary* (Basingstoke: Palgrave Macmillan).

Schmidl, E. (2000), 'The Evolution of Peace Operations from the Nineteenth Century', in E. Schmidl (ed.), *Peace Operations Between War and Peace* (London: Frank Cass), pp. 4–20.

Schmitter, P. and Terry Lynne Karl (1991) 'What Democracy is ... And is Not', *Journal of Democracy*, 2 (3), 75–88.

Schmitter, P. and Terry Lynne Karl (1994) 'The Conceptual Travels of Transitologists and Consolodologists: How Far East Should They Attempt to Go?', *Slavic Review*, 53(1): 173–85.

Schnabel, A. and Farr, V. (2012) 'Returning to the Development Roots of Security Sector Reform', in A. Schnabel and V. Farr (eds), *Back to the Roots: Security Sector Reform and Development* (Zürich and Berlin: LIT).

Schnabel, R. and Rocca, F. (2005) *The Next Superpower?: The Rise of Europe and Its Challenge to the United States* (Lanham, MD: Rowman & Littlefield).

Schreuder, Y. (2009) *The Corporate Greenhouse: Climate Change Policy in a Globalizing World* (London: Zed Books).

Schreurs, M. and Tiberghien, Y. (2007) 'Multi-Level Reinforcement: Explaining European Union Leadership in Climate Change Mitigation', *Global Environmental Politics*, 7(4): 19–46.

Schultz, J. (1998) *Reviving the Fourth Estate: Democracy, Accountability and the Media* (Cambridge: Cambridge University Press).

Schuman, R. (1950) 'The Schuman Declaration', available at http://europa.eu/abc/symbols/9-may/decl_en.htm.

Schumpeter, J. (2010 [1943]) *Capitalism, Socialism and Democracy* (London: Routledge).

Scott, W. (1995) *Institutions and Organizations* (London: Sage).

Securities and Exchange Commission (2009) '17 CFR Parts 240, 243, and 249b Re-Proposed Rules for Nationally Recognized Statistical Rating Organizations; Amendments to Rules for Nationally Recognized Statistical Rating Organizations; Final Rule and Proposed Rule', *Federal Register,* 74 (25) 9 February: 6456–84.

*Security Dialogue*, Special Section, various authors, 'What is Human Security?', *Security Dialogue,* 35:3 (2004): 345–72.

Seib, P. 2004. 'The News Media and the "Clash of Civilizations"', *Parameters,* Winter 2004–5: 71–85.

Seybolt, T. (2007) *Humanitarian Military Intervention: The Conditions for Success and Failure* (Oxford: Oxford University Press for SIPRI).

Shani, G., Makoto Sato and Mustapha Kamal Pasha (eds) (2007) *Protecting Human Security in a Post 9/11 World: Critical and Global Insights* (Basingstoke: Palgrave Macmillan).

Shawcross, William (2000) *Deliver us From Evil. Peacekeepers, Warlords and a World of Endless Conflict* (New York, NY: Simon & Schuster).

Sheehan, J.(2008) *Where Have All the Soldiers Gone? The Transformation of Modern Europe* (Boston, MA: Houghton Mifflin).

Sheehan, M. (2005) *International Security. An Analytical Survey* (Boulder, CO: Lynne Rienner) pp. 177–8.

Shenker, J. (2012) 'Council of Europe Demands Policy Overhaul to Stop Migrant Boat Deaths', *The Guardian*, 24 April. Accessed at: http://www.guardian.co.uk/world/2012/apr/24/council-of-europe-migrant-boat-deaths?INTCMP=SRCH

Siebert, F., Peterson, T. and Schramm, W. (1956) *Four Theories of the Press: The Authoritarian, Libertarian, Social Responsibility and Soviet Concepts of What the Press Should Be and Do* (Chicago, IL: University of Illinois Press).

Simmons, B. and Elkins, Z. (2004) 'The Globalization of Liberalization: Policy Diffusion in the International Political Economy', *American Political Science Review*, 98 (1): 171–89.

Simpson, G. (2004) *Great Powers and Outlaw States* (Cambridge: Cambridge University Press).

Sinclair, T. (2004) *Global Governance: Critical Concepts in Political Science* (London: Routledge).

Sinclair, T. (2005) *The New Masters of Capital: American Bond Rating Agencies and the Politics of Creditworthiness* (Ithaca, NY: Cornell University Press).

Sinclair, T. (2009) 'The Queen and the Perfect Bicycle', *Inside Story*, 12 August. Available at: http://inside.org.au/the-queen-and-the-perfect-bicycle/.

Sinclair, U. (2001 [1908]) *The Moneychangers* (New York, NY: Prometheus Books).

Singer, H. (1950) 'The Distribution of Gains from Trade between Investing and Borrowing Countries', *American Economic Review*, 40: 473–85.

Singer P.W. (2009) *Wired for War. The Robotics Revolution and Conflict in the 21st Century* (Harmondsworth: Penguin).

Sjoberg, L. (2010) 'Introduction', in L. Sjoberg (ed.), *Gender and International Security: Feminist Perspectives* (New York and Oxford: Routledge).

Sjoberg, L. and Gentry, C. (2007) *Mothers, Monsters, Whores: Women's Violence in Global Politics* (London, New York: Zed Books).

Sklair, L. (1989) *Assembling for Development: The Maquila Industry in Mexico and the United States* (Boston, MA: Unwin & Hyman).

Sklair, L.(2000) *The Transnational Capitalist Class* (Oxford: Blackwell).

Slaughter, A. (2004) *A New World Order* (Princeton, NJ: Princeton University Press).

Slaughter, A. (2009) 'America's Edge: Power in the Networked Century', *Foreign Affairs*, Jan/Feb.

Slaughter, A. (2011) 'Reflections on the 9/11 Decade', *RUSI Journal*, August/September, 156( 4).

Slaughter, A. (2012) 'How to Halt the Butchery in Syria', *The New York Times*, 23 February.

Smith, A. (1986) *The Ethnic Origins of Nations* (New York, NY: Basil Blackwell).

Smith, A. (2001) *Nationalism: Theory, Ideology, History* (Cambridge: Polity Press).

Smith, H. (2012) 'Greek Crackdown on Illegal Immigrants Leads to Mass Arrests', *The Guardian*, 7 August. Accessed at: http://www.guardian.co.uk/world/2012/aug/07/greece-crackdown-illegal-immigrants-arrest?INTCMP=SRCH.

Smith, M. (2010) *International Security: Politics, Policy, Prospects* (Basingstoke: Palgrave Macmillan).

Smith, R. (2006) *The Utility of Force: The Art of War in the Modern Age* (New York, NY: Knopf).

Smith, S. (2005) 'The Contested Concept of Security', in K. Booth (ed.) *Critical Security Studies and World Politics* (Boulder, CO: Lynne Rienner).

Söderbaum, F. (2008) 'Consolidating Comparative Regionalism: From Euro-centrism to Global Comparison', Paper for the GARNET 2008 Annual Conference, Sciences Po Bordeaux, University of Bordeaux 17–19 September. Available at http://garnet.science-spobordeaux.fr/Garnet%20papers%20PDF/SODERBAUM%20Fredrik.pdf. [Accessed 3 June 2009.]

Söderbaum, F. and Van Langenhove, L. (2006) 'The EU as a Global Actor and the Role of Interregionalism', Special Issue of *Journal of European Integration*, 27 (3).

Soederberg, S., Menz, G. and Cerny, P. (eds) (2005) *Internalizing Globalization: The Rise of Neoliberalism and the Erosion of National Varieties of Capitalism* (London and New York, NY: Palgrave Macmillan).

Solomon, M. (2005) 'International Migration Management through Inter-State Consultation Mechanisms: Focus on Regional Consultative Processes on Migration, IOM's International Dialogue on Migration and the Berne Initiative', Paper prepared for the United Nations Expert Group Meeting on International Migration and Development, 6–8 July (Geneva: IOM).

Specht, I. and Attree, L. (2006) 'The Reintegration of Teenage Girls and Young Women', *Intervention* 4:3 (219–28).

Spence, M. (2011) *The Next Convergence: The Future of Economic Growth in a Multispeed World* (New York, NY: Farrar, Straus & Giroux).

Spruyt, H. (1994) *The Sovereign State and Its Competitors: An Analysis of Systems Change* (Princeton, NJ: Princeton University Press).

Sreberny, A. and Paterson, C. (2004) 'Shouting from the Rooftops: Reflections on International News in the 21st Century', in C. Paterson and A. Sreberny (eds), *International News in the 21st Century* (Newport, VT: John Libbey Publishing), pp. 3–27.

Stambouli, A. (2011) 'Algerian Renewable Energy Assessment: The Challenge of Sustainability', *Energy Policy*, 39: 4507–19.

Steans, J. (2006) *Gender and International Relations* (Cambridge: Polity Press).

Stepan, A. (2012) 'Tunisia's Transition and the Twin Tolerations', *Journal of Democracy,* 23(2), 89–103.

Stepan, A. and Skach, C. (1993) 'Constitutional Frameworks and Democratic Consolidation: Parliamentarism versus Presidentialism', *World Politics*, 46(1) : 1–22.

Stepanova, E. (2011) 'The Role of Information Communication Technologies in the "Arab Spring"', PONARS Eurasia Policy Memo No.159.

Stern, N. (2007) *The Economics of Climate Change* (Cambridge: Cambridge University Press).

Stern, N. (2009) *A Blueprint for a Safer Planet* (London: Bodley Head).

Stiglitz, J. (2002) *Globalization and Its Discontents* (New York, NY: Norton).

Stockmann, D. and Gallagher, M.E. (2011) 'Remote Control: How the Media Sustain Authoritarian Rule in China', *Comparative Political Studies*, 44(4): 436–67.

Stone, D. (2001) (ed.) *Banking on Knowledge: The Genesis of the Global Development Network* (London: Routledge).

Stone, D. (2008) 'Global Public Policy, Transnational Policy Communities and their Networks', *Policy Studies Journal*, 36 (10): 19–38.

Stone, D. and Wright, C. (2006) (eds) *The World Bank and Governance* (London: Routledge).

Strachan, H. and Scheipers, S. (eds) (2011) *The Changing Character of War* (Oxford: Oxford University Press).

Strange, S. (1998) *Mad Money: When Markets Outgrow Governments* (Ann Arbor, MI: University of Michigan Press).

Streeck, W. (1997) 'German Capitalism: Does it Exist? Can it Survive?' *New Political Economy*, 2 (2): 237–56.

Streeck, W. (2011) 'The Crises of Democratic Capitalism', *New Left Review*, 71(Sept/Oct): 5–29.

Subramanian, A. (2011) *Eclipse: Living in the Shadow of China's Economic Dominance* (Washington, DC: IIE Press).

Suhrke, A. (2003) 'Human security and the protection of refugees', in E. Newman and J. van Selm (eds), *Refugees and Forced Displacement: International Security, Human Vulnerability, and the State* (Tokyo: UNU Press).

Sullivan, A. (2001) 'This *is* a Religious War', *New York Times*, 7 October.

Sumner, A. (2004) 'Epistemology and "Evidence" in Development Studies: A Review of Dollar and Kraay', *Third World Quarterly*, 25(6): 1160–74.

Sumner, A. (2010) *Global Poverty and the New Bottom Billion* (Brighton: IDS Working Paper no. 349).

Sutherland, P. (2005) 'Correcting Misperceptions', *Foreign Affairs*, 84(7) (December).

Sylvester, C. (1994) *Feminist Theory and International Relations in a Postmodern Era* (Cambridge: Cambridge University Press).

Szporluk, R. (1998) 'Thoughts about Change: Ernest Gellner and the History of Nationalism', in J. Hall (ed.), *The State of the Nation: Ernest Gellner and the History of Nationalism*(Cambridge: Cambridge University Press).

Tadjbakhsh, S. and Chenoy, A. (2007) *Human Security: Concepts and Implications* (London: Routledge).

Taras, R. and Ganguly, R. (2009) *Understanding Ethnic Conflict*, 4th edn (New York, NY: Longman).

Telo, M. (2009) *International Relations: A European Perspective* (London: Ashgate).

Teorell, J. (2010) *Determinants of Democratization: Explaining Regime Change in the World, 1972–2006* (Cambridge: Cambridge University Press).

Terry, T. (2007) *Understanding Global Media* (Basingstoke: Palgrave Macmillan).

Tesón, F.R. (1997) *Humanitarian Intervention: An Inquiry into Law and Morality*, 2nd edn (New York, NY: Transnational Publishers).

Tesón, F. (2003) 'The Liberal Case for Humanitarian Intervention', in J. Holzgrefe and R. Keohane (eds), *Humanitarian Intervention: Ethical, Legal and Political Dilemmas* (Cambridge: Cambridge University Press).

Thakur, R. (2004) 'Iraq and the Responsibility to Protect', *Behind the Headlines*, 62 (1): 1–16.

Thakur, R. and Newman, E. (2004) 'Introduction: Non-Traditional Security in Asia', in R. Thakur and E. Newman (eds), *Broadening Asia's Security Discourse and Agenda: Political, Social, and Environmental Perspectives* (Tokyo: UN University Press), pp. 1–15.

Thakur, R. and Singh Sidhu, W. (2006) 'Iraq's Challenge to World Order', in R. Thakur and W. Singh Sidhu (eds) *The Iraq Crisis and World Order: Structural, Institutional and Normative Challenges* (New York, NY: United Nations University Press).

Thiessen, M. (2009) 'Obama's Inheritance – Al Qaeda in Retreat', *World Affairs*, 172 (1): 74–83.

Thomas, C. (2000) *Global Governance, Development and Human Security* (London: Pluto).

Thomas, C. (2002) 'Global Governance and Human Security', in R. Wilkinson and S. Hughes (eds), *Global Governance. Critical Perspectives* (London: Routledge).

Thomas, N. and W. Tow (2002) 'The Utility of Human Security: Sovereignty and Human Intervention', *Security Dialogue*, 33(2): 177–92.

Thompson, M. (1995) *The Anti-Marcos Struggle: Personalistic Rule and Democratic Transition in the Philippines* (New Haven, CT: Yale University Press).

Tickell, O. (2008) *Kyoto 2* (London: Zed Books).

Tickner, A. (1992) *Gender in International Relations: Feminist Perspectives on Achieving Global Security* (New York, NY: Columbia University Press).

Tilly, C. (ed.) (1975) *The Formation of National States in Western Europe* (Princeton, NJ: Princeton University Press).

*Time Asia Edition* (2001) 'People Power Redux' , 29 January.

Tissot, R. (2009) 'Energy Security in Latin America', in A. Wenger, R. Orttung and J. Perovic (eds), *Energy and the Transformation of International Relations* (Oxford: Oxford University Press).

Tonelson, A. (2006) 'The Real Lessons in the Doha Round's Failure', *American Economics Alert* (August 15); available at http://www.americaneconomicalert.org/view_art.asp? Prod_ID=2537.

Townsend, M.E. (1941) *European Colonial Expansion since 1871* (Chicago, IL: Lippincott).

Traub, J. (2006) *The Best of Intentions: Kofi Annan and the UN in an Era of American World Power* (London: Bloomsbury).

Treasury, Department of (US) (2008) *Final Monthly Treasury Statement* (Washington, DC: USGPO).

Treasury, Department of (US) (2011) 'Joint Statement of Timothy Geithner, Secretary of the Treasury, and Jacob Lew, Director of the Office of Management And Budget, on Budget Results for Fiscal Year 2011', Washington, DC: 14 October.

Truong, T.D., S. Wieringa and A. Chhachhi (eds) (2007), *Engendering Human Security: Feminist Perspectives* (Basingstoke: Palgrave Macmillan).

Tsai, K.S. (2007) *Capitalism without Democracy: The Private Sector in Contemporary China* (Ithaca, NY: Cornell University Press).

Tsingou, E. (2004) *Policy Preferences in Financial Governance: Public-Private Dynamics and the Prevalence of Market-Based Arrangements in the Banking Industry,* University of Warwick: Centre for the Study of Globalisation and Regionalisation, Working Paper 131/04.

Tsingou, E. (2010) 'Transnational Governance Networks in the Regulation of Finance –The Making of Global Regulation and Supervision Standards in the Banking Industry', in M. Ougaard (ed.), *Theoretical Perspectives on Business and Global Governance: Bridging Theoretical Divides* (London: Routledge).

Tuastad, D. (2003) 'Neo-Orientalism and the New Barbarism Thesis: Aspects of Symbolic Violence in the Middle East Conflict(s)', *Third World Quarterly,* 24 (4): 591–9.

Turner, A. (2009) *The Turner Review: A Regulatory Response to the Global Banking Crisis* (London: FSA): at http://www.fsa.gov.uk/pages/Library/Corporate/turner/index.shtml

Turner, G. (2002) 'Public Relations', in S. Cunningham. and G. Turner, *The Media and Communications in Australia* (Sydney: Allen & Unwin).

Ullman, R. (1983) 'Redefining Security', *International Security*, 8(1).

UN (2000) *We the Peoples: The Role of the United Nations in the 21st Century* (New York: United Nations).

UNCTAD (2002a) *Trade and Development Report 2002* (Geneva: UNCTAD).

UNCTAD (2002b) *World Investment Report 2002* (Geneva: UNCTAD).

UNCTAD (2007) *World Investment Report 2007* (Geneva: UNCTAD).

UNCTAD (2010) *World Investment Report 2010* (Geneva: UNCTAD).

UNDP (1994) *Human Development Report 1994* (New York: Oxford University Press).

UNDP (2001) *Human Development Report* (New York; Oxford: Oxford University Press /UNDP).

UNEP (United Nations Environment Programme) (2011) *Bridging the Emissions Gap*, http://www.unep.org/publications/ebooks/bridgingemissionsgap/.

UNFCCC (2012) http://cdm.unfccc.int/about/index.html.

UNHCR (1999) *Refugees and Others of Concern to UNHCR: 1998 Statistical Overview* (Geneva: UNHCR, July).

UNHCR (2000) *The State of the World's Refugees 2000* (Oxford: Oxford University Press).

UNHCR (2001) 'Care Urged in Balancing Security and Refugee Protection Needs', press release (Geneva: UNHCR, 1 October 2001).

UNHCR (2004) *Proposal to Establish an Assistant High Commissioner (Protection) Post in UNHCR* (Geneva: EXCOM 55th session, A/AC.96/992/Add.1, 2 September 2004).

UNHCR (2006a) *Asylum Levels and Trends in Industrialized Countries, 2005: Overview of Asylum Applications Lodged in Europe and Non-European Industrialized Countries in 2005* (Geneva: UNHCR, 17 March 2006).

UNHCR (2006b) *2005 Global Refugee Trends: Statistical Overview of Populations of Refugees, Asylum-Seekers, Internally Displaced Persons, Stateless Persons, and Other Persons of Concern* (Geneva: UNHCR, 9 June 2006).

UNHCR (2011a) Statistical Yearbook 2010: Trends in Displacement, Protection and *Solutions*, 10th Edition (Geneva: UNHCR).

UNHCR (2011b) *Asylum Levels and Trends in Industrialized Countries 2010: Statistical Overview of Asylum Applications Lodged in Europe and Selected Non-European Countries* (Geneva: UNHCR, 28 March).

UNHCR (2012) *Asylum Levels and Trends in Industrialized Countries 2011: Statistical Overview of Asylum Applications Lodged in Europe and Selected Non-European Countries* (Geneva: UNHCR, 27 March).

United Kingdom (2011) 'Leveson Inquiry: Culture, Practice and Ethics of the Press', Terms of Reference www.levesoninquiry.org.uk.

United Nations (2000) 'Resolution 55/2', available at: www.un.org/millennium/declaration/ares552e.pdf.

United Nations (2008) *Security, Peace and Development: The Role of the United Nations in Supporting Security Sector Reform*, Report of the Secretary-General (New York: UN General Assembly Security Council).

United Nations Commission of Experts on Reforms of the International Monetary and Financial System (2009) *Recommendations* (19 March 2009), http://www.un.org/ga/president/63/letters/recommendationExperts200309.pdf.

United Nations Security Council (UNSC) (2004) Meeting Record on the topic of Sudan, S/PV.4988 11 June.

Vayrynen, R. (2003) 'Regionalism: Old and New', *International Studies Review,* 5(1): 25–52.

Verkuyten, M. (2005) *The Social Psychology of Ethnic Identity* (Hove: Psychology Press).

Victor, D. *et al.* (eds) (2006) *Natural Gas and Geopolitics* (Cambridge : Cambridge University Press).

Vogel, S. (2006) *Japan Remodeled: How Government and Industry Are Reforming Japanese Capitalism* (Ithaca, NY: Cornell University Press).

Vogler, J. (2011) 'The European Union as a Global Environmental Policy Actor: Climate Change', in R. Wurzel and J. Connelly (eds), *The European Union as a Leader in International Climate Politics* (London: Routledge), pp. 21–37.

Wade, R. (2000) 'Wheels within wheels: Rethinking the Asian Crisis and the Asian Model', *Annual Review of Political Science,* 3: 85–115.

Wade, R. (2003a) 'The Disturbing Rise in Poverty and Inequality: Is It All a "Big Lie"?', in D. Held and M. Koenig-Archibugi (eds), *Taming Globalization* (Cambridge: Polity), pp.18–46.

Wade, R. (2003b) *Governing the Market: Economic Theory and the Role of Government in East Asian Industrialization* (Princeton, NJ: Princeton University Press).

Wade, R. (2010) 'After the Crisis: Industrial Policy and the Developmental State in Low-Income Countries', *Global Policy,* 1(2): 150 61.

Wade, R. and Veneroso, F. (1998) 'The Asian Crisis: The High Debt Model versus the Wall Street-Treasury Complex', *The New Left Review,* 228, March–April: 3–23.

Wæver, O., Buzan, B., Kelstrup, M. and Lemaitre, P. (1993) *Identity, Migration and the New Security Agenda in Europe* (London: Pinter).

Waldman, M. (2010) 'Sun in the Sky: The Relationship between Pakistan's ISI and Afghan Insurgents', Crisis States Research Centre Discussion Paper 18, June.

Waldman, T. (2007) 'British Post-Conflict Operations in Iraq: Into the Heart of Strategic Darkness, *Civil Wars,* 9 (1), March.

Waldman, T. (2010) 'Politics and War: Clausewitz's Paradoxical Equation', *Parameters,* 40 (3), Autumn.

Waldman, T. (2012) *War, Clausewitz and the Trinity* (London: Ashgate).

Walker, R. (1992) *Inside/Outside: International Relations as Political Theory* (Cambridge: Cambridge University Press).

Wallace, H. (2002) 'Europeanisation and Globalisation: Complementary or Contradictory Trends?', in S. Breslin, C. Hughes, N. Phillips and B. Rosamond (eds), *New Regionalisms in the Global Political Economy: Theories and Cases* (London: Routledge) pp. 137–49.

Walt, S. (1991) 'The Renaissance of Security Studies', *International Studies Quarterly,* 35(2), 1991: 211–39.

Walt, S. (2004) *Taming American Power: The Global Response to US Primacy* (New York, NY: W.W. Norton).

Walt, S. (2011) 'The End of the American Era', *The National Interest,* 116, Nov–Dec.

Waltz, K. (1979) *Theory of International Politics* (Reading, MA: Addison-Wesley).

Waltz, K. (2000) 'Structural Realism after the Cold War', *International Security,* 25(1): 5–41.

Walzer, M. (2006) *Just and Unjust Wars* (New York, NY: Basic Books).

Wang, G. (2011) 'Paradigm Shift and the Centrality of Communication Discipline', *International Journal of Communication,* 5: 1458–66.

Warbrick, C. (2006) 'States and Recognition in international Law', in M. Evans (ed.), *International Law* (Oxford: Oxford University Press).

Warwick Commission (2007) *The Multilateral Trade Regime: Which Way Forward?* University of Warwick, at http://go.warwick.ac.uk/go/warwickcommission.

Watts, A. (2001) 'The Importance of International Law', in M. Byers (ed.) *The Role of International Law in International Politics* (Oxford: Oxford University Press).

Weaver, K. (2008) *The Hypocrisy Trap: The World Bank and the Poverty of Reform* (Princeton, NJ: Princeton University Press.)

Weiner, M. (1987) 'Empirical Democratic Theory', in M. Weiner and E. Ozbudun (eds), *Competitive Elections in Developing Countries* (Durham, NC: Duke University Press), pp. 3–36.

Weiss, M. (2006) *Protest and Possibilities: Civil Society and Coalitions for Political Change in Malaysia* (Stanford, CA: Stanford University Press).

Weiss, T. (2004) 'The Sunset of Humanitarian Intervention? The Responsibility to Protect in a Unipolar Era', *Security Dialogue*, 35 (2).

Weiss, T. (2007) *Humanitarian Intervention: Ideas into Action* (Cambridge: Polity Press).

Weiss, T. (2009) *What's Wrong With the United Nations and How to Fix It* (Cambridge: Polity).

Weiss, T. (2011) 'R2P Alive and Well After Libya', *Ethics and International Affairs*, 25(3): 287–92.

Weller, M. (2002) 'Undoing the Global Constitution: UN Security Council Action on the International Criminal Court', *International Affairs*, 87(4): 693–712.

Welsh, J. (ed.) (2004) *Humanitarian Intervention and International Relations* (Oxford: Oxford University Press).

Wheeler, N. (2000) Saving Strangers: Humanitarian Intervention in International Society (Oxford: Oxford University Press).

Wheeler, N. (2001) 'The Legality of NATO's Intervention in Kosovo', in K. Booth (ed.), The Kosovo Tragedy: The Human Rights Dimensions (London: Frank Cass).

White, N. (2004) 'The Will and Authority of the Security Council After Iraq', *Leiden Journal of International Law*, 17(4): 645–72.

White House (2002) 'The National Security Strategy of the United States of America', *The White House Website*, 17 September.

Williams, P. (ed.) (2008) *Security Studies: An Introduction* (London: Routledge).

Whitworth, S. (1997) *Feminism and International Relations: Towards a Political Economy of Gender in Interstate and Non-Governmental Institutions* (London: Macmillan).

Williamson, J. (1994) 'In Search of a Manual for Technopols', in J. Williamson, *The Political Economy of Policy Reform* (Washington, DC: Institute for International Economics), pp. 11–28.

Wilson, W. (2006) 'Appeal for Support of the League of Nations at Pueblo, Colorado', in M. DiNunzio (ed.) *Woodrow Wilson: Essential Writings and Speeches of the Scholar-President* (New York, NY: New York University Press), pp. 411–20.

Wohlforth, W. (1999) 'The Stability of a Unipolar World', *International Security* 24(1): 5–41.

Wolf, M. (2004) *Why Globalization Works* (New Haven, CT: Yale University Press).

Wolf, M. (2009) 'The Cautious Approach to Fixing Banks Will Not Work', *Financial Times*, 30 June.

Wolfers, A. (1952) 'National Security as an Ambiguous Symbol', *Political Science Quarterly*, 67(4): 481–502.

Woods, N. (2000) 'The Challenge of Good Governance for the IMF and the World Bank Themselves', *World Development*, 28 (5): 823–41.

Woods, N. (2006) *The Globalizers: The IMF, the World Bank and their Borrowers* (Ithaca, NY: Cornell University Press).

Wooldridge, A. (2012) 'The Visible Hand: Special Report on the Rise of State Capitalism', *The Economist*, 21 January.

World Bank (1997) *World Development Report 1997: The State in a Changing World* (New York, NY: Oxford University Press).

World Bank (2002) *Globalization, Growth and Poverty* (Oxford: Oxford University Press).

World Bank (2011a) *Russian Economic Report*, No. 25, June.

World Bank (2011b) *Migration and Remittances Factbook 2011*, 2nd edn (Washington, DC: World Bank).

World Bank (2011c) *State and Trends of the Carbon Market 2011*, June (Washington, DC: World Bank).

World Bank (2012) 'About Us: What We Do' *web.worldbank.org*, at http://go.worldbank.org/7Q47C9KOZ0. [Accessed March 2012.]

Wright, L. (2006) *The Looming Tower Al-Qaeda's Road to 9/11* (Harmondsworth: Penguin).

WTO (2005) *International Trade Statistics* (Geneva: WTO).

WTO (2007) *World Trade Report: Six Decades of Multilateral Trade Cooperation-What Have we Learned?* (Geneva: WTO).

WTO (2012) 'Understanding the WTO > The Uruguay Round', *www.wto.org/english*, at http://www.wto.org/english/thewto_e/whatis_e/tif_e/fact5_e.htm. [Accessed March 2012.]

Wurzel, R. and Connelly, J. (2011) 'Introduction: European Union Political Leadership in International Climate Change Politics', in R. Wurzel and J. Connelly (eds), *The European Union as a Leader in International Climate Politics* (London: Routledge), pp. 3–20.

Yergin, D. (2008) *The Prize: The Epic Quest for Oil, Money, and Power* (New York, NY: Simon & Shuster), p. 587.

Yergin, D. (2011). *The Quest: The Quest: Energy, Security, and the Remaking of the Modern World* (New York, NY: Penguin).

York, J. C. (2011) 'The Revolutionary Force of Facebook and Twitter', Neiman Reports <http://www.nieman.harvard.edu/reports/article/102681/The-Revolutionary-Force-of-Facebook-and-Twitter.aspx>.

Young, O. (2002) *The Institutional Dimensions of Environmental Change: Fit, Interplay, and Scale* (Cambridge, MA: MIT Press).

Youngs, R. (2009) *Energy Security: Europe's New Foreign Policy Challenge* (London: Routledge).

Youngs, R. (2009) Nabucco : The Sequel [Onine] Available at: http://www.europeanenergyreview.eu/site/pagina.php?id_mailing=257&toegang=d96409bf894217686ba124d7356686c9&id=1491. [Accessed 09 March 2012.]

Youngs, R. (2010) *Europe's Decline and Fall: The Struggle Against Global Irrelevance* (London: Profile).

Zakaria, F. (2003) *The Future of Freedom: Illiberal Democracy at Home and Abroad,* (New York, NY: W.W. Norton).

Zakaria, F. (2008), *The Post-American World* (New York, NY: W.W. Norton).

Zalasiewicz, J., Williams, M., Steffen, W. and Crutzen, P. (2010) 'The New World of the Anthropocene', *Environmental Science & Technology*, 44(7): 2228–31.

Zarate, J.C. and David A. Gordon (2011) 'The Battle for Reform with Al-Qaeda', *The Washington Quarterly,* 34 (3):103–22.

Zhao, S. (2010) 'The China Model: Can It Replace the Western Model of Modernization?', *Journal of Contemporary China,* 19(65): 419 –36.

Zheng, Z. (2002) 'China's Terms of Trade in World Manufactures, 1993-2000', UNCTAD Discussion Paper no.161, pp.1–61.

Zhu, Y. (2011) '"Performance Legitimacy" and China's Political Adaption strategy', *Journal of Chinese Political Science*, 16(2): 123–40.

Zysman, J. (1983) *Governments, Markets, and Growth: Financial Systems and the Politocs of Industrial Change* (Ithaca, NY: Cornell University Press).

# Index

Afghanistan, 78, 93–4, 96–104
  media reports, 266, 274
  reconstruction, 25
  refugees, 165
  terrorism, 121, 123–4, 126–31, 134
  Soviet invasion, 195
  state failure, 218
  US foreign policy, 24, 40
  US military strategy, 2, 21, 288
African Union, 60, 65, 169, 256
Ahmadinejad, Mahmoud, 238
Akerlof, George, 83
Alaska, 200
Albania, 78
Albright, Madeleine, 294
Algeria, 1, 123, 202
Allied South-East Asia Command, 64
al Huq, Zia, 123
al-Qaeda, 6, 10, 122, 124–32
Afghanistan, 96
  CIA, 100
  9/11 attacks, 42, 104, 196
  see also September 11 attacks
Andean Community of Nations, 65
Anderson, Benedict, 212, 269
Angola, 78, 109
Annan, Kofi, 116, 252, 260
apartheid, 70, 258
Arab–Israeli war, 164, 266
Arab Spring, 1, 3, 7
  democracy 130, 247
  explanations 25, 41
  intervention, 93 106
  media, 263, 269–70, 275
Arafat, Yasser, 123
Argentina, 78, 157, 222, 240
  authoritarianism, 238
  financial crisis, 75, 85
Armed Non-State Actors (ANSAs), 227–8
Armenia, 78, 216
Asia, 2, 8, 16, 60
  Central Asia, 28, 126, 204, 235, 243
  climate change 184
  defence spending, 28
  democracy, 36, 235
  East Asia, 54, 62, 65, 70, 74–5, 77, 152,
    154, 278–9, 282–4, 294–5
  emerging power, 14, 16–29
  energy security, 197, 204
  failed states, 218
  nationalism, 217
    North East Asia, 147
  regionalism, 60, 62, 64–5, 69, 70–1,
    74–8
  South Asia, 77, 126, 129, 131, 147, 223
  Southeast Asia, 6, 28, 64, 242

  Southwest Asia, 24
    war, 101, 122, 132, 167
Asian Development Bank, 155, 158
Asian Financial Crisis, 51, 53–4, 70, 80, 85–6
'Asian tigers', 16
'Asian values', 86
Asia Pacific Economic Cooperation (APEC),
    49, 65, 70, 78
Asia-Pacific Partnership on Clean Development
    and Climate, 184
Association of Southeast Asian Nations
    (ASEAN), 25
  non-interference, 242
  regionalism, 62, 65, 69–71, 74–5, 77–8
Assad, Bashar Hafez al-, 1
  see also Syria
Assange, Julian,
Augustus (Emperor), 211
Australasia, 65, 278
Australia, 15, 24, 27, 78, 282
  asylum seekers, 166
  climate change, 182–4, 191
  energy, 196
Australia–New Zealand Closer Economic
    Relations (CER), 77
Austria, 78, 168
Austria-Hungarian Empire, 215
authoritarianism, 26, 245–6
Azerbaijan, 78, 204

Baader-Meinhof Group, 123
Bahrain, 18, 78, 260
Baker, Dean, 86
balance of power, 3, 6, 38, 41, 136
Bangladesh, 78, 148, 163, 180
Ban Ki-moon, 116–7, 118
Bank of England, 87
Bank for International Settlements (BIS), 50
Basques, 216
Battle of the Boyne, 212
Battle of Kosovo, 212
Beeson, Mark, 12, 26
Beijing Conference on Women, 244
Beijing Consensus, 286–9
Belgium, 15, 78, 185, 216
Bellamy, Alex, 9, 258–9
Bellin, Eva, 237
Ben Ali, Zine El Abidine, 7,
  see also Tunisia
'benevolent imperialism', 259
Berlin Wall, 120, 235
Beslan, 125, 130
biodiversity, 177
biopolitics, 31
Birmingham, 219
Bisley, Nick, 8, 285, 292

Bismarck, Otto von, 214–15
'Black Hawk Down', 109
    *see also* Somalia; humanitarian intervention
Black September, 123
Blair, 112, 115, 185, 251, 254
Bobbitt, Philip, 213–4, 221
Booth, Ken, 137
Bosnia, 94–5, 106, 109, 112–13, 165, 210
Botswana, 78, 238
Bouazizi, Mohammed, 1
    *see also* Tunisia
*bourgeoisie*, 35, 41, 237
Brahimi, Lakhdar, 109–10
Brazil, 222, 239, 248, 260
    BRIC, 41, 14
    climate change, 189–90
    emerging power, 4, 18, 23–7, 147
    'gobal South', 55
    inequality, 157
    regionalism 78
Breslin, Shaun, 9
Bretons, 216
Bretton Woods System, 6, 8, 47–8, 50–3, 84
    alternatives, 160
    breakdown, 9, 80, 90
    post-Bretton Woods, 280, 284, 295
BRICS (Brazil, Russia, India, China, South
        Africa), 14, 19, 28, 41 197, 290
Britain, 2, 15, 27, 30, 36, 40, 64, 123, 126, 150,
        164
    democracy, 237
    economic liberalization, 278, 282
    energy policy, 198, 206
    Iraq, 196
    media, 270
    nationalism, 219
    national interest, 284
    Royal Air Force, 195
British Special Boat Service, 103
British Petroleum (BP), 200
British Isles, 120
Brundtland Commission, 139
Brussels, 219
Bulgaria, 78, 203
Bull, Benedict, 72
Burma/Myanmar, 65, 168, 237, 240
Burundi, 213, 218
Bush, George H W, 94, 183
Bush, George W, 100, 115
    administration, 125, 129
    climate change, 181–5
    collective security
    democracy, 242, 246
    international law, 251, 253, 258–9
    'war on terror' 96
Buzan, Barry, 139, 141, 173
Byers, Michael, 117
Byrd–Hagel resolution, 187

Cambodia, 65, 78, 109, 114, 245

Canada, 15, 65, 78, 298
    climate change, 182–3, 190–1
    energy policy, 198, 200, 203
    nationalism, 216, 119
capitalism, 2, 4, 12, 13, 26, 277–89
    China, 294
    crisis of, 91, 160
    gender, 231
    globalization, 32–3, 39, 43, 45, 63, 75
    liberal democracy, 120, 133, 292, 295
'carbon commodification', 188
Caribbean, 168, 218
Carothers, Thomas, 242, 250
Carter doctrine, 196
Carter, Neil, 11, 291
Case, William, 11
Caspian basin, 204
Caspian Development Corporation, 204
Catalans, 216
CDM, *see* 'Clean Development Mechanism'
Central African Republic, 148, 218
Central America, 65, 72, 78, 101, 232
Central American Common Market, 65
Central Asia, *see* Asia
Central Intelligence Agency (CIA), 100
Cerny, Philip, 8, 18, 45, 221, 281, 293
Chad, 78, 165, 218
Charlesworth, Hilary, 261–2
Chavez, Hugo, 160, 201
Chechen separatists, 125, 210, 260
Chechnya, 94–95, 228
Chesterman, Simon, 114, 117, 256, 262
Chevron, 200
Chiang Mai Initiative, 70
Chile, 78, 157
China, 1, 2, 3
    democracy, 235, 242, 246–7
    development, 24, 55, 73, 154–7, 159, 293–4
    drones, 100
    climate change, 25, 183–4, 186–7, 189–90
    energy, 25, 201–2, 206
    influence, 14, 17, 71, 293–4
    international law, 255, 257
    intervention, 113, 117
    media, 272, 275,
    nationalism, 211, 222
    population, 167, 168
    relations with US, 5, 25
    regionalism, 65, 70–1, 73, 75–6, 78
    rise of, 2, 3, 5, 8, 12, 13–14, 16–29, 41, 71,
        147–8, 298–9, 285–9, 290–1, 294–5
    terrorism, 125, 133
China–Africa summits, 26
    *see also* Shanghai Cooperation
        Organization (SCO)
Chinese Communist Party, 5
Christopher, Warren, 216
Churchill, Winston, 41
citizenship, 214, 244
civil liberties, 132, 236, 241, 243, 245–6, 248

civil society, 6
democracy, 237, 240–4
global economy, 52, 56–7, 59
international law, 250
media, 264, 272, 276
non-state actors, 32–3
security, 144
Clausewitz, Carl von, 97, 102–3, 105, 126
'clash of civilizations', 126, 220
*see also* Huntington, Samuel
Clean Development Mechanism (CDM), 183, 188–9
climate change, 3, 6, 8, 10–11, 21, 25, 177–91, 290–1
energy, 192, 197, 206–7, 208
migration, 165–6, 174
security, 139, 145, 147–9
Clinton, Bill, 183,
Clinton, Hillary, 270
$CO_2$ emissions, 178, 183, 187–9, 194, 197, 203–4
Coker, Christopher, 100
Cold War, 2, 9, 295–6
capitalism, 279, 285
democracy, 235, 241, 247
development, 150
energy, 197
great powers, 15–17
gender, 229
globalisation, 39
international law, 251, 252, 255 8, 261
media, 271
migration, 164–8
multilateral trade, 52
nationalism, 210, 216–17
peace operations, 108–10, 114–15, 119
post-Cold War era, 60, 92, 94–5
security 135–40
terrorism, 122, 126, 132–3
Colombia, 157, 222, 227
'colour revolutions', 41
COMECON, *see* Council for Mutual Economic Assistance
Committee of European Securities Regulators, 87
'common but differentiated responsibilities', 181–3, 186
Common Economic Space, 64
*see also* Soviet Union
Commonwealth of, Christopher, 100
communism, 2, 12, 70, 120, 235
'competition state', 44–5, 221
'complex interdependence', 35, 39–40, 45, 69
'compromise of embedded liberalism', 279
Concert of Europe, 49, 108
Conference of Versailles, *see* Versailles Conference
Congo, 78, 106, 113, 154, 168, 218
*see also* Democratic Republic of Congo
Connor, Walker, 211
'consolidology', 240

'contingent democrats', 237
'contraction and convergence', 62
Cooper, George, 83
'coordinated market economies', 282
Copenhagen Conference, 11, 25, 179, 181,189–90, 196–7
Copenhagen School, 141, 146, 176
Cornish, Paul, 99
Corsicans, 216
cosmopolitan democracy, 57, 244
Coted'Ivoire, 78, 113, 118, 218
Council for Mutual Economic Assistance (COMECON), 78
Counter-insurgency Field Manual, FM 3–40, 97

counter-insurgency (COIN), 9, 93, 97–9, 102, 104, 127
counter-terrorism, 102
Cox, Robert, 146
Credit Rating Agency Reform Act (2006), 87–8
Crimean War, 214
Critical Security Studies, 146
Croatia, 106
Cuba, 78, 96, 113,
Czechoslovakia, 78, 114
Czech Republic, 78

Dahl, Robert, 236, 244
Darfur, 106, 113–14, 165, 255, 260
deforestation, 177–8
Delors, Jacques, 68
democracy, 96, 235–50, 293, 297
capitalism, 276, 285
nationalism, 214–15
international law, 258
media 272–3
security, 138, 160
terrorism, 120, 125, 128, 131, 133
war, 101
Deng, Francis, 115–16
Deng Xiaoping, 287
Denmark, 78, 168, 182
dependency theory, 150–2, 157
deregulation, 12, 138, 207, 281
development, 229, 230, 234, 237–42, 248
models 277–89
Diamond, Larry, 236–7, 240, 243, 245, 250
Direct Action, 123
Doha Round (2001), 53, 222–3
Dow Jones, 84
drones, 9, 94, 99–100, 103, 133, 259

East Africa, 65, 222,
Eastern Europe, 40, 41
democracy, 240
climate change, 177, 182, 186
migration, 164, 170
regionalism, 40, 64–7
colour revolutions, 41
*see also* Europe; European Union

East Timor, 106, 109, 113, 165
Economic Community of West African States
    (ECOWAS), 65, 109
*Economist, The*, 29
Egypt, 1, 7, 27, 78, 247–8, 269–70
    terrorism, 120, 123, 130.
    *see also* Mubarak, Hosni El Sayed; Arab
        Spring
'embedded emissions', 187
emissions trading system (ETS), 183, 185, 191
Emmott, Bill, 29
'end of history', 2, 120, 132–3, 235
    *see also* Fukuyama, Francis
Energy Bill, 184
    *see also* Byrd–Hagel resolution
energy security, 3, 8, 190, 192–209
Enlightenment, 235
Enloe, Cynthia, 227, 234
Enron bankruptcy (2001–2), 80, 86–9
'epistemic communities', 43, 180
equity, 180, 186–7
Ethiopia, 218, 252
ethnicity, 11, 38
    identity, 210–24, 225, 230, 237–8
ETS, *see* emissions trading system (ETS)
Etzioni, Amitai, 215
Eurasian Economic Community, 78
Europe, 9, 14–15, 26, 30, 34–6, 39, 51, 55, 158,
        277, 279, 286–7, 290, 297
    climate change, 181–2, 185–6, 188, 196
    democracy, 235 238, 242
    energy, 21, 198, 200–1, 204, 206–9
    financial crisis, 13, 20, 51, 54, 88–90, 160,
        292, 296
    integration, 61–3, 67, 77, 186
    monetary union, 77
    nationalism, 214–19, 222–3
    population, 162–4, 166–8, 170–1, 173–5,
        220
    regionalism, 53, 60–1, 64–78
    terrorism, 122–3, 125, 260
    wars, 40, 43, 94
    *see also* Eastern Europe; European Union
European Coal and Steel Community (ECSC),
        61, 65–8
European Commission, 68, 88–9, 186, 201, 204
European Economic Community, 65, 68
*European Energy Review*, 204
European Exchange Rate Mechanism (ERM),
        84–5
European integration, 61–3, 68, 77, 186
European Parliament, 61, 87, 89, 186
European Union, 32–3, 196
    financial crisis, 288
    gender, 229
    intervention, 196
    regionalism, 40, 49, 67
Europeanization, 68
Exxon, 5, 194, 200

Falk, Richard, 251
FDI, *see* Foreign Direct Investment
Federal Reserve, *see* US Federal Reserve
femininity, 228.
    *see also* gender
Ferguson, Niall, 54, 223
feudalism, 34–6, 214
Fiji, 78, 244
financial crisis, 2–4, 80–91
    *see also* Global Financial Crisis; Great
        Recession; East Asian Financial Crisis
financial markets, 6
    global economy, 54
    global financial crisis, 81–3, 85–7, 90
    globalization, 31, 39, 43
    *see also* Global Financial Crisis
Financial Stability Board, 32
Financial Stability Forum, 32
Finland, 78, 182, 185
First United Nations Emergency Force (UNEF
        I), 108
First World War, 15, 47, 122, 215–16, 223, 297
Fischer, Joschka, 185
Flemish, 216
floating exchange rate, 50, 84, 280
Foreign Direct Investment (FDI), 17, 18, 284
    development, 154, 157–8, 172
    energy, 199
*Foreign Policy*, 218
Foucault, Michel, 31
France, 2, 15, 27, 30, 35–6, 40
    climate change, 182, 185, 190
    democracy 247
    energy, 203, 205–6
    international law 256
    intervention, 100, 109
    regionalism, 67, 78
    migration, 168
    nationalism 216, 219–20
Freedom House, 249
Free Trade Areas (FTAs), 65, 68, 74–5
French Revolution, 213
Friedman, Milton, 81, 82, 280
Friedman, Thomas, 218
Fukuyama, Francis, 2, 120, 132, 139, 235
functionalism, 67–9, 71, 76

G7/8, 14, 20, 32, 55, 177
G20, 8, 13, 18, 23, 25–6, 32, 51–2, 55, 59
Galbraith, John Kenneth, 91, 278
gas, 18
    *see also* energy
Gaza, 246
Gellner, Ernest, 212, 213
gender, 7, 11, 38, 139, 144, 225–34, 236
General Agreement on Tariffs and Trade
        (GATT), 47–9, 52–3
Georgians, 216
German Democratic Republic, *see* Germany
German unification, 214

Germany, 27, 30, 36, 39, 126, 127, 182, 185,
      195, 205–6, 219, 119, 241, 260, 282
   East, 78
   regionalism, 67, 78,
   West, 71
global civil society, 6, 32–3, 52, 56, 59,
      243–4
Global Financial Crisis (2007–12), 3, 4, 9,
      11–12,13–14, 16, 17, 20, 23, 32, 47,
      80–91, 175, 277, 292, 296
   regionalism, 60, 62, 75
global governance, 6, 15, 39, 53, 55, 56–7, 215,
      234, 293–4
   economic 47–8, 55–6
'global village', 31–2, 39, 42
globalization, 2–4, 7–8, 10, 18–19, 23–4, 27–8,
      30–46, 47, 54, 56, 58, 73–5, 80, 90, 108,
      112, 116, 121, 127, 132, 134, 138,
      149–50, 152–3, 156, 159, 161, 162, 165,
      210, 216–18, 220–4, 231–4, 236, 248,
      272, 279, 281, 285, 293, 296
   anti-globalization movements, 6, 51, 53,
      222
Goldman Sachs, 5, 14, 28
Goldsmith, Lord, 251
Gore, Al, 183
'governmentality', 35, 45
Gray, Colin, 94
Great Depression, 52, 54, 91, 293, 296
   capitalism, 277, 288
   financial crisis, 81, 82, 83–4, 89
   gender, 223
Great Recession, 2, 3, 13, 14, 16, 20, 22, 26,
      54.
   *see also* global financial crisis
Greece, 2, 13, 51, 66, 78, 223, 292
   democracy, 235, 240
   immigrants, 167, 174
Greenspan, Alan, 278
Gulf Cooperation Council (GCC), 70, 77–8
Gulf state states, 76, 238
Gulf War (1990–91), 196, 274
Gulf War (2003), 131, 274

Hadfield, Amelia, 11
Haas, Ernst, 67
Haas, Hein de , 164
Haass, Richard, 21, 27
Hague Conference (COP-6), 183
Haiti, 106, 110, 112, 166, 218, 256
Hall, Peter A., 289
Hall, Rodney Bruce, 213
Hamas, 100
Hamburg, 219
Hammerstad, Anne, 10
Hardin, Garret, 179
Hayek, Friedrich von, 81
Hegel, Friedrich, 214–15
Hehir, Aidan, 12
Held, David, 161, 243–4, 250

Hezbollah, 6
Higgott, Richard, 8, 9
Hispanics, 220
Hitler, Adolf, 114–15
HIV/AIDS, 144
Holland, 85
Holy Roman Empire, 35
Hong Kong, 78
humanitarian intervention, 106–19
   forced migration, 166
   legality, 251, 257
   media, 265, 271
   use of force, 102, 138
   war, 92, 93
Hungary, 78, 215
Huntington, Samuel, 250
   assimilation, 220
   'clash of civilizations', 126, 210
   nationalism 223–4
   'universal opposition', 237–9
   'waves', 235, 241
Hurrell, Andrew, 46, 71, 79, 255
Hurricane Katrina, 184

Iceland, 2
Ignatieff, Michael, 101
'imagined community', 212, 213
Imperialism, European, 4, 15, 34, 40.
   *see also* 'benevolent imperialism'
Import Substitution Industrialization (ISI), 151,
      159, 279
India, 2, 4, 8
   democracy, 237–8
   climate change, 183–4, 186–7, 189–90
   emerging power, 14, 16, 171–9, 22–8, 41,
      147
   gender, 233
   global South, 55
   international law, 260
   migration, 163–4, 167, 170
   nationalism, 222
   post-colonialism, 36
   regionalism, 65, 76, 78
   terrorism, 131
   underdevelopment, 149, 155–6
India–Brazil–South Africa (IBSA), 25
Indonesia, 18, 26–7, 78, 85, 128, 239, 242
inequality, 28, 149, 161, 291
   democracy, 249
   climate change, 187
   ethnicity, 212
   migration, 162
Institutional Revolutionary Party, 240, 245
integration, *see* European integration, regional
      integration
intergovernmentalism, 68–9
Intergovernmental Panel on Climate Change
      (IPCC), 181
International Commission on Intervention and
      State Sovereignty (ICISS), 166, 145

International Criminal Court (ICC), 15, 57
    international law, 251, 255–6, 259–62
    peace operations, 116
International Energy Agency (IEA), 195, 205
International Labour Organization (ILO), 171
International Monetary Fund (IMF), 6, 13–14,
        16, 25, 32, 293
    capitalism, 283
    democracy, 243
    development, 156
    multilateralism, 47
International Organization of Securities
        Commissions (IOSCO), 50
International Security Assistance Force (ISAF),
        99, 131
International Telegraph Union, 49
Inuits, 216
Iran, 18, 147, 167, 238, 246
    drones, 100
    climate change, 186
    energy, 199–200, 203
    identity, 32
    intervention, 113
    religion, 41
    regionalism, 70, 78
    nuclear weapons, 26
    *see also*  Iranian Revolution
Iranian Revolution, 123, 175, 195
Iraq, 2, 18, 78, 296
    climate change, 186
    democracy, 242, 246
    energy, 196, 203
    humanitarian intervention, 112, 114
    international law, 251–2, 254, 256–9
    media, 264, 268, 274
    migration, 165–166
    nationalism, 217–218
    terrorism, 121, 124–5, 127–31, 134
    US foreign policy, 288
    war, 21, 40, 42, 69, 93–8, 101–4
Ireland, 13, 78, 120, 171, 223
ISE, *see* Import Substitution Industrialization
        (ISI)
Islamism, 219, 239
Israel, 1, 21
    energy 195
    international law, 256–7
    media, 266
    regionalism 74
    statehood, 32
    terrorism, 123–4, 164
    war, 100
Israeli–Palestinian conflict, 21, 123
Italy, 36, 223, 241, 252, 292
    drones, 100
    environment, 185
    financial crisis, 2, 13, 66
    migration 174
    regionalism, 78
Ivory Coast, *see* Côte d'Ivoire

Jamaica, 237
Janus, 30, 38, 45
Japan, 2, 39, 64–5, 127
    capitalism, 279, 282, 287–8
    climate change, 182–4
    currency, 84
    democracy, 239, 241
    economic growth, 14, 17, 23
    economic rise, 26–7
    energy, 20–1, 192, 201, 205
    great powers, 36
    human security, 143, 148
    international law, 260, 279
    nationalism, 211, 218
    refugees, 164
    regionalism, 70–1, 78
    trade deficits, 52
jihad, 123–32, 134, 219
J. P. Morgan, 84
JUSCANZ (Japan, USA, Canada, Australia and
        New Zealand), 183
Just War theory, 112

Kant, Immanuel, 112, 251
Kashmir, 108, 131
Kennedy, Caroline, 9
Kennedy, David, 261–2
Kennedy, Paul, 40
Keohane, Robert Owen, 45, 48, 57, 77
Keynesianism, 45, 53, 280
Keynes, John Maynard, 82–3, 90–1, 279–80
Kiely, Ray, 10, 19, 161, 291
Kilcullen, David, 100, 134
Kony, Joseph, 103
Korea, *see* North Korea; South Korea.
Kosovo, 212, 257, 258
    intervention, 107, 109, 112, 115–16
    migration, 165
    war, 92–5
Kossuth, Lajos, 214
Kunz, Rahel, 11
Kurds, 210, 213, 260
Kuwait, 18, 24, 78, 196, 203, 253
Kyoto Protocol, 177, 179, 181, 182–91,
        203
    post-Kyoto, 11, 177, 184, 185–6
    *see also* climate change

Lansing, Robert, 215
Laos, 65, 78
Lasswell, Harold, 59
Latvia, 78, 210
League of Nations, 49, 108, 252
Lebanon, 78, 129, 238, 246
Lehman Brothers, 85
Leiken, Robert, 219
Lenin, Vladimir Ilyich, 123
liberal capitalism, 279.
    *see also*  neoliberal capitalism
liberalism, 223, 279, 287

Liberation Tigers of Tamil Eelam (LTTE), 122, 227
Liberia, 78, 95, 106, 113
Libya, 1
Lijphart, Arend, 238
Lindberg, Todd, 117
Lipset, Seymour Martin, 238
Lithuania, 78
lobbying, 68
London, 51, 165
    bombings (2005), 126, 130
'Londonistan', 219
Los Angeles, 220
Luck, Edward, 117

Maastricht Treaty (1992), 68, 74
Madrid, 219
    bombing (2004), 125, 130
Mahathir bin Mohamad, 242, 245
Mahbubani, Kishore, 29
Malaysia, 17, 78, 85, 237–9, 242, 245
Mali, 78, 189, 238
Mansbach, Richard W., 11
'Manhattan raid', 120
Mao Zedong, 123
Marchand, Marianne H., 11, 231, 234
Marcos, Ferdinand, 240, 246
'market failure', 87, 89, 208, 281
'market-state', 221
Marseilles, 219
Marxism, 133
Marx, Karl, 3–4, 82, 291
Mattli, Walter, 68
Mayall, James, 214
Mazzini, Giuseppe, 214
McChrystal, Stanley, 98
McLeod, Ross, 249
McLuhan, Marshall, 39
Mercosur, 65, 78
Mexicans, 66, 220
Mexico, 18, 26–7
    climate change, 187
    democracy, 233–4, 240, 245
    energy, 192, 200 203
    gender, 230, 232
    migration, 163
    nationalism, 220, 223
    regionalism, 65–6, 72
Microsoft, 5
Middle East, 1, 3, 7, 15, 36, 101, 285
    climate change, 181, 183
    democracy, 246, 248
    energy security, 195, 202, 207
    intervention, 106–8
    media, 266, 269
    nationalism, 218–19, 223
    terrorism, 122–5, 127–8, 130–1
migration, 10, 162–76
    climate change, 181
    globalization, 31, 39

human security, 135, 138–9
    nationalism, 218–20, 223
Milan, 219
Millennium Development Goals (MDG), 58, 153
Milosevic, Slobodan, 215, 260
'minilateralism, 58–9
Mitrany, David, 67, 76–7
Moldova, 78, 210
Moldovan, 216
monetarism, 280–1
Monnet, Jean, 63, 68
Moody's, 88
Moore, Barrington, 237
Morocco, 78, 171
Moscow, 125, 130
Mubarak, Muhammad Hosni El Sayed, 1
    *see also* Egypt
Murdoch, Rupert, 267
multilateralism, 8, 33, 47–59, 63, 74, 75, 222–3
multinational corporations (MNCs), 5–6, 39, 43, 263, 279
Mumbai, 19
Munich Olympics, 123
Mussolini, Benito, 215

Naim, Moisés, 58
Nagl, John, 97
Napoleon Bonaparte, 214–15
Napoleonic Continental System, 64
Napoleonic wars, 121, 213
National Endowment for Democracy (NED), 241
National Liberation Front (NLF), 122
national self-determination, 122, 214, 215–6
'nation-building', 32, 36
nationalism, 3, 5, 11, 31–3, 67, 210–24
    democracy, 239
    resource, 198–9
Nationally Recognized Statistical Rating
    Organizations (NRSROs), 87, 88, 89
native Americans, 216
NATO, 92, 98, 174
    international law, 257–8
    intervention, 106, 110, 112, 115–16
    terrorism, 125–6
neoliberal capitalism, 12, 75, 285, 294
    *see also* liberal capitalism
neoliberal institutionalism, 77
neoliberalism, 31, 45, 153, 157, 160, 192, 231
    post-neoliberalism, 277–89
Net Capital Rule, 87
Netherlands, 15, 78, 84, 168, 180
New Deal reforms, 87
Newman, Edward, 10, 297
new wars, 9, 92, 93, 94–5, 97–8, 101, 104
New York, 42, 171, 270
New York Stock Exchange, 84
*New York Times*, 268

New Zealand, 15, 77, 78, 183, 191
Nigeria, 18, 26–7, 78, 101, 103, 148, 192,
    197–9, 203, 218
non-governmental organizations (NGOs), 6, 32,
    48, 50, 73, 95, 241
non-state actors, 26–7, 37, 57, 69, 71, 120
    climate change, 180
    regionalism, 72–3
    terrorism, 130, 132
    *see also* Armed Non-State Actors (ANSAs)
non-traditional security, 62, 76, 138–42, 144–8
North Africa, 1, 164, 167, 207, 219
    energy, 195, 202
    protests, 1, 247–8
North America, 66, 122, 166, 168, 184, 219,
    290
North American Free Trade Agreement
    (NAFTA), 49, 65, 68, 78, 208
North Korea, 148, 295
North–South Divide, 149, 187
Norway, 168, 171, 194, 198
Nye, Joseph, 45, 77

Oakeshott, Michael, 38
Obama, Barak, 22, 98–9, 184, 189, 259
    administration, 130
Oceania, 77
O'Donnell, Guillermo, 239–40, 250
Ohmae, Kenichi, 73
'old wars', 9
Oman, 1
Operation Chastise, 195
Operation Desert Storm, 196
Organization of Central Asian Cooperation, 64,
    74
Organisation for Economic Co-operation and
    Development (OECD), 55, 195, 197,
    206, 229
Organization of Petroleum Exporting Countries
    (OPEC), 195, 196–7, 199–201, 208
Organization for Security and Cooperation in
    Europe (OSCE), 169
Osama bin Laden, 10, 96, 103, 124, 130–1, 266
Ottoman Empire, 106, 108
ozone depletion, 177

Pacific Islands Forum (1995), 69
Pakistan
    Afghanistan, 98
    drones, 94, 100, 103
    refugees, 167, 218
    regionalism, 78, 114, 237, 245
    nationalism, 222
    terrorism, 123, 131
    United States, 133
Palestine, 78, 164, 260
    Palestinian people, 21, 108, 123, 260, 266
Palestinian Liberation Organization (PLO), 123
Palme Commission, 139
Panama, 241

Panetta, Leon, 131
Papua New Guinea, 78
Paraguay, 78
Parekh, Bhikhu, 113
Partnoy, Frank, 88
'path dependency', 45, 281, 287, 291
peace operations, 9, 102, 106–19
Peace of Westphalia, 35, 136
    post-Westphalian system, 138
peacekeeping, 43, 95, 107, 108–11, 119
Pentagon, 98, 120
People Power II, 237, 246
People's Alliance for Democracy (PAD), 237
Peron, Juan, 238
Peru, 78, 84, 244
Petraeus, David, 97
Philippines, 78
    democracy, 235, 237, 239–40, 242, 246, 249
    migration, 171
Phillips, Andrew, 10, 134
Poland, 78, 164, 175, 186, 196, 203, 219
Polanyi, Karl, 82, 91
Pol Pot regime, 114
'polyarchal democracy', 236
populism, 237, 238
Portugal, 13, 78, 182, 219, 223, 235, 239
postcolonialism, 30, 36
post-Kyoto, 11, 177, 184–6, 189
'post-Washington consensus', 284
poverty, 3, 7, 51, 53, 297
    capitalism, 283
    development, 153, 155–61
    gender, 227, 229
    human security, 135, 138, 139, 143–6, 149
    nationalism, 218
Powell, Enoch, 164
Power, Samantha, 111
Prebisch, Raul, 151, 159
Prebisch–Singer thesis, 159
procedural democracy, 236, 250
precision guided munitions (PGMs), 133
Provisional Irish Republican Army (PIRA), 120
Prussia, 214
'public choice theory', 281
purchasing power parity (PPP), 155–6
Putin, Vladimir, 184, 210, 242, 245

Qaddafi, Muammar Muhammad Abu Minyar
    al-, 1
    *see also* Libya

Rabushka, Alvin, 238,
Ramo, Joshua Cooper, 286
Ramsey, Paul, 112
Reagan, Ronald, 241, 280
realism, 70–1, 77, 141
'rebel terror', 122, 128, 132
Red Army, 64, 123
Red Brigades, 291
*reformasi*, 242

Regional Consultative Processes (RCPs), 169–70
Regional Greenhouse Gas Initiative, 184
regional integration, 54, 60–1, 75–9
   economic, 73–5
   empire, 64
   European, 61–3
   identity, 64–6
   'new regionalism', 71–2
   non-European, 68–71
   theory, 67–8
Reilly, Benjamin, 238
religion, 38, 132, 211, 213, 217, 230
Renan, Ernest 211, 212
resource nationalism, 198–9
Responsibility to Protect (R2P), 1, 107, 112, 115–19
   human security, 138, 143–4
   refugees, 166
Revolution in Military Affairs (RMA), 93, 95, 104
Rio Earth Summit (1992), 181
Roberts, David, 146
Robertson, Geoffrey, 255
Roman Empire, 35
Romania, 78
Rome, 162, 211
Rome Statute, 255
Rosamond, Ben, 77
Rosenau, James, 43–4, 215
Rostow, Walt, 150, 161
Rothberg, Ronald, 218
Rotterdam, 219
Ruggie, John, 48, 54, 77, 279
Ruhr, 108, 195
Rupert, Mark, 222
Russia, 1, 4, 8, 36, 40–1, 84,
   climate change, 182, 184–5
   democracy, 235, 242, 245–6
   drones, 100
   energy, 192, 195, 197–201, 203–4, 207–8
   international law, 255, 257, 2
   intervention, 117
   nationalism, 210, 216, 219, 222
   population, 168
   regionalism, 64, 70, 75, 78,
   rise, 14, 17, 18, 19, 21, 23, 25–8, 285
   terrorism, 122, 125–6
Russians, 216
Russia–Ukraine transit, 208
Rustow, Dankwart, 239, 250
Rwanda, 92, 9495, 106, 109, 165, 216
Rwandan genocide, 106, 112–13, 256
Rwandan Patriotic Front (RPF), 106

Sachs, Jeffrey, 17
Sadat, Anwar, 123
San Diego, 72
Sarkozy, Nicholas, 186, 223,
SARs, *see* Severe Acute Respiratory Syndrome

Sassen, Saskia, 46, 232
Saudi Arabia, 18, 78, 120, 125, 197, 200, 203, 256
Scandinavia, 168, 241
Schmitter, Philippe, 236, 239, 240, 250
Schuman, Robert, 68
Scots, 216
Second World War, 36, 42, 120, 127, 136, 297
   American power, 4
   democracy, 235, 242
   energy, 192, 195, 197
   financial crisis, 84–5, 90–1
   intervention, 108
   migration, 164
   nationalism, 219
   post-war liberalism, 274, 279
   post-war international organization, 6, 25, 47–9, 50–2, 54, 84
   regionalism, 60, 63, 66
Secure Fence Act, 163
Securities and Exchange Commission (SEC), 87
security, 2, 3, 8, 10–11, 28, 42, 103–4, 110, 112, 117, 150, 252–4, 256, 293, 297
   alliances, 63
   collective security, 108
   gender, 226–31
   human security, 135–48, 102, 107, 248
   national, 60, 93, 106–7, 173–6, 246
   nationalism, 217
   private, 94, 98, 281
   populations, 162, 165–6, 169, 170–1
   regional, 63–4, 67, 71, 76–7, 79
   terrorism, 120, 123, 125–6, 129, 132–3
   *see also* non-traditional security; energy security
security sector reform (SSR), 102, 226–7, 229, 230
Sen, Amartya, 248–9
September 11 attacks, 9, 76, 93, 95, 96–9, 104
   international law, 251, 258
   media, 264–5, 271
   migration, 163, 170–2, 174, 176
   terrorism, 120, 123–2, 139
Serbia, 92, 95, 168, 216
Severe Acute Respiratory Syndrome (SARS), 76
Shanghai, 18
Shanghai Cooperation Organization (SCO), 23, 25, 126, 130
*sharia* law, 124
Sheehan, James, 40,
Shepsle, Kenneth, 238
Sierra Leone, 78, 95, 106, 109
Sinai, 108
Sinclair, Timothy, J., 9, 91, 293
Singapore, 17, 78, 237–9, 245
Singer, Hans, 151
Singer, P. W, 99
Slaughter, Ann-Marie, 22, 46, 104

Smith, Adam, 81
Smith, Anthony, 212,
Smith, Michael, 148
Smith, Rupert, 104
Smith, Steve, 141
social networking, 12
'soft power', 32, 92, 264, 266, 271
    *see also* Nye, Joseph
Solomon Islands, 78
Somalia, 118, 148, 218, 256
    aid, 101, 111
    failed state, 40, 107
    intervention 92, 109
    refugees, 165, 168
    regionalism, 78
    terrorism, 129
    war, 94–5, 106
Soros, George, 84
South Africa, 25, 26
    climate change 189, 190
    international law 260
    population movement, 163, 167–71, 173
    law, 260
    regionalism, 65, 69–70, 78
South African Development Community
        (SADC), 65
South Korea, 17–18, 27, 152, 235
    climate change, 184, 187, 190–1
    democracy, 222, 239, 242
    drones, 100
    energy, 201
    regionalism, 65, 78
    traditional security, 148
Southern African Development Community
        (1992), 69–70
sovereignty, 3, 9, 11, 41, 62
    authority, 57
    climate change, 177, 180
    democracy, 243, 248
    human security, 143
    international law, 257–8, 287
    intervention, 111–18, 132, 138–9
    nationalism, 213–14, 221
    regionalism, 67, 69, 75
    religion, 53
    state power, 27, 35, 38, 67
Soviet Union, 50, 137, 164, 295
    Afghanistan, 195–6
    disintegration, 92, 216
    globalization, 39, 40
    international law, 252, 255
    regionalism, 64–5, 78
Spain, 36, 78, 167, 216, 219, 235, 239–40
spillover, 68–9, 139
Srebrenica, 95, 109
Sri Lanka, 95, 216, 260
St Augustine, 112
stagflation, 280
Standard Oil Co. of New York (Socony), 200
state-building, 32, 35, 97–8, 109

statehood, 30–46
Stern Review, 165, 179, 191
Stockholm United Nations Conference on the
        Human Environment (1972), 177
Sudan, 18
    conflict, 106, 114–16, 118, 154, 216, 218
    development, 242
    International Criminal Court, 255
    regionalism, 78
Suez Canal, 123
Suez Crisis (1956), 108
Suharto, 249
Summers, Larry, 17,
Sweden, 78,
Syria, 1, 195, 247, 257, 260

Taiwan, 5, 17, 152, 235, 239, 240–1
Taliban, 96–9, 126, 129, 266
Tampere Conclusion, 170
terrorism, 3, 10, 31 41–2, 80, 193
    counter-terrorism, 100, 102
    human security, 135, 139, 144, 147–8
    migration, 171,174, 218, 223
    justice, 258–69
    religious, 246
    transnational terrorism, 120–34
    war, 170
Thailand, 17, 78, 237, 245–6, 249
Thatcher, Margaret, 280–1
Thaksin Shinawatra, 249
Thompson, Mark, 240
Tibetans, 210
Tickner, Ann, 234
Tijuana, 72
Tilly, Charles, 43
Tsarist Russia, 122
Tsar, Nicholas, 210
Tunisia, 1
Turkey, 1, 18, 26–7, 244
    drones, 100
    energy, 204
    refugees, 167
    reglionalism, 78

Uganda, 78, 103
Ukraine, 203–4, 208, 222
*ummah*, 124, 127, 129
unipolar, 17, 258, 259, 277, 292
United Kingdom, 78,
United Malays National Organization (UMNO),
        240
United Nations, 9, 32–3, 36, 95, 106, 114, 177,
        244, 251–2, 293
    'safe area' 109;
United Nations High Commission for Refugees
        (UNHCR), 165, 166, 169, 171, 175–6
United States, 30, 36, 39, 40, 42, 292
    American dominance, 2, 13, 21, 27, 277,
        279
    democracy, 237, 241–2

development, 150
economy, 2
energy, 195–6, 198
financial crisis, 87, 88, 89, 91
nationalism, 215, 219–20, 222–3
regionalism, 78
war, 94, 99, 102, 104
Uppsala Conflict Data Program (UCDP), 110
US Agency for International Development
    (USAID), 241
US Federal Reserve, 82, 85, 278
US Special Forces, 99
uranium, 193
Uzbekistan, 78, 126

van Onselen, Peter, 12
'varieties of capitalism', 45, 277–89
Venezuela, 160, 285
    intervention, 113
    primary resources, 18, 197, 204
    regionalism, 65, 78
Versailles Conference, 215
Vietnam, 20, 42, 65, 78, 114
Vietnam War, 21, 40, 50, 274

Waldman, Thomas, 9
Wall Street, 84, 293
Walt, Stephen, 140
Waltz, Kenneth, 30
war, 1, 9, 22, 31, 40–3, 46, 67, 85, 89, 90,
    136–40, 144, 147, 279, 295–8
    climate change, 186
    cyber-warfare, 135, 140
    democracy, 235, 240–2, 247, 249
    energy, 192, 195–7
    gender, 226, 228–9
    intervention, 106–12, 114–15, 118–19
    international law, 251–6, 258–9, 261–7
    nationalism, 210, 214–19, 223
    media, 264–5, 269, 274
    population, 162–8, 170, 174–5
    terrorism, 120–34
    21st century, 92–105
'war on terror', 96, 126–34, 251, 257
Warsaw Pact, 64
Warwick Commission, 58

'Washington Consensus', 75, 283–5, 287–8
weapons of mass destruction (WMD), 96, 114,
    124, 196
Weber, Max, 44, 211
Weberian state, 45
Weiner, Myron, 237
Weiss, Thomas, 113
welfare state, 44–5, 231
Welsh School, 142
Western Europe, 54, 67, 122–3, 125, 168, 279
Wikileaks, 12
Williams, Paul, 232
Williams, Michael, 148
Williamson, John, 232, 283
Wilson, Woodrow, 215
'working peace system', 67
World Bank, 6, 7, 47
    decision-making, 48
    development, 51–2, 155–6, 161, 283–4
    gender, 229, 243
    international regimes, 32
    migration, 169, 172
world order, 20, 48, 295
    multipolar, 26
    regionalism, 63, 77
    new, 92, 94
    threat, 131
    UN-centred, 258
    Western-centric, 27
World Order Models Project, 136
World Trade Order, 120
World Trade Organization (WTO), 6, 7, 25–6,
    47, 50–3, 58
    democracy, 243
    development, 160–1
    regionalism, 77
    protectionism, 222

xenophobia, 218

Yemen, 1, 78, 106, 218, 247
Yugoslavia, 106, 168, 216, 251, 256

Zawahiri, Ayman Mohammed Rabie al-, 124,
    130
Zimbabwe, 78, 113, 163, 168, 171, 218